Jumping Frogs

UNDISCOVERED, REDISCOVERED, AND CELEBRATED WRITINGS OF MARK TWAIN

Named after one of Mark Twain's best-known and beloved short stories, the Jumping Frogs series of books brings neglected treasures from Mark Twain's pen to readers.

1. *Is He Dead? A Comedy in Three Acts,* by Mark Twain. Edited with Foreword, Afterword, and Notes by Shelley Fisher Fishkin. Text Established by the Mark Twain Project, The Bancroft Library. Illustrations by Barry Moser.

2. *Mark Twain's Helpful Hints for Good Living: A Handbook for the Damned Human Race,* by Mark Twain. Edited by Lin Salamo, Victor Fischer, and Michael B. Frank of the Mark Twain Project, The Bancroft Library.

3. *Mark Twain's Book of Animals,* by Mark Twain. Edited with Introduction, Afterword, and Notes by Shelley Fisher Fishkin. Texts Established by the Mark Twain Project, The Bancroft Library. Illustrations by Barry Moser.

The publisher gratefully acknowledges
the generous support of the Humanities Endowment Fund
of the University of California Press Foundation.

The publisher also gratefully acknowledges
the generous support of Robert and Beverly Middlekauff
as members of the Literati Circle
of the University of California Press Foundation.

Mark Twain's Book of Animals

Mark Twain's Book of Animals

Edited with Introduction, Afterword, & Notes
by Shelley Fisher Fishkin

Illustrations by Barry Moser

TEXTS ESTABLISHED BY THE MARK TWAIN PROJECT,
THE BANCROFT LIBRARY

UNIVERSITY OF CALIFORNIA PRESS
BERKELEY • LOS ANGELES • LONDON

University of California Press, one of the most distinguished university presses in the United States, enriches lives around the world by advancing scholarship in the humanities, social sciences, and natural sciences. Its activities are supported by the UC Press Foundation and by philanthropic contributions from individuals and institutions. For more information, visit www.ucpress.edu.

University of California Press
Berkeley and Los Angeles, California

University of California Press, Ltd.
London, England

Library of Congress Cataloging-in-Publication Data

Twain, Mark, 1835–1910.
    Mark Twain's book of animals / by Mark Twain ; edited with introduction, afterword, and notes by Shelley Fisher Fishkin ; texts established by The Mark Twain Project, The Bancroft Library ; illustrations by Barry Moser.
        p.   cm.—(Jumping frogs ; 3)
    "The Mark Twain Project is a research and editorial project housed with the Mark Twain Papers at the Bancroft Library, Univ. of Calif., Berkeley."
    Includes bibliographical references and index.
    ISBN 978-0-520-24855-7 (cloth : alk. paper)
    1. Animal behavior—Anecdotes.   2. American wit and humor.   3. Animal rights.   I. Fishkin, Shelley Fisher.   II. Bancroft Library. Mark Twain Project.   III. Title.
PS1302.F5   2009
818'.409—dc22   2009004264

Manufactured in the United States of America

19 18 17 16 15 14 13 12 11 10
10 9 8 7 6 5 4 3 2 1

The paper used in this publication meets the minimum requirements of ANSI/NISO Z39.48-1992 (R 1997) (*Permanence of Paper*).

Contents

Contents   VII

ILLUSTRATIONS

Apart from the two original drawings of cats by Mark Twain in "A Cat-Tale,"
all of the following wood engravings were created by Barry Moser for this book.

INTRODUCTION

ANIMALS WERE INTEGRAL to Mark Twain's work as a writer from the first story that earned him national renown to pieces he wrote during his final years that remained unpublished at his death. Twain is famous for having crafted amusing and mordant quips about animals, as well as for having brought to life a cavalcade of animals who are distinctive, quirky, vividly drawn, and memorable. He is less known for being the most prominent American of his day to throw his weight firmly behind the movement for animal welfare.

Mark Twain's Book of Animals brings together in one volume writings that span more than fifty years, nearly the full range of Twain's career. It includes familiar stories as well as pieces that have never appeared in print before. We encounter Twain at his silliest and at his most philosophical, at his most sentimental and most sardonic, Twain having fun and Twain seething in anger. We read texts that are playful and texts that are dark, texts that are appealing and texts that are repulsive. We get glimpses of Twain as a child and as a parent, artist, thinker, and activist. Twain's writings on animals, in short, are as complex and variegated as the author himself.

Mark Twain came of age as a writer at a time when Western culture was struggling to assimilate and grasp the significance of the links that Charles Darwin posited between humans and other animals. Twain himself often weighed in on this reexamination of humankind's place in creation, even limning a delightful post-Darwinian Eden in which Adam hypothesizes that the newest small animal in the neighborhood (we recognize it as his baby son) must be a new kind of fish.[1] Adam decides that it must be some other kind of animal only after he throws it in the water and it sinks. But the question that stumps Twain's Adam seriously troubled Twain and his peers, as well: what kind of animal *was* man after all? And what obligations—if any—did he owe the other creatures with whom he shared the earth?

These questions percolated throughout the last third of the nineteenth century, and they surface again and again in the work of Mark Twain, where a broad range of animals take center stage with the human animals who populate the planet alongside them. A long-jumping frog, a churchgoing poodle, ravenous coyotes, and loquacious blue-jays are just a few of the memorable animals we meet in his work. But while Twain often found animals to be a reliable source of humor at the start of his career, they soon became much more: an Archimedean point from which to view—and evaluate—humans. Twain's astute observations of nonhuman animals, and of the ways they were treated, enabled him to train a cynical eye on human animals, and find them wanting. It turns out that the Lowest Animal—as he came to call man—did not stack up so well against the rest of the animal kingdom.

This introduction opens with an overview of Mark Twain's personal experience with actual animals and then looks at the roles animals played in his work, moving chronologically through the three periods into which the selections in this book are divided, the 1850s–1860s, the 1870s–1880s, and the 1890s–1910. The afterword discusses the cultural conversation about animals that Twain's writings entered and, in turn, helped shape.

Animals in Mark Twain's Life

A home without a cat—and a well-fed, well-petted and properly revered cat—
may be a perfect home, perhaps, but how can it prove title?
—*The Tragedy of Pudd'nhead Wilson*, chap. 1

TWAIN WAS SURROUNDED by animals from childhood through the last years of his life. His mother's compassion for all animals made a big impression on young Sam. He tells us in his autobiography that

One day in St. Louis she walked out into the street and greatly surprised a burly cartman who was beating his horse over the head with the butt of his heavy whip; for she took the whip away from him and then made such a persuasive appeal in behalf of the ignorantly offending horse that he was tripped into saying he was to blame; and also into volunteering a promise which of course he couldn't keep, for he was not built in that way—a promise that he wouldn't ever abuse a horse again. That sort of interference in behalf of abused animals was a common thing with her all her life. . . . All the race of dumb animals had a friend in her.[2]

The sympathy Jane Clemens held for stray cats was striking. "By some subtle sign," Twain wrote, "the homeless, hunted, bedraggled, and disreputable cat recognized her at a glance as the born refuge and champion of his sort—and followed her home. His instinct was right, he was as welcome as the prodigal son."[3] At one point in 1845 the family had nineteen cats; according to Twain, "there wasn't one in the lot that had any character, not one that had any merit, except the cheap and tawdry merit of being unfortunate. They were a vast burden to us all—including my mother—but they were out of luck, and that was enough; they had to stay." Cats were the only pets Jane Clemens permitted her children to have. They were "not allowed to have caged ones." "An imprisoned creature was out of the question," Twain recalled. "My mother would not have allowed a rat to be restrained of its liberty."[4] Albert Bigelow Paine, Mark Twain's official biographer, called Jane Clemens's "sense of pity" "abnormal," writing that "She refused to kill even flies, and punished the cat for catching mice."[5]

To a large extent, Jane Clemens's son Sam shared his mother's revulsion at the thought of inflicting pain on animals—but not as a result of her supplications. In the unpublished "A Family Sketch" (1901), he recalled that "for more than fifty-five years I have not wantonly injured a dumb creature" but credited that fact not "to home, school or pulpit, but to a momentary outside influence."

When I was a boy my mother pleaded for the fishes and birds and tried to persuade me to spare them, but I went on taking their lives unmoved, until at last I shot a bird that sat in a high tree, with its head tilted back, and pouring out a grateful song from an innocent heart. It toppled from its perch and came floating down limp and forlorn and fell at my feet, its song quenched and its unoffending life extinguished. I had not needed that harmless creature, I had destroyed it wantonly, and I felt all that an assassin feels, of grief and remorse when his deed comes home to him and he wishes he could undo it and have his hands and his soul clean again from accusing blood.[6]

(If we take Twain at his word that this childhood experience made him loath to "wantonly [injure] a dumb creature ever after," then we must assume that if—as he claims in *Roughing It*—he took a shot at a jackrabbit in the Nevada desert to scare him and watch the velocity at which he'd speed off, then he really did intend to miss.[7] Although Twain condemned cruelty to animals when he saw others inflicting it, on this occasion, at least, he seems to have been blind to the cruelty of his own behavior. Then again, since Twain never exempted himself from the flaws of which he accused mankind, he may have had behavior like his own in mind when he wrote, "Of all the animals, man is the only one that is cruel.")[8] His close friend William Dean Howells recalled that Twain "abhorred the dull and savage joy of the sportsman in a lucky shot," adding that "once when I met him in the country he had just been sickened by the success of a gunner in bringing down a blackbird, and he described the poor, stricken, glossy thing, how it lay throbbing its life out on the grass, with such pity as he might have given a wounded child."[9]

Some eight years before Twain wrote about his own regret at killing a bird when he was a child, he had Huck Finn reflect on a similar experience (in *Tom Sawyer Abroad*). Here is Huck, in his own voice, describing how it felt to shoot a bird:

. . . I see a bird setting on a limb of a high tree, singing, with its head tilted back and his mouth open, and before I thought I fired, and his song stopped and he fell straight down from the limb, all limp like a rag, and I run and picked him up, and he was dead, and his body was warm in my hand, and his head rolled about, this way and that, like his neck was broke, and there was a little white skin over his eyes, and one little drop of blood on the side of his head, and laws! I couldn't see nothing more for the tears; and I hain't never murdered no creature since, that warn't doing me no harm, and I ain't going to.[10]

(Despite his disapproval of the wanton cruelty that hunting as a sport condoned, Twain did not object to killing animals for food, a view underlying his humorous piece "Hunting the Deceitful Turkey," in which the turkey clearly gets the better of the narrator trying to catch him.)[11] Given that adults in the nineteenth century often viewed boys' killing small wild animals with approval—as "a rehearsal for the activities of manhood," as Katherine Grier has observed—Twain's revulsion from hunting as sport or pastime is notable.[12]

When Twain himself became a parent, he retained the prohibition on caged pets that had prevailed throughout his childhood, and also made sure there were always plenty of cats. He wrote in an 1884 letter to Charlie Webster, "There is nothing so valuable in a home as a baby—& no young home is complete *without* a baby—a baby & a cat. Some people scorn a cat & think it not an essential; but the Clemens tribe are not of these."[13] His daughter Clara recalled that if for any reason she had to disturb her father while he was at work, it was "expedient to be accompanied by a kitten."[14] Twain couldn't bear to be without pet cats during a summer stay in Dublin, New Hampshire, so he rented four cats from the wife of a neighboring farmer. "They have been good company," Twain wrote in an autobiographical dictation, claiming that they liked hearing him speak French "with a Missouri accent," and particularly enjoyed hearing him make "impassioned speeches in that language."[15] His daughter Susy once commented that "The difference between papa and mama is, that mama loves morals and papa loves cats."[16] His Hartford pastor and close friend Joseph Twichell recalled that Twain "could scarcely meet a cat on the street without stopping to make its acquaintance."[17]

The family had cats named "Stray Kit, Abner, Motley, Freulein [sic], Lazy, Bufalo Bill [sic], Soapy Sall, Cleveland, Sour Mash, and Pestilence and Famine."[18] Also Billiards, Babylon, Ananda, Annanci, Sindbad, Bones, Appollinaris, Zoroaster, Blatherskite, Socrates, and Belchazar.[19] And "at one time when the children were small," they "had a very black mother-cat named Satan, and Satan had a small black offspring named Sin."[20] The family had eleven or twelve cats at Quarry Farm in Elmira, New York, where they spent summers, and several more at their home in Hartford.[21] Susy noted that her father was fond of carrying around on his shoulder a grey cat named Lazy whose color matched his "grey coat and hair."[22] In his home in Redding, Twain tolerated with good humor a cat named Tammany who was fond of squeezing himself into a corner-pocket of Twain's billiard table and spoiling shots with his paw.[23] Other family pets at various times included a pet dog named Flash, a pet calf named Jumbo, horses named Max Clemens, Scott, and Fix, and a pet donkey named Cadichon.[24] For a while Clara kept two pet squirrels she had tamed in a cubicle off the third-floor billiard room where Twain wrote in Hartford.[25] The Clemens family's affection for their pets reflected attitudes held by much of mainstream America. As Katherine Grier notes in *Pets in America: A History*, there was wide consensus in America during this era on the importance of pets in shaping a child's character—a consensus reflected in child-rearing advice books, parenting guides, and children's magazines.[26]

The stable of the Hartford home, presided over by Patrick McAleer, the family coachman, was a favorite retreat of the children's.[27] "The children had a deep admiration for Patrick," Twain recalled in "A Family Sketch." "To them he seemed to know everything and how to do everything."[28] The family kept a flock of garden ducks which the children would help Patrick drive down to the stream that "lazily flowed through the grounds" and then bring them back to the stable at sunset. Twain tells us that Patrick allowed the children

to look on and shrink and shiver and compassionately exclaim, when he had a case of surgery on hand—which was rather frequent when the ducks were youthful. They would go to sleep on the water, and the mud-turtles would get them by the feet and chew until Patrick happened along and released them. Then he brought them up the slope and sat in the shade of the long quarter-deck called "the ombra" and bandaged the stumps of the feet with rags while the children helped the ducks do the suffering.[29]

But Patrick also "slaughtered a mess of birds for the table pretty frequently, and this conduct got him protests and rebukes." Twain writes,

Once Jean said—
   "I wonder God lets us have so much ducks, Patrick kills them so."
   A proper attitude for one who was by and by, in her sixteenth year, to be the founder of a branch of the Society for the Prevention of Cruelty to Animals.[30]

Neither Twain nor Jean avoided eating meat. But the issue Jean raised in this conversation of the cosmic justice underlying what—and who—becomes "supper" would trouble Twain well into his later years, as a piece like "The Victims" clearly demonstrates.[31]

Twain's letters throughout his life show him regaling family and friends with anecdotes about various pets. For example, to his friend Franklin Whitmore, a Hartford real estate and insurance agent, he wrote, during a summer in Elmira in 1881, "That cat of ours went down to town—3 miles, through the woods, in the night,—& attended a colored people's church festival where she didn't even know the deacons—was gone 48 hours, & marched home again this morning. Now think of that! That cat is not for sale. Talented cat. Religious cat. And no color prejudices, either."[32] To his friend Charles S. Fairchild, an attorney, who had presented the Clemens family with a pet dog named Rab, Twain wrote in 1881,

   Alas! Rab has acquired an evil reputation already. He takes position on the lawn, & thence darts forth & greets every horse & wagon & street car that goes along—three hundred of 'em a day—always in the friendliest spirit, of course, but he has caused a couple of runaways & come near causing many more; & he can't be persuaded to leave off his diversion. People threaten his life daily; so we've got to part, for his sake as well as our own. You wanted him back in case this state of things occurred. . . .[33]

After explaining how he would get the dog back to Fairchild, Twain added, "I am mighty sorry it has turned out so, for he *is* a noble dog."

Twain wrote his mother from Elmira in 1887 that he and his family had "put in this whole Sunday forenoon teaching the new dog to let the cats alone, & it has been uncommonly lively for those 5 cats. They have spent the most of the time in the trees, swearing."[34] His letters to the Angelfish, the little girls whose visits brightened his final years, were filled with news of pets, as well.[35]

Twain's daughters developed an empathy for animals as intuitive and strong as their grandmother's. As a child, when Jean was shown a book about the Lisbon earthquake, she showed little interest in a picture of people "being swallowed up." But when a picture on the next page "showed a number of animals being overwhelmed," her nurse recalled, she had exclaimed "Poor things!" Questioned as to why she didn't say that about the people, Jean answered, "Oh, they could speak." The "dumb" animals had a special claim on her sympathies. "She was a loyal friend to all animals," Twain recalled after her death, "and she loved them all, birds, beasts, and everything—even snakes— an inheritance from me. She became a member of various humane societies when she was still a little girl—both here and abroad—and she remained an active member to the last. She founded two or three societies for the protection of animals, here and in Europe."[36]

Twain recalled that his eldest daughter, Susy,

was born with humane feelings for the animals, and compassion for their troubles. This enabled her to see a new point in an old story once, when she was only six years old—a point which had been overlooked by older and perhaps duller people for many ages. Her mother told her the moving story of the sale of Joseph by his brethren, the staining of his coat with the blood of the slaughtered kid, and the rest of it. She dwelt upon the inhumanity of the brothers, their cruelty toward their helpless young brother, and the unbrotherly treachery which they practiced upon him; for she hoped to teach the child a lesson in gentle pity and mercifulness which she would remember. Apparently her desire was accomplished, for the tears came into Susy's eyes and she was deeply moved. Then she said, "Poor little kid!" [37]

Twain recalled, in "A Family Sketch," that "I admonished the children not to hurt animals; also to protect weak animals from stronger ones." "When Clara was small," he recalled, "small enough to wear a shoe the size of a cowslip—she suddenly brought this shoe down with determined energy, one day, dragged it rearward with an emphatic rake, then stooped down to examine the results. We inquired, and she explained—'The naughty big ant was trying to kill the little one!' Neither of them survived the generous interference."[38]

Mark Twain sometimes identified with animals in a personal, visceral way. In 1868 he had learned that his friend Mary Mason Fairbanks and her family had named a dog after him. "How is the dog?" he inquired in a letter. "If he neglects to wipe his feet on the mat before he comes in, & is in all places & at all times blundering & heedless, he will do no discredit to his name. But don't *chain* him. It makes me restive to think of it."[39] In their correspondence, his daughters Susy and Jean commonly addressed Clemens as "Dearest Grenouille."[40] Whether the sobriquet was paying homage to the celebrated author of the "Celebrated Jumping Frog" or not (more likely not, since that was not one of his daughters' favorite pieces), the Clemens daughters must have had their own reasons for addressing their father as a frog, albeit a French one, in letters otherwise written in English. And in an 1899 letter to his friend William Dean Howells, in which he berated himself for having bragged about selling a particular stock at a "fine profit" only to watch it advance to "$60,000 more than I sold it for," Twain wrote, "My tail hangs low."[41]

In the Missouri farm country where Sam Clemens spent his childhood, mosquitoes, flies, ants, fish, frogs, snakes, bats, and bees were even more plentiful than the ubiquitous cats, horses, and pigs. Twain's travels around the world exposed him to camels, exotic birds, porpoises, monkeys, and a wide variety of other creatures—animals that sometimes irritated him and sometimes intrigued him—but that always captured his attention, and often found their way into his books.[42]

Animals in Mark Twain's Work

If you pick up a starving dog and make him prosperous, he will not bite you.
This is the principal difference between a dog and a man.
—The Tragedy of Pudd'nhead Wilson, chap. 16

FROM HIS EARLIEST WRITINGS to his latest, nonhuman animals provided a vehicle through which Twain could comment on his fellow human beings. Describing animal behavior in terms usually reserved for humans was, from early on, a source of broad humor for Twain. But when he described the human flaws and foibles that the animals appeared to replicate, the joke was on the humans, not the animals: Twain found that making fun of animals for qualities that showed them as all too human could be a useful ploy for mounting genial critiques of human behavior. By the same token, Twain found that shining a spotlight on the cruelty with which humans treated animals could be a useful strategy for illuminating human hypocrisy, misplaced moral pride, and unwarranted senses of entitlement and superiority—qualities that became increasingly salient for Twain as the years wore on. No matter how much they may resemble humans, however, Twain's animals in the selections in this book are usually recognizable as animals—animals with familiar human personality traits and qualities, perhaps—but animal nonetheless.

Twain's animals communicate, but unlike the animals one finds in Aesop's fables or animal trickster tales common to African American and Native American folklore, they rarely "talk." Twain occasionally hypothesizes what animals might be saying if they *could* talk (as when he imagines what the ravens in *A Tramp Abroad* or the crows in *Following the Equator* might be saying about *him*); but they usually don't talk to each other. Indeed, the relatively rare occasions when Twain does write fables that feature talking animals—as in "A Fable," "Some Learned Fables," or "The Fable of the Yellow Terror"—the result is a rather pedestrian conversation among generally interchangeable disembodied "animal" voices shorn of any real distinctiveness. Since these pieces tend to be rather clumsy, long-winded, and not especially well-crafted, and since they are readily available elsewhere, they are omitted here.[43] (I have, however, made three exceptions: I have included "The Jungle Discusses Man," a tale from the 1890s that was published for the first time in 2009; "The Victims," a little-known but important piece from the early 1900s that was first published in 1972; and portions of the 1906 novella, *A Horse's Tale*—all three feature animals that talk to each other.)

If Twain's animals do not generally talk to each other, in one text in this book they *write* to each other: "Letters from a Dog to Another Dog Explaining and Accounting for Man. Author, Newfoundland Smith. Translated from the Original Doggerel by M.T." And in two others—*A Horse's Tale* and "A Dog's Tale"—they speak directly to *us*. While *A Horse's Tale* contains a fair amount of interpolated text that is *not* from the horse's point of view, "A Dog's Tale" is narrated almost in its entirety (until the last few lines) by an engaging and sympathetic dog who, like Huck, begins by introducing herself to the reader: "My father was a St. Bernard, my mother was a collie, but I am a Presbyterian."

Mark Twain enjoyed both fiction and nonfiction about animals.[44] His dog was called Rab in homage to the eponymous hero of a novella by his friend the Scottish doctor John Brown, *Rab and His Friends* (1858), a book he greatly admired.[45] He was fascinated by Darwin's descriptions of animal behavior in *The Descent of Man* (1871), as his copious marginal notes in that book make clear.[46] He was a great fan of the animal fables that Ambrose Bierce published in *Fun* in the 1870s (the famous blue-jay yarn Twain published in 1880 may well have reprised a scenario he had first encountered in Bierce's 1873 story, "The Robin and the Woodpecker").[47] Twain purchased a copy of John James Audubon's *Birds of America* in 1880; when his friend George Washington Cable visited him in Hartford in 1884 the two men consulted it "to identify a strange & beautiful bird" that they had seen through the library window.[48] Twain called Kipling's *Jungle Book* (1894) "incomparable" and entertained his family one evening in 1906 with a reading from Kipling's story "Red Dog."[49]

He praised Robert Williams Wood's 1908 *Animal Analogues. Verse and Illustrations* as "a cunning book."[50] He presented his daughter Jean with *The Kindred of the Wild; A Book of Animal Life* by Charles Roberts in 1903, and gave her a copy of Audubon's *Birds of North America* in 1906.[51] His own writing on animals, however, while reminiscent, now and then, of work by others, is more variegated in form, function, and content than that of any of his peers.

The selections in this book are arranged roughly in the chronological order in which they were written (although not necessarily the order in which they were published: some pieces are printed here for the first time). The fact that the second section (devoted to writing from the 1870s and 1880s) is longer than the first (focused on writing from the previous two decades), and that the final section (work from the 1890s until Twain's death) is the longest by far reflects the increasingly important role that writing on animals came to play in Twain's work as he grew older.

1850s and 1860s

You never see a frog so modest and
straightfor'ard as he was, for all he was so gifted.
—"Jim Smiley and His Jumping Frog"

IN 1856, in a letter home, nine years before a story about a man who'd bet on frogs, bull-pups, and one-eyed cows won him his first national fame, twenty-one-year-old Sam Clemens spun this inventive description of the bugs that tormented him as he worked at a printing press at 2 A.M. in Keokuk, Iowa:

They at first came in little social crowds of a dozen or so, but soon increased in numbers, until a religious mass meeting of several millions was assembled on the board before me, presided over by a venerable beetle, who occupied the most prominent lock of my hair as his chair of state, while innumerable lesser dignitaries of the same tribe were clustered around him, keeping order, and at the same time endeavoring to attract the attention of the vast assemblage to their own importance by industriously grating their teeth.[52]

Here Twain is punning on the similar sound of the name of a church official and the name of a familiar insect—beadles and beetles. Of course it's whimsical anthropomorphism to interpret this gathering of insects as a grand "religious mass meeting." But while perhaps the first description we have from Twain of a religious gathering happened to be a fantasy about insects, it clearly prefigures the famous church scene in *Tom Sawyer*, where Twain would reprise this image of a religious service in which the teachers, the students, and the preacher—everyone, in fact—was trying to attract attention to their own importance by showing off. This fact suggests that writing about animals may have sometimes been a rehearsal for things Twain would later write about humans.

Mark Twain first achieved national fame for a sketch based on a story he heard from a man named Ben Coon in Angels Camp in Calaveras County, California, about an inveterate gambler named Jim Smiley. "Jim Smiley and His Jumping Frog" appeared in the New York *Saturday Press* on 18 November 1865, and was reprinted by Bret Harte in the *Californian* on 16 December 1865. Prior to the publication of "Jumping Frog," Twain had a growing but largely regional reputation in the West, principally in California and Nevada, where he had lived and worked as a journalist since 1862. In the story, Simon Wheeler, a master of western deadpan humor, infuriates and befuddles a genteel visitor from the East with stories about an inveterate gambler named Jim Smiley, who

said all a frog wanted was education, and he could do most anything—and I believe him. Why, I've seen him set Dan'l Webster down here on this floor—Dan'l Webster was the name of the frog—and sing out, "Flies! Dan'l, flies," and quicker'n you could wink, he'd spring straight up, and snake a fly off'n the counter there, and flop down on the floor again as solid as a gob of mud, and fall to scratching the side of his head with his hind foot as indifferent as if he hadn't no idea he'd done any more'n any frog might do. You never see a frog so modest and straightfor'ard as he was, for all he was so gifted.[53]

The humor in the story comes not from the eponymous frog himself (or from the other animals in the piece) but from the story Simon Wheeler tells and the eastern visitor's failure to realize that he is being "had." "Jumping Frog" reverses the dynamics of the usual "frame story," in which educated narrator and readers are amused by the ignorant speech and antics of rustics who are their social and intellectual inferiors. Here it is the effete, impatient, and humorless eastern visitor, not the loquacious and colloquial Simon Wheeler, who is out of his depth. The story (which appeared under a number of different titles) provided the title to Twain's first book in 1867—*The Celebrated Jumping Frog of Calaveras County and Other Sketches*—which sported a "gorgeous gold frog" on its cover.[54]

The "Jumping Frog" story signaled one important way in which animals would figure in Twain's work: as comic foils to a deft vernacular storyteller. (A jumping frog would also become an emblem for the author himself: posters advertising his readings and lectures after the story appeared sometimes featured the image of Twain riding a jumping frog, the same image that appears on the first page of this book.) But Twain would also write a great deal about animals that was not comic. His travel books, for example, are filled with many straight descriptive passages about animals. And his writing on the topic of cruelty to animals—a body of work that includes journalism, essays, short stories, and a novella—would eventually make him the most well-known American advocate of animal welfare of his era.

Twain published his earliest short squib on the topic in the San Francisco *Daily Morning Call* in September 1864 under the heading "Cruelty to Animals." It skewers the driver of a truck wagon for trying (unsuccessfully) to make a horse pull a load "nearly as heavy as an ordinary church."[55] Another form of abuse was featured in an 1866 piece Twain published in the Virginia City *Territorial Enterprise* about a horse whose owner fed him only "old newspapers and sometimes a basket of shavings," leading the starving animal to eat anything—including neighborhood cats.[56] Twain again used the title "Cruelty to Animals" for his first extended article devoted solely to the issue of animal welfare, which appeared in the San Francisco *Daily Alta California* in 1867, the year he published his first book. His 1867 article, which Twain filed from New York, heaps praise on the recently founded American Society for the Prevention of Cruelty to Animals:

One of the most praiseworthy institutions in New York, and one which must plead eloquently for it when its wickedness shall call down the anger of the gods, is the Society for the Prevention of Cruelty to Animals. Its office is located on the corner of Twelfth street and Broadway, and its affairs are conducted by humane men who take a genuine interest in their work, and who have got worldly wealth enough to make it unnecessary for them to busy themselves about anything else. They have already put a potent check upon the brutality of draymen and others to their horses, and in future will draw a still tighter rein upon such abuses, a late law of the Legislature having quadrupled their powers, and distinctly marked and specified them. You seldom see a horse beaten or otherwise cruelly used in New York now, so much has the society made itself feared and respected. Its members promptly secure the arrest of guilty parties and relentlessly prosecute them.[57]

The article describes how the society works, and what other projects it is undertaking on behalf of animals. Twain even evidently followed its founder,

Henry Bergh, on a mission to get a theatre manager to discontinue what Bergh viewed as the abuse of an animal on stage during a show. It would be hard to find a more laudatory portrait than the one Twain limns here of Bergh.

Shortly after filing this story, Mark Twain left on the cruise of the *Quaker City*, which he chronicled in newspaper articles during the trip. That material would form the core of his first travel book, *The Innocents Abroad*, published in 1869; the remaining selections in part 1 are from that volume. Twain's travels and the books that resulted are key to his writing on animals, and much of the basic pattern is established in *Innocents Abroad*. Travel provided Twain with the opportunity to be exposed to animals he hadn't seen before—like the camels he encounters in Syria or the oddly pious-looking bird he sees in a zoo in Marseilles; his readers were unlikely to have seen such creatures either, and Twain undertook the challenge of describing them with sufficient detail and wit to allow his readers to see them in their mind's eyes. Travel also gave Twain the chance to observe familiar animals in unfamiliar contexts (like the dogs of Constantinople), and to pay attention to how humans and animals interacted in fresh circumstances—such as watching how the horses were treated both by the Arabs who rented them out and by his fellow American tourists who were their customers. Twain directs harsh criticism at both groups. Of his compatriots, he writes,

Properly, with the sorry relics we bestrode, it was a three days' journey to Damascus. It was necessary that we should do it in less than two. It was necessary because our three pilgrims would not travel on the Sabbath day. . . . We pleaded for the tired, ill-treated horses, and tried to show that their faithful service deserved kindness in return, and their hard lot compassion. . . . Nothing could move the pilgrims. They *must* press on. . . . they must enter upon holy soil next week, with no Sabbath-breaking stain upon them. . . . Apply the Testament's gentleness, and charity, and tender mercy to a toiling, worn and weary horse?—Nonsense—these are for God's human creatures, not His dumb ones. . . .

We satisfied our pilgrims by making those hard rides from Baalbec to Damascus, but Dan's horse and Jack's were so crippled we had to leave them behind and get fresh animals for them. The dragoman says Jack's horse died.[58]

When Twain needs to swap horses because his own horse is worn out, he tells us that he chooses the one he chooses because he has "not seen his back":

I do not wish to see it. I have seen the backs of all the other horses, and found most of them covered with dreadful saddle-boils which I know have not been washed or doctored for years. The idea of riding all day long over such ghastly inquisitions of torture is sickening. My horse must be like the others, but I have at least the consolation of not knowing it to be so. [59]

These early comments by Twain on cruelty to animals prefigure a theme that will become increasingly salient for him in later decades.

1870s and 1880s

*Of all God's creatures there is only one that cannot be made the
slave of the lash. That one is the cat. If man could be crossed with
the cat it would improve man, but it would deteriorate the cat.*
—Notebook 33, typescript pp. 56–57

MUCH OF TWAIN'S most interesting writing on animals during this period appears in the travel books *Roughing It* (1872) and *A Tramp Abroad* (1880), and the novel *The Adventures of Tom Sawyer* (1876). But there are also memorable passages in *Adventures of Huckleberry Finn* (1885), *A Connecticut Yankee in King Arthur's Court* (1889), and sketches written for his children.

In *Roughing It*, the saga of Twain's trip out west by stagecoach, we meet two of Twain's most memorable animals, the coyote and the jackrabbit, animals who have left an indelible mark on American popular culture. Chuck Jones, the legendary Warner Brothers animation director who created the Road Runner cartoons and was one of the creators of Bugs Bunny, acknowledges in his autobiography, *Chuck Amuck*, the seminal role that Twain's coyote and jackrabbit played in the creation of both Wile E. Coyote and Bugs Bunny. On page 34 of *Chuck Amuck* is an image of Wile E. Coyote chasing after his famous prey, Road Runner, with a knife and fork in his hand and a determined glint in his eye. The artist's caption reads "The Coyote—Mark Twain discovered him first." Jones writes that "One fateful day our family moved into a rented house, furnished with a complete set of Mark Twain, and my life changed forever."[60] What particularly impressed Jones was Twain's ability to portray quirky, funny, and yet totally plausible *character* in animals—particularly one memorable coyote he encountered while devouring *Roughing It* at age seven. Twain had written that

The cayote is a long, slim, sick and sorry-looking skeleton, with a gray wolf-skin stretched over it, a tolerably bushy tail that forever sags down with a despairing expression of forsakenness and misery, a furtive and evil eye, and a long, sharp face, with slightly lifted lip and exposed teeth. He has a general slinking expression all over. The cayote is a living, breathing allegory of Want. He is *always* hungry.[61]

In Mark Twain's coyote, we can glimpse a prototype of Wile E. Coyote. Whenever Road Runner races past, Wile E. Coyote imagines him on a platter, steaming hot, evenly browned, garnished with vegetables and potatoes. The madcap chase is always fueled by a hunger as vast as the craggy chasms of the desert landscape in which the action takes place—a chase Coyote is always doomed to lose, his abject humiliation immediately giving way to new plots to trap his opponent. Although Road Runner is clearly a bird, he takes his character and abilities from several of Mark Twain's portraits of nonfeathered creatures in *Roughing It*, among them the jackrabbit, as Jones notes. He tells us that Twain's chapter on jackrabbits in *Roughing It* "gave [him] the clue to the speed of the Road Runner."[62] When he perceives himself being shot at, Twain's jackrabbit "dropped his ears, set up his tail, and left for San Francisco at a speed which can only be described as a flash and a vanish! Long after he was out of sight we could hear him whiz."[63] Jones came to understand that "Mark Twain used words the way the graphic artist uses line control."[64] Through his influence on Jones and others, Twain would shape the Saturday mornings of American children for generations to come.

In *Roughing It*, Twain occasionally interpolates memories of animals from other times and places as they come to mind—an artistic strategy that he will employ with more and more frequency in later years. Here this openness to digression allows him to have another pass at the Syrian camel he first described in *Innocents Abroad*. The train of thought that takes him there matters little: what matters is that *this* time Twain does not constrain himself to description or even description that descends into hyperbole as he did in *Innocents Abroad*; instead, he superimposes on the distinctive image in his head—of a camel chewing—a comic edifice so elaborate that it would collapse under its own weight if it weren't so funny.[65] His mind also wanders back to a "former crisis" of his life set in a different time and a different place in which a horse that was understandably a creature of habit caused Twain excruciating embarrassment. Here, as in so many of Twain's animal stories, the horse is presented respectfully (we are told that he "had just retired from a long and honorable career as the moving impulse of a milk wagon") while Twain makes fun of his own desire to impress the "aristocratic young lady" who is his date. When the habits of a sensible horse who is set in his ways clash comically with Twain's attempts at social climbing, it is Twain's vanity rather than the horse that is made to appear ridiculous.[66]

Tom Sawyer includes several memorable passages about animals, but surely the most iconic is the encounter between the poodle and the pinch-bug in church on a languid summer morning during an interminable sermon. During the dull service, Tom remembers a treasure he has in his pocket and gets it out.

It was a large black beetle with formidable jaws—a "pinch-bug," he called it. It was in a percussion-cap box. The first thing the beetle did was to take him by the finger. A natural fillip followed, the beetle went floundering into the aisle and lit on its back, and the hurt finger went into the boy's mouth. The beetle lay there working its helpless legs, unable to turn over. . . . Presently a vagrant poodle dog came idling along, sad at heart, lazy with the summer softness and the quiet, weary of captivity, sighing for change. He spied the beetle; the drooping tail lifted and wagged. He surveyed the prize; walked around it; smelt at it from a safe distance; walked around it again; grew bolder, and took a closer smell; then lifted his lip and made a gingerly snatch at it, just missing it; made another, and another; began to enjoy the diversion; subsided to his stomach with the beetle between his paws, and continued his experiments; grew weary at last, and then indifferent and absent-minded. His head nodded, and little by little his chin descended and touched the enemy, who seized it. There was a sharp yelp, a flirt of the poodle's head, and the beetle fell a couple of yards away, and lit on its back once more. The neighboring spectators shook with a gentle inward joy . . . and Tom was entirely happy. The dog looked foolish, and probably felt so; but there was resentment in his heart, too, and a craving for revenge. So he went to the beetle and began a wary attack on it again; jumping at it from every point of a circle, lighting with his forepaws within an inch of the creature, making even closer snatches at it with his teeth, and jerking his head till his ears flapped again. But he grew tired once more, after a while; tried to amuse himself with a fly but found no relief; followed an ant around, with his nose close to the floor, and quickly wearied of that; yawned, sighed, forgot the beetle entirely, and sat down on it! Then there was a wild yelp of agony and the poodle went sailing up the aisle; the yelps continued, and so did the dog. . . . till presently he was but a woolly comet moving in its orbit with the gleam and the speed of light. . . . By this time the whole church was red-faced and suffocating with suppressed laughter, and the sermon had come to a dead stand-still.[67]

Part of what makes this passage so brilliant is that the dog acts like a dog and the bug acts like a bug and the people act like people. One can imagine that it may well have been scenes like this that helped make *Tom Sawyer* the favorite book of Walt Disney, the man who went on to create the modern animated cartoon. Disney, who grew up in Marceline, Missouri, down the road from Hannibal, adored *Tom Sawyer*—in fact, Tom Sawyer's Island is the only part of Disneyland that Walt Disney himself completely designed. Since Disney was more of a storyteller than an artist, it is hard to believe that scenes like this one from *Tom Sawyer* did not play a key role as he developed his distinctive cast of animated animals.[68]

The 1880s brought us "A Cat-Tale," a whimsical story Twain spun for his daughters (1880); the travel books *A Tramp Abroad* (1880), which chronicled a second journey to Europe, and *Life on the Mississippi* (1883), which included Twain's report of a sojourn in New Orleans; and the novels *Huckleberry Finn* (1885) and *Connecticut Yankee* (1889). Although it could not possibly be more different in tone from "Jumping Frog," "A Cat-Tale" has one thing in common with its famous predecessor: it is more about the skill of the gifted storyteller telling the tale than it is about the animals allegedly at its center. One might be tempted to say that "Jim Baker's Blue-jay Yarn" in *A Tramp Abroad* is also more about the gifts of the storyteller than about blue-jays—but Twain manages to capture something so *right* about the birds that it's hard to write them off as mere foils (*A Tramp Abroad* contains some memorable portraits of other birds with real personality, as well).

Twain's observations on ants in *A Tramp Abroad* inaugurate a new stance for Twain regarding writing on animals: a willingness to observe animal behavior with the patience and attention to detail of a naturalist (a stance to which he will return in a later essay on bees). He watches an ant capture "something which can be of no sort of use to himself or anybody else" and "is usually seven times bigger than it ought to be."

... he hunts out the awkwardest place to take hold of it; he lifts it bodily up in the air by main force, and starts: not toward home, but in the opposite direction; not calmly and wisely, but with a frantic haste which is wasteful of his strength; he fetches up against a pebble, and instead of going around it, he climbs over it backward dragging his booty after him, tumbles down on the other side, jumps up in a passion, kicks the dust off his clothes, moistens his hands, grabs his property viciously, yanks it this way then that, shoves it ahead of him a moment, turns tail and lugs it after him another moment, gets madder and madder, then presently hoists it into the air and goes tearing away in an entirely new direction; comes to a weed; it never occurs to him to go around it; no, he must climb it; and he does climb it, dragging his worthless property to the top ... when he gets up there he finds that that is not the place; takes a cursory glance at the scenery and either climbs down again or tumbles down, and starts off once more—as usual, in a new direction. At the end of half an hour, he fetches up within six inches of the place he started from. . . . [69]

Similar attention to detail comes out in Twain's description of a cock-fight in New Orleans in *Life on the Mississippi.* Although Twain disapproves of cock-fighting, the apparent interest that the birds themselves seem to take in the fight makes him hesitant to condemn it outright the way he condemns hunting for sport. Twain seems unaware of the cruel regimen of training and breeding that lay behind the "enjoyment" the cocks appeared to take in fighting. During the next two decades Twain will become much more sensitive to issues of cruelty to animals. In 1883, however, he seems to believe that the jury is still out on cock-fighting.

But if Twain is not ready to condemn the people who attend and enjoy the cock-fight he witnesses in New Orleans, he has no hesitation conveying just how degraded the loafers that Huck encounters in Bricksville are by telling us how they treat pigs and dogs:

All the streets and lanes was just mud, they warn't nothing else *but* mud—mud as black as tar, and nigh about a foot deep in some places; and two or three inches deep in *all* the places. The hogs loafed and grunted around, everywheres. You'd see a muddy sow and a litter of pigs come lazying along the street and whollop herself right down in the way, where folks had to walk around her, and she'd stretch out, and shut her eyes, and wave her ears, whilst the pigs was milking her, and look as happy as if she was on salary. And pretty soon you'd hear a loafer sing out, "Hi! *so* boy! sick him, Tige!" and away the sow would go, squealing most horrible, with a dog or two swinging to each ear, and three or four dozen more a-coming; and then you would see all the loafers get up and watch the thing out of sight, and laugh at the fun and look grateful for the noise. Then they'd settle back again, till there was a dog-fight. There couldn't anything wake them up all over, and make them happy all over, like a dog-fight—unless it might be putting turpentine on a stray dog and setting fire to him, or tying a tin to his tail and see him run himself to death.[70]

One effective measure of civilization, Twain suggests here, may be how men treat the nonhuman animals that are around them. (On this issue, as on many others, Twain was inconsistent. While the Bricksville loafers' interest in dog-fights makes them repugnant, the fondness with which Simon Wheeler recalls dog-fights starring the bull-pup Andrew Jackson in "Jim Smiley and His Jumping Frog" is not designed to make readers think any less of him.)

During the 1880s, Twain occasionally chose to leave the naturalist's precincts entirely, weaving impossible animals into preposterous fantasies. He claims to have written "A Cat-Tale" as a soporific for his daughters at bedtime. The cats are hardly animals at all, but rather imaginative constructs that Twain enlists for the project at hand—as are the "royal cats" that are considered for a moment as a substitute for a hereditary human monarchy in *A Connecticut Yankee*.[71] This latter piece, "A Prescription for Universal Peace," is a fanciful exploration of a theme to which Twain will return with greater and greater frequency—and seriousness—in the decades that follow: the idea that in important ways, nonhuman animals are superior to human beings.

1890s–1910

Concerning the difference between man and the jackass.
Some observers hold that there isn't any. But this wrongs the jackass.
—Notebook 42, typescript p. 72

MARK TWAIN PRODUCED more writing focused on animals during the last two decades of his life than he had in his entire career up to that point. These writings range from the charming and humorous to the darkly sardonic. Occasionally these disparate moods coexist (somewhat uneasily) in one text, as is the case with the first piece in this section, "Letters from a Dog to Another Dog Explaining and Accounting for Man" by "Author, Newfoundland Smith. Translated from the Original Doggerel by M.T." Written in 1891 but left unfinished, it is printed here for the first time. There is, to be sure, a fair measure of endearing whimsy in this piece, as when the dog "writing" the letters urges the friend to whom they are addressed to "sponge your mind clear of prejudice, ostensible information, and dogly tradition concerning Man and what he is for and why he was invented and whether he is worth while,—in a word make yourself a puppy again, with all which that implies of receptivity and hospitable welcome to any new thing." But more mordant undertones soon surface, as when the dog-author asks his friend, a Saint Bernard, to

Try to conceive of a nation of Men worthy to be nick-named St. Bernards! Contemplate the countenances of your great race, dear admirable friend of mine. All gracious traits are to be found there. . . . What nobility of mind, what benevolence, what honesty, what sincerity, what simplicity, what stainless purity of heart, what unselfishness, what truthfulness, . . . what gentle and winning humility, what loving welcome. . . .

Does this describe the rare & far-between St. Bernard Dog only? No, it describes every member of the race.

Try to imagine this benignant face distorted by hate, malice, envy; or framing itself to purposes of deceit; or to give expression to insolence, arrogance, egotism, vanity; or to frown away the supplicant, the friendless, the forsaken. . . .

Think of any nation among Men making serious claim to being the moral equals of the St. Bernard Dog. I mean as a nation, as a whole. Now and then, at long intervals, a Man has appeared in the earth who was a St. Bernard Dog in all but the name & shape, but no whole nation of Men has risen to a recognizable resemblance to that unrivaled race.[72]

"Letters from a Dog" soon begins to sound like an early draft of Twain's acerbic 1896 invective, "Man's Place in the Animal World," especially when the dog-author writes, "Malice resides in no animal but one—Man. . . . Ambition deforms and defiles the character of no animal but one—Man. . . . Cruelty—the inflicting of pain upon the feelings or the body for the mere pleasure of inflicting it—is an infamous characteristic which is found in no animal but one—Man." The relatively early date of this piece reminds us that Twain was comparing animals and humans to the disadvantage of the latter before the years when he became well known for his bleak view of humankind.

The round-the-world trip Twain took in 1895–1896 to repay his debts introduced him to a broad range of people, societies, and customs; but the birds he met on that trip—crows, magpies, laughing jackasses (better known today as kookaburras), nightingales, owls, coppersmiths—turned out to be more memorable, in some cases, than the people. In his final travel book, *Following the Equator* (1897), Twain admits to having become "infatuated" with "The Bird of Birds, the Indian Crow":

In his straddling wide forward-step, and his springy side-wise series of hops, and his impudent air, and his cunning way of canting his head to one side upon occasion, he reminds one of the American blackbird. But the sharp resemblances stop there. . . . The blackbird is a perfect gentleman, in deportment and attire, and is not noisy, I believe, except when holding religious services and political conventions in a tree; but this Indian sham Quaker is just a rowdy, and is always noisy when awake—always chaffing, scolding, scoffing, laughing, ripping and cursing and carrying on about something or other. I never saw such a bird for delivering opinions.[73]

Like so much of Twain's writing on animals, this passage blends attentive observation and description with anthropomorphic interpretation. But on this occasion, as on so many others, the blend works splendidly.

If I sat on one end of the balcony, the crows would gather on the railing at the other end and talk about me; and edge closer, little by little, till I could almost reach them; and they would sit there, in the most unabashed way, and talk about my clothes, and my hair, and my complexion, and probable character and vocation and politics, and how I came to be in India, and what I had been doing, and how many days I had got for it, and how I had happened to go unhanged so long . . . and so on, and so on, until I could not longer endure the embarrassment of it; then I would shoo them away, and they would circle around in the air a little while, laughing and deriding and mocking, and presently settle on the rail and do it all over again. . . . [74]

Twain conveys the loud and boisterous behavior of the crows by letting us know what it feels like to be the object of their comments. Are they talking about *him?* Well, yes: his presence prompts their unruly outburst. Are they expressing "thoughts" like the ones Twain ascribes to them? We can't know. We don't speak their language. But Twain persuades us that they *have* a language, and helps us hear what they're "saying" as if we were there ourselves.

Twain also tells us about the Australian magpie, famous for "never coming when he is called, always coming when he isn't, and studying disobedience as an accomplishment." He likes the magpie's "talent, and cuteness, and impudence," and recalls with fondness a domesticated magpie who "knew a number of tunes, and could sing them in perfect time and tune; and would do it, too, at any time that silence was wanted; and then encore himself and do it again; but if he was asked to sing he would go out and take a walk."[75] His affection for this bird seems to stem, at least in part, from the fact that it is as independent-minded as a cat, an animal whose virtues Twain never tires of singing. (As he put it on one occasion, "Of all God's creatures there is only one that cannot be made the slave of the lash. That one is the cat. If a man could be crossed with the cat it would improve man, but it would deteriorate the cat.")[76]

Readers of *Following the Equator* are treated to memorable descriptions of creatures as common as crows and magpies, and as uncommon as the curious ornithorhynchus, and are presented with vivid pictures of "pious" chameleons, "marvelous" moas, and the phosphorescent flash of porpoises frolicking in the moonlight. Twain provides vivid aural portraits as well as visual ones:

The song of the nightingale is the deadliest known to ornithology. That demoniacal shriek can kill at thirty yards. The note of the cue-owl is infinitely soft and
sweet—soft and sweet as the whisper of a flute. But penetrating—oh, beyond belief;
it can bore through boiler-iron. It is a lingering note, and comes in triplets, on the
one unchanging key: *hoo-o-o, hoo-o-o, hoo-o-o;* then a silence of fifteen seconds, then
the triplet again; and so on, all night. At first it is divine; then less so; then trying;
then distressing; then excruciating; then agonizing, and at the end of two hours
the listener is a maniac.[77]

As maddening as these birds are, however, they are not the most infuriat-
ing creatures in the animal kingdom for Twain. There is only one creature
on the planet who consistently incurs Twain's wrath: the housefly, the insect
who "hunts up patients suffering from loathsome and deadly diseases; wades
in their sores, gaums its legs with a million death-dealing germs; then comes
to that healthy man's table and wipes these things off on the butter and discharges a bowel-load of typhoid germs and excrement on his batter-cakes.
The housefly wrecks more human constitutions and destroys more human
lives than all God's multitude of misery-messengers and death-agents put
together."[78] With no hesitation, Twain asserts, in "The Supremacy of the House
Fly" (1906),

Of all the animals that inhabit the earth, the air, and the waters, I hate only one—
and that is the house fly. But I do hate him. I hate him with a hatred that is not
measurable with words. I always spare the snake and the spider, and the others,
and would not intentionally give them pain, but I would go out of my way, and
put aside my dearest occupation, to kill a fly, even if I knew it was the very last
one.[79]

(Twain follows this statement with an interesting confession: "I can even bear
to see a fly suffer for an entire minute—even two minutes, if it is one that I
have spent an hour hunting around the place with a wet towel—but that is
the limit. I would like to see him suffer a year, and would do it, and gladly, if I
could restrict the suffering to himself; but after it reaches a certain point, and
the bulk of it begins to fall to my share, I have to call a halt and put him out
of his misery, for I am like the rest of my race—I am merciful to a fellow-creature upon one condition only: that its pain shall not confer pain upon *me.*")[80]
Twain may have hated the common housefly early and often, but by the end
of his life he came to truly *loathe* above all others one member of the housefly
family, the blood-sucking tsetse fly, who plagued much of Africa in his day

with sleeping sickness—and who continues to threaten some sixty million Africans daily with the dread disease.[81]

The author known to have quipped that "nothing is made in vain, but the fly came near it" found flies useful to satirize the apparent willingness of the Russians to be ruled by an autocratic czar ("Flies and Russians," 1904–1905). Interestingly, although Twain was a sworn enemy of flies, he genuinely admired fleas, and wrote a paean to the physical prowess of the lowly flea in *Tom Sawyer Abroad* (1894).[82]

Twain had fun imagining how Adam and Eve understood their fellow creatures in the Garden of Eden in "Extracts from Adam's Diary" (1901), the "Autobiography of Eve" (1901), and "Eve's Diary" (1905). He committed to paper amusing anecdotes about deceitful turkeys and clever crows (1906), about how his wife's scheme for ridding the house of flies backfired (1906), and about the time he was sent an elephant for Christmas (1908).[83] Occasionally he digested and summarized the writings of naturalists in his own words—as in his essay "The Bee" (c. 1902), which is indebted, in part, to Sir John Lubbock's investigations of this insect.

But the whimsical, playful, and descriptive pages from these decades are outnumbered by the darker ones. As Twain grew increasingly disillusioned and pessimistic about his country and about humankind more generally, animals came to figure more and more prominently in his consciousness. He paid increasing attention to animal intelligence and emotions, and grew more and more dubious about the idea that human beings were a priori superior to the nonhuman animals they hunted and killed for sport, abandoned with impunity to certain death, or conducted painful and often unnecessary laboratory experiments on. Pieces in this book from this period that reflect these serious doubts include "Letters from a Dog to Another Dog Explaining and Accounting for Man" (1891), "The Sailors and the St. Bernard" (1896), "Man's Place in the Animal World" (1896), "Letter to the London Anti-Vivisection Society" (1899), "The Victims" (early 1900s), "The Jungle Discusses Man" (c. 1902), "Was the World made for Man?" (1903), "A Dog's Tale" (1903), "The Edisons of the Animal World" (1906), and *A Horse's Tale* (1906).

Sometimes darkness and whimsy go together—as in "Little Bessie Would Assist Providence" (1908 or 1909) and "The Victims" (early 1900s), two corrosive pieces that invoke the universality of predation in the animal kingdom. In "Little Bessie," a satire on Christian views of the purpose of suffering, a three-year-old reports having been told by Mr. Hollister, a man her mother calls a "scandalous person," that "there isn't a bird or fish or reptile or any other animal that hasn't got an enemy that Providence has sent to bite it and chase it and pester it, and kill it, and suck its blood and discipline it and make it good and religious."[84] Mr. Hollister has also told her that

the wasps catch spiders and cram them down into their nests on the ground—*alive*, mamma!—and there they live and suffer days and days and days, and the hungry little wasps chewing their legs and gnawing into their bellies all the time, to make them good and religious and praise God for his infinite mercies. . . . And mamma, he says the spider is appointed to catch the fly, and drive her fangs into his bowels, and suck and suck and suck his blood to discipline him and make him a Christian.[85]

(This passage is reminiscent of Twain's comment in *Innocents Abroad* about all the Church did to turn barbarians into Christians: "first by twisting their thumbs out of joint with a screw; then by nipping their flesh with pincers . . . ; then by skinning them alive a little, and finally, by roasting them in public. They always convinced those barbarians. The true religion, properly administered, as the good Mother Church used to administer it, is very, very soothing. It is wonderfully persuasive, also.")[86]

In "The Victims," the young offspring of a range of increasingly complex anthropomorphized creatures beg and beg their mothers to let them go to a picnic that "all the nicest creatures" were going to attend. The mamma says yes, and tells her beloved child to "be good, and behave, and be sure and be home before sundown" and "be careful," since "it would break mamma's heart if any harm came to her darling." She then promises "to have something nice for his supper when he got home." The "darling" leaves for the picnic and mamma leaves "to hunt the kind of game he preferred for supper." Inevitably, the "game" that mamma hunts is the "darling" of some other creature, who is also on its way to the picnic. For example,

Little Dora Sparrow begged
   So little Dora went to the picnic and mamma Sparrow went out to hunt little Sammy Pinch-Bug and harpooned him with her beak
   Little Harry Weasel begged
   So little Harry went to the picnic, and mamma Weasel went out to hunt and joined her teeth together in the person of little Dora Sparrow[87]

But the tenor changes when we come to Little Jimmy Gem-of-the-Creation Man, making one suspect that the other creatures' acts of hunting were an extended set-up for the following bit of searing social and moral critique:

Little Jimmy Gem-of-the-Creation Man begged

So little Jimmy went to the picnic and papa Gem-of-the-Creation went out to hunt for—for anything that might contain life and be helpless—

and hid behind a rock and shot little Jumbo Jackson dead with a magazine rifle and took his tusks and traded them to an Arab land-pirate for a cargo of captive black women and children and sold them to a good Christian planter who promised to give them religious instruction and considerable to do, and blest the planter and shook hands good-bye, and said "By cracky this is the way to extend our noble civilization," and loaded up again and Went for More.[88]

In "The Victims" Twain links Man to the rest of creation by having all the parents hunt for supper for their offspring; but at the same time he sets Man off from the other animals by making him the only animal who hunts armed with both insatiable greed and lofty rationales. The other animals, after all, unlike "papa Gem-of-the-Creation Man," neither "Went for More" nor justified their taking life for any purpose other than "supper."

Hunting and killing for "supper" was vastly more understandable in Twain's view than hunting for greed and material gain ("More"); and it was infinitely preferable to hunting for "sport," a practice Twain increasingly came to abhor, as this comparison of an earl with an anaconda underlines:

In the course of my reading I had come across a case where, many years ago, some hunters on our Great Plains organized a buffalo hunt for the entertainment of an English earl—that, and to provide some fresh meat for his larder. They had charming sport. They killed seventy-two of those great animals; and ate part of one of them and left the seventy-one to rot. In order to determine the difference between an anaconda and an earl—if any—I caused seven young calves to be turned into the anaconda's cage. The grateful reptile immediately crushed one of them and swallowed it, then lay back satisfied. It showed no further interest in the calves, and no disposition to harm them. I tried this experiment with other anacondas; always with the same result. The fact stood proven that the difference between an earl and an anaconda is, that the earl is cruel and the anaconda isn't; and that the earl wantonly destroys what he has no use for, but the anaconda doesn't.[89]

Twain dryly concludes, "This seemed to suggest that the anaconda was not descended from the earl. It also seemed to suggest that the earl was descended from the anaconda and had lost a good deal in the transition."[90] While several pieces Twain wrote in the 1890s attack hunting for sport (such as the passage about Huck killing a bird in *Tom Sawyer Abroad*), Twain's condemnations of hunting are relatively mild in comparison with his other attacks on cruelty to animals, a subject that he had addressed in various ways in print since 1867.

From 1899 until his death in 1910, Mark Twain lent his pen to reform efforts on both sides of the Atlantic and became the best-known American author—and, indeed, the most famous American celebrity in any field—to give outspoken, public support to agitation for animal welfare. This chapter of his life, however, has been largely neglected by biographers and critics.[91] To understand the factors that influenced Twain's thinking about issues of animal intelligence and animal emotions and that motivated his involvement in the animal welfare movement, it is helpful to examine the cultural conversation about animals going on around him that his own writing entered. This topic is the focus of the afterword to this book. For now, I'll simply give a brief overview of three key polemical pieces on the subject written during the last decade of Twain's life: his letter to the London Anti-Vivisection Society (1899), "A Dog's Tale" (1903), and A Horse's Tale (1907).

Twain was strongly opposed to vivisection, the practice of medical experimentation and demonstration on live animals (the history of the movement against vivisection and Twain's engagement in it is surveyed in more detail in the afterword). In 1899, as he prepared to move his family from Vienna to London, Twain wrote a letter to Sidney G. Trist, secretary of the London Anti-Vivisection Society, condemning vivisection in the strongest language he could muster. Trist gave the letter wide circulation in the press, and also had numerous copies printed as a pamphlet sold to benefit the society. "I believe I am not interested to know whether Vivisection produces results that are profitable to the human race or doesn't," Twain wrote.

To know that the results are profitable to the race would not remove my hostility to it. The pains which it inflicts upon unconsenting animals is the basis of my enmity towards it, & is to me sufficient justification of the enmity without looking further. It is so distinctly a matter of feeling with me, & is so strong & so deeply rooted in my make & constitution that I am sure I could not even see a vivisector vivisected with anything more than a sort of qualified satisfaction. I do not say I should not go & look on; I only mean that I should almost surely fail to get out of it the degree of contentment which it ought of course to be expected to furnish.[92]

Twain's dramatic, widely circulated 1899 letter gave the London Anti-Vivisection Society an eloquent and important endorsement that was reprinted frequently in periodicals in the United States and Britain.[93] It was also published as a freestanding pamphlet called The Pains of Lowly Life in 1900 by the London

Anti-Vivisection Society, which sold it for tuppence. The New York Anti-Vivisection Society also published it as a pamphlet entitled *Mark Twain on Vivisection* around 1905, and the New England Anti-Vivisection Society published it as a pamphlet around the same time.[94] Twain's letter continues to have an impact on social thought and activism: excerpts from it appear on over a thousand animal welfare and animal rights Web sites around the world today.[95]

What—and who—might have led him to write it? Twain had been responding to animals with curiosity and compassion throughout his career, and had been exposing cruelty to animals whenever he encountered it. But others who shared those views did not necessarily become animal welfare activists. A look at Twain's reading, at his friendships with men who were committed antivivisectionists, and at the state of vivisection in fin de siècle Vienna might help us understand the origins of this famous text (all of these issues are addressed in the afterword).

Four years after publishing his letter to the London Anti-Vivisection Society, in the winter of 1903, Twain turned his pen to the subject of vivisection once again with his publication of "A Dog's Tale" in the Christmas issue of *Harper's.* (Some possible reasons why Twain may have written "A Dog's Tale" when he did are addressed in the afterword.) "A Dog's Tale" is narrated by a charming and articulate dog. But while the narrator is endearing, the story she tells is chilling. She is celebrated for the quick intelligence and courage that she showed when she rescued her master's child from a fire.[96] Her owner proclaims that, were it not "for the beast's intelligence—it's *reason*, I tell you!—the child would have perished!" But he and his friends have an amateur interest in the science of optics, and are curious about "whether a certain injury to the brain would produce blindness or not." To resolve their debate, they take the dog's beloved puppy to the laboratory in their home. The mother dog, who was lamed when she rescued her master's child, tells us that when her puppy was taken to the laboratory, she

limped three-leggedly along, too, feeling proud, for any attention shown to the puppy was a pleasure to me, of course. They discussed and experimented, and then suddenly the puppy shrieked, and they set him on the floor, and he went staggering around, with his head all bloody, and the master clapped his hands and shouted:

"There, I've won—confess it! He's a blind as a bat!"[97]

At the story's close, the mother dog does not grasp that the man whose child she saved has killed *her* child. But words that she doesn't understand carry "something cold to [her] heart." Often dismissed as "pathetic" and "sentimental," the story might just as reasonably be read as a deft and wrenching parable about the treatment of the self-sacrificing Mammy's own children under slavery, as well as a scathing condemnation of vivisection. (This resonance may be less surprising when we recall that in Britain at least, early opponents of vivisection were often veteran activists of the movement to end slavery, and that after Britain abolished slavery, the radical wing of the antivivisection movement adopted the term "abolitionists" to describe themselves.) Once again—as was the case with his letter to the London Anti-Vivisection Society—"A Dog's Tale" was reprinted in pamphlet form and sold for the benefit of antivivisection societies.[98] On occasion the reprinting of the story as a pamphlet was treated as news in its own right: the *Christian Observer* reported in 1904 that "Harper & Brothers have been requested to supply several thousand specially bound copies of Mark Twain's story, 'A Dog's Tale,' which appeared in *Harper's Magazine* for December, to the Hon. Stephen Coleridge, Honorary Secretary of the National Anti-Vivisection Society of England for distribution there as a powerful argument against vivisection."[99] The London and Provincial Antivivisection society issued it as a pamphlet, as well. Harper and Brothers also published it as a book in 1904 with illustrations by W. T. Smedley.[100] It was reprinted in all the editions of Twain's collected works.

The story attracted its share of controversy when it first appeared. An unsigned "Topic of the Times" column in the *New York Times* in December 1903 claimed that "every one of the medical journals" opined "that, in regard at least to vivisection, its methods and its objects, Mr. Clemens is a very ignorant person." [101] The *Times* referred to the "complete misunderstanding it reveals as to how and why seekers of knowledge resort to the dissection of living animals." It is true that by choice Twain himself had little firsthand contact with vivisection. But *was* the story as off base as the *Times* writer claimed? Ten years earlier, after all, in 1894, Dr. Albert Leffingwell had documented an experiment in Jersey City, New Jersey, in which an experimenter had dropped "a great number of dogs" 141 times from a height of more than two stories "to produce the greatest amount of injury to the spinal cord and its attachments without killing the animal outright."[102] Leffingwell quotes "the highest European authority upon medical questions" as maintaining that this experiment "*is a record of the most wanton and stupidest cruelty we have ever seen chronicled under the guise of scientific experiments.*" The document he quotes goes on to ask,

What conclusions can be drawn from these unscientific experiments? That dogs falling from a height of twenty-four feet were liable to rupture or injure lungs, liver, kidneys, viscera, blood-vessels, or bones? Is there anything new or useful in this grand discovery? That pathological changes rarely occurred in the spinal cord? Does this help us to any similar conclusion, after totally dissimilar railway accidents to man? Not the least. Badly planned and without a chance of teaching us anything, *and carried out in a wholesale cruel way, we cannot but feel ashamed of the work as undertaken by a member of our profession.*[103]

Dr. Leffingwell wrote letters to the presidents of American colleges and universities asking whether the universities had *"placed any limitations to painful experimentation on living animals?* Are students . . . permitted to carry their investigations *to any extent* inclination may suggest?"[104] The presidents of Stanford, Yale, Harvard, Princeton, the University of Chicago, Tufts, the University of California, etc. all wrote back with some variation on the unashamed assertion that no such restrictions existed at their institutions.[105]

While the anonymous critic in the *Times* had negative things to say about "A Dog's Tale" when it appeared in *Harper's* in 1903, when the story came out as a book in 1904, it received almost uniformly positive reviews. The *Charleston Sunday News* noted that the "terrible indictment of the vivisectionists created a real sensation when it appeared a year ago in *Harper's Magazine*" and predicted that the "attractive little volume" in which it was republished "may be trusted to do an effective work in its appeal to the hearts of its readers. . . . we should not like to be the man who could read this story and remain uninvolved."[106] Most but not all reviewers shared the opinion of the *Detroit Free Press* that Twain's blend of "humor and pathos" in the book was successful; *Congregationalist and Christian World* called it "a most effective plea against the excesses of vivisection."[107]

In addition to letting antivivisection organizations on both sides of the Atlantic promote their cause with pamphlets reprinting his writings, Twain wrote an anti-bullfighting novella, *A Horse's Tale*, in 1905, at the request of animal welfare activist and actress Minnie Maddern Fiske.[108] Fiske, known for performing both Ibsen and light comedy, was a militant animal welfare activist who protested issues ranging from the steel traps used to capture animals for fur coats to the treatment of mules in oil fields.[109] She forbade other actresses appearing with her onstage to wear furs or feather-decorated hats offstage or on, and was known for collecting stray cats in towns in which she played while on tour.[110] Fiske had been moved by "A Dog's Tale" and asked Twain to do something to help save the horses cruelly sacrificed in the Spanish bullring after years of faithful service. "I have lain awake nights very often wondering if I dare ask you to write a story of an old horse that is finally given over to the bull-ring," Fiske wrote, adding, "The story you would write would do more good than all the laws we are trying to have made and enforced for the prevention of cruelty to animals in Spain. We would translate and circulate the story in that country. I have wondered if you would ever write it."[111] Twain replied promptly: "I shall certainly write the story."[112]

Twain began work on the piece immediately. In a letter to his editor at *Harper's Magazine*, where he submitted it for serial publication the year before Harper and Brothers published it as a book, he explains how he had put in "a good deal of work on it," even trying to get the bugle calls right by having his secretary play them on the orchestrelle. He was particularly interested in the story once he realized, after the work was well under way, that he had based the heroine on "my small daughter Susy, whom we lost."[113] The letter he sent with the manuscript makes it clear that Twain was anxious that it reach the largest audience possible. "Don't you think you can get it into the Jan. & Feb. numbers & issue it as a dollar booklet just after the middle of Jan. when you issue the Feb. number?" he asked his publisher, adding, "Why not sell simultaneous rights, for this once, to the Ladies' Home Journal or Collier's, or both, & recoup yourself?—for I would like to get it to classes that can't afford Harper's. Although it doesn't preach, there's a sermon concealed in it."[114] A year after it was published, Fiske "sent him her grateful acknowledgments, and asked permission to have it printed for pamphlet circulation in Spain" as part of her anti-bullfighting crusade.[115] *A Horse's Tale* is marred by a melodramatic plot, and an excess of sentimentality, and could have stood some heavy editing (an abridged version of the novella is included here). But it has some moments that are vintage Twain—simultaneously engaging, entertaining, and compelling.[116] And it clearly moved some of its readers, one of whose letters Twain included in an autobiographical dictation. "Dear 'Mark Twain,'" wrote the correspondent (who was a stranger to him) on August 25, 1906,

Please don't write any more such heart-breaking stories. I have just been reading Soldier Boy's story in Harper's. I don't think I would have read it had I known what was to come to [the horse named] Soldier Boy. . . .

   When your story of the poor dog was published in Harper's I read it—and I can't tell you what I felt. I have never re-read it and I try not to remember it, but I can't help it. And now this story of Soldier Boy. It sinks into my heart. I feel like stretching out my hand to you and saying "I, too, feel these things, the dumb helpless pain of all the poor animals, and my soul protests against it, mightily but impotently, like yours."[117]

In an autobiographical dictation, Twain adds his own response to this letter, saying, "I have explained my case to the lady as follows."

Dear Madam:

I know it is a pity to wring the poor human heart, and it grieves me to do it; but it is the only way to move some people to reflect.

The "Horse's Tale" has a righteous purpose. It was not written for publication here, but in Spain. I was asked to write it to assist a band of generous ladies and gentlemen of Spain who have set themselves the gracious task of persuading the children of that country to renounce and forsake the cruel bull-fight. This is in the hope that these children will carry on the work when they grow up. It is a great and fine cause, and if this story, distributed abroad in Spain in translation can in any degree aid it, I shall not be sorry that I complied with the request with which I was honored.[118]

Although the book version of the tale in English that came out in 1907 never achieved the readership of an earlier story told from the horse's point of view, Anna Sewell's *Black Beauty* (several million copies of which were distributed free by animal welfare organizations), *A Horse's Tale* got glowing reviews in both the United States and Britain. The *Birmingham Post* (U.K.) wrote that the book "indicates that Mark Twain has lost nothing of his fine humanity, his gift of vivid description, his mastery of quaint American dialogue," adding, "Of his humour there is less to be said, for the story is not humorous."[119] The *Louisville Courier-Journal* asserted that "Our beloved Mr. Clemens has here combined his most delicate veins of humor and pathos."[120] A reviewer in the *New York Times* wrote that the book combined "some of the best flavor of Mark Twain's peculiar humor with sentiment borrowed partly from standard nursery literature and partly from the tracts of the Society for the Prevention of Cruelty to Animals."[121] *Book News Monthly* called the book "one of the most important published this fall in fiction."[122] A British publication, *Bookman*, saw the resonances between *A Horse's Tale* and "A Dog's Tale," viewing both as emblematic of an increasingly significant dimension of Twain's career, his role as advocate for animal welfare: "All our lives we have known Mark Twain as an ever-welcome humorist; but of late years we have learnt that he has additions to this early virtue. We see him now as a lover and champion of animals."[123]

TEN YEARS EARLIER, in 1896, in "Man's Place in the Animal World," a text published posthumously in *Letters from the Earth,* Twain had written,

I have been scientifically studying the traits and dispositions of the "lower animals" (so-called,) and contrasting them with the traits and dispositions of man. I find the results profoundly humiliating to me. For it obliges me to renounce my allegiance to the Darwinian theory of the Ascent of Man from the Lower Animals; since it now seems plain to me that the theory ought to be vacated in favor of a new and truer one, this new and truer one to be named the *Descent* of Man from the Higher Animals.

He supports this idea with some of the observations that have led him to this conclusion, such as,

Of all the animals, man is the only one that is cruel. He is the only one that inflicts pain for the pleasure of doing it. It is a trait not known to the higher animals. . . . Man is the Religious Animal. He is the only Religious Animal. He is the only animal that has the True Religion—several of them. He is the only animal that loves his neighbor as himself, and cuts his throat if his theology isn't straight. He has made a graveyard of the globe in trying his honest best to smooth his brother's path to happiness and heaven.[124]

Perhaps Twain's most succinct summary of this position is his famous comment (from this same essay), "man is the Animal that Blushes. He is the only one that does it—or has occasion to."[125]

Twain had explored similar ideas in "Letters from a Dog to Another Dog Explaining and Accounting for Man" in which the dog-narrator, Newfoundland Smith, suggests that Darwin's theory of evolution has it backwards: "Man's new claim is obviously untenable," he writes. "It would be the reverse of difficult to show that in true nobleness and fineness of character his stage of development is far below that of the other animals"; Smith supports this assertion with a litany of man's sordid qualifications:

Lust of vengeance for old treasured injury is found in the character of no animal but one—Man. . . .

Base spirit, boot-licking servility. These degradations are found in the characters of no animals but two—Man and the Dog. And the Dog was free of them until he took to comradeship with Man.

Slavery. No animal inflicts it but Man and the Ant. . . .

Captivity, mutilation and death for opinions' sake. No animal has had experience of this sort but one—Man.

This creature has invented a heaven. And from it has excluded all the animals but himself.

Our own philosophy has always taught that Man was on his tedious and patient way upward toward the moral heights attained by the other animals—with a considerable distance to climb yet; and so far I see nothing the matter with that theory.[126]

Twain saw "nothing the matter with that theory" either. Indeed, events that he witnessed during the last two decades of his life confirmed its validity: he watched—appalled—as his country embraced imperialism with the enthusiasm of all the other imperialist nations, and he watched so-called "civilized" nations manifest ever-increasing hypocrisy, nationalism, and greed. Twain's awareness of his fellow human beings' willingness to disregard the welfare of animals became an integral part of this broader disillusionment and despair. "The dog is a gentleman," he wrote William Dean Howells in 1899; "I hope to go to his heaven, not man's."[127]

Twain's rejection of the theory of evolution—from a moral standpoint at least—did not dim his interest in reading the latest books on it. In 1903, Twain acquired a book by a physician, S. V. Clevenger, entitled *The Evolution of Man and His Mind. A History and Science of the Evolution and Relation of the Mind and Body of Man and Animals*. Twain often scribbled his disagreement with authors in the margins of their books. But he must have approved of what Clevenger wrote on page 404 (in chap. 11, "Development of the Brain"), since he marked the passage without quibbling about Clevenger's syntax or sense: "Mark Twain will, in all future ages, be recognized as one who educated his readers to important, yes, vital matters, while amusing them."[128] Not bad, as literary epitaphs go. Twain must have been pleasantly surprised to find something so accurate in a book about evolution. It is my hope that *Mark Twain's Book of Animals* will help Twain continue to teach his readers about "important, yes, vital matters, while amusing them."

Part One: 1850s and 1860s

Bugs!

BUGS! YES, B-U-G-S! What of the bugs? Why, perdition take the bugs! That is all. Night before last I stood at the little press until nearly 2 o'clock, and the flaring gas light over my head attracted all the varieties of bugs which are to be found in natural history, and they all had the same praiseworthy recklessness about flying into the fire. They at first came in little social crowds of a dozen or so, but soon increased in numbers, until a religious mass meeting of several millions was assembled on the board before me, presided over by a venerable beetle, who occupied the most prominent lock of my hair as his chair of state, while innumerable lesser dignitaries of the same tribe were clustered around him, keeping order, and at the same time endeavoring to attract the attention of the vast assemblage to their own importance by industriously grating their teeth. It must have been an interesting occasion— perhaps a great bug jubilee commemorating the triumph of the locusts over Pharaoh's crops in Egypt many centuries ago. At least, good seats, commanding an unobstructed view of the scene, were in great demand; and I have no doubt small fortunes were made by certain delegates from Yankee land by disposing of comfortable places on my shoulders at round premiums. In fact, the advantages which my altitude afforded were so well appreciated that I soon began to look like one of those big cards in the museum covered with insects impaled on pins.

The big "president" beetle (who, when he frowned, closely resembled Isbell when the pupils are out of time) rose and ducked his head and, crossing his arms over his shoulders, stroked them down to the tip of his nose several times, and after thus disposing of the perspiration, stuck his hands under his wings, propped his back against a lock of hair, and then, bobbing his head at the congregation, remarked, "B-u-z-z!" To which the congregation devoutly responded, "B-u-z-z!" Satisfied with this promptness on the part of his flock, he took a more imposing perpendicular against another lock of hair and, lifting his hands to command silence, gave another melodious "b-u-z-z!" on a louder key (which I suppose to have been the key-note) and after a moment's silence the whole congregation burst into a grand anthem, three dignified daddy longlegs, perched near the gas burner, beating quadruple time during the performance. Soon two of the parts in the great chorus maintained silence, while a treble and alto duet, sung by forty-seven thousand mosquitoes and twenty-three thousand house flies, came in, and then, after another chorus, a tenor and bass duet by thirty-two thousand locusts and ninety-seven thousand pinch bugs was sung—then another grand chorus, "Let Every Bug Rejoice and Sing" (we used to sing "heart" instead of "bug"), terminated the performance, during which eleven treble singers split their throats from head to heels, and the patriotic "daddies" who beat time hadn't a stump of a leg left.

It would take a ream of paper to give all the ceremonies of this great mass meeting [. . . .]

❧

Cruelty to Animals I

PROBABLY THERE IS no law against it. A large truck wagon, with a load on it nearly as heavy as an ordinary church, came to a stand-still on the slippery cobble stones in front of the Russ House, yesterday, simply because the solitary horse attached to it found himself unable to keep up his regular gait with it. A street car and other vehicles were delayed some time by the blockade. It was natural to expect that a "streak" of lightning would come after the driver out of the cloudless sky, but it did not. It is likely Providence wasn't noticing.

❧

Jim Smiley and His Jumping Frog

MR. A. WARD,
Dear Sir:—Well, I called on good-natured, garrulous old Simon Wheeler, and inquired after your friend, Leonidas W. Smiley, as you requested me to do, and I hereunto append the result. If you can get any information out of it you are cordially welcome to it. I have a lurking suspicion that your Leonidas W. Smiley is a myth—that you never knew such a personage, and that you only conjectured that if I asked old Wheeler about him it would remind him of his infamous *Jim* Smiley, and he would go to work and bore me nearly to death with some infernal reminiscence of him as long and tedious as it should be

useless to me. If that was your design, Mr. Ward, it will gratify you to know that it succeeded.

I found Simon Wheeler dozing comfortably by the bar-room stove of the little old dilapidated tavern in the ancient mining camp of Boomerang, and I noticed that he was fat and bald-headed, and had an expression of winning gentleness and simplicity upon his tranquil countenance. He roused up and gave me good-day. I told him a friend of mine had commissioned me to make some inquiries about a cherished companion of his boyhood named Leonidas W. Smiley—Rev. Leonidas W. Smiley—a young minister of the gospel, who he had heard was at one time a resident of this village of Boomerang. I added that if Mr. Wheeler could tell me anything about this Rev. Leonidas W. Smiley, I would feel under many obligations to him.

Simon Wheeler backed me into a corner and blockaded me there with his chair—and then sat down and reeled off the monotonous narrative which follows this paragraph. He never smiled, he never frowned, he never changed his voice from the quiet, gently-flowing key to which he tuned the initial sentence, he never betrayed the slightest suspicion of enthusiasm—but all through the interminable narrative there ran a vein of impressive earnestness and sincerity, which showed me plainly that so far from his imagining that there was anything ridiculous or funny about his story, he regarded it as a really important matter, and admired its two heroes as men of transcendent genius in finesse. To me, the spectacle of a man drifting serenely along through such a queer yarn without ever smiling was exquisitely absurd. As I said before, I asked him to tell me what he knew of Rev. Leonidas W. Smiley, and he replied as follows. I let him go on in his own way, and never interrupted him once:

There was a feller here once by the name of *Jim* Smiley, in the winter of '49—or maybe it was the spring of '50—I don't recollect exactly, some how, though what makes me think it was one or the other is because I remember the big flume wasn't finished when he first come to the camp; but anyway, he was the curiosest man about always betting on anything that turned up you ever see, if he could get anybody to bet on the other side, and if he couldn't he'd change sides—any way that suited the other man would suit *him*—any way just so's he got a bet, *he* was satisfied. But still, he was lucky—uncommon lucky; he most always come out winner. He was always ready and laying for a chance; there couldn't be no solitry thing mentioned but what that feller'd offer to bet on it—and take any side you please, as I was just telling you: if there was a horse race, you'd find him flush or you find him busted at the end of it; if there was a dog-fight, he'd bet on it; if there was a cat-fight, he'd bet on it; if there was a chicken-fight, he'd bet on it; why if there was two birds setting on a fence, he would bet you which one would fly first—or if there was a camp-meeting he would be there reglar to bet on parson Walker, which he judged to be the best exhorter about here, and so he was, too, and a good man; if he even see a straddle-bug start to go any wheres, he would bet you how long it would take him to get wherever he was going to, and if you took him up he would foller that straddle-bug to Mexico but what he would find out where he was bound for and how long he was on the road. Lots of the boys here has seen that Smiley and can tell you about him. Why, it never made no difference to *him*—he would bet on *anything*—the dangdest feller. Parson Walker's wife laid very sick, once, for a good while, and it seemed as if they warn't going to save her; but one morning he come in and Smiley asked him how she was, and he said she was considerable better—thank the Lord for his inf'nit mercy—and coming on so smart that with the blessing of Providence she'd get well yet—and Smiley, before he thought, says, "Well, I'll resk two-and-a-half that she don't, anyway."

Thish-yer Smiley had a mare—the boys called her the fifteen-minute nag, but that was only in fun, you know, because, of course, she was faster than that—and he used to win money on that horse, for all she was so slow and always had the asthma, or the distemper, or the consumption, or something of that kind. They used to give her two or three hundred yards' start, and then pass her under way; but always at the fag-end of the race she'd get excited and desperate-like, and come cavorting and spraddling up, and scattering her legs around limber, sometimes in the air, and sometimes out to one side amongst the fences, and kicking up m-o-r-e dust, and raising m-o-r-e racket with her coughing and sneezing and blowing her nose—and always fetch up at the stand just about a neck ahead, as near as you could cipher it down.

And he had a little small bull-pup, that to look at him you'd think he warn't worth a cent, but to set around and look ornery, and lay for a chance to steal something. But as soon as money was up on him he was a different dog—his under-jaw'd begin to stick out like the for'castle of a steamboat, and his teeth would uncover, and shine savage like the furnaces. And a dog might tackle him, and bully-rag him, and bite him, and throw him over his shoulder two or three times, and Andrew Jackson—which was the name of the pup—Andrew Jackson would never let on but what he was satisfied, and hadn't expected nothing else—and the bets being doubled and doubled on the other side all the time, till the money was all up—and then all of a sudden he would grab that other dog just by the joint of his hind legs and freeze to it—not chaw, you understand, but only just grip and hang on till they threw up the sponge, if it was a year. Smiley always came out winner on that pup till he harnessed a dog once that didn't have no hind legs because they'd been sawed off in a circular saw, and when the thing had gone along far enough, and the money was all up, and he came to make a snatch for his pet holt, he saw in a minute how he'd been imposed on, and how the other dog had him in the door, so to speak, and he 'peared surprised, and then he looked sorter discouraged like, and didn't try no more to win the fight, and so he got shucked out bad. He gave Smiley a look as much as to say his heart was broke, and it was *his* fault, for putting up a dog that hadn't no hind legs for him to take holt of, which was his main dependence in a fight, and then he limped off a piece, and laid down and died. It was a good pup, was that Andrew Jackson, and would have made a name for hisself if he'd lived, for the stuff was in him, and he had genius—I know it, because he hadn't had no opportunities to speak of, and it don't stand to reason that a dog could make such a fight as he could under them circumstances, if he hadn't no talent. It always makes me feel sorry when I think of that last fight of his'on, and the way it turned out.

Well, thish-yer Smiley had rat-tarriers and chicken cocks, and tom-cats, and all of them kind of things, till you couldn't rest, and you couldn't fetch nothing for him to bet on but he'd match you. He ketched a frog one day and took him home and said he cal'lated to educate him; and so he never done nothing for three months but set in his back yard and learn that frog to jump. And you bet you he *did* learn him, too. He'd give him a little hunch behind, and the next minute you'd see that frog whirling in the air like a doughnut—see him turn one summerset, or maybe a couple, if he got a good start, and come down flat-footed and all right, like a cat. He got him up so in the matter of ketching flies, and kept him in practice so constant, that he'd nail a fly every time as far as he could see him. Smiley said all a frog wanted was education, and he could do most anything—and I believe him. Why, I've seen him set Dan'l Webster down here on this floor—Dan'l Webster was the name of the frog—and sing out, "Flies! Dan'l, flies," and quicker'n you could wink, he'd spring straight up, and snake a fly off'n the counter there, and flop down on the floor again as solid as a gob of mud, and fall to scratching the side of his head with his hind foot as indifferent as if he hadn't no idea he'd done any more'n any frog might do. You never see a frog so modest and straightfor'ard as he was, for all he was so gifted. And when it come to fair-and-square jumping on a dead level, he could get over more ground at one straddle than any animal of his breed you ever see. Jumping on a dead level was his strong suit, you understand, and when it come to that, Smiley would ante up money on him as long as he had a red. Smiley was monstrous proud of his frog, and well he might be, for fellers that had travelled and ben everywheres all said he laid over any frog that ever *they* see.

Well, Smiley kept the beast in a little lattice box, and he used to fetch him down town sometimes and lay for a bet. One day a feller—a stranger in the camp, he was—come across him with his box, and says:

"What might it be that you've got in the box?"

And Smiley says, sorter indifferent like, "It might be a parrot, or it might be a canary, maybe, but it ain't—it's only just a frog."

And the feller took it, and looked at it careful, and turned it round this way and that, and says, "H'm—so 'tis. Well, what's *he* good for?"

"Well," Smiley says, easy and careless, "He's good enough for *one* thing I should judge—he can out-jump ary frog in Calaveras county."

The feller took the box again, and took another long, particular look, and give it back to Smiley and says, very deliberate, "Well—I don't see no points about that frog that's any better'n any other frog."

"Maybe you don't," Smiley says. "Maybe you understand frogs, and maybe you don't understand 'em; maybe you've had experience, and maybe you ain't only a amature, as it were. Anyways, I've got *my* opinion, and I'll resk forty dollars that he can outjump ary frog in Calaveras county."

And the feller studied a minute, and then says, kinder sad, like, "Well—I'm only a stranger here, and I ain't got no frog—but if I had a frog I'd bet you."

And then Smiley says, "That's all right—that's all right—if you'll hold my box a minute I'll go and get you a frog;" and so the feller took the box, and put up his forty dollars along with Smiley's, and set down to wait.

So he set there a good while thinking and thinking to hisself, and then he got the frog out and prized his mouth open and took a teaspoon and filled him full of quail-shot—filled him pretty near up to his chin—and set him on the floor. Smiley he went to the swamp and slopped around in the mud for a long time, and finally he ketched a frog and fetched him in and give him to this feller and says:

"Now if you're ready, set him alongside of Dan'l, with his fore-paws just even with Dan'l's, and I'll give the word." Then he says, "one—two—three—jump!" and him and the feller touched up the frogs from behind, and the new frog hopped off lively, but Dan'l give a heave, and hysted up his shoulders—so—like a Frenchman, but it wasn't no use—he couldn't budge; he was planted as solid as a anvil, and he couldn't no more stir than if he was anchored out.

Smiley was a good deal surprised, and he was disgusted too, but he didn't have no idea what the matter was, of course.

The feller took the money and started away; and when he was going out at the door he sorter jerked his thumb over his shoulder—this way—at Dan'l, and says again, very deliberate, "Well—*I* don't see no points about that frog that's any better'n any other frog."

Smiley he stood scratching his head and looking down at Dan'l a long time, and at last he says, "I do wonder what in the nation that frog throwed off for—I wonder if there ain't something the matter with him—he 'pears to look mighty baggy, somehow"—and he ketched Dan'l by the nap of the neck, and lifted him up and says, "Why blame my cats if he don't weigh five pound"—and turned him upside down, and he belched out about a double-handful of shot. And then he see how it was, and he was the maddest man—he set the frog down and took out after that feller, but he never ketched him. And—

[Here Simon Wheeler heard his name called from the front-yard, and got up to go and see what was wanted.] And turning to me as he moved away, he said: "Just sit where you are, stranger, and rest easy—I ain't going to be gone a second."

But by your leave, I did not think that a continuation of the history of the enterprising vagabond Jim Smiley would be likely to afford me much information concerning the Rev. Leonidas W. Smiley, and so I started away.

At the door I met the sociable Wheeler returning, and he buttonholed me and recommenced:

"Well, thish-yer Smiley had a yaller one-eyed cow that didn't have no tail only just a short stump like a bannanner, and—"

"O, curse Smiley and his afflicted cow!" I muttered, good-naturedly, and bidding the old gentleman good-day, I departed.

Yours, truly,
Mark Twain.

ꝫ

Fitz Smythe's Horse

YESTERDAY, AS I was coming along through a back alley, I glanced over a fence, and there was Fitz Smythe's horse. I can easily understand, now, why that horse always looks so dejected and indifferent to the things of this world. They feed him on old newspapers. I had often seen Smythe carrying "dead loads" of old exchanges up town, but I never suspected that they were to be put to such a use as this. A boy came up while I stood there, and said, "That hoss belongs to Mr. Fitz Smythe, and the old man—that's my father, you know—the old man's going to kill him."

"Who, Fitz Smythe?"

"No, the hoss—because he et up a litter of pups that the old man wouldn't a taken forty dol—"

"Who, Fitz Smythe?"

"No, the hoss—and he eats fences and everything—took our gate off and carried it home and et up every dam splinter of it; you wait till he gets done with them old *Altas* and *Bulletins* he's a chawin' on now, and you'll see him branch out and tackle a-n-y-thing he can shet his mouth on. Why, he nipped a little boy, Sunday, which was going home from Sunday school; well, the boy got loose, you know, but that old hoss got his bible and some tracts, and them's as good a thing as *he* wants, being so used to papers, you see. You put anything to eat anywheres, and that old hoss'll shin out and get it—and he'll eat anything he can bite, and he don't care a dam. He'd climb a tree, he would, if you was to put anything up there for him—cats, for instance—he likes cats—he's et up every cat there was here in four blocks—he'll take more chances—

why, he'll bust in anywheres for one of them fellers; I see him snake a old tom cat out of that there flower-pot over yonder, where she was a sunning of her-self, and take her down, and she a hanging on and a grabbling for a holt on something, and you could hear her yowl and kick up and tear around after she was inside of him. You see Mr. Fitz Smythe don't give him nothing to eat but them old newspapers and sometimes a basket of shavings, and so you know, he's got to prospect or starve, and a hoss ain't going to starve, it ain't likely, on account of not wanting to be rough on cats and sich things. Not that hoss, anyway, you bet you. Because *he* don't care a dam. You turn him loose once on this town, and don't you know he'd eat up m-o-r-e goods-boxes, and fences, and clothing-store things, and animals, and all them kind of valu-ables? Oh, you bet he would. Because that's his style, you know, and he don't care a dam. But you ought to see Mr. Fitz Smythe ride him around, prospect-ing for them items—you ought to see him with his soldier coat on, and his mustashers sticking out strong like a cat-fish's horns, and them long laigs of his'n standing out so, like them two prongs they prop up a step-ladder with, and a jolting down street at four mile a week—oh, what a guy!—sets up stiff like a close pin, you know, and thinks he looks like old General Macdowl. But the old man's a going to hornisswoggle that hoss on account of his goblin up them pups. Oh, you bet your life the old man's *down* on him. Yes, sir, coming!" and the entertaining boy departed to see what the "old man" was calling him for. But I am glad that I met the boy, and I am glad I saw the horse taking his literary breakfast, because I know now why the animal looks so discouraged when I see Fitz Smythe rambling down Montgomery street on him—he has altogether too rough a time getting a living to be cheerful and frivolous or anyways frisky.

℘

Cruelty to Animals II

ONE OF THE most praiseworthy institutions in New York, and one which must plead eloquently for it when its wickedness shall call down the anger of the gods, is the Society for the Prevention of Cruelty to Animals. Its office is located on the corner of Twelfth street and Broadway, and its affairs are con-ducted by humane men who take a genuine interest in their work, and who have got worldly wealth enough to make it unnecessary for them to busy themselves about anything else. They have already put a potent check upon the brutality of draymen and others to their horses, and in future will draw a still tighter rein upon such abuses, a late law of the Legislature having quadrupled their powers, and distinctly marked and specified them. You seldom see a horse beaten or otherwise cruelly used in New York now, so much has the society made itself feared and respected. Its members promptly secure the arrest of guilty parties and relentlessly prosecute them.

The new law gives the Society power to designate an adequate number of agents in every county, and these are appointed by the Sheriff, but work independently of all other branches of the civil organization. They can make arrests of guilty persons on the spot, without calling upon the regular police, and what is better, they can compel a man to stop abusing his horse, his dog, or any other animal, at a moment's warning. The object of the Society, as its name implies, is to prevent cruelty to animals, rather than punish men for being guilty of it.

They are going to put up hydrants and water tanks at convenient distances all over the city, for drinking places for men, horses and dogs.

Mr. Bergh, the President of the Society, is a sort of enthusiast on the subject of cruelty to animals—or perhaps it would do him better justice to say he is full of honest earnestness upon the subject. Nothing that concerns the happiness of a brute is a trifling matter with him—no brute of whatever position or standing, however plebeian or insignificant, is beneath the range of his merciful interest. I have in my mind an example of his kindly solicitude for his dumb and helpless friends.

He went to see the dramatic version of "Griffith Gaunt" at Wallack's Theatre. The next morning he entered the manager's office and the following conversation took place:

Mr. Bergh—"Are you the manager of this theatre?"

Manager—"I am, sir. What can I do for you?"

Mr. B.—"I am President of the Society for the Prevention of Cruelty to Animals, and I have come to remonstrate against your treatment of that pig in the last act of the play last night. It is cruel and wrong, and I beg that you will leave the pig out in future."

"That is impossible! The pig is necessary to the play."

"But it is cruel, and you could alter the play in some way so as to leave the pig out."

"It cannot possibly be done, and besides I do not see anything wrong about it at all. What is it you complain of?"

"Why, it is plain enough. They punch the pig with sticks, and chase him and harass him, and contrive all manner of means to make him unhappy. The poor thing runs about in its distress, and tries to escape, but is met at every turn by its tormentors and its hopes blighted. The pig does not understand it. If the pig understood it, it might be well enough, but the pig does not know it is a play, but takes it all as reality, and is frightened and bewildered by the crowd of people and the glare of the lights, and yet no time is given it for reflection—no time is given it to arrive at a just appreciation of its circumstances—but its persecutors constantly assail it and keep its mind in such a chaotic state that it can form no opinion upon any point in the case. And besides, the pig is cast in the play without its consent, is forced to conduct itself in a manner which cannot but be humiliating to it, and leaves that stage every night with a conviction that it would rather die than take a character in a theatrical performance again. Pigs are not fitted for the stage; they have no dramatic talent; all their inclinations are toward a retired and unostentatious career in the humblest walks of life, and—"

Manager—"Say no more, sir. The pig is yours. I meant to have educated him for tragedy and made him a blessing to mankind and an ornament to his species, but I am convinced, now, that I ought not to do this in the face of his marked opposition to the stage, and so I present him to you, who will treat him well, I am amply satisfied. I am the more willing to part with him, since the play he performs in was taken off the stage last night, and I could not conveniently arrange a part for him in the one we shall run for the next three weeks, which is Richard III."

Mr. Bergh does everything in the behest of the Society with the very best of intentions and the most honest motives. He makes mistakes, sometimes, like all other men. He complained against a Jewish butcher, and required his arrest, for cutting the throat of an ox instead of knocking it on the head; said he was cruelly slow about terminating the animal's life. Of course, people smiled, because the religious law which compels Jewish butchers to slaughter with a consecrated knife is as old as the Pyramids of Egypt, and Mr. Bergh would have to overthrow the Pentateuch itself to accomplish his point.

ॐ

The Pilgrim

IN THE GREAT Zoological Gardens, we found specimens of all the animals the world produces, I think, including a dromedary, a monkey ornamented with tufts of brilliant blue and carmine hair—a very gorgeous monkey he was—a hippopotamus from the Nile, and a sort of tall, long-legged bird with a beak like a powder-horn, and close-fitting wings like the tails of a dress coat. This fellow stood up with his eyes shut and his shoulders stooped forward a little, and looked as if he had his hands under his coat tails. Such tranquil stupidity, such supernatural gravity, such self-righteousness, and such ineffable self-complacency as were in the countenance and attitude of that gray-bodied, dark-winged, bald-headed, and preposterously uncomely bird! He was so ungainly, so pimply about the head, so scaly about the legs; yet so serene, so unspeakably satisfied! He was the most comical looking creature that can be imagined. It was good to hear Dan and the doctor laugh—such natural and such enjoyable laughter had not been heard among our excursionists since our ship sailed away from America. This bird was a god-send to us, and I should be an ingrate if I forgot to make honorable mention of him in these pages. Ours was a pleasure excursion; therefore we stayed with that bird an hour, and made the most of him. We stirred him up occasionally, but he only unclosed an eye and slowly closed it again, abating no jot of his stately piety of demeanor or his tremendous seriousness. He only seemed to say, "Defile not Heaven's anointed with unsanctified hands." We did not know his name, and so we called him "The Pilgrim."

❧

The Dogs of Constantinople

I AM HALF WILLING to believe that the celebrated dogs of Constantinople have been misrepresented—slandered. I have always been led to suppose that they were so thick in the streets that they blocked the way; that they moved about in organized companies, platoons and regiments, and took what they wanted by determined and ferocious assault; and that at night they drowned

all other sounds with their terrible howlings. The dogs I see here cannot be those I have read of.

I find them everywhere, but not in strong force. The most I have found together has been about ten or twenty. And night or day a fair proportion of them were sound asleep. Those that were not asleep always looked as if they wanted to be. I never saw such utterly wretched, starving, sad-visaged, broken-hearted looking curs in my life. It seemed a grim satire to accuse such brutes as these of taking things by force of arms. They hardly seemed to have strength enough or ambition enough to walk across the street—I do not know that I have seen one walk that far yet. They are mangy and bruised and mutilated, and often you see one with the hair singed off him in such wide and well defined tracts that he looks like a map of the new Territories. They are the sorriest beasts that breathe—the most abject—the most pitiful. In their faces is a settled expression of melancholy, an air of hopeless despondency. The hairless patches on a scalded dog are preferred by the fleas of Constantinople to a wider range on a healthier dog; and the exposed places suit the fleas exactly. I saw a dog of this kind start to nibble at a flea—a fly attracted his attention, and he made a snatch at him; the flea called for him once more, and that forever unsettled him; he looked sadly at his flea-pasture, then sadly looked at his bald spot. Then he heaved a sigh and dropped his head resignedly upon his paws. He was not equal to the situation.

The dogs sleep in the streets, all over the city. From one end of the street to the other, I suppose they will average about eight or ten to a block. Sometimes, of course, there are fifteen or twenty to a block. They do not belong to anybody, and they seem to have no close personal friendships among each other. But they district the city themselves, and the dogs of each district, whether it be half a block in extent, or ten blocks, have to remain within its bounds. Woe to a dog if he crosses the line! His neighbors would snatch the balance of his hair off in a second. So it is said. But they don't look it.

They sleep in the streets these days. They are my compass—my guide. When I see the dogs sleep placidly on, while men, sheep, geese, and all moving things turn out and go around them, I know I am not in the great street where the hotel is, and must go further. In the Grand Rue the dogs have a sort of air of being on the lookout—an air born of being obliged to get out of the way of many carriages every day—and that expression one recognizes in a moment. It does not exist upon the face of any dog without the confines of that street. All others sleep placidly and keep no watch. They would not move, though the Sultan himself passed by.

In one narrow street (but none of them are wide) I saw three dogs lying coiled up, about a foot or two apart. End to end they lay, and so they just bridged the street neatly, from gutter to gutter. A drove of a hundred sheep came along. They stepped right over the dogs, the rear crowding the front, impatient to get on. The dogs looked lazily up, flinched a little when the impatient feet of the sheep touched their raw backs—sighed, and lay peacefully down again. No talk could be plainer than that. So some of the sheep jumped over them and others scrambled between, occasionally chipping a leg with their sharp hoofs, and when the whole flock had made the trip, the dogs sneezed a little, in the cloud of dust, but never budged their bodies an inch. I thought I was lazy, but I am a steam engine compared to a Constantinople dog. But was not that a singular scene for a city of a million inhabitants?

These dogs are the scavengers of the city. That is their official position, and a hard one it is. However, it is their protection. But for their usefulness in partially cleansing these terrible streets, they would not be tolerated long. They eat anything and everything that comes in their way, from melon rinds and spoiled grapes up through all the grades and species of dirt and refuse to their own dead friends and relatives—and yet they are always lean, always hungry, always despondent. The people are loath to kill them—do not kill them, in fact. The Turks have an innate antipathy to taking the life of any dumb animal, it is said. But they do worse. They hang and kick and stone and scald these wretched creatures to the very verge of death, and then leave them to live and suffer.

Once a Sultan proposed to kill off all the dogs here, and did begin the work—but the populace raised such a howl of horror about it that the massacre was stayed. After a while, he proposed to remove them all to an island in the Sea of Marmara. No objection was offered, and a shipload or so was taken away. But when it came to be known that somehow or other the dogs never got to the island, but always fell overboard in the night and perished, another howl was raised and the transportation scheme was dropped.

So the dogs remain in peaceable possession of the streets. I do not say that they do not howl at night, nor that they do not attack people who have not a red fez on their heads. I only say that it would be mean for *me* to accuse them of these unseemly things who have not seen them do them with my own eyes or heard them with my own ears.

৯৯

Syrian Camels I

THE ROAD WAS filled with mule trains and long processions of camels. This reminds me that we have been trying for some time to think what a camel looks like, and now we have made it out. When he is down on all his knees, flat on his breast to receive his load, he looks something like a goose swimming; and when he is upright he looks like an ostrich with an extra set of legs. Camels are not beautiful, and their long under-lip gives them an exceedingly "gallus"* expression. They have immense, flat, forked cushions of feet, that make a track in the dust like a pie with a slice cut out of it. They are not particular about their diet. They would eat a tombstone if they could bite it. A thistle grows about here which has needles on it that would pierce through leather, I think; if one touches you, you can find relief in nothing but profanity. The camels eat these. They show by their actions that they enjoy them. I suppose it would be a real treat to a camel to have a keg of nails for supper [. . . .]

A camel is as tall as any ordinary dwelling house in Syria—which is to say a camel is from one to two, and sometimes nearly three feet taller than a

---

*Excuse the slang—no other word will describe it.

good-sized man. In this part of the country his load is oftenest in the shape of colossal sacks—one on each side. He and his cargo take up as much room as a carriage. Think of meeting this style of obstruction in a narrow trail. The camel would not turn out for a King. He stalks serenely along, bringing his cushioned stilts forward with the long, regular swing of a pendulum, and whatever is in the way must get out of the way peaceably, or be wiped out forcibly by the bulky sacks. It was a tiresome ride to us, and perfectly exhausting to the horses. We were compelled to jump over upwards of eighteen hundred donkeys, and only one person in the party was unseated less than sixty times by the camels. This seems like a powerful statement, but the poet has said "things are not what they seem." I cannot think of anything, now, more certain to make one shudder, than to have a soft-footed camel sneak up behind him and touch him on the ear with its cold, flabby under-lip. A camel did this for one of the boys, who was drooping over his saddle in a brown study. He glanced up and saw the majestic apparition hovering above him, and made frantic efforts to get out of the way, but the camel reached out and bit him on the shoulder before he accomplished it. This was the only pleasant incident of the journey.

The Remarkable "Jericho"

[. . .]I HAVE a horse now by the name of "Jericho." He is a mare. I have seen remarkable horses before, but none so remarkable as this. I wanted a horse that could shy, and this one fills the bill. I had an idea that shying indicated spirit. If I was correct, I have got the most spirited horse on earth. He shies at everything he comes across, with the utmost impartiality. He appears to have a mortal dread of telegraph poles, especially; and it is fortunate that these are on both sides of the road, because as it is now, I never fall off twice in succession on the same side. If I fell on the same side always, it would get to be monotonous after a while. This creature has scared at everything he has seen to-day, except a haystack. He walked up to that with an intrepidity and a recklessness that were astonishing. And it would fill any one with admiration to see how he preserves his self-possession in the presence of a barley sack. This dare-devil bravery will be the death of this horse some day.

He is not particularly fast, but I think he will get me through the Holy Land. He has only one fault. His tail has been chopped off or else he has sat down on it too hard, some time or other, and he has to fight the flies with his heels. This is all very well, but when he tries to kick a fly off the top of his head with his hind foot, it is too much variety. He is going to get himself into trouble that way some day. He reaches around and bites my legs too. I do not care particularly about that, only I do not like to see a horse too sociable.

I think the owner of this prize had a wrong opinion about him. He had an idea that he was one of those fiery, untamed steeds, but he is not of that character. I know the Arab had this idea, because when he brought the horse out for inspection in Beirout, he kept jerking at the bridle and shouting in Arabic, "Ho! will you? Do you want to run away, you ferocious beast, and break your neck?" when all the time the horse was not doing anything in the world, and only looked like he wanted to lean up against something and think. Whenever he is not shying at things, or reaching after a fly, he wants to do that yet. How it would surprise his owner to know this.

ॐ

Pilgrims on Horseback

PROPERLY, WITH THE sorry relics we bestrode, it was a three days' journey to Damascus. It was necessary that we should do it in less than two. It was necessary because our three pilgrims would not travel on the Sabbath day. We were all perfectly willing to keep the Sabbath day, but there are times when to keep the *letter* of a sacred law whose spirit is righteous, becomes a sin, and this was a case in point. We pleaded for the tired, ill-treated horses, and tried to show that their faithful service deserved kindness in return, and their hard lot compassion. But when did ever self-righteousness know the sentiment of pity? What were a few long hours added to the hardships of some over-taxed brutes when weighed against the peril of those human souls? It was not the most promising party to travel with and hope to gain a higher veneration for religion through the example of its devotees. We said the Savior who pitied dumb beasts and taught that the ox must be rescued from the mire even on the Sabbath day, would not have counseled a forced march like this. We said the "long trip" was exhausting and therefore dangerous in the blistering heats of summer, even when the ordinary days' stages were traversed, and if we persisted in this hard march, some of us might be stricken down with the fevers of the country in consequence of it. Nothing could move the pilgrims. They *must* press on. Men might die, horses might die, but they must enter upon holy soil next week, with no Sabbath-breaking stain upon them. Thus they were willing to commit a sin against the spirit of religious law, in order that they might preserve the letter of it. It was not worth while to tell them "the letter kills." I am talking now about personal friends; men whom I like; men who are good citizens; who are honorable, upright, conscientious; but whose idea of the Savior's religion seems to me distorted. They lecture our shortcomings unsparingly, and every night they call us together and read to us chapters from the Testament that are full of gentleness, of charity, and of tender mercy; and then all the next day they stick to their saddles clear up to the summits of these rugged mountains, and clear down again. Apply the Testament's gentleness, and charity, and tender mercy to a toiling, worn and weary horse?—Nonsense—these are for God's human creatures, not His dumb ones[. . . .]

We satisfied our pilgrims by making those hard rides from Baalbec to Damascus, but Dan's horse and Jack's were so crippled we had to leave them behind and get fresh animals for them. The dragoman says Jack's horse died. I swapped horses with Mohammed, the kingly-looking Egyptian who is our Ferguson's lieutenant. By Ferguson I mean our dragoman Abraham, of course. I did not take this horse on account of his personal appearance, but because I have not seen his back. I do not wish to see it. I have seen the backs of all the other horses, and found most of them covered with dreadful saddle-boils which I know have not been washed or doctored for years. The idea of riding all day long over such ghastly inquisitions of torture is sickening. My horse must be like the others, but I have at least the consolation of not knowing it to be so.

ℒ

Arabs and Their Steeds

I HOPE THAT in future I may be spared any more sentimental praises of the Arab's idolatry of his horse. In boyhood I longed to be an Arab of the desert and have a beautiful mare, and call her Selim or Benjamin or Mohammed, and feed her with my own hands, and let her come into the tent, and teach her to caress me and look fondly upon me with her great tender eyes; and I wished that a stranger might come at such a time and offer me a hundred thousand dollars for her, so that I could do like the other Arabs—hesitate, yearn for the money, but overcome by my love for my mare, at last say, "Part with thee, my beautiful one! Never with my life! Away, tempter, I scorn thy gold!" and then bound into the saddle and speed over the desert like the wind!

But I recall those aspirations. If these Arabs be like the other Arabs, their love for their beautiful mares is a fraud. These of my acquaintance have no love for their horses, no sentiment of pity for them, and no knowledge of how to treat them or care for them. The Syrian saddle-blanket is a quilted mattrass two or three inches thick. It is never removed from the horse, day or night. It gets full of dirt and hair, and becomes soaked with sweat. It is bound to breed sores. These pirates never think of washing a horse's back. They do not shelter the horses in the tents, either; they must stay out and take the weather as it comes. Look at poor cropped and dilapidated "Baalbec," and weep for the sentiment that has been wasted upon the Selims of romance!

ℒ

Part Two: 1870s and 1880s

The Cayote, Allegory of Want

THE CAYOTE IS a long, slim, sick and sorry-looking skeleton, with a gray wolf-skin stretched over it, a tolerably bushy tail that forever sags down with a despairing expression of forsakenness and misery, a furtive and evil eye, and a long, sharp face, with slightly lifted lip and exposed teeth. He has a general slinking expression all over. The cayote is a living, breathing allegory of Want. He is *always* hungry. He is always poor, out of luck and friendless. The meanest creatures despise him, and even the fleas would desert him for a velocipede. He is so spiritless and cowardly that even while his exposed teeth are pretending a threat, the rest of his face is apologizing for it. And he is *so* homely!—so scrawny, and ribby, and coarse-haired, and pitiful. When he sees you he lifts his lip and lets a flash of his teeth out, and then turns a little out of the course he was pursuing, depresses his head a bit, and strikes a long, soft-footed trot through the sage-brush, glancing over his shoulder at you, from time to time, till he is about out of easy pistol range, and then he stops and takes a deliberate survey of you; he will trot fifty yards and stop again—another fifty and stop again; and finally the gray of his gliding body blends with the gray of the sage-brush, and he disappears. All this is when you make no demonstration against him; but if you do, he develops a livelier interest in his journey, and instantly electrifies his heels and puts such a deal of real estate between himself and your weapon, that by the time you have raised the hammer you see that you need a minie rifle, and by the time you have got him in line you need a rifled cannon, and by the time you have "drawn a bead" on him you see well enough that nothing but an unusually long-winded streak of lightning could reach him where he is now. But if you start a swift-footed dog after him, you will enjoy it ever so much—especially if it is a dog that has a good opinion of himself, and has been brought up to think he knows something about speed. The cayote will go swinging gently off on that deceitful trot of his, and every little while he will smile a fraudful smile over his shoulder that will fill that dog entirely full of encouragement and worldly ambition, and make him lay his head still lower to the ground, and stretch his neck further to the front, and pant more fiercely, and stick his tail out straighter behind, and move his furious legs with a yet wilder frenzy, and leave a broader and broader, and higher and denser cloud of desert sand smoking behind, and marking his long wake across the level plain! And all this time the dog is only a short twenty feet behind the cayote, and to save the soul of him he cannot understand why it is that he cannot get perceptibly closer; and he begins to get aggravated, and it makes him madder and madder to see how gently the cayote glides along and never pants or sweats or ceases to smile; and he grows still more and more incensed to see how shamefully he has been taken in by an entire stranger, and what an ignoble swindle that long, calm, soft-footed trot is; and next he notices that he is getting fagged, and that the cayote actually has to slacken speed a little to keep from running away from him—and *then* that town-dog is mad in earnest, and he begins to strain and weep and swear, and paw the sand higher than ever, and reach for the cayote with concentrated and desperate energy. This "spurt" finds him six feet behind the gliding enemy, and two miles from his friends. And then, in the instant that a wild new hope is lighting up his face, the cayote turns and smiles blandly upon him once more, and with a something about it which seems to say: "Well, I shall have to tear myself away from you, bub—business is business, and it will not do for me to be fooling along this way all day"—and forthwith there is a rushing sound, and the sudden splitting of a long crack through the atmosphere, and behold that dog is solitary and alone in the midst of a vast solitude!

It makes his head swim. He stops, and looks all around; climbs the nearest sand-mound, and gazes into the distance; shakes his head reflectively, and then, without a word, he turns and jogs along back to his train, and takes up a humble position under the hindmost wagon, and feels unspeakably mean, and looks ashamed, and hangs his tail at half-mast for a week. And for as much as a year after that, whenever there is a great hue and cry after a cayote, that dog will merely glance in that direction without emotion, and apparently observe to himself, "I believe I do not wish any of the pie."

The cayote lives chiefly in the most desolate and forbidding deserts, along with the lizard, the jackass rabbit and the raven, and gets an uncertain and precarious living, and earns it. He seems to subsist almost wholly on the carcases of oxen, mules and horses that have dropped out of emigrant trains and died, and upon windfalls of carrion, and occasional legacies of offal bequeathed to him by white men who have been opulent enough to have something better to butcher than condemned army bacon. He will eat anything in the world that his first cousins, the desert-frequenting tribes of Indians will, and they will eat anything they can bite. It is a curious fact that these latter are the only creatures known to history who will eat nitro-glycerine and ask for more if they survive.

The cayote of the deserts beyond the Rocky Mountains has a peculiarly hard time of it, owing to the fact that his relations, the Indians, are just as apt to be the first to detect a seductive scent on the desert breeze, and follow the fragrance to the late ox it emanated from, as he is himself; and when this occurs he has to content himself with sitting off at a little distance watching those people strip off and dig out everything edible, and walk off with it. Then he and the waiting ravens explore the skeleton and polish the bones. It is considered that the cayote, and the obscene bird, and the Indian of the desert, testify their blood kinship with each other in that they live together in the waste places of the earth on terms of perfect confidence and friendship, while hating all other creatures and yearning to assist at their funerals. He does not mind going a hundred miles to breakfast, and a hundred and fifty to dinner, because he is sure to have three or four days between meals, and he can just as well be traveling and looking at the scenery as lying around doing nothing and adding to the burdens of his parents.

We soon learned to recognize the sharp, vicious bark of the cayote as it came across the murky plain at night to disturb our dreams among the mailsacks; and remembering his forlorn aspect and his hard fortune, made shift to wish him the blessed novelty of a long day's good luck and a limitless larder the morrow.

ʝə

With a Flash and a Whiz

As THE SUN was going down, we saw the first specimen of an animal known familiarly over two thousand miles of mountain and desert—from Kansas clear to the Pacific Ocean—as the "jackass rabbit." He is well named. He is just like any other rabbit, except that he is from one-third to twice as large, has longer legs in proportion to his size, and has the most preposterous ears that ever were mounted on any creature *but* a jackass. When he is sitting quiet, thinking about his sins, or is absent-minded or unapprehensive of danger, his majestic ears project above him conspicuously; but the breaking of a twig will scare him nearly to death, and then he tilts his ears back gently and starts for home. All you can see, then, for the next minute, is his long gray form stretched out straight and "streaking it" through the low sage-brush, head erect, eyes right, and ears just canted a little to the rear, but showing you where the animal is, all the time, the same as if he carried a jib. Now and then he makes a marvelous spring with his long legs, high over the stunted sage-brush, and scores a leap that would make a horse envious. Presently he comes down to a long, graceful "lope," and shortly he mysteriously disappears. He has crouched behind a sage-bush, and will sit there and listen and tremble until you get within six feet of him, when he will get under way again. But one must shoot at this creature once, if he wishes to see him throw his heart into his heels, and do the best he knows how. He is frightened clear through, now, and he lays his long ears down on his back, straightens himself out like a yard-stick every spring he makes, and scatters miles behind him with an easy indifference that is enchanting.

Our party made this specimen "hump himself," as the conductor said. The Secretary started him with a shot from the Colt; I commenced spitting at him with my weapon; and all in the same instant the old "Allen's" whole broadside let go with a rattling crash, and it is not putting it too strong to say that the rabbit was frantic! He dropped his ears, set up his tail, and left for San Francisco at a speed which can only be described as a flash and a vanish! Long after he was out of sight we could hear him whiz.

ℛ

Syrian Camels II

SAGE–BRUSH IS very fair fuel, but as a vegetable it is a distinguished failure. Nothing can abide the taste of it but the jackass and his illegitimate child the mule. But their testimony to its nutritiousness is worth nothing, for they will eat pine knots, or anthracite coal, or brass filings, or lead pipe, or old bottles, or anything that comes handy, and then go off looking as grateful as if they had had oysters for dinner. Mules and donkeys and camels have appetites that anything will relieve temporarily, but nothing satisfy. In Syria, once, at the head-waters of the Jordan, a camel took charge of my overcoat while the tents were being pitched, and examined it with a critical eye, all over, with as much interest as if he had an idea of getting one made like it; and then, after he was done figuring on it as an article of apparel, he began to contemplate it as an article of diet. He put his foot on it, and lifted one of the sleeves out with his teeth, and chewed and chewed at it, gradually taking it in, and all the while opening and closing his eyes in a kind of religious ecstasy, as if he had never tasted anything as good as an overcoat before, in his life. Then

he smacked his lips once or twice, and reached after the other sleeve. Next
he tried the velvet collar, and smiled a smile of such contentment that it was
plain to see that he regarded that as the daintiest thing about an overcoat.
The tails went next, along with some percussion caps and cough candy, and
some fig-paste from Constantinople. And then my newspaper correspondence
dropped out, and he took a chance in that—manuscript letters written for the
home papers. But he was treading on dangerous ground, now. He began to
come across solid wisdom in those documents that was rather weighty on
his stomach; and occasionally he would take a joke that would shake him up
till it loosened his teeth; it was getting to be perilous times with him, but he
held his grip with good courage and hopefully, till at last he began to stumble
on statements that not even a camel could swallow with impunity. He began
to gag and gasp, and his eyes to stand out, and his forelegs to spread, and in
about a quarter of a minute he fell over as stiff as a carpenter's work-bench,
and died a death of indescribable agony. I went and pulled the manuscript
out of his mouth, and found that the sensitive creature had choked to death
on one of the mildest and gentlest statements of fact that I ever laid before a
trusting public.

༄

The Genuine Mexican Plug

I RESOLVED TO have a horse to ride. I had never seen such wild, free, magnificent horsemanship outside of a circus as these picturesquely-clad Mexicans,
Californians and Mexicanized Americans displayed in Carson streets every
day. How they rode! Leaning just gently forward out of the perpendicular,
easy and nonchalant, with broad slouch-hat brim blown square up in front,
and long *riata* swinging above the head, they swept through the town like the
wind! The next minute they were only a sailing puff of dust on the far desert.
If they trotted, they sat up gallantly and gracefully, and seemed part of the
horse; did not go jiggering up and down after the silly Miss-Nancy fashion of
the riding-schools. I had quickly learned to tell a horse from a cow, and was
full of anxiety to learn more. I was resolved to buy a horse.

While the thought was rankling in my mind, the auctioneer came skurrying through the plaza on a black beast that had as many humps and corners

on him as a dromedary, and was necessarily uncomely; but he was "going, going, at twenty-two!—horse, saddle and bridle at twenty-two dollars, gentlemen!" and I could hardly resist.

A man whom I did not know (he turned out to be the auctioneer's brother) noticed the wistful look in my eye, and observed that that was a very remarkable horse to be going at such a price; and added that the saddle alone was worth the money. It was a Spanish saddle, with ponderous *tapaderas*, and furnished with the ungainly sole-leather covering with the unspellable name. I said I had half a notion to bid. Then this keen-eyed person appeared to me to be "taking my measure;" but I dismissed the suspicion when he spoke, for his manner was full of guileless candor and truthfulness. Said he:

"I know that horse—know him well. You are a stranger, I take it, and so you might think he was an American horse, maybe, but I assure you he is not. He is nothing of the kind; but—excuse my speaking in a low voice, other people being near—he is, without the shadow of a doubt, a Genuine Mexican Plug!"

I did not know what a Genuine Mexican Plug was, but there was something about this man's way of saying it, that made me swear inwardly that I would own a Genuine Mexican Plug, or die.

"Has he any other—er—advantages?" I inquired, suppressing what eagerness I could.

He hooked his forefinger in the pocket of my army-shirt, led me to one side, and breathed in my ear impressively these words:

"He can out-buck anything in America!"

"Going, going, going—at *twent–ty*-four dollars and a half, gen—"

"Twenty-seven!" I shouted, in a frenzy.

"And sold!" said the auctioneer, and passed over the Genuine Mexican Plug to me.

I could scarcely contain my exultation. I paid the money, and put the animal in a neighboring livery-stable to dine and rest himself.

In the afternoon I brought the creature into the plaza, and certain citizens held him by the head, and others by the tail, while I mounted him. As soon as they let go, he placed all his feet in a bunch together, lowered his back, and then suddenly arched it upward, and shot me straight into the air a matter of three or four feet! I came as straight down again, lit in the saddle, went instantly up again, came down almost on the high pommel, shot up again, and came down on the horse's neck—all in the space of three or four seconds. Then he rose and stood almost straight up on his hind feet, and I, clasping his lean neck desperately, slid back into the saddle, and held on. He came down, and immediately hoisted his heels into the air, delivering a vicious kick at the sky, and stood on his forefeet. And then down he came once more, and began the original exercise of shooting me straight up again. The third time I went up I heard a stranger say:

"Oh, *don't* he buck, though!"

While I was up, somebody struck the horse a sounding thwack with a leathern strap, and when I arrived again the Genuine Mexican Plug was not there. A Californian youth chased him up and caught him, and asked if he might have a ride. I granted him that luxury. He mounted the Genuine, got lifted into the air once, but sent his spurs home as he descended, and the horse darted away like a telegram. He soared over three fences like a bird, and disappeared down the road toward the Washoe Valley.

I sat down on a stone, with a sigh, and by a natural impulse one of my hands sought my forehead, and the other the base of my stomach. I believe I never appreciated, till then, the poverty of the human machinery—for I still needed a hand or two to place elsewhere. Pen cannot describe how I was jolted up. Imagination cannot conceive how disjointed I was—how internally, externally and universally I was unsettled, mixed up and ruptured. There was a sympathetic crowd around me, though.

One elderly-looking comforter said:

"Stranger, you've been taken in. Everybody in this camp knows that horse. Any child, any Injun, could have told you that he'd buck; he is the very worst devil to buck on the continent of America. You hear *me*. I'm Curry. *Old* Curry. Old *Abe* Curry. And moreover, he is a simon-pure, out-and-out, genuine d—d Mexican plug, and an uncommon mean one at that, too. Why, you turnip, if you had laid low and kept dark, there's chances to buy an *American* horse for mighty little more than you paid for that bloody old foreign relic."

I gave no sign; but I made up my mind that if the auctioneer's brother's funeral took place while I was in the Territory I would postpone all other recreations and attend it.

After a gallop of sixteen miles the Californian youth and the Genuine Mexican Plug came tearing into town again, shedding foam-flakes like the spume-spray that drives before a typhoon, and, with one final skip over a wheelbarrow and a Chinaman, cast anchor in front of the "ranch."

Such panting and blowing! Such spreading and contracting of the red equine nostrils, and glaring of the wild equine eye! But was the imperial beast subjugated? Indeed he was not. His lordship the Speaker of the House thought he was, and mounted him to go down to the Capitol; but the first dash the creature made was over a pile of telegraph poles half as high as a church; and his time to the Capitol—one mile and three-quarters—remains unbeaten to this day. But then he took an advantage—he left out the mile, and only did the three-quarters. That is to say, he made a straight cut across lots, preferring fences and ditches to a crooked road; and when the Speaker got to the Capitol he said he had been in the air so much he felt as if he had made the trip on a comet.

In the evening the Speaker came home afoot for exercise, and got the Genuine towed back behind a quartz wagon. The next day I loaned the animal to the Clerk of the House to go down to the Dana silver mine, six miles, and *he* walked back for exercise, and got the horse towed. Everybody I loaned him to always walked back; they never could get enough exercise any other way. Still, I continued to loan him to anybody who was willing to borrow him, my idea being to get him crippled, and throw him on the borrower's hands, or killed, and make the borrower pay for him. But somehow nothing ever happened to him. He took chances that no other horse ever took and survived, but he always came out safe. It was his daily habit to try experiments that had always before been considered impossible, but he always got through. Sometimes he miscalculated a little, and did not get his rider through intact, but *he* always got through himself. Of course I had tried to sell him; but that was a stretch of simplicity which met with little sympathy. The auctioneer stormed up and down the streets on him for four days, dispersing the populace, interrupting business, and destroying children, and never got a bid—at least never any but the eighteen-dollar one he hired a notoriously substanceless bummer to make. The people only smiled pleasantly, and restrained their desire to buy, if they had any. Then the auctioneer brought in his bill, and I withdrew the horse from the market. We tried to trade him off at private vendue next, offering him at a sacrifice for second-hand tombstones, old iron, temperance tracts—any kind of property. But holders were stiff, and we retired from the market again. I never tried to ride the horse any more. Walking was good enough exercise for a man like me, that had nothing the matter with him except ruptures, internal injuries, and such things. Finally I tried to *give* him away. But it was a failure. Parties said earthquakes were handy enough on the Pacific coast—they did not wish to own one. As a last resort I offered him to the Governor for the use of the "Brigade." His face lit up eagerly at first, but toned down again, and he said the thing would be too palpable.

Just then the livery-stable man brought in his bill for six weeks' keeping—stall-room for the horse, fifteen dollars; hay for the horse, two hundred and fifty! The Genuine Mexican Plug had eaten a ton of the article, and the man said he would have eaten a hundred if he had let him.

I will remark here, in all seriousness, that the regular price of hay during that year and a part of the next was really two hundred and fifty dollars a ton. During a part of the previous year it had sold at five hundred a ton, in gold, and during the winter before that there was such scarcity of the article that in several instances small quantities had brought eight hundred dollars a ton in coin! The consequence might be guessed without my telling it: people turned their stock loose to starve, and before the spring arrived Carson and Eagle valleys were almost literally carpeted with their carcases! Any old settler there will verify these statements.

I managed to pay the livery bill, and that same day I gave the Genuine Mexican Plug to a passing Arkansas emigrant whom fortune delivered into my hand. If this ever meets his eye, he will doubtless remember the donation.

Now whoever has had the luck to ride a real Mexican plug will recognize the animal depicted in this chapter, and hardly consider him exaggerated—but the uninitiated will feel justified in regarding his portrait as a fancy sketch, perhaps.

The Retired Milk Horse

We rode horseback all around the island of Hawaii (the crooked road making the distance two hundred miles), and enjoyed the journey very much. We were more than a week making the trip, because our Kanaka horses would not go by a house or a hut without stopping—whip and spur could not alter their minds about it, and so we finally found that it economized time to let them have their way. Upon inquiry the mystery was explained: the natives are such thorough-going gossips that they never pass a house without stopping to swap news, and consequently their horses learn to regard that sort of thing as an essential part of the whole duty of man, and his salvation not to be compassed without it. However, at a former crisis of my life I had once taken an aristocratic young lady out driving, behind a horse that had just retired from a long and honorable career as the moving impulse of a milk wagon, and so this present experience awoke a reminiscent sadness in me in place of the exasperation more natural to the occasion. I remembered how helpless I was that day, and how humiliated; how ashamed I was of having intimated to the girl that I had always owned

the horse and was accustomed to grandeur; how hard I tried to appear easy, and even vivacious, under suffering that was consuming my vitals; how placidly and maliciously the girl smiled, and kept on smiling, while my hot blushes baked themselves into a permanent blood-pudding in my face; how the horse ambled from one side of the street to the other and waited complacently before every third house two minutes and a quarter while I belabored his back and reviled him in my heart; how I tried to keep him from turning corners, and failed; how I moved heaven and earth to get him out of town, and did not succeed; how he traversed the entire settlement and delivered imaginary milk at a hundred and sixty-two different domiciles, and how he finally brought up at a dairy depot and refused to budge further, thus rounding and completing the revealment of what the plebeian service of his life had been; how, in eloquent silence, I walked the girl home, and how, when I took leave of her, her parting remark scorched my soul and appeared to blister me all over: she said that my horse was a fine, capable animal, and I must have taken great comfort in him in my time—but that if I would take along some milk-tickets next time, and appear to deliver them at the various halting places, it might expedite his movements a little. There was a coolness between us after that.

ஃ

An Invention to Make Flies Curse

HARTFORD, CONN., MARCH 3, 1873.

Mr. White,—Dear Sir:

There is nothing that a just & right feeling man rejoices in more than to see a mosquito imposed on & put down, & brow-beaten & aggravated,—& this ingenious contrivance will do it. And it is a rare thing to worry a fly with, too. A fly will stand off & curse this invention till language utterly fails him. I have seen them do it hundreds of times. I like to dine in the air on the back porch in summer, & so I would not be without this portable net for anything; when you have got it hoisted, the flies have to wait for the second table. We shall see the summer day come when we shall all sit under our nets in church & slumber peacefully, while the discomfited flies club together & take it out of the minister. There are heaps of ways of getting priceless enjoyment out of these charming things, if I had time to point them out & dilate on them a little.

Mark Twain.

୫ð

Peter and the Pain-Killer

Becky Thatcher had stopped coming to school [. . . .] She was ill. What if she should die! There was distraction in the thought. He no longer took an interest in war, nor even in piracy. The charm of life was gone; there was nothing but dreariness left. He put his hoop away, and his bat; there was no joy in them any more. His aunt was concerned. She began to try all manner of remedies on him. She was one of those people who are infatuated with patent medicines and all new-fangled methods of producing health or mending it. She was an inveterate experimenter in these things. When something fresh in this line came out she was in a fever, right away, to try it; not on herself, for she was never ailing, but on anybody else that came handy. She was a subscriber for all the "Health" periodicals and phrenological frauds; and the solemn ignorance they were inflated with was breath to her nostrils. All the "rot" they contained about ventilation, and how to go to bed, and how to get up, and what to eat, and what to drink, and how much exercise to take, and what frame of mind to keep one's self in, and what sort of clothing to wear, was all gospel to her, and she never observed that her health-journals of the current month customarily upset everything they had recommended the month before. She was as simple-hearted and honest as the day was long, and so she was an easy victim. She gathered together her quack periodicals and her quack medicines, and thus armed with death, went about on her pale horse, metaphorically speaking, with "hell following after." But she never suspected that she was not an angel of healing and the balm of Gilead in disguise, to the suffering neighbors.

The water treatment was new, now, and Tom's low condition was a windfall to her. She had him out at daylight every morning, stood him up in the woodshed and drowned him with a deluge of cold water; then she scrubbed him down with a towel like a file, and so brought him to; then she rolled him up in a wet sheet and put him away under blankets till she sweated his soul clean and "the yellow stains of it came through his pores"—as Tom said.

Yet notwithstanding all this, the boy grew more and more melancholy and pale and dejected. She added hot baths, sitz baths, shower baths and plunges. The boy remained as dismal as a hearse. She began to assist the water with a slim oatmeal diet and blister plasters. She calculated his capacity as she would a jug's, and filled him up every day with quack cure-alls.

Tom had become indifferent to persecution, by this time. This phase filled the old lady's heart with consternation. This indifference must be broken up at any cost. Now she heard of Pain-Killer for the first time. She ordered a lot at once. She tasted it and was filled with gratitude. It was simply fire in a liquid form. She dropped the water treatment and everything else, and pinned her faith to Pain-Killer. She gave Tom a tea-spoonful and watched with the deepest anxiety for the result. Her troubles were instantly at rest, her soul at peace again; for the "indifference" was broken up. The boy could not have shown a wilder, heartier interest, if she had built a fire under him.

Tom felt that it was time to wake up; this sort of life might be romantic enough, in his blighted condition, but it was getting to have too little sentiment and too much distracting variety about it. So he thought over various plans for relief, and finally hit upon that of professing to be fond of Pain-Killer. He asked for it so often that he became a nuisance, and his aunt ended by telling him to help himself and quit bothering her. If it had been Sid, she would have had no misgivings to alloy her delight; but since it was Tom, she watched the bottle clandestinely. She found that the medicine did really diminish, but it did not occur to her that the boy was mending the health of a crack in the sitting-room floor with it.

One day Tom was in the act of dosing the crack when his aunt's yellow cat came along, purring, eyeing the tea-spoon avariciously, and begging for a taste. Tom said:

"Don't ask for it unless you want it, Peter."

But Peter signified that he did want it.

"You better make sure."

Peter was sure.

"Now you've asked for it, and I'll give it to you, because there ain't anything mean about *me*; but if you find you don't like it, you mustn't blame anybody but your own self."

Peter was agreeable. So Tom pried his mouth open and poured down the Pain-Killer. Peter sprang a couple of yards into the air, and then delivered a war-whoop and set off round and round the room, banging against furniture, upsetting flower pots and making general havoc. Next he rose on his hind feet and pranced around, in a frenzy of enjoyment, with his head over his shoulder and his voice proclaiming his unappeasable happiness. Then he went tearing around the house again spreading chaos and destruction in his path. Aunt Polly entered in time to see him throw a few double summersets, deliver a final mighty hurrah, and sail through the open window, carrying the rest of the flower-pots with him. The old lady stood petrified with astonishment, peering over her glasses; Tom lay on the floor expiring with laughter.

"Tom, what on earth ails that cat?"

"I don't know, aunt," gasped the boy.

"Why I never see anything like it. What *did* make him act so?"

"Deed I don't know aunt Polly; cats always act so when they're having a good time."

"They do, do they?" There was something in the tone that made Tom apprehensive.

"Yes'm. That is, I believe they do."

"You *do?*"

"Yes'm."

The old lady was bending down, Tom watching, with interest emphasized by anxiety. Too late he divined her "drift." The handle of the tell-tale teaspoon was visible under the bed-valance. Aunt Polly took it, held it up. Tom winced, and dropped his eyes. Aunt Polly raised him by the usual handle—his ear—and cracked his head soundly with her thimble.

"Now, sir, what did you want to treat that poor dumb beast so, for?"

"I done it out of pity for him—because he hadn't any aunt."

"Hadn't any aunt!—you numscull. What has that got to do with it?"

"Heaps. Because if he'd a had one she'd a burnt him out herself! She'd a roasted his bowels out of him 'thout any more feeling than if he was a human!"

Aunt Polly felt a sudden pang of remorse. This was putting the thing in a new light; what was cruelty to a cat *might* be cruelty to a boy, too. She began to soften; she felt sorry. Her eyes watered a little, and she put her hand on Tom's head and said gently:

"I was meaning for the best, Tom. And, Tom, it *did* do you good."

Tom looked up in her face with just a perceptible twinkle peeping through his gravity:

"I know you was meaning for the best, aunty, and so was I with Peter. It done *him* good, too. I never see him get around so since—"

"O, go 'long with you, Tom, before you aggravate me again. And you try and see if you can't be a good boy, for once, and you needn't take any more medicine."

The Pinch-bug and the Poodle

THE MINISTER GAVE out his text and droned along monotonously through
an argument that was so prosy that many a head by and by began to nod—
and yet it was an argument that dealt in limitless fire and brimstone and
thinned the predestined elect down to a company so small as to be hardly
worth the saving. Tom counted the pages of the sermon; after church he
always knew how many pages there had been, but he seldom knew anything else about the discourse. However, this time he was really interested for
a little while. The minister made a grand and moving picture of the assem-
bling together of the world's hosts at the millennium when the lion and the
lamb should lie down together and a little child should lead them. But the
pathos, the lesson, the moral of the great spectacle were lost upon the boy; he
only thought of the conspicuousness of the principal character before the on-
looking nations; his face lit with the thought, and he said to himself that he
wished he could be that child, if it was a tame lion.

Now he lapsed into suffering again, as the dry argument was resumed.
Presently he bethought him of a treasure he had and got it out. It was a large
black beetle with formidable jaws—a "pinch-bug," he called it. It was in a percussion-cap box. The first thing the beetle did was to take him by the finger.
A natural fillip followed, the beetle went floundering into the aisle and lit on
its back, and the hurt finger went into the boy's mouth. The beetle lay there
working its helpless legs, unable to turn over. Tom eyed it, and longed for
it; but it was safe out of his reach. Other people uninterested in the sermon,
found relief in the beetle, and they eyed it too. Presently a vagrant poodle
dog came idling along, sad at heart, lazy with the summer softness and the
quiet, weary of captivity, sighing for change. He spied the beetle; the drooping tail lifted and wagged. He surveyed the prize; walked around it; smelt at
it from a safe distance; walked around it again; grew bolder, and took a closer
smell; then lifted his lip and made a gingerly snatch at it, just missing it; made
another, and another; began to enjoy the diversion; subsided to his stomach with the beetle between his paws, and continued his experiments; grew
weary at last, and then indifferent and absent-minded. His head nodded, and
little by little his chin descended and touched the enemy, who seized it. There
was a sharp yelp, a flirt of the poodle's head, and the beetle fell a couple of
yards away, and lit on its back once more. The neighboring spectators shook
with a gentle inward joy, several faces went behind fans and handkerchiefs,
and Tom was entirely happy. The dog looked foolish, and probably felt so; but

there was resentment in his heart, too, and a craving for revenge. So he went to the beetle and began a wary attack on it again; jumping at it from every point of a circle, lighting with his forepaws within an inch of the creature, making even closer snatches at it with his teeth, and jerking his head till his ears flapped again. But he grew tired once more, after a while; tried to amuse himself with a fly but found no relief; followed an ant around, with his nose close to the floor, and quickly wearied of that; yawned, sighed, forgot the beetle entirely, and sat down on it! Then there was a wild yelp of agony and the poodle went sailing up the aisle; the yelps continued, and so did the dog; he crossed the house in front of the altar; he flew down the other aisle; he crossed before the doors; he clamored up the home-stretch; his anguish grew with his progress, till presently he was but a woolly comet moving in its orbit with the gleam and the speed of light. At last the frantic sufferer sheered from its course, and sprang into its master's lap; he flung it out of the window, and the voice of distress quickly thinned away and died in the distance.

By this time the whole church was red-faced and suffocating with sup-pressed laughter, and the sermon had come to a dead stand-still. The dis-course was resumed presently, but it went lame and halting, all possibility of impressiveness being at an end; for even the gravest sentiments were con-stantly being received with a smothered burst of unholy mirth, under cover of some remote pew-back, as if the poor parson had said a rarely facetious thing. It was a genuine relief to the whole congregation when the ordeal was over and the benediction pronounced.

Tom Sawyer went home quite cheerful, thinking to himself that there was some satisfaction about divine service when there was a bit of variety in it. He had but one marring thought; he was willing that the dog should play with his pinch-bug, but he did not think it was upright in him to carry it off.

૪๑

Bugs and Birds and Tom in the Morning

WHEN TOM AWOKE in the morning, he wondered where he was. He sat up and rubbed his eyes and looked around. Then he comprehended. It was the cool gray dawn, and there was a delicious sense of repose and peace in the deep pervading calm and silence of the woods. Not a leaf stirred; not a sound obtruded upon great Nature's meditation. Beaded dew-drops stood upon the leaves and grasses. A white layer of ashes covered the fire, and a thin blue breath of smoke rose straight into the air. Joe and Huck still slept.

Now, far away in the woods a bird called; another answered; presently the hammering of a woodpecker was heard. Gradually the cool dim gray of the morning whitened, and as gradually sounds multiplied and life manifested itself. The marvel of Nature shaking off sleep and going to work unfolded itself to the musing boy. A little green worm came crawling over a dewy leaf, lifting two-thirds of his body into the air from time to time and "sniffing around," then proceeding again—for he was measuring, Tom said; and when the worm approached him, of its own accord, he sat as still as a stone, with his hopes rising and falling, by turns, as the creature still came toward him or seemed inclined to go elsewhere; and when at last it considered a painful moment with its curved body in the air and then came decisively down upon Tom's leg and began a journey over him, his whole heart was glad—for that meant that he was going to have a new suit of clothes—without the shadow of a doubt a gaudy piratical uniform. Now a procession of ants appeared, from nowhere in particular, and went about their labors; one struggled manfully by with a dead spider five times as big as itself in its arms, and lugged it straight up a tree-trunk. A brown spotted lady-bug climbed the dizzy height of a grass-blade, and Tom bent down close to it and said, "Lady-bug, lady-bug, fly away home, your house is on fire, your children's alone," and she took wing and went off to see about it—which did not surprise the boy, for he knew of old that this insect was credulous about conflagrations and he had practiced upon its simplicity more than once. A tumble-bug came next, heaving sturdily at its ball, and Tom touched the creature, to see it shut its legs against its body and pretend to be dead. The birds were fairly rioting, by this time. A cat-bird, the northern mocker, lit in a tree over Tom's head, and trilled out her imitations of her neighbors in a rapture of enjoyment; then a shrill jay swept down, a flash of blue flame, and stopped on a twig almost within the boy's reach, cocked his head to one side and eyed the strangers with a consuming curiosity; a gray squirrel and a big fellow of the "fox" kind came skurrying along, sitting up at intervals to inspect and chatter at the boys, for the wild things had probably never seen a human being before and scarcely knew whether to be afraid or not. All Nature was wide awake and stirring, now; long lances of sunlight pierced down through the dense foliage far and near, and a few butterflies came fluttering upon the scene.

A Cat-Tale*

ONCE THERE WAS a noble big cat, whose Christian name was Catasauqua—because she lived in that region—but she did not have any surname, because she was a short-tailed cat—being a Manx—and did not need one. It is very just and becoming in a long-tailed cat to have a surname, but it would be very ostentatious, and even dishonorable, in a Manx. Well, Catasauqua had a beautiful family of catlings; and they were of different colors, to harmonize with their characters. Cattaraugus, the eldest, was white, and he had high impulses and a pure heart; Catiline, the youngest, was black, and he had a self-seeking nature, his motives were nearly always base, he was truculent and insincere. He was vain and foolish, and often said he would rather be what he was, and live like a bandit, yet have none above him, than be a cat-o-nine-tails and eat with the King. He hated his harmless and unoffending little catercousins, and frequently drove them from his presence with imprecations, and at times even resorted to violence.

Susie—What are catercousins, papa?

Quarter-cousins—it is so set down in the big dictionary. You observe I refer to it every now and then. This is because I do not wish to make any mistakes, my purpose being to instruct as well as entertain. Whenever I use a word which you do not understand, speak up and I will look and find out what it means. But do not interrupt me except for cause, for I am always excited when I am erecting history, and want to get on. Well, one day Catasauqua met with a misfortune; her house burned down. It was the very day after it had been insured for double its value, too—how singular! yes, and how lucky! This often happens. It teaches us that mere loading a house down with insurance isn't going to save it. Very well, Catasauqua took the insurance money and built a new house; and a much better one, too; and what is more, she had money left to add a gaudy concatenation of extra improvements with. O, I tell you! what she didn't know about catalactics no other cat need ever try to acquire.

Clara—What is catalactics, papa?

The dictionary intimates, in a nebulous way, that it is a sort of demi-synonym for the science commonly called political economy.

---

* My little girls—Susie, aged eight, and Clara, six and a half—often require me to help them go to sleep, nights, by telling them original tales. They think my tales are better than paregoric, and quicker. While I talk, they make comments and ask questions, and we have a pretty good time. I thought maybe other little people might like to try one of my narcotics—so I offer this one. M.T.

Clara—Thank you, papa.

Yes, behind the house she constructed a splendid large catadrome, and enclosed it with a caterwaul about nine feet high, and in the centre was a spacious grass-plot where—

Clara—What is a catadrome, papa?

I will look. Ah, it is a race-course; I thought it was a ten-pin alley. But no matter; in fact it is all the better; for cats do not play ten-pins, when they are feeling well, but they *do* run races, you know; and the spacious grass-plot was for cat-fights, and other free exhibitions; and for ball-games—three-cornered cat, and all that sort of thing; a lovely spot, lovely. Yes, indeed; it had a hedge of dainty little catkins around it, and right in the centre was a splendid great categorematic in full leaf, and—

Susie—What is a categorematic, papa?

I think it's a kind of a shade-tree, but I'll look. No—I was mistaken; it is a *word*; "a word which is capable of being employed by itself as a term."

Susie—Thank you, papa.

Don't mention it. Yes, you see, it wasn't a shade tree; the good Catasauqua didn't know that, else she wouldn't have planted it right there in the way; you can't run over a word like that, you know, and not cripple yourself more or less. Now don't forget that definition, it may come handy to you some day—there is no telling—life is full of vicissitudes. Always remember, a categorematic is a word which a cat can use by herself as a term; but she mustn't try to use it along with another cat, for that is not the idea. Far from it. We have authority for it, you see—Mr. Webster; and he is dead, too, besides. It would be a noble good thing if his dictionary was, too. But that is too much to expect. Yes; well, Catasauqua filled her house with internal improvements—cat-calls in every room, and they are O ever so much handier than bells; and cat-amounts to mount the stairs with, instead of those troublesome elevators which are always getting out of order; and civet-cats in the kitchen, in place of the ordinary sieves, which you can't ever sift anything with, in a satisfactory way; and a couple of tidy ash-cats to clean out the stove and keep it in order; and—catenated on the roof—an alert and cultivated pole-cat to watch the flag-pole and keep the banner a-flying. Ah yes—such was Catasauqua's country residence; and she named it Kamscatka—after her dear native land far away.

Clara—What is catenated, papa?

Chained, my child. The pole-cat was attached by a chain to some object upon the roof contiguous to the flag-pole. This was to retain him in his position.

Clara—Thank you, papa.

The front garden was a spectacle of sublime and bewildering magnificence. A stately row of flowering catalpas stretched from the front door clear to the gate, wreathed from stem to stern with the delicate tendrils and shining scales of the cat's foot ivy, whilst ever and anon the enchanted eye wandered from congeries of lordly cat-tails and kindred catapetalous blooms too deep for utterance, only to encounter the still more entrancing vision of catnip without number and without price, and swoon away in ecstasy unutterable, under the blissful intoxication of its too too fragrant breath!

Both Children—O, how lovely!

You may well say it. Few there be that shall look upon the like again. Yet was not this all; for hither to the north boiled the majestic cataract in unimaginable grandiloquence, and thither to the south sparkled the gentle catadupe in serene and incandescent tranquillity, whilst far and near the halcyon brooklet flowed between!

Both Children—O, how sweet! What is a catadupe, papa?

Small waterfall, my darlings. Such is Webster's belief. All things being in readiness for the house-warming, the widow sent out her invitations, and then proceeded with her usual avocations. For Catasauqua was a widow—sorrow cometh to us all. The husband-cat—Catullus was his name—was no more. He was of a lofty character, brave to rashness, and almost incredibly unselfish. He gave eight of his lives for his country, reserving only one for himself. Yes—the banquet having been ordered, the good Catasauqua tuned up for the customary morning-song, accompanying herself on the catarrh, and her little ones joined in. These were the words:

> There was a little cat,
> And she caught a little rat,
> Which she dutifully rendered to her mother,
> Who said "Bake him in a pie,
> For his flavor's rather high—
> Or confer him on the poor, if you'd druther."

Catasauqua sang soprano, Catiline sang tenor, Cattaraugus bass. It was exquisite melody; it would make your hair stand right up.

Susie—Why, papa, I didn't know cats could sing.

O, can't they, though! Well, these could. Cats are packed full of music—just as full as they can hold; and when they die, people remove it from them and sell it to the fiddle-makers. O yes indeed. Such is life.

Susie—O, here is a picture! Is it a picture of the music, papa?

Only the eye of prejudice could doubt it, my child.

Susie—Did you draw it, papa?

I am indeed the author of it.

Susie—How wonderful! What is a picture like this called, papa?

A work of art, my child. There—do not hold it so close; prop it up on the chair, *three steps away*; now then— that is right; you see how much better and stronger the expression is than when it is close by. It is because some of this picture is drawn in perspective.

Clara—Did you always know how to draw, papa?

Yes. I was born so. But of course I could not draw at first as well as I can now. These things require study—and practice. Mere talent is not sufficient. It takes a person a long time to get so he can draw a picture like this.

Clara—How long did it take you, papa?

Morning-Song

Many years—thirty years, I reckon. Off and on—for I did not devote myself exclusively to art. Still, I have had a great deal of practice. Ah, practice is the great thing!—it accomplishes wonders. Before I was twenty-five, I had got so I could draw a cork as well as anybody that ever was. And many a time I have drawn a blank in a lottery. Once I drew a check that wouldn't go; and after the war I tried to draw a pension—but this was too ambitious. However, the most gifted must fail sometimes. Do you observe those things that are sticking up, in this picture? They are not bones, they are paws; it is very hard to express the difference between bones and paws, in a picture.

Susie—Which is Cattaraugus, papa?

The little pale one that almost has the end of his mother's tail in his mouth.

Susie—But papa, that tail is not right. You know Catasauqua was a Manx, and had a short one.

It is a just remark, my child; but a long tail was necessary, here, to express a certain passion—the passion of joy. Therefore the insertion of a long tail is permissible; it is called a poetic licence. You cannot express the passion of joy with a short tail. Nor even extraordinary excitement. You notice that Cattaraugus is brilliantly excited; now nearly all of that verve, spirit, *elan*, is owing to his tail; yet if I had been false to Art to be true to Nature, you would see there nothing but a poor little stiff and emotionless stump on that cat that would have cast a coldness over the whole scene; yet Cattaraugus was a Manx, like his mother, and had hardly any more tail than a rabbit. Yes, in art, the office of the tail is to express feeling; so, if you wish to portray a cat in repose, you will always succeed better by leaving out the tail. Now here is a striking illustration of the very truth which I am trying to impress upon you. I proposed to draw a cat recumbent and in repose; but just as I had finished the front end of her, she got up and began to gaze passionately at a bird and wriggle her tail in a most expressively wistful way. I had to finish her with that end standing, and the other end lying. It greatly injures the picture. For, you see, it confuses two passions together—the passion of standing up, and the passion of lying down. These are incompatible; and they convey a bad effect to the picture by rendering it unrestful to the eye. In my opinion a cat in a picture ought to be doing one thing or the other—lying down, or standing up; but not both. I ought to have laid this one down again, and put a brick or something on her; but I did not think of it at the time. Let us now separate these conflicting passions in this cat, so that you can see each by itself, and the more easily study it. Lay your hand on the picture, to where I have made those dots, and cover the rear half of it

Effects Married but not Mated

from sight—now you observe how reposeful the front end is. Very well; now lay your hand on the front end and cover *it* from sight—do you observe the eager wriggle in that tail?—it is a wriggle which only the presence of a bird can inspire.

Susie—You must know a wonderful deal, papa.

I have that reputation—in Europe; but here the best minds think I am superficial. However, I am content; I make no defense; my pictures show what I am.

Susie—Papa, I should think you would take pupils.

No, I have no desire for riches. Honest poverty and a conscience torpid through virtuous inaction are more to me than corner lots and praise.

But to resume. The morning-song being over, Catasauqua told Catiline and Cattaraugus to fetch their little books, and she would teach them how to spell.

Both Children—Why, papa! do cats have books?

Yes—catechisms. Just so. Facts are stubborn things. After lesson, Catasauqua gave Catiline and Cattaraugus some rushes, so that they could earn a little circus-money by building cat's-cradles, and at the same time amuse themselves and not miss her; then she went to the kitchen and dining-room to inspect the preparations for the banquet.

The moment her back was turned, Catiline put down his work and got out his cat-pipe for a smoke.

Susie—Why, how naughty!

Thou hast well spoken. It was disobedience; and disobedience is the flagship of the fleet of sin. The gentle Cattaraugus sighed and said—

"For shame, Catiline! How often has our dear mother told you not to do that!

Ah, how can you thus disregard the commandments of the author of your being?"

Susie—Why, what beautiful language, for such a little thing—*wasn't* it, papa?

Ah, yes indeed. That was the kind of cat he was—Cultivated, you see. He had sat at the feet of Rollo's mother; and in the able "Franconia Series" he had not failed to observe how harmoniously gigantic language and a microscopic topic go together. Catiline heard his brother through, and then replied with the contemptuous ejaculation—

"S'scat!"

It means the same that Shakspeare means when he says "Go to." Nevertheless, Catiline's conscience was not at rest. He murmured something about Where was the harm, since his mother would never know? But Cattaraugus said, sweetly but sadly—

"Alas, if we but do the right under restraint of authoritative observance, where then is the merit?"

Susie—How *good* he was!

Monumentally so. The more we contemplate his character the more sublime it appears. But Catiline, who was coarse and worldly, hated all lofty sentiments, and especially such as were stated in choice and lofty terms; he wished to resent this one, yet compelled himself to hold his peace; but when Cattaraugus said it *over* again, partly to enjoy the sound of it, but mainly for his brother's good, Catiline lost his patience, and said—

"O, take a walk!"

Yet he still felt badly; for he knew he was doing wrong. He began to pretend he did not know it was against the rule to smoke his cat-pipe; but Cattaraugus, without an utterance, lifted an accusing paw toward the wall, where, among the illuminated mottoes, hung this one—

"No Smoking Strictly Prohibited."

Catiline turned pale; and, murmuring in a broken voice, "I am undone—forgive me, brother," laid the fatal cat-pipe aside and burst into tears.

Clara—Poor thing! It was cruel—*wasn't* it, papa?

Susie—Well but he oughtn't to done so, in the first place. Cattaraugus wasn't to blame.

Clara—Why, *Susie!* If Catiline didn't *know* he wasn't allowed—

Susie—Catiline did know it—Cattaraugus told him so; and besides, Catiline—

Clara—Cattaraugus only told Catiline that if—

Susie—Why *Clara!* Catiline didn't *need* for Cattaraugus to say one single—

O, hold on!—it's all a mistake! Come to look in the dictionary, we are proceeding from false premises. The Unabridged says a cat-pipe is "a squeaking
instrument used in play-houses to condemn plays." So you see it wasn't a pipe
to smoke, after all; Catiline *couldn't* smoke it; therefore it follows that he was
simply pretending to smoke it, to stir up his brother, that's all.

Susie—But papa, Catiline might as well smoke as stir up his brother.

Clara—Susie, you don't like Catiline, and so whatever he does, it don't suit
you—it ain't right; and he is only a little fellow, anyway.

Susie—I don't *approve* of Catiline, but I *like* him well enough; I only say—

Clara—What is approve?

Susie—Why it's as if you did something, and I said it was all right. So *I* think
he might as well smoke as stir up his brother. Isn't it so, papa?

Looked at from a strictly mathematical point of view, I don't know but it *is*
a case of six-in-one-and-half-a-dozen-in-the-other. Still, *our* business is mainly
with the historical facts; if we only get *them* right, we can leave posterity to
take care of the moral aspects of the matter. To resume the thread of the narrative—when Cattaraugus saw that Catiline had not been smoking at all, but
had only been making believe, and this too with the avowed object of fra-
ternal aggravation, he was deeply hurt; and by his heat was beguiled into
recourse to that bitter weapon, sarcasm; saying—

"The Roman Catiline would have betrayed his foe; it was left to the Catasau-
quian to refine upon the model and betray his friend."

"O, a gaudy speech!—and very erudite and swell!" retorted Catiline, deri-
sively, "but just a *little* catachrestic."

Susie—What is catachrestic, papa?

"Far-fetched," the dictionary says. The remark stung Cattaraugus to the
quick, and he called Catiline a Catapult; this infuriated Catiline beyond
endurance, and he threw down the gauntlet and called Cattaraugus a catso.
No cat will stand that; so at it they went. They spat and clawed and fought
until they dimmed away and finally disappeared in a flying fog of cat-fur.

Clara—What is a catso, papa?

"A base fellow, a rogue, a cheat," says the dictionary. When the weather
cleared, Cattaraugus, ever ready to acknowledge a fault, whether committed
by himself or another, said—

"I was wrong, brother—forgive me. A cat may err—to err is cattish; but
toward even a foreigner, even a wildcat, a catacaustic remark is in ill taste;
how much more so, then, when a brother is the target! Yes, Catiline, I was
wrong; I deeply regret the circumstance. Here is my hand—let us forget the
dark o'erclouded past in the bright welkin of the present, consecrating our-

selves anew to its nobler lessons, and sacrificing ourselves yet again, and forever if need be, to the thrice-armed beacon that binds them in one!"

Susie—He was a splendid talker, *wasn't* he, papa? Papa, what is catacaustic?

Well, a catacaustic remark is a bitter, malicious remark—a sort of a—sort of—or a kind of a—well, let's look in the dictionary; that is cheaper. O, yes, here it is: "Catacaustic, *n;* a caustic curve formed by reflection of light." O, yes, that's it.

Susie—Well, papa, what does *that* mean?

The Presumptuous Ravens

One never tires of poking about in the dense woods that clothe all those lofty Neckar hills to their tops. The great deeps of a boundless forest have a beguiling and impressive charm in any country; but German legends and fairy tales have given these an added charm. They have peopled all that region with gnomes, and dwarfs, and all sorts of mysterious and uncanny creatures. At the time I am writing of, I had been reading so much of this literature that sometimes I was not sure but that I was beginning to believe in the gnomes and fairies as realities.

One afternoon I got lost in the woods about a mile from the hotel, and presently fell into a train of dreamy thought about animals which talk, and kobolds, and enchanted folk, and the rest of the pleasant legendary stuff; and so, by stimulating my fancy, I finally got to imagining I glimpsed small flitting shapes here and there down the columned aisles of the forest. It was a place which was peculiarly meet for the occasion. It was a pine wood, with so thick and soft a carpet of brown needles that one's footfall made no more sound than if he were treading on wool; the tree-trunks were as round and straight and smooth as pillars, and stood close together; they were bare of branches to a point about twenty-five feet above ground, and from there upward so thick with boughs that not a ray of sunlight could pierce through. The world was bright with sunshine outside, but a deep and mellow twilight reigned in there, and also a silence so profound that I seemed to hear my own breathings.

When I had stood ten minutes, thinking and imagining, and getting my

spirit in tune with the place, and in the right mood to enjoy the supernatural, a raven suddenly uttered a horse croak over my head. It made me start; and then I was angry because I started. I looked up, and the creature was sitting on a limb right over me, looking down at me. I felt something of the same sense of humiliation and injury which one feels when he finds that a human stranger has been clandestinely inspecting him in his privacy and mentally commenting upon him. I eyed the raven, and the raven eyed me. Nothing was said during some seconds. Then the bird stepped a little way along his limb to get a better point of observation, lifted his wings, stuck his head far down below his shoulders toward me, and croaked again—a croak with a distinctly insulting expression about it. If he had spoken in English he could not have said any more plainly than he did say in raven, "Well, what do *you* want here?" I felt as foolish as if I had been caught in some mean act by a responsible being, and reproved for it. However, I made no reply; I would not bandy words with a raven. The adversary waited a while, with his shoulders still lifted, his head thrust down between them, and his keen bright eye fixed on me; then he threw out two or three more insults, which I could not understand, further than that I knew a portion of them consisted of language not used in church.

I still made no reply. Now the adversary raised his head and called. There was an answering croak from a little distance in the wood,—evidently a croak of inquiry. The adversary explained with enthusiasm, and the other raven dropped everything and came. The two sat side by side on the limb and discussed me as freely and offensively as two great naturalists might discuss a new kind of bug. The thing became more and more embarrassing. They called in another friend. This was too much. I saw that they had the advantage of me, and so I concluded to get out of the scrape by walking out of it. They enjoyed my defeat as much as any low white people could have done. They craned their necks and laughed at me, (for a raven *can* laugh, just like a man,) they squalled insulting remarks after me as long as they could see me. They were nothing but ravens—I knew that,—what they thought about me could be a matter of no consequence,—and yet when even a raven shouts after you, "What a hat!" "O, pull down your vest!" and that sort of thing, it hurts you and humiliates you, and there is no getting around it with fine reasoning and pretty arguments.

ৡৡ

Birds with a Sense of Humor

ANIMALS TALK to each other, of course. There can be no question about that; but I suppose there are very few people who can understand them. I never knew but one man who could. I knew he could, however, because he told me so himself. He was a middle-aged, simple-hearted miner who had lived in a lonely corner of California, among the woods and mountains, a good many years, and had studied the ways of his only neighbors, the beasts and the birds, until he believed he could accurately translate any remark which they made. This was Jim Baker. According to Jim Baker, some animals have only a limited education, and use only very simple words, and scarcely ever a comparison or a flowery figure; whereas, certain other animals have a large vocabulary, a fine command of language and a ready and fluent delivery; consequently these latter talk a great deal; they like it; they are conscious of their talent, and they enjoy "showing off." Baker said, that after long and careful observation, he had come to the conclusion that the blue-jays were the best talkers he had found among birds and beasts. Said he:

"There's more *to* a blue-jay than any other creature. He has got more moods, and more different kinds of feelings than other creatures; and mind you, whatever a blue-jay feels, he can put into language. And no mere commonplace language, either, but rattling, out-and-out book-talk—and bristling with metaphor, too—just bristling! And as for command of language—why *you* never see a blue-jay get stuck for a word. No man ever did. They just boil out of him! And another thing: I've noticed a good deal, and there's no bird, or cow, or anything that uses as good grammar as a blue-jay. You may say a cat uses good grammar. Well, a cat does—but you let a cat get excited, once; you let a cat get to pulling fur with another cat on a shed, nights, and you'll hear grammar that will give you the lockjaw. Ignorant people think it's the *noise* which fighting cats make that is so aggravating, but it ain't so; it's the sickening grammar they use. Now I've never heard a jay use bad grammar but very seldom; and when they do, they are as ashamed as a human; they shut right down and leave.

"You may call a jay a bird. Well, so he is, in a measure—because he's got feathers on him, and don't belong to no church, perhaps; but otherwise he is just as much a human as you be. And I'll tell you for why. A jay's gifts, and instincts, and feelings, and interests, cover the whole ground. A jay hasn't got any more principle than a Congressman. A jay will lie, a jay will steal, a jay will deceive, a jay will betray; and four times out of five, a jay will go back on his solemnest promise. The sacredness of an obligation is a thing which you can't cram into no blue-jay's head. Now on top of all this, there's another thing: a jay can out-swear any gentleman in the mines. You think a cat can swear. Well, a cat can; but you give a blue-jay a subject that calls for his reserve-powers, and where is your cat? Don't talk to *me*—I know too much about this thing. And there's yet another thing: in the one little particular of scolding—just good, clean, out-and-out scolding—a blue-jay can lay over anything, human or divine. Yes, sir, a jay is everything that a man is. A jay can cry, a jay can laugh, a jay can feel shame, a jay can reason and plan and discuss, a jay likes gossip and scandal, a jay has got a sense of humor, a jay knows when he is an ass just as well as you do—maybe better. If a jay ain't human, he better take in his sign, that's all. Now I'm going to tell you a perfectly true fact about some blue-jays."

Baker's Blue-Jay Yarn

"When I first begun to understand jay language correctly, there was a little incident happened here. Seven years ago, the last man in this region but me, moved away. There stands his house,—been empty ever since; a log house, with a plank roof—just one big room, and no more; no ceiling—nothing between the rafters and the floor. Well, one Sunday morning I was sitting out here in front of my cabin, with my cat, taking the sun, and looking at the blue hills, and listening to the leaves rustling so lonely in the trees, and thinking of the home away yonder in the States, that I hadn't heard from in thirteen years, when a blue jay lit on that house, with an acorn in his mouth, and says, 'Hello, I reckon I've struck something.' When he spoke, the acorn dropped out of his mouth and rolled down the roof, of course, but he didn't care; his mind was all on the thing he had struck. It was a knot-hole in the roof. He cocked his head to one side, shut one eye and put the other one to the hole, like a 'possum looking down a jug; then he glanced up with his bright eyes, gave a wink or two with his wings—which signifies gratification, you understand,— and says, 'It looks like a hole, it's located like a hole,—blamed if I don't believe it *is* a hole!'

"Then he cocked his head down and took another look; he glances up per- fectly joyful, this time; winks his wings and his tail both, and says, 'O, no, this ain't no fat thing, I reckon! If I ain't in luck!—why it's a perfectly elegant hole!' So he flew down and got that acorn, and fetched it up and dropped it in, and was just tilting his head back, with the heavenliest smile on his face, when all of a sudden he was paralyzed into a listening attitude and that smile faded gradually out of his countenance like breath off'n a razor, and the queerest look of surprise took its place. Then he says, 'Why, I didn't hear it fall!' He cocked his eye at the hole again, and took a long look; raised up and shook his head; stepped around to the other side of the hole and took another look from that side; shook his head again. He studied a while, then he just went into the *de*tails—walked round and round the hole and spied into it from every point of the compass. No use. Now he took a thinking attitude on the comb of the roof and scratched the back of his head with his right foot a minute, and finally says, 'Well, it's too many for *me*, that's certain; must be a mighty long hole; however, I ain't got no time to fool around here, I got to 'tend to business; I reckon it's all right—chance it, anyway.'

"So he flew off and fetched another acorn and dropped it in, and tried to flirt his eye to the hole quick enough to see what become of it, but he was too late. He held his eye there as much as a minute; then he raised up and sighed, and says, 'Consound it, I don't seem to understand this thing, no way; how- ever, I'll tackle her again.' He fetched another acorn, and done his level best to see what become of it, but he couldn't. He says, 'Well, *I* never struck no such a hole as this, before; I'm of the opinion it's a totally new kind of a hole.' Then he begun to get mad. He held in for a spell, walking up and down the comb of the roof and shaking his head and muttering to himself; but his feelings got the upper hand of him, presently, and he broke loose and cursed himself black in the face. I never see a bird take on so about a little thing. When he got through he walks to the hole and looks in again for half a minute; then he says, 'Well, you're a long hole, and a deep hole, and a mighty singular hole altogether—but I've started in to fill you, and I'm d—d if I *don't* fill you, if it takes a hundred year!'

"And with that, away he went. You never see a bird work so since you was born. He laid into his work like a nigger, and the way he hove acorns into that hole for about two hours and a half was one of the most exciting and aston- ishing spectacles I ever struck. He never stopped to take a look anymore— he just hove 'em in and went for more. Well at last he could hardly flop his wings, he was so tuckered out. He comes a-drooping down, once more, sweat- ing like an ice-pitcher, drops his acorn in and says, '*Now* I guess I've got the bulge on you by this time!' So he bent down for a look. If you'll believe me, when his head come up again he was just pale with rage. He says, 'I've shov- eled acorns enough in there to keep the family thirty years, and if I can see a sign of one of 'em I wish I may land in a museum with a belly full of sawdust in two minutes!'

"He just had strength enough to crawl up onto the comb and lean his back agin the chimbly, and then he collected his impressions and begun to free his mind. I see in a second that what I had mistook for profanity in the mines was only just the rudiments, as you may say.

"Another jay was going by, and heard him doing his devotions, and stops to inquire what was up. The sufferer told him the whole circumstance, and says, 'Now yonder's the hole, and if you don't believe me, go and look for your- self.' So this fellow went and looked, and comes back and says, 'How many did you say you put in there?' 'Not any less than two tons,' says the sufferer. The other jay went and looked again. He couldn't seem to make it out, so he raised a yell, and three more jays come. They all examined the hole, they all made the sufferer tell it over again, then they all discussed it, and got off as many leather-headed opinions about it as an average crowd of humans could have done.

"They called in more jays; then more and more, till pretty soon this whole region 'peared to have a blue flush about it. There must have been five thou- sand of them; and such another jawing and disputing and ripping and cuss- ing you never heard. Every jay in the whole lot put his eye to the hole and delivered a more chuckle-headed opinion about the mystery than the jay that went there before him. They examined the house all over, too. The door was standing half open, and at last one old jay happened to go and light on it and look in. Of course, that knocked the mystery galley-west in a second. There lay the acorns, scattered all over the floor. He flopped his wings and raised a whoop. 'Come here!' he says, 'Come here, everybody; hang'd if this fool hasn't been trying to fill up a house with acorns!' They all came a-swooping down like a blue cloud, and as each fellow lit on the door and took a glance, the whole absurdity of the contract that that first jay had tackled hit him home and he fell over backwards suffocating with laughter, and the next jay took his place and done the same.

"Well, sir, they roosted around here on the house-top and the trees for an hour, and guffawed over that thing like human beings. It ain't any use to tell me a blue-jay hasn't got a sense of humor, because I know better. And memory, too. They brought jays here from all over the United States to look down that hole, every summer for three years. Other birds too. And they could all see the point, except an owl that come from Nova Scotia to visit the Yo Semite, and he took this thing in on his way back. He said he couldn't see anything funny in it. But then he was a good deal disappointed about Yo Semite, too."

৪৯

The Idiotic Ant

NOW AND THEN, while we rested, we watched the laborious ant at his work. I found nothing new in him,—certainly nothing to change my opinion of him. It seems to me that in the matter of intellect the ant must be a strangely over-rated bird. During many summers, now, I have watched him, when I ought to have been in better business, and I have not yet come across a living ant that seemed to have any more sense than a dead one. I refer to the ordinary ant, of course; I have had no experience of those wonderful Swiss and African ones which vote, keep drilled armies, hold slaves, and dispute about religion. Those particular ants may be all that the naturalist paints them, but I am persuaded that the average ant is a sham. I admit his industry, of course; he is the hardest working creature in the world,—when anybody is looking,—but his leather-headedness is the point I make against him. He goes out foraging, he makes a capture, and then what does he do? Go home? No,—he goes anywhere but home. He doesn't know where home is. His home may be only three feet away,—no matter, he can't find it. He makes his capture, as I have said; it is generally something which can be of no sort of use to himself or

anybody else; it is usually seven times bigger than it ought to be; he hunts
out the awkwardest place to take hold of it; he lifts it bodily up in the air by
main force, and starts: not toward home, but in the opposite direction; not
calmly and wisely, but with a frantic haste which is wasteful of his strength;
he fetches up against a pebble, and instead of going around it, he climbs over
it backwards dragging his booty after him, tumbles down on the other side,
jumps up in a passion, kicks the dust off his clothes, moistens his hands,
grabs his property viciously, yanks it this way then that, shoves it ahead of
him a moment, turns tail and lugs it after him another moment, gets madder
and madder, then presently hoists it into the air and goes tearing away in an
entirely new direction; comes to a weed; it never occurs to him to go around
it; no, he must climb it; and he does climb it, dragging his worthless property to the top—which is as bright a thing to do as it would be for me to carry
a sack of flour from Heidelberg to Paris by way of Strasburg steeple; when
he gets up there he finds that that is not the place; takes a cursory glance
at the scenery and either climbs down again or tumbles down, and starts
off once more—as usual, in a new direction. At the end of half an hour, he
fetches up within six inches of the place he started from and lays his burden
down; meantime he has been over all the ground for two yards around, and
climbed all the weeds and pebbles he came across. Now he wipes the sweat
from his brow, strokes his limbs, and then marches aimlessly off, in as violent
a hurry as ever. He traverses a good deal of zig-zag country, and by and by
stumbles on his same booty again. He does not remember to have ever seen
it before; he looks around to see which is not the way home, grabs his bun-
dle and starts; he goes through the same adventures he had before; finally
stops to rest, and a friend comes along. Evidently the friend remarks that a
last year's grasshopper leg is a very noble acquisition, and inquires where he
got it. Evidently the proprietor does not remember exactly where he did get it,
but thinks he got it "around here somewhere." Evidently the friend contracts
to help him freight it home. Then, with a judgment peculiarly antic, (pun
not intentional,) they take hold of opposite ends of that grasshopper leg and
begin to tug with all their might in opposite directions. Presently they take
a rest and confer together. They decide that something is wrong, they can't
make out what. Then they go at it again, just as before. Same result. Mutual
recriminations follow. Evidently each accuses the other of being an obstruc-
tionist. They lock themselves together and chew each other's jaws for a while;
then they roll and tumble on the ground till one loses a horn or a leg and
has to haul off for repairs. They make up and go to work again in the same
old insane way, but the crippled ant is at a disadvantage; tug as he may, the

other one drags off the booty and him at the end of it. Instead of giving up, he hangs on, and gets his shins bruised against every obstruction that comes in the way. By and by, when that grasshopper leg has been dragged all over the same old ground once more, it is finally dumped at about the spot where it originally lay, the two perspiring ants inspect it thoughtfully and decide that dried grasshopper legs are a poor sort of property after all, and then each starts off in a different direction to see if he can't find an old nail or something else that is heavy enough to afford entertainment and at the same time valueless enough to make an ant want to own it.

There in the Black Forest, on the mountain side, I saw an ant go through with such a performance as this with a dead spider of fully ten times his own weight. The spider was not quite dead, but too far gone to resist. He had a round body the size of a pea. The little ant—observing that I was noticing—turned him on his back, sunk his fangs into his throat, lifted him into the air and started vigorously off with him, stumbling over little pebbles, stepping on the spider's legs and tripping himself up, dragging him backwards, shoving him bodily ahead, dragging him up stones six inches high instead of going around them, climbing weeds twenty times his own height and jumping from their summits,—and finally leaving him in the middle of the road to be confiscated by any other fool of an ant that wanted him. I measured the ground which this ass traversed, and arrived at the conclusion that what he had accomplished inside of twenty minutes would constitute some such job as this,—relatively speaking,—for a man; to wit: to strap two eight-hundred pound horses together, carry them eighteen hundred feet, mainly over (not around) boulders averaging six feet high, and in the course of the journey climb up and jump from the top of one precipice like Niagara, and three steeples, each a hundred and twenty feet high; and then put the horses down, in an exposed place, without anybody to watch them, and go off to indulge in some other idiotic miracle for vanity's sake.

Science has recently discovered that the ant does not lay up anything for winter use. This will knock him out of literature, to some extent. He does not work, except when people are looking, and only then when the observer has a green, naturalistic look, and seems to be taking notes. This amounts to deception, and will injure him for the Sunday schools. He has not judgment enough to know what is good to eat from what isn't. This amounts to ignorance, and will impair the world's respect for him. He cannot stroll around a stump and find his way home again. This amounts to idiotcy, and once the damaging fact is established, thoughtful people will cease to look up to him, the sentimental will cease to fondle him. His vaunted industry is but a vanity and of no effect, since he never gets home with anything he starts with. This disposes of the last remnant of his reputation and wholly destroys his main usefulness as a moral agent, since it will make the sluggard hesitate to go to him any more. It is strange beyond comprehension, that so manifest a humbug as the ant has been able to fool so many nations and keep it up so many ages without being found out.

The ant is strong, but we saw another strong thing, where we had not suspected the presence of much muscular power before. A toadstool—that vegetable which springs to full growth in a single night—had torn loose and lifted a matted mass of pine needles and dirt of twice its own bulk into the air, and supported it there, like a column supporting a shed. Ten thousand toadstools, with the right purchase, could lift a man, I suppose. But what good would it do?

❧

Cock-fight in New Orleans

We went to a cock-pit in New Orleans, on a Saturday afternoon. I had never seen a cock-fight before. There were men and boys there of all ages and all colors, and of many languages and nationalities. But I noticed one quite conspicuous and surprising absence—the traditional brutal faces. There were no brutal faces. With no cock-fighting going on, you could have played the gathering on a stranger for a prayer meeting; and after it began, for a revival—provided you blindfolded your stranger; for the shouting was something prodigious.

A negro and a white man were in the ring—everybody else outside. The cocks were brought in in sacks; and when time was called, they were taken out by the two bottle-holders, stroked, caressed, poked toward each other, and finally liberated. The big black cock plunged instantly at the little gray one and struck him on the head with his spur. The gray responded with spirit. Then the babel of many-tongued shoutings broke out, and ceased not, thenceforth. When the cocks had been fighting some little time, I was expecting them, momently, to drop dead; for both were blind, red with blood, and so exhausted that they frequently fell down. Yet they would not give up, neither would they die. The negro and the white man would pick them up, every few seconds, wipe them off, blow cold water on them in a fine spray, and take their heads in their mouths and hold them there a moment—to warm back the perishing-life perhaps; I do not know. Then, being set down again, the dying creatures would totter gropingly about, with dragging wings, find each other, strike a guess-work blow or two, and fall exhausted once more.

I did not see the end of the battle. I forced myself to endure it as long as I could; but it was too pitiful a sight; so I made frank confession to that effect, and we retired. We heard afterward that the black cock died in the ring, and fighting to the last.

Evidently there is abundant fascination about this "sport" for such as have had a degree of familiarity with it. I never saw people enjoy anything more than this gathering enjoyed this fight. The case was the same with old gray-heads and with boys of ten. They lost themselves in frenzies of delight. The "cocking-main" is an inhuman sort of entertainment, there is no question about that; still, it seems a much more respectable and far less cruel sport than fox-hunting—for the cocks like it; they experience, as well as confer, enjoyment; which is not the fox's case.

༄

The Bricksville Loafers

ALL THE STREETS and lanes was just mud, they warn't nothing else *but* mud—mud as black as tar, and nigh about a foot deep, in some places; and two or three inches deep in *all* the places. The hogs loafed and grunted around, everywheres. You'd see a muddy sow and a litter of pigs come lazying along the street and whollop herself right down in the way, where folks had to walk around her, and she'd stretch out and shut her eyes, and wave her ears, whilst the pigs was milking her, and look as happy as if she was on salary. And pretty soon you'd hear a loafer sing out, "Hi! *so* boy! sick him, Tige!" and away the sow would go, squealing most horrible, with a dog or two swinging to each ear, and three or four dozen more a-coming; and then you would see all the loafers get up and watch the thing out of sight, and laugh at the fun and look grateful for the noise. Then they'd settle back again, till there was a dog-fight. There couldn't anything wake them up all over, and make them happy all over, like a dog-fight—unless it might be putting turpentine on a stray dog and setting fire to him, or tying a tin pan to his tail and seeing him run himself to death.

≈

A Prescription for Universal Peace

CLARENCE WAS WITH ME, as concerned the revolution, but in a modified way. His idea was a Republic, without privileged orders, but with a hereditary royal family at the head of it instead of an elective chief magistrate. He believed that no nation that had ever known the joy of worshiping a royal family could ever be robbed of it and not fade away and die of melancholy. I urged that kings were dangerous. He said, then have cats. He was sure that a royal family of cats would answer every purpose. They would be as useful as any other royal family, they would know as much, they would have the same virtues and the same vices, the same fidelities and the same treacheries, the same disposition to get up shindies with other royal cats, they would be laughably vain and absurd and never know it, they would be wholly inexpensive; finally, they would have as sound a divine right as any other royal house, and "Tom VII, or Tom XI, or Tom XIV by the grace of God King," would sound as well as it would when applied to the ordinary royal tomcat with tights on. "And as a rule," said he, in his neat modern English, "the character of these cats would be considerably above the character of the average king, and this would be an immense moral advantage to the nation, for the reason that a nation always models its morals after its monarch's. The worship of royalty being founded in unreason, these graceful and harmless cats would easily become as sacred as any other royalties, and indeed more so, because it would presently be noticed that they hanged nobody, beheaded nobody, imprisoned nobody, inflicted no cruelties or injustices of any sort, and so must be worthy of a deeper love and reverence than the customary human king, and would certainly get it. The eyes of the whole harried world would soon be fixed upon this humane and gentle system, and royal butchers would presently begin to disappear; their subjects would fill the vacancies with catlings from our own royal house; we should become a factory; we should supply the thrones of the world; within forty years all Europe would be governed by cats, and we should furnish the cats. The reign of universal peace would begin, then, to end no more forever. . . . . . *Me-e-e-yow-ow-ow-ow—FZT!-wow!*"

Hang him, I supposed he was in earnest, and was beginning to be persuaded by him, until he exploded that cat-howl and startled me almost out of my clothes. But he never could be in earnest. He didn't know what it was. He had pictured a distinct and perfectly rational and feasible improvement upon constitutional monarchy, but he was too feather-headed to know it, or care anything about it, either.

ℒ

Part Three: 1890s–1910

Letters from a Dog to Another Dog Explaining and Accounting for Man

Author, Newfoundland Smith.
Translated from the Original Doggerel by M. T.

[Foot-notes by Bull Wilkerson and Tige Lathrop; trustworthy generally,
but sometimes crude and ignorant. M.T.]

DEAR ST. BERNARD—

The questions you ask me are hard to answer, but I will try. I understand
the matter perfectly myself, for I have devoted my whole life to the closest
study of it; but I am not sure that I can convey to another, fully and clearly,
all I know.

As a help to my attempt, I must ask you to sponge[1] your mind clear of prejudice, ostensible information and dogly tradition concerning Man and what
he is for and why he was invented and whether he is worth while,—in a word
make yourself a puppy again, with all which that implies of receptivity and
hospitable welcome to any new thing.

Now, then, I begin. I begin by placing before you this maxim, so to call
it, and with it the requirement that you accept it and force yourself to
believe it:

All things considered, a Man is as good as a Dog.

Be patient—notice the qualification "all things considered." I claim and do
honestly believe, that it is chiefly Man's environment that makes him ridiculous; and not, as has always been taught and believed, his fundamental inca-
pacity to be otherwise than ridiculous. I claim that a Dog placed in Man's
situation, and hampered by the myriad pathetic slaveries to which he is subject from his cradle, would gradually and surely deteriorate, and at last turn
into a thing which would be to all intents and purposes a Man. Take just one
detail, for example, to start with:

*No Man has ever possessed that common and inviolable heritage of our race, Freedom of
Conscience, Freedom of Speech, Freedom of Action.*

I ask you, what would a Dog be without these? Where would his character
be? How could he have a character at all, with nothing to build it on? Imagine yourself so situated that while holding views of your own you must pre-

---

1. *Sponge.* A kind of vegetable rag which grows in drugstores and barber shops, and is used
to wash dogs and rub things out with.

tend to hold the views of your neighbors; bark in your party's[1] key or your church's[2] key or your monarch's[3] key or bark not at all; and as for freedom of action—why a Man's cook can put limits to that.

Now there you have in a nutshell the thing—at least the most important thing—which differentiates Man from Dog. To speak broadly, one might perhaps say, Give a Man freedom of conscience, freedom of speech, freedom of action, and he is a Dog; take them from a Dog and he is a Man.

Chapter II

Now that you understand the foundation upon which Man's character is built, it ought to be possible, by painstaking explanation and illustration, to presently make you understand the bizarre edifice that rests upon it. Please keep that foundation in mind, otherwise we shall achieve nothing, we shall arrive nowhere. It is the Key, mind you, the key to Man. Everything he thinks and does and says must be referred to it—then it is intelligible; but without the key all his thoughts, his speeches, his acts are grotesque, irrational, amazing, unaccountable, and the study of them would result in hydrophobia.

Now we will take one more step. Man, as we see, is a slave, from his cradle to his grave. What does slavery naturally impose upon its victim? The necessity of being always on the alert, of always looking out for himself, of always fending off the encroachments of his fellow-slaves and his masters, of always appeasing his own necessities, no matter at whose cost—is not this true? Very well—out of this springs naturally and of necessity the most gigantic upheaval, the most far-shining and conspicuous summit in the whole broad landscape of Man's character—*Selfishness*. If we say that all Men are selfish—which is true—we do not need to add that all Men are also *cruel;* for that follows without argument.

Chapter III

In two brief lessons you have possessed yourself of three great and luminous facts: Man is wholly without liberties, and is selfish and cruel. He has other qualities, and better ones, as we shall see as we go along—foot-hills, ver-

---

1. Organized band of political slaves who think one way and vote another, as a rule, by command of the proprietor, who is usually called Boss.

2. Similar kind of property, owned by persons called Priests, Popes, Grand Lamas, and so on.

3. A select and peculiar kind of slave-proprietor who does not get his property by purchase, or trick, or beguilement, but inherits it—from an ancestor who stole it.

dant, pleasant, inconspicuous, scattered along the base of those mountains. And dulled and dimmed and chilled by the blanket shadows flung across them by those mountains—as a rule.

Well, would you suppose that an animal of this description has a good opinion of itself? You shall judge. Man has exactly reversed our ancient Dog-philosophy of late, and claims that he has *ascended*—note that word—from *us!* From us and the rest of what he calls the "lower" animals. Meaning, observe you, that this ascent has been from false to true, from coarse to fine, from ignoble to noble. It is certainly very odd, very curious, that Man, who, during all these ages and aeons, has been universally and without dissent considered the base original from whom all the other animals have ascended, patiently conquering their way toward the perfection which they finally achieved, suddenly steps to the front and claims place as the latest result himself! Isn't it gigantic—the complacency of it, I mean. If we stop a moment and consider—

Chapter IV

I was interrupted. Pip Lapierre was running along the grassy bank of the little river, clodding a wounded muskrat, and fell in; I tore down the hill and jumped in and saved him. I fetched him ashore and climbed the bank, holding him upside down by the slack of his breeches, and laid him down on the grass, and stood over him wagging my tail in a gratified way, and giving a bark now and then to remind him that I was there and he needn't worry; and pretty soon his low-down father, half drunk, arrived in a profane fury, and when the boy sat up and began to beg, (I helping him with all my might with wagging tail and pleasing eyes,) and said it wasn't his fault—that he was going along not doing anything in the world, and I came tearing by and hit him a-purpose and knocked him in—that Frenchman took me suddenly on the side of the head with his stick and I shot howling up the hill and around the stable, saying to myself "there's my *other* ear torn, now." For I had had an ear torn by that very boy two weeks ago to-day—torn with a brickbat—a most curious circumstance, for I wasn't doing anything to him, in fact didn't notice that he was around. As a rule we all do notice when he is around, except Bull Wilkerson, for if we don't he makes us regret it, but this time he slipped up on me while I was absorbed in a procession that was going by.[1]

But as I was saying when interrupted, if we stop a moment to consider,

---

1. He struck me once—for amusement; but there must have been something about the quantity or the quality of it that disappointed him.—B.W.

Man's new claim is obviously untenable. It would be the reverse of difficult to show that in true nobleness and fineness of character his stage of development is far below that of the other animals. Let us note a few particulars in this connection.

Malice resides in no animal but one—Man.

Envy is found in no animal but one—Man.

Ambition deforms and defiles the character of no animal but one—Man.

Lust of vengeance for old treasured injury is found in the character of no animal but one—Man.

Cruelty—the inflicting of pain upon the feelings or the body for the mere pleasure of inflicting it—is an infamous characteristic which is found in no animal but one—Man.

Murder. All animals kill, but only Man murders.

Immodesty. This is restricted to Man; no other animal has it.

Base spirit, boot-licking servility. These degradations are found in the characters of no animals but two—Man and the Dog. And the Dog was free of them until he took to comradeship with Man.

Slavery. No animal inflicts it but Man and the Ant; no animal endures it with contentment and transmits it to his posterity without shame but Man alone.

Captivity, mutilation and death for opinion's sake. No animal has had experience of this sort but one—Man.

This creature has invented a heaven. And from it has excluded all the animals but himself.

Our own philosophy has always taught that Man was on his tedious and patient way upward toward the moral heights attained by the other animals— with a considerable distance to climb yet; and so far I see nothing the matter with that theory.

Chapter V

You now have the salient facts of Man's character before you. Talk, gossip, illustration—these will do the rest. Almost before you are aware of it you will begin to understand Man, marvel at him, acquire an insatiable interest in him, and churn your brains to butter trying to reconcile him with the maxim that all things are made for a purpose and none for fun.

As we go along you would be likely to notice without my calling your attention to it, that Men, like Dogs, are grouped, and the several groups classified by the sharply defined stages of development to which they have attained. These groups have names, and are referred to as Germans, French, English, Irish, Pawnees, Turks, Americans, Russians, and so on, just as we refer to our groups as St. Bernards, Black-and-Tans, Pugs, and so forth. Some Men have imagined close correspondences of character between certain of their groups and certain of ours—a sufficiently humorous idea, truly, but that is the most that one can say of it. Try to conceive of a nation of Men worthy to be nick-named St. Bernards! Contemplate the countenances of your great race, dear and admirable friend of mine. All gracious traits are to be found there. Inspect, examine, analyze; these thoughts and these words will surely follow. What nobility of mind, what benevolence, what honesty, what sincerity, what simplicity, what stainless purity of heart, what unselfishness, what trustfulness, what truth, what sweetness, what gentle and winning humility, what loving welcome to all comers,—in a word, what unapproachable beauty and perfection of character, what unhaloed and unconscious saintship!

Does this describe the rare and far-between St. Bernard Dog only? No, it describes every member of the race.

Try to imagine this benignant face distorted by hate, malice, envy; or framing itself to purposes of deceit; or to give expression to insolence, arrogance, egotism, vanity; or to frown away the supplicant, the friendless, the forsaken; try to imagine these soft indulgent eyes refusing forgiveness to an offender; and finally, try to imagine this noble "brute" drunk, wallowing in filth, hiccoughing forth obscene words, nasty images, and blaspheming God with every breath.

Think of any nation among Men making serious claim to being the moral equals of the St. Bernard Dog. I mean as a nation, as a whole. Now and then, at long intervals, a Man has appeared in the earth who was a St. Bernard Dog in all but the name and shape, but no whole nation of Men has risen to a recognizable resemblance to that unrivaled race.

Bull Wilkerson thinks there is no great difference between the Black-and-Tan terriers and the French, and he also thinks that in manners, general style and personal appearance the Pug is much like an Englishman, but I think that these resemblances are but dim and fanciful rather than distinct and real. To compliment the Englishman and the Frenchman may be admissible, but this oversteps the limit and amounts to flattery.

Bull Wilkerson says the English themselves do not claim to be like Pugs, but like Bulldogs. Now think what it is to make such a claim. Look at Bull Wilkerson himself—as fine a character as I know anywhere, and all his tribe are similar. Bull Wilkerson is a handsome figure—chunky, stocky, all muscle and gristle, stands as square and firm as a work bench, and is the very impersonation of sturdy independence. There is a permanent smile on his placid face, on account of his under jaw projecting and his lower teeth overlapping his upper lip. He has a good heart and a kindly and loving spirit, and will bear without a murmur all the rough treatment that children inflict upon him in their rude and thoughtless play. He is loyal, faithful to his duties, willing, accommodating, open to persuasion. He troubles nobody, interferes with no one's affairs, takes the world as he finds it, and makes the best of it, without whining or complaint. He invites no quarrel, provokes no quarrel; but if one is put upon him the business end of his disposition comes to the fore, and he will stay by that misunderstanding as long as there is anything left of the party that introduced it. Certainly there are Englishmen like this, but is it the rule? Bull Wilkerson allows no other Bulldog to make a doormat of him on plea of rank and birth. Is that English? Bull Wilkerson was born in a stable, Bull Tanner was born in the State House, and so were his father and his grandfather and his great-grandfather, but does Bull Tanner think a Capitol-born Dog is necessarily any better Dog than a stable-born Dog? He would never think of such a thing. All the Dogs in the land would laugh at him.

Now I will tell you something that Bull Wilkerson did. Puss Wilkerson had a family of four wee little weak-legged stumbling kittens, nine days old, in the bin in the hayloft about fifty yards from the house. The Wilkerson children brought them to the house while Puss Wilkerson was out visiting somewhere, and they played with them on the porch for an hour while Bull looked on and superintended and saw that things went right. Then it was nightfall, and the children went off to bed and left the helpless little creatures to creep and stumble aimlessly about the porch and cry for their mother. Bull Wilkerson reflected over the situation, then he took the kittens one at a time in his mouth and carried them across the grounds and up to the hayloft and dropped them in the bin. Four trips. Is that English? Would an Englishman carry kittens in his mouth? Not any that I have struck. Not the nobility, anyway.

Chapter VI

Kingship, nobility? Yes, I will talk about these now, though if you had let me alone I should have come to them in their proper turn. These two institutions are among the most grotesque and unaccountable of all the odd inventions of men. They take their rise in this way. First, there will be a lot of savages scattered over a country. They quarrel—about nothing; then they try to settle it with a fight, tribe against tribe. One man in a tribe shows superior ability; they elect him chief, that is, leader, to hold that place during their pleasure. One tribe beats another, and peace ensues. The victorious chief is praised, glorified, by his tribe. He gets up war after war, subdues tribe after tribe, brings them under his government, takes possession of their lands. His glory is supreme, he is become the idol of the people. His course, now, is simple and easy. He is the custodian, in trust, of all the powers, treasures and public domain of the consolidated nation. He takes advantage of his opportunity—seizes upon these valuables and makes them his personal property by the strong hand. It is not difficult; for he has only to buy up the capablest men of the several tribes by distributing inalienable lands and permanent honors and privileges among them, and his game is won. And there you have it: he is king—in perpetuity; those minor chiefs are "nobles"—in perpetuity; the nation are slaves—in perpetuity. The king, you see, has turned a temporary loan of power into a permanent and transmissible possession by force—and all the nation recognize this as robbery pure and simple; he has given some of the swag in perpetuity to his nobles—and the nation has wit enough to know that he has given away what was not his to give.

But now you shall see what use and habit can do, among men, in reconciling them to outrage. Within fifty years the sons and daughters of those highwaymen will be peaceably enjoying those stolen properties and powers as *rights*; and the dull and patient nation will be found acquiescing in that view. A hundred years later, the descendents of the highwaymen will be looking down in scorn upon the masses of the robbed nation, and there will be nobody to find fault with that attitude. Next, *reverence* for the descendants of those highwaymen will begin to be required of the people; it will be granted, and it will grow. Century after century it will go on growing. It will become worship—apparently. Think of that. In that day the descendants of the robbed people will stand ready at all times to froth at the mouth with indignation if any shall attack the "rights" of their nobility, and will also stand ready to lay down their very lives, cheerfully and proudly, to maintain the "rights" of the descendants of the head highwayman of the olden time. Isn't it funny?

To the canine mind, it is inconceivably funny. Barney, I tell you this, and it is true: there is not a monarch in the earth to-day but sits upon a stolen throne and represents a thief; yet there is not one among them who is not revered, held sacred, regarded as something in a sense divine. In fact, a royal "right" stolen five hundred years ago is called a "divine" right to-day. God himself is made a conspirator, an accessory to the theft.

Consider the Czar of Russia. His powers are a theft to-day, just as they were when they came originally into his family. His portrait hangs everywhere that you may go, throughout his dominions. His eighty million slaves, instead of being privileged to clod it with mud wherever they find it, and say "This is the posterity of that highwayman that robbed our fathers," are actually required to take their hats off when they come into its presence, and humbly salute it. And yet, do you know, a Russian would rather be a Russian than a Dog. It seems incredible, but I have it from a Russian terrier who lives over the way from our house and says he *knows* Russians are not ashamed of being Russians, and has often heard them speak contemptuously of Dogs. Look—this is from a newspaper:

To Check Desertions: It is well known in the Russian army that death follows desertion. A deserter was lately shot who got away a year ago and had traveled 4,000 miles. It cost the Government over $3,000 to find him, but it would have paid $20,000 sooner than let him get away. Over 30,000 soldiers were assembled to see him shot.

You understand, the soldier didn't go into that army because he wanted to; he went into it because the Czar required him to do it. The Czar requires every Russian to spend the fifteen best and most efficient years of his life in the army; and then turns him adrift without pension and ignorant of all ways of sustaining life except by killing people.

This reminds me of a curious thing. A monarch always keeps a vast and expensive army on hand all the time to protect himself from his own people. But he doesn't confess that that is his reason. He says it is to protect the people themselves from other nations. Now those monarchs know that they could get up a Royal Highwaymans' Union, exchange hostages, and disband those armies without apprehension tomorrow if there was any truth in their pretence.

Now you are going to ask me what has become of all that reverence for the monarch, and anxiety to die for his "rights," which I have just been saying is the hereditary subject's attitude toward his master, if it is true that the monarch is afraid of the subject and keeps an army as a protection against him. I only answer that that reverence and that loyalty are mainly sham, are but skin deep, and would quickly disappear if the abolition of the army rendered the opposite attitude safe. I think so because, when they had a revolution in France a hundred years ago, the reversal of the attitude of a thousand years was instantaneous and complete. Reverence for king and respect for noble disappeared in a day. These sentiments had actually been a sham for a thousand years.

If armies are merely useful to protect nations, not kings and nobles, why doesn't America keep one? The truth is, when a *nation* wants to protect itself, an army *always exists*. Maybe it isn't under wages; maybe it isn't in uniform; maybe it isn't visible anywhere: but you hoist the danger-signal and tap the drum once! You'll see.

ఎ

The Phenomenal Flea

JIM SAID HE reckoned a balloon was a good deal the fastest thing in the world, unless it might be some kinds of birds—a wild pigeon, maybe, or a railroad.

But Tom said he had read about railroads in England going nearly a hundred miles an hour for a little ways, and there never was a bird in the world that could do that—except one, and that was a flea.

"A flea? Why, Mars Tom, in de fust place he ain't a bird, strickly speakin'—"

"He ain't a bird, ain't he? Well, then, what is he?"

"I don't rightly know, Mars Tom, but I speck he's only jist a animal. No, I reckon dat won't do, nuther, he ain't big enough for a animal. He mus' be a bug. Yassir, dat's what he is, he's a bug."

"I bet he ain't, but let it go. What's your second place?"

"Well, in de second place, birds is creturs dat goes a long ways, but a flea don't."

"He don't, don't he? Come, now, what *is* a long distance, if you know?"

"Why, it's miles, en lots of 'em—anybody knows dat."

"Can't a man walk miles?"

"Yassir, he kin."

"As many as a railroad?"

"Yassir, if you give him time."

"Can't a flea?"

"Well,—I s'pose so—ef you gives him heaps of time."

"Now you begin to see, don't you, that *distance* ain't the thing to judge by, at all; it's the time it takes to go the distance *in*, that *counts*, ain't it?"

"Well, hit do look sorter so, but I wouldn't a b'lieved it, Mars Tom."

"It's a matter of *proportion*, that's what it is; and when you come to gage a thing's speed by its size, where's your bird and your man and your railroad,

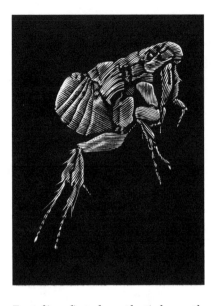

alongside of a flea? The fastest man can't run more than about ten miles in an hour—not much over ten thousand times his own length. But all the books says any common ordinary third-class flea can jump a hundred and fifty times his own length; yes, and he can make five jumps a second too,—seven hundred and fifty times his own length, in one little second—for he don't fool away any time stopping and starting—he does them both at the same time; you'll see, if you try to put your finger on him. Now that's a common ordinary third-class flea's gait; but you take an Eyetalian *first*-class, that's been the pet of the nobility all his life and hasn't ever knowed what want or sickness or exposure was, and he can jump more than three hundred times his own length, and keep it up all day, five such jumps every second, which is fifteen hundred times his own length. Well, suppose a man could go fifteen hundred times his own length in a second—say, a mile and a half? It's ninety miles a minute; it's considerable more than five thousand miles an hour. Where's your man *now*?—yes, and your bird, and your railroad, and your balloon? Laws, they don't amount to shucks 'longside of a flea. A flea is just a comet biled down small."

❧

Huck Kills a Bird

[. . .]I SEE A BIRD setting on a dead limb of a high tree, singing, with his head tilted back and his mouth open, and before I thought I fired, and his song stopped and he fell straight down from the limb, all limp like a rag, and I run and picked him up, and he was dead, and his body was warm in my hand, and his head rolled about, this way and that, like his neck was broke, and there was a white skin over his eyes, and one little drop of blood on the side of his head, and laws! I couldn't see nothing more for the tears; and I hain't never murdered no creature since, that warn't doing me no harm, and I ain't going to.

* formula*

The Bird with the Best Grammar

NOW THERE IS MORE to the blue-jay than any other animal. He has got more different kinds of feeling. Whatever a blue-jay feels he can put into language, and not mere commonplace language, but straight out and out book talk, and there is such a command of language. You never saw a blue-jay get stuck for a word. He is a vocabularized geyser. Now, you must call a jay a bird, and so he is in a measure, because he wears feathers and don't belong to any church, but otherwise he is just as human nature made him. A blue-jay hasn't any more principle than an ex-congressman, and he will steal, deceive and betray four times out of five; and as for the sacredness of an obligation, you cannot scare him in the detail of principle. He talks the best grammar of all the animals. You may say a cat talks good grammar. Well, a cat does; but you let a cat get excited, you let a cat get at pulling fur with another cat on a shed nights and you will hear grammar. A blue-jay is human; he has got all a man's faculties and a man's weakness. He likes especially scandal; he knows when he is an ass as well as you do.

formula

Ants and the True Religion

IN JEYPOOR [Jaipur, India] I tried several of Sir John Lubbock's experiments & got results similar to his. Then I tried some experiments of my own. These latter proved that the ant is peculiarly intelligent in the higher concerns of life. I constructed four miniature houses of worship—a Mohammedan mosque, a Hindu temple, a Jewish synagogue & a Xn cathedral, & placed them in a row. I then marked 15 ants with red paint & turned them loose. They made several trips to & fro, glancing in at the several places of worship, but not entering. I turned loose 15 more, painted blue. They acted just as the red ones had done. I now gilded 15 & turned them loose. No change in result: the 45 traveled back & forth in an eager hurry, persistently & continuously visiting each fane but never entering. This satisfied me that these ants were without religious prejudices—just what I wished; for under no other condition w^d my next & greater experiment be valuable.

I now placed a small square of white paper within the door of each fane; upon the mosque-paper I put a pinch of putty, upon the temple-paper a dab of tar, upon the synagogue-paper a trifle of turpentine, & upon the cathedral-paper a small cube of sugar. First I liberated the red ants. They examined & rejected the putty, the tar & the turpentine, & then took to the sugar with zeal & apparently sincere conviction. I next liberated the blue ants. They did exactly as the red ones had done. The gilded ants followed. The preceding results precisely repeated. This seemed to prove beyond question that ants destitute of religious prejudices will always prefer Christianity to any of the other great creeds.

However, to make sure, I removed the ants & put the putty in the cathedral & the sugar in the mosque. I now liberated the ants in a body, & they rushed tumultuously to the cathedral. I was very touched & gratified, & went in the back room to write down the event; but when I came back the ants had all apostatised & gone over to the Mohammedan communion. I saw that I had been too hasty in my conclusions, & naturally felt rebuked & humbled. With diminished confidence I went on with the test to the finish. I placed the sugar first in one house of worship then another till I had tried them all. With this result: that whatever church I put the sugar in, that was the one the ants straightway joined. This was proof, beyond shadow of doubt, that in religious matters the ant is the opposite of man: for man cares for but one thing, to find the only true church; whereas the ant hunts for the one with the sugar in it.

છ

The Sailors and the St. Bernard

WE GOT INTO that place by a judgment—judgment on the captain of the ship. It was this way. We were becalmed, away down south, dead summer time, middle of December, 1853. The vessel was a brig, and a fairly good sailer;

name, *Mabel Thorpe*; loaded with provisions and blasting powder for the new gold mines in Australia; Elliot Cable master, a rough man and hard-hearted, but he *was* master, and that is the truth. When he laid down the law there wasn't pluck enough in the whole ship to take objections to it.

Now to go back a little. About two months before, when we were lying at the dock the day we sailed, a lovely big beautiful dog came aboard and went racing around with his nose down hunting for somebody that had been there—his owner, I reckon—and the crew caught him and shut him up below, and we sailed in an hour. He was a darling, that dog. He was full of play, and fun, and affection and good nature, the dearest and sweetest disposition that ever was. Inside of two days he was the pet of the whole crew. We bedded him like the aristocracy, and there wasn't a man but would divide his dinner with him, and he was ever so loving and grateful. And smart, too; smart and willing. He elected of his own notion to stand watch and watch with us. He was in the larboard watch, and he would turn out at eight bells without anybody having to tell him it was "Yo-ho, the larboard watch!" And he would tug at the ropes and help make sail or take it in, and seemed to know all about it, just like any old veteran. The crew were proud of him—well, of course they would be.

And so, as I was saying, we got becalmed when we were out about two months. It was warm that night, and still and drowsy and lazy; and the sails hung idle, and the deck-watch and the lookout and everybody else was sound asleep, including the dog, for it was his trick below and he had turned in at midnight. Well, along about an hour after midnight there was a tremendous scratching and barking at the captain's door, and he jumped out of his bunk, and that dog was just wild with excitement, and rushed off, and just as good as *told* the captain to come along and come *quick*. You see, the ship was afire down in the hold, and he had discovered it. Down the captain plunged, and the dog rushed off waking up the others.

Dear, dear, it was the closest fit! The fire was crowding a pile of the powder-kegs close, and in another minute or two it would have had them and we should have been blown into the sky. The captain snatched the pile of kegs out of reach in half a second, and we were safe; because the bulk of the powder was away up forward. And by this time we all came tearing down—white?—oh, white as ghosts when we saw what a close shave we had had. Well, then we started in and began to hug the dog. And wasn't he a proud dog?—and happy?—why, if he had had speech he couldn't have expressed it any better. The captain snarled at us and said:

"You may well hug him, you worthless hounds! he saved my life, not you,

you lazy rips. I've never cared for dogs before, but next time I hear people talking against them I'll put in a word for this one, anyway."

Overboard went that little batch of powder kegs, and then we flew around getting food and water and compass and sextant and chart and things for the boat; and the dog helped, just like anybody else. He did a grown man's work carrying things to the boat, and then went dancing around *superintending* whilst we launched her. Bright?—oh, you can't think how bright he was, and intelligent.

When everybody was in the boat but the captain, and the flames were soaring up and lighting the whole ocean, he tied the dog to the foot of the mainmast and then got in himself and took the tiller and said—

"All ready. Give way!"

We were all struck dumb, for a second, then all shouted at once—

"Oh, *captain!*—going to leave the dog?"

He roared out in a fury—

"Didn't you hear the order? Give way!"

Well, the tears began to run down our faces; and we said, Why, he saved our *lives*—we *can't* leave him. Please, captain! please let him come.

"What, in this little tub of a boat? You don't know what you are talking about. He'd be more in the way than a family of children; and he can eat as much as a family of children, too. Now, men, you know *me*"—and he pulled an old pepper-box revolver and pointed it—"give *way!*"

Well, it was pitiful, the way that poor dog acted. At first he was dancing and capering and barking, happy and proud and gay; but when he saw us going away he stopped and stood still, gazing; it seemed as if he was trying to believe it, and couldn't. And dear, dear, how noble and handsome he was, in that red glare. He was a huge big St. Bernard, with that gentle good face and that soft loving eye that they've got.

Well, pretty soon when he saw that he *was* left, he seemed to go kind of crazy; and he rose on his hind legs in the strong light, and strained and lunged and tugged at his rope, and begged and moaned and yelped—why it was as plain as if he was *saying* Oh, *don't* leave me, *please* don't leave me, *I* haven't done any harm. And then presently the fire swept down on him and swallowed him up, and he sent up two or three awful shrieks, and it was all over. And the men sat there crying like children.

And deep down in our hearts we believed a judgment would come on the captain for this. And it did; as you will see.

II

We were in the Indian ocean when we lost the ship—about five hundred miles south of Port Natal, and about the same distance east by south from Cape Town, South Africa. The captain set his course by the stars and struck north, because he believed we were a little south of the track of ships bound for either Natal or Australia. A smart breeze sprung up and we went along at a good rate. In about four hours day broke, and the first thing that showed up on the westward sea-line was the hazy top-hamper of a ship! She was east-ward-bound, and making straight across our course. We raised a cheer, and altered our course to go and meet her. And there wasn't as much heart in the cheer as you might expect, for the thing we were thinking about was, that our poor dog had been done to death for no use; if he had been allowed to come with us he wouldn't have cost us any inconvenience, and no food that we couldn't spare.

The captain had an idea that he was born lucky, and he said something to the mate about it now; he said running across this ship here was pure luck—nobody else could have had such luck. Well, it certainly did look so; but at the same time we said to ourselves, how about this ship's luck that's coming? Our idea was that our captain would bring bad luck to her, and trouble to himself and us, too, on account of the way he treated the dog that saved our lives. And that is what happened, as I have said before.

In about an hour we were aboard that ship; and it happened that we knew her, and knew her crew, too; for she was sister to our ship and belonged to the same house, and was loaded at the same dock with us, and with the same kind of cargo—provisions for the new mines almost altogether, and a few other odds and ends of mining supplies, like candles and powder and fuse, and such things. By name she was the *Adelaide*. She had left port a week or ten days ahead of us, but we could outsail her on a wind. Her captain had been dead about a month, now—died of a sickness of some kind—and Mrs. Mose-ley, his young widow, was broken-hearted, and cried pretty much all the time, and was in terror lest something should happen to her little girl, and then she would be desolate indeed. Two of the *Adelaide*'s crew had died of the sickness, also; so that left mate, second mate and five men aboard. When we joined, that made it seventeen men, one woman and a child.

Our captain took command straight away, and began to give orders, with-out a by-your-leave to anybody—for that was his style. It wasn't the right way to go about it, and it made bad blood.

The captain allotted the watches and the ship continued on her course for Australia. The wind freshened, the sky grew dark, and inside of an hour there was a terrific gale blowing. We stripped the ship and she drove help-less before it, straight south-east. And so, night and day and day and night for eighteen days we drove, and never got a sight of the sun or the moon or the stars in all that time—hundreds and hundreds and hundreds of miles we wallowed through the wild seas, with never a notion of where we were but what we got from the dead reckoning.

For the last two or three days the captain had got to looking pretty white; and by this time he was just ghastly. Then we found out the reason, from the mates: the captain judged that we must be south of Kerguelan's Land, and maybe nearly half way between that and the Antarctic Circle. Well, that news turned the rest of us white; for if it was true, we were getting into the neigh-borhood of the Devil's Race-Track! [. . .]

[. . .] We were in a trap; and that trap was the Everlasting Sunday.

There was no need to say it; everybody knew it. And everybody shuddered, too, and was in a cold despair. For a week we drifted little by little around the cloud-wall, and further and further away from it; and when we seemed to have gotten ten or fifteen miles from it we appeared to have stopped dead still. We threw empty bottles overboard and watched them. There was really no motion—at any rate in any one direction. Sometimes a bottle would stay where we threw it; sometimes after the end of an hour we could see that it had moved five or six yards ahead or as many aft.

The stillness was horrible; and the absence of life. There was not a bird or a creature of any kind in sight, the slick surface of the water was never bro-ken by a fin, never a breath of wind fanned the dead air, and there was not a sound of any kind, even the faintest—the silence of death was everywhere. We showed no life ourselves, but sat apart, each by himself, and brooded and brooded, and scarcely ever moved [. . . .]

Try to escape? Why, none of us wanted to try. What could be the use? Of course the captain tried; it would be just like him. He manned one of the boats and started. He disappeared in the cloud-wall for a while; got lost in it, of course—compass no use—and came near getting swamped by the heavy seas. He was not in there long; the currents soon swept him back into the Everlasting Sunday. Our ship was pretty far away, but still in sight; so he came aboard, and never said a word. *His* spirit was broken, too, you see, like ours; so after that he moped around again, like the rest—and prayed for death, I reckon. We all did.

One morning when we had been in there seven months and gradually get-ting further and further toward the middle, an inch at a time, there was a sudden stir and excitement—the first we had known for so long that it seemed strange and new and unnatural—like something we hadn't ever experienced before; it was like corpses getting excited—corpses that had been dead many years and had forgotten the feel of it and didn't understand it. A sailor came flying along the deck blubbering and shouting, "A ship! a ship!"

The dull people sitting moping and dreaming here and there and yonder looked up at him in a kind of a drowse, and not pleasantly; for his racket and activity pained their heads and distressed them; and their brains were so blunted and sodden that at first his words couldn't find their way in to their understandings, all practice in talk having ceased so long ago. But of course we did understand, presently, and then we woke up and got wildly excited, as I was telling you.

Away off yonder we made out a ship, sure enough; and as the daylight brightened we made out another; and then another, and still another and another and another—a whole fleet, scattered around, a mile or so apart. We were full of amazement. When did they come, and how did they get there in that sudden way, and so many of them? We were full of joy; for maybe here was rescue for us. If they came in there on purpose, they must know the trick of how to get out again.

Well, everything was bustle and hurry, now. We got out our boats, and I pulled stroke in the chief mate's. I was twenty-three and a half years old, and big and strong and an experienced sailor. We hoisted a flag, first, in the mizzen halliards—union down, of course—and left the young widow and the little girl standing under it crying for happiness when we pulled away in the frosty bright morning [. . . .]

You will know beforehand what we found: barring the frosty litter of decaying wreckage that strewed the deck, just the counterpart of our own ship, as you might say—men lying here and there and yonder, and two or three sitting, with elbow on knee and hand under chin—just as natural! No, not men—leathery shriveled-up effigies of them. Dead these dozen years. It was what we had been seeing for seven months; we would come to be like these, by and by. It was our fate foreshadowed [. . . .]

ç℈

Man's Place in the Animal World

[*Page 1 of the manuscript, containing "telegrams," has been lost. Mark Twain copied out the following quotations, from unidentified sources, on pages 2 and 3 of the manuscript.*]

In August, 1572, similar things were occurring in Paris and elsewhere in France. In this case it was Christian against Christian. The Roman Catholics, by previous concert, sprung a surprise upon the unprepared and unsuspecting protestants, and butchered them by thousands—both sexes and all ages. This was the memorable St. Bartholomew's Day. At Rome the Pope and the Church gave public thanks to God when the happy news came.

During several centuries hundred of heretics were burned at the stake every year because their religious opinions were not satisfactory to the Roman Church.

In all ages the savages of all lands have made the slaughtering of their neighboring brothers and the enslaving of their women and children the common business of their lives.

Hypocrisy, envy, malice, cruelty, vengefulness, seduction, rape, robbery, swindling, arson, bigamy, adultery, and the oppression and humiliation of the poor and the helpless in all ways, have been and still are more or less common among both the civilized and uncivilized peoples of the earth.

For many centuries "the common brotherhood of man" has been urged— on Sundays—and "patriotism" on Sundays and weekdays both. Yet patriotism *contemplates the opposite of a common brotherhood.*

Woman's equality with man has never been conceded by any people, ancient or modern, civilized or savage.

I HAVE BEEN scientifically studying the traits and dispositions of the "lower animals" (so-called,) and contrasting them with the traits and dispositions of man. I find the result profoundly humiliating to me. For it obliges me to renounce my allegiance to the Darwinian theory of the Ascent of Man from the Lower Animals; since it now seems plain to me that that theory ought to be vacated in favor of a new and truer one, this new and truer one to be named the *Descent* of Man from the Higher Animals.

In proceeding toward this unpleasant conclusion I have not guessed or speculated or conjectured, but have used what is commonly called the scientific method. That is to say, I have subjected every postulate that presented itself, to the crucial test of actual experiment, and have adopted it or rejected it according to the result. Thus I verified and established each step of my course in its turn before advancing to the next. These experiments were made in the London Zoölogical Gardens, and covered many months of pains-taking and fatiguing work.

Before particularizing any of the experiments, I wish to state one or two things which seem to more properly belong in this place than further along. This in the interest of clearness. The massed experiments established to my satisfaction certain generalizations, to wit:

1. That the human race is of one distinct species. It exhibits slight variations—in color, stature, mental calibre, and so on—due to climate, environment, and so forth; but it is a species by itself, and not to be confounded with any other.

2. That the quadrupeds are a distinct family, also. This family exhibits variations—in color, size, food-preferences and so on; but it is a family by itself.

3. That the other families—the birds, the fishes, the insects, the reptiles, etc., are more or less distinct, also. They are in the procession. They are links in the chain which stretches down from the higher animals to man at the bottom.

Some of my experiments were quite curious. In the course of my reading I had come across a case where, many years ago, some hunters on our Great Plains organized a buffalo hunt for the entertainment of an English earl—that, and to provide some fresh meat for his larder. They had charming sport. They killed seventy-two of those great animals; and ate part of one of them and left the seventy-one to rot. In order to determine the difference between an anaconda and an earl—if any—I caused seven young calves to be turned into the anaconda's cage. The grateful reptile immediately crushed one of them and swallowed it, then lay back satisfied. It showed no further interest in the calves, and no disposition to harm them. I tried this experiment with other anacondas; always with the same result. The fact stood proven that the difference between an earl and an anaconda is, that the earl is cruel and the anaconda isn't; and that the earl wantonly destroys what he has no use for, but the anaconda doesn't. This seemed to suggest that the anaconda was not descended from the earl. It also seemed to suggest that the earl was descended from the anaconda, and had lost a good deal in the transition.

I was aware that many men who have accumulated more millions of money than they can ever use, have shown a rabid hunger for more, and have not scrupled to cheat the ignorant and the helpless out of their poor savings in order to partially appease that appetite. I furnished a hundred different kinds of wild and tame animals the opportunity to accumulate vast stores of food, but none of them would do it. The squirrels and bees and certain birds made accumulations, but stopped when they had gathered a winter's supply, and could not be persuaded to add to it either honestly or by chicane. In order to bolster up a tottering reputation the ant pretended to store up supplies, but I was not deceived. I know the ant. These experiments convinced me that there is this difference between man and the higher animals: he is avaricious and miserly, they are not.

In the course of my experiments I convinced myself that among the animals man is the only one that harbors insults and injuries, broods over them, waits till a chance offers, then takes revenge. The passion of revenge is unknown to the higher animals.

Roosters keep harems, but it is by consent of their concubines; therefore no wrong is done. Men keep harems, but it is by brute force, privileged by atrocious laws which the other sex were allowed no hand in making. In this matter man occupies a far lower place than the rooster.

Cats are loose in their morals, but not consciously so. Man, in his descent from the cat, has brought the cat's looseness with him but has left the unconsciousness behind—the saving grace which excuses the cat. The cat is innocent, man is not.

Indecency, vulgarity, obscenity—these are strictly confined to man; he invented them. Among the higher animals there is no trace of them. They hide nothing; they are not ashamed. Man, with his soiled mind, covers himself. He will not even enter a drawing room with his breast and back naked, so alive is he and his mates to indecent suggestion. Man is "the Animal that Laughs." But so does the monkey, as Mr. Darwin pointed out; and so does the Australian bird that is called the laughing jackass. No—man is the Animal that Blushes. He is the only one that does it—or has occasion to.

At the head of this article we see how "three monks were burnt to death" a few days ago, and a prior "put to death with atrocious cruelty." Do we inquire into the details? No; or we should find out that the prior was subjected to unprintable mutilations. Man—when he is a North American Indian—gouges out his prisoner's eyes; when he is King John, with a nephew to render untroublesome, he uses a red-hot iron; when he is a religious zealot dealing with heretics in the Middle Ages, he skins his capture alive and scatters salt on his back; in the first Richard's time he shuts up a multitude of Jew families in a tower and sets fire to it; in Columbus's time he captures a family of Spanish Jews and—but *that* is not printable; in our day in England a man is fined ten shillings for beating his mother nearly to death with a chair, and another man is fined forty shillings for having four pheasant eggs in his possession without being able to satisfactorily explain how he got them. Of all the animals, man is the only one that is cruel. He is the only one that inflicts pain for the pleasure of doing it. It is a trait that is not known to the higher animals. The

cat plays with the frightened mouse; but she has this excuse, that she does not know that the mouse is suffering. The cat is moderate—unhumanly moderate: she only scares the mouse, she does not hurt it; she doesn't dig out its eyes, or tear off its skin, or drive splinters under its nails—man-fashion; when she is done playing with it she makes a sudden meal of it and puts it out of its trouble. Man is the Cruel Animal. He is alone in that distinction.

The higher animals engage in individual fights, but never in organized masses. Man is the only animal that deals in that atrocity of atrocities, War. He is the only one that gathers his brethren about him and goes forth in cold blood and with calm pulse to exterminate his kind. He is the only animal that for sordid wages will march out, as the Hessians did in our Revolution, and as the boyish Prince Napoleon did in the Zulu war, and help to slaughter strangers of his own species who have done him no harm and with whom he has no quarrel.

Man is the only animal that robs his helpless fellow of his country—takes possession of it and drives him out of it or destroys him. Man has done this in all the ages. There is not an acre of ground on the globe that is in possession of its rightful owner, or that has not been taken away from owner after owner, cycle after cycle, by force and bloodshed.

Man is the only Slave. And he is the only animal who enslaves. He has always been a slave in one form or another, and has always held other slaves in bondage under him in one way or another. In our day he is always some man's slave for wages, and does that man's work; and this slave has other slaves under him for minor wages, and they do *his* work. The higher animals are the only ones who exclusively do their own work and provide their own living.

Man is the only Patriot. He sets himself apart in his own country, under his own flag, and sneers at the other nations, and keeps multitudinous uniformed assassins on hand at heavy expense to grab slices of other people's countries, and keep *them* from grabbing slices of *his*. And in the intervals between campaigns he washes the blood off his hands and works for "the universal brotherhood of man"—with his mouth.

Man is the Religious Animal. He is the only Religious Animal. He is the only animal that has the True Religion—several of them. He is the only animal that loves his neighbor as himself, and cuts his throat if his theology isn't straight. He has made a graveyard of the globe in trying his honest best to smooth his brother's path to happiness and heaven. He was at it in the time of the Caesars, he was at it in Mahomet's time, he was at it in the time of the Inquisition, he was at it in France a couple of centuries, he was at it in England in Mary's day, he has been at it ever since he first saw the light, he is at it today in Crete—as per the telegrams quoted above—he will be at it somewhere else tomorrow. The higher animals have no religion. And we are told that they are going to be left out, in the Hereafter. I wonder why? It seems questionable taste.

Man is the Reasoning Animal. Such is the claim. I think it is open to dispute. Indeed, my experiments have proven to me that he is the Unreasoning Animal. Note his history, as sketched above. It seems plain to me that whatever he is he is *not* a reasoning animal. His record is the fantastic record of a maniac. I consider that the strongest count against his intelligence is the fact that with that record back of him he blandly sets himself up as the head animal of the lot; whereas by his own standards he is the bottom one.

In truth, man is incurably foolish. Simple things which the other animals easily learn, he is incapable of learning. Among my experiments was this. In an hour I taught a cat and a dog to be friends. I put them in a cage. In another hour I taught them to be friends with a rabbit. In the course of two days I was able to add a fox, a goose, a squirrel and some doves. Finally a monkey. They lived together in peace; even affectionately.

Next, in another cage I confined an Irish Catholic from Tipperary, and as soon as he seemed tame I added a Scotch Presbyterian from Aberdeen. Next a Turk from Constantinople; a Greek Christian from Crete; an Armenian; a Methodist from the wilds of Arkansaw; a Buddhist from China; a Brahmin from Benares. Finally, a Salvation Army Colonel from Wapping. Then I stayed away two whole days. When I came back to note results, the cage of Higher Animals was all right, but in the other there was but a chaos of gory odds and ends of turbans and fezzes and plaids and bones and flesh—not a specimen left alive. These Reasoning Animals had disagreed on a theological detail and carried the matter to a Higher Court.

One is obliged to concede that in true loftiness of character, Man cannot claim to approach even the meanest of the Higher Animals. It is plain that he is constitutionally incapable of approaching that altitude; that he is constitutionally afflicted with a Defect which must make such approach forever impossible, for it is manifest that this defect is permanent in him, indestructible, ineradicable.

I find this Defect to be THE MORAL SENSE. He is the only animal that has it. It is the secret of his degradation. It is the quality *which enables him to do wrong*. It has no other office. It is incapable of performing any other function. It could never have been intended to perform any other. Without it, man could do no wrong. He would rise at once to the level of the Higher Animals.

Since the Moral Sense has but the one office, the one capacity—to enable man to do wrong—it is plainly without value to him. It is as valueless to him as is disease. In fact it manifestly *is* a disease. *Rabies* is bad, but it is not so bad as this disease. Rabies enables a man to do a thing which he could not do when in a healthy state: kill his neighbor with a poisonous bite. No one is the better man for having rabies. The Moral Sense enables a man to do wrong. It enables him to do wrong in a thousand ways. Rabies is an innocent disease, compared to the Moral Sense. No one, then, can be the better man for having the Moral Sense. What, now, do we find the Primal Curse to have been? Plainly what it was in the beginning: the infliction upon man of the Moral Sense; the ability to distinguish good from evil; and with it, necessarily, the ability to *do* evil; for there can be no evil act without the presence of consciousness of it in the doer of it.

And so I find that we have descended and degenerated, from some far ancestor,—some microscopic atom wandering at its pleasure between the mighty horizons of a drop of water perchance,—insect by insect, animal by animal, reptile by reptile, down the long highway of smirchless innocence, till we have reached the bottom stage of development—nameable as the Human Being. Below us—nothing. Nothing but the Frenchman.

There is only one possible stage below the Moral Sense; that is the Immoral Sense. The Frenchman has it. Man is but little lower than the angels. This definitely locates him. He is between the angels and the French.

Man seems to be a rickety poor sort of a thing, any way you take him; a kind of British Museum of infirmities and inferiorities. He is always undergoing repairs. A machine that was as unreliable as he is would have no market. On top of his specialty—the Moral Sense—are piled a multitude of minor infirmities; such a multitude, indeed, that one may broadly call them countless. The higher animals get their teeth without pain or inconvenience. Man gets his through months and months of cruel torture; and at a time of life when he is but ill able to bear it. As soon as he has got them they must all be pulled out again, for they were of no value in the first place, not worth the loss of a night's rest. The second set will answer for a while, by being reinforced occasionally with rubber or plugged up with gold; but he will never get a set which can really be depended on till a dentist makes him one. This set will be called "false" teeth—as if he had ever worn any other kind.

In a wild state—a natural state—the Higher Animals have a few diseases; diseases of little consequence; the main one is old age. But man starts in as a child and lives on diseases till the end, as a regular diet. He has mumps, measles, whooping cough, croup, tonsilitis, diphtheria, scarlet fever, almost as a matter of course. Afterward, as he goes along, his life continues to be threatened at every turn: by colds, coughs, asthma, bronchitis, itch, cholera, cancer, consumption, yellow fever, bilious fever, typhus fevers, hay fever, ague, chilblains, piles, inflammation of the entrails, indigestion, toothache, earache, deafness, dumbness, blindness, influenza, chicken pox, cow pox, small pox, liver complaint, constipation, bloody flux, warts, pimples, boils, carbuncles, abscesses, bunions, corns, tumors, fistulas, pneumonia, softening of the brain, melancholia and fifteen other kinds of insanity; dysentery, jaundice, diseases of the heart, the bones, the skin, the scalp, the spleen, the kidneys, the nerves, the brain, the blood; scrofula, paralysis, leprosy, neuralgia, palsy, fits, headache, thirteen kinds of rheumatism, forty-six of gout, and a formidable supply of gross and unprintable disorders of one sort and another. Also—but why continue the list. The mere names of the agents appointed to keep this shackly machine out of repair would hide him from sight if printed on his body in the smallest type known to the founder's art. He is but a basket of festering offal provided for the support and entertainment of swarming armies of bacilli,—armies commissioned to rot him and destroy him, and each army equipped with a special detail of the work. The process of waylaying him, persecuting him, rotting him, killing him, begins with his first breath, and there is no mercy, no pity, no truce till he draws his last one.

Look at the workmanship of him, in certain of its particulars. What are his tonsils for? They perform no useful function; they have no value. They have no business there. They are but a trap. They have but the one office, the one industry: to provide tonsilitis and quinzy and such things for the possessor of them. And what is the vermiform appendix for? It has no value; it cannot perform any useful service. It is but an ambuscaded enemy whose sole interest in life is to lie in wait for stray grape seeds and employ them to breed strangulated hernia. And what are the male's mammals for? For business, they are out of the question; as an ornament, they are a mistake. What is his beard for? It performs no useful function; it is a nuisance and a discomfort; all nations hate it; all nations persecute it with the razor. And because it is a nuisance and a discomfort, Nature never allows the supply of it to fall short, in any man's case, between puberty and the grave. You never see a man bald-headed on his chin. But his hair! It is a graceful ornament, it is a comfort, it is the best of all protections against certain perilous ailments, man prizes it above emeralds and rubies. And because of these things Nature puts it on, half the time, so that it won't stay. Man's sight, smell, hearing, sense of locality—how inferior they are. The condor sees a corpse at five miles; man has no telescope that can do it. The bloodhound follows a scent that is two days old. The robin hears the earth-worm burrowing his course under the ground. The cat, deported in a closed basket, finds its way home again through twenty miles of country which it has never seen.

Certain functions lodged in the other sex perform in a lamentably inferior way as compared with the performance of the same functions in the Higher Animals. In the human being, menstruation, gestation and parturition are terms which stand for horrors. In the Higher Animals these things are hardly even inconveniences.

For style, look at the Bengal tiger—that ideal of grace, beauty, physical perfection, majesty. And then look at Man—that poor thing. He is the Animal of the Wig, the Trepanned Skull, the Ear Trumpet, the Glass Eye, the Pasteboard Nose, the Porcelain Teeth, the Silver Windpipe, the Wooden Leg—a creature that is mended and patched all over, from top to bottom. If he can't get renewals of his bricabrac in the next world, what will he look like?

He has just one stupendous superiority. In his intellect he is supreme. The Higher Animals cannot touch him there. It is curious, it is noteworthy, that no heaven has ever been offered him wherein his one sole superiority was provided with a chance to enjoy itself. Even when he himself has imagined a heaven, he has never made provision in it for intellectual joys. It is a striking omission. It seems a tacit confession that heavens are provided for the Higher Animals alone. This is matter for thought; and for serious thought. And it is

full of a grim suggestion: that we are not as important, perhaps, as we had all
along supposed we were.

જ

The Marvelous Moa

THE NATURALIST SAID that the oddest bird in Australasia was the Laughing
Jackass, and the biggest the now extinct Great Moa. The Moa stood thirteen
feet high, and could step over an ordinary man's head or kick his hat off; and
his head too, for that matter. He said it was wingless, but a swift runner. The
natives used to ride it. It could make forty miles an hour, and keep it up for
four hundred miles and come out reasonably fresh. It was still in existence
when the railway was introduced into New Zealand; still in existence, and
carrying the mails. The railroad began with the same schedule it has now:
two expresses a week—time, twenty miles an hour. The company exterminated the moa to get the mails.

જ

The Inimitable Ornithorhynchus

SPEAKING OF THE indigenous coneys and bactrian camels, the naturalist said
that the coniferous and bacteriological out put of Australasia was remarkable
for its many and curious departures from the accepted laws governing these
species of tubercles, but that in his opinion Nature's fondness for dabbling in
the erratic was most notably exhibited in that curious combination of bird,
fish, amphibian, burrower, crawler, quadruped and Christian called the Ornithorhynchus—grotesquest of animals, king of the animalculæ of the world for
versatility of character and make-up. Said he—

"You can call it anything you want to, and be right. It is a fish, for it lives in the
river half the time; it is a land animal, for it resides on the land half the time; it is an
amphibian, since it likes both and does not know which it prefers; it is a hybernian,

for when times are dull and nothing much going on it buries itself under the mud at the bottom of a puddle and hybernates there a couple of weeks at a time; it is a kind of duck, for it has a duck-bill and four webbed paddles; it is fish and quadruped together, for in the water it swims with the paddles and on shore it paws itself across country with them; it is a kind of seal, for it has a seal's fur; it is carnivorous, herbivorous, insectivorous, and vermifuginous, for it eats fish and grass and butterflies, and in the season digs worms out of the mud and devours them; it is clearly a bird, for it lays eggs and hatches them; it is clearly a mammal, for it nurses its young; and it is manifestly a kind of Christian, for it keeps the Sabbath when there is anybody around, and when there isn't, doesn't. It has all the tastes there are except refined ones, it has all the habits there are except good ones.

"It is a survival—a survival of the fittest. Mr. Darwin invented the theory that goes by that name, but the Ornithorhynchus was the first to put it to actual experiment and prove that it could be done. Hence it should have as much of the credit as Mr. Darwin. It was never in the Ark; you will find no mention of it there; it nobly stayed out and worked the theory. Of all creatures in the world it was the only one properly equipped for the test. The Ark was thirteen months afloat, and all the globe submerged; no land visible above the flood, no vegetation, no food for a mammal to eat, nor water for a mammal to drink; for all mammal-food was destroyed, and when the pure floods from heaven and the salt oceans of the earth mingled their waters and rose above the mountain tops, the result was a drink which no bird or beast of ordinary construction could use and live. But this combination was nuts for the Ornithorhynchus, if I may use a term like that without offence. Its river home had always been salted by the flood-tides of the sea. On the face of the Noachian deluge innumerable forest trees were floating. Upon these the Ornithorhynchus voyaged in peace; voyaged from clime to clime, from hemisphere to hemisphere, in contentment and comfort, in virile interest in the constant change of scene, in humble thankfulness for its privileges, in ever-increasing enthusiasm in the development of the great theory upon whose validity it had staked its life, its fortunes and its sacred honor, if I may use such expressions without impropriety in connection with an episode of this nature.

"It lived the tranquil and luxurious life of a creature of independent means. Of things actually necessary to its existence and its happiness not a detail was wanting. When it wished to walk, it scrambled along the tree-trunk; it mused in the shade of the leaves by day, it slept in their shelter by night; when it wanted the refreshment of a swim, it had it; it ate leaves when it wanted a vegetable diet, it dug under the bark for worms and grubs; when it wanted fish it caught them, when it wanted eggs it laid them. If the grubs gave out in one tree it swam to another; and as for fish, the very opulence of the supply was an embarrassment. And finally, when it was thirsty it smacked its chops in gratitude over a blend that would have slain a crocodile.

"When at last, after thirteen months of travel and research in all the zones it went aground on a mountain-summit, it strode ashore, saying in its heart, 'Let them that come after me invent theories and dream dreams about the Survival of the Fittest if they like, but I am the first that has *done* it!'

"This wonderful creature dates back, like the kangaroo and many other Australian hydrocephalous invertebrates, to an age long anterior to the advent of man upon the earth; they date back, indeed, to a time when a cause way hundreds of miles wide and thousands of miles long joined Australia to Africa and the animals of the two countries were alike and all belonged to that remote geological epoch known to science as the Old Red Grindstone Post-Pleosaurian. Later the cause way sank under the sea; subterranean convulsions lifted the African continent a thousand feet higher than it was before, but Australia kept her old level. In Africa's new climate the animals necessarily began to develop and shade off into new forms and families and species, but the animals of Australia as necessarily remained stationary, and have so remained until this day. In the course of some millions of years the African Ornithorhynchus developed and developed and developed, and sluffed off detail after detail of its make-up until at last the creature became wholly disintegrated and scattered. Whenever you see a bird or a beast or a seal or an otter in Africa you know that he is merely a sorry surviving fragment of that sublime original of whom I have been speaking—that creature which was everything in general and nothing in particular—the opulently endowed *E Pluribus Unum* of the animal world.

"Such is the history of the most hoary, the most ancient, the most venerable creature that exists in the earth to-day—*Ornithorhynchus Platypus Extraordinariensis*—whom God preserve!"

When he was strongly moved he could rise and soar like that with ease. And not only in the prose form but in the poetical as well. He had written many pieces of poetry in his time, and these manuscripts he lent around among the passengers, and was willing to let them be copied. It seemed to me that the least technical one in the series, and the one which reached the loftiest note, perhaps, was his

Invocation
"Come forth from thy oozy couch
O, Ornithorhynchus dear!
And greet with a cordial claw
The stranger that longs to hear

"From thy own own lips the tale
Of thy origin all unknown:
Thy misplaced bone where flesh should be
And flesh where should be bone;

"And fishy fin where should be paw,
And beaver-trowel tail,
And snout of beast equip'd with teeth
Where gills ought *to* prevail.

"Come, Kangaroo, the good and true!
Foreshortened as to legs,
And body tapered like a churn,
And sack marsupial, i' fegs,

"And tell us why you linger here,
Thou relic of a vanished time,
When all your friends as fossils sleep,
Immortalized in lime!"

The Laughing Jackass of Adelaide

In the Zoological Gardens of Adelaide I saw the only laughing jackass that ever showed any disposition to be courteous to me. This one opened his head wide and laughed like a demon; or like a maniac who was consumed with humorous scorn over a cheap and degraded pun. It was a very human laugh. If he had been out of sight I could have believed that the laughter came from a man. It is an odd-looking bird, with a head and beak that are much too large for its body. In time man will exterminate the rest of the wild creatures of Australia, but this one will probably survive, for man is his friend and lets him alone. Man always has a good reason for his charities toward wild things, human or animal—when he has any. In this case the bird is spared because he kills snakes. If L. J. will take my advice he will not kill all of them.

ℒ

The Phosphorescent Sea-Serpent

Sept. 15—night. Close to Australia now. Sydney 50 miles distant.

That note recals an experience. The passengers were sent for, to come up in the bow and see a fine sight. It was very dark. One could not follow with the eye the surface of the sea more than fifty yards in any direction—it dimmed away and became lost to sight at about that distance from us. But if you patiently gazed into the darkness a little while, there was a sure reward for you. Presently, a quarter of a mile away you would see a blinding splash or explosion of light on the water—a flash so sudden and so astonishingly brilliant that it would make you catch your breath; then that blotch of light would instantly extend itself and take the cork-screw shape and imposing length of the fabled sea-serpent, with every curve of its body and the "break" spreading away from its head and the wake following behind its tail clothed in a fierce splendor of living fire. And my, but it was coming at a lightning gait! Almost before you could think, this monster of light, fifty feet long, would go flaming and storming by, and suddenly disappear. And out in the distance whence he came you would see another flash; and another and another and another, and see them turn into sea-serpents on the instant; and once sixteen flashed up at the same time and came tearing toward us, a swarm of wiggling curves, a moving conflagration, a vision of bewildering beauty, a spectacle of fire and energy whose equal the most of those people will not see again until after they are dead.

It was porpoises—porpoises aglow with phosphorescent light. They presently collected in a wild and magnificent jumble under the bows, and there they played for an hour, leaping and frolicking and carrying on, turning summersaults in front of the stem or across it and never getting hit, never making a miscalculation, though the stem missed them only about an inch as a rule. They were porpoises of the ordinary length—eight or ten feet—but every twist of their bodies sent a long procession of united and glowing curves astern. That fiery jumble was an enchanting thing to look at and we stayed out the performance; one cannot have such a show as that twice in a lifetime. The porpoise is the kitten of the sea; he never has a serious thought, he cares for nothing but fun and play. But I think I never saw him at his winsomest until that night. It was near a centre of civilization, and he could have been drinking.

$\S$

The Independent-Minded Magpie

HE IS A HANDSOME large creature, with snowy white decorations, and is a singer; he has a murmurous rich note that is lovely. He was once modest, even diffident; but he lost all that when he found out that he was Australia's sole musical bird. He has talent, and cuteness, and impudence; and in his tame state is a most satisfactory pet—never coming when he is called, always coming when he isn't, and studying disobedience as an accomplishment. He is not confined, but loafs all over the house and the grounds, like the laughing jackass. I think he learns to talk, I know he learns to sing tunes, and his friends say that he knows how to steal without learning. I was acquainted with a tame magpie in Melbourne. He had lived in a lady's house several years, and believed he owned it. The lady had tamed him, and in return he had tamed the lady. He was always on deck when not wanted, always having his own way, always tyrannizing over the dog, and always making the cat's life a slow sorrow and a martyrdom. He knew a number of tunes, and could sing them in perfect time and tune; and would do it, too, at any time that silence was wanted; and then encore himself and do it again; but if he was asked to sing he would go out and take a walk.

୫ର

The Bird of Birds

THE BIRD OF BIRDS—the Indian crow. I came to know him well, by and by, and be infatuated with him. I suppose he is the hardest lot that wears feathers. Yes, and the cheerfulest, and the best satisfied with himself. He never arrived at what he is by any careless process, or any sudden one; he is a work of art, and "art is long;" he is the product of immemorial ages, and of deep calculation; one can't make a bird like that in a day. He has been re-incarnated more times than Shiva; and he has kept a sample of each incarnation, and fused it into his constitution. In the course of his evolutionary promotions, his sublime march toward ultimate perfection, he has been a gambler, a low comedian, a dissolute priest, a fussy woman, a blackguard, a scoffer, a liar, a thief, a spy, an informer, a trading politician, a swindler, a professional hypocrite, a patriot for cash, a reformer, a lecturer, a lawyer, a conspirator, a rebel, a royalist, a democrat, a practicer and propagator of irreverence, a meddler, an intruder, a busy-body, an infidel, and a wallower in sin for the mere love of it. The strange result, the incredible result, of this patient accumulation of all damnable traits is, that he does not know what care is, he does not know what sorrow is, he does not know what remorse is, his life is one long thundering ecstasy of happiness, and he will go to his death untroubled, knowing that he will soon turn up again as an author or something, and be even more intolerably capable and comfortable than ever he was before.

In his straddling wide forward-step, and his springy side-wise series of hops, and his impudent air, and his cunning way of canting his head to one side upon occasion, he reminds one of the American blackbird. But the sharp resemblances stop there. He is much bigger than the blackbird; and he lacks the blackbird's trim and slender and beautiful build and shapely beak; and of course his sober garb of gray and rusty black is a poor and humble thing compared with the splendid lustre of the blackbird's metallic sables and shifting and flashing bronze glories. The blackbird is a perfect gentleman, in deportment and attire, and is not noisy, I believe, except when holding religious services and political conventions in a tree; but this Indian sham Quaker is just a rowdy, and is always noisy when awake— always chaffing, scolding, scoffing, laughing, ripping and cursing and carrying on about something or other. I never saw such a bird for delivering opinions. Nothing escapes him; he notices everything that happens, and brings out his opinion about it, particularly if it is a matter that is none of his business. And it is never a mild opinion, but always violent—violent and profane—the presence of ladies does not affect him. His opinions are not the outcome of reflection, for he never thinks about anything, but heaves out the opinion that is on top in his mind, and which is often an opinion about some quite different thing and does not fit the case. But that is his way; his main idea is to get out an opinion, and if he stopped to think he would lose chances.

I suppose he has no enemies among men. The whites and Mohammedans never seemed to molest him; and the Hindoos, because of their religion, never take the life of any creature, but spare even the snakes and tigers and fleas and rats. If I sat on one end of the balcony, the crows would gather on the railing at the other end and talk about me; and edge closer, little by little, till I could almost reach them; and they would sit there, in the most unabashed way, and talk about my clothes, and my hair, and my complexion, and probable character and vocation and politics, and how I came to be in India, and what I had been doing, and how many days I had got for it, and how I had happened to go unhanged so long, and when would it probably come off, and might there be more of my sort where I came from, and when would *they* be hanged,—and so on, and so on, until I could not longer endure the embarrassment of it; then I would shoo them away, and they would circle around in the air a little while, laughing and deriding and mocking, and presently settle on the rail and do it all over again.

They were very sociable when there was anything to eat—oppressively so. With a little encouragement they would come in and light on the table and help me eat my breakfast; and once when I was in the other room and they found themselves alone, they carried off everything they could lift; and they were particular to choose things which they could make no use of after they got them. In India their number is beyond estimate, and their noise is in proportion. I suppose they cost the country more than the government does; yet that is not a light matter. Still, they pay; their company pays; it would sadden the land to take their cheerful voice out of it.

᪥

The Deadliest Song Known to Ornithology

FROM THE WOODS all about came the songs of birds—among them the contributions of a couple of birds which I was not then acquainted with: the brain-fever bird and the coppersmith. The song of the brain-fever demon starts on a low but steadily rising key, and is a spiral twist which augments in intensity and severity with each added spiral, growing sharper and sharper, and more and more painful, more and more agonizing, more and more maddening, intolerable, unendurable, as it bores deeper and deeper and deeper into the listener's brain, until at last the brain fever comes as a relief and the man dies. I am bringing some of these birds home to America. They will be a great curiosity there, and it is believed that in our climate they will multiply like rabbits.

The coppersmith-bird's note, at a certain distance away, has the ring of a sledge on granite; at a certain other distance the hammering has a more metallic ring, and you might think that the bird was mending a copper kettle; at another distance it has a more woodeny thump; but it is a thump that is full of energy, and sounds just like starting a bung. So he is a hard bird to name with a single name; he is stone-breaker, coppersmith and bung-starter, and even then he is not completely named; for when he is close by, you find that there is a soft, deep, melodious quality in his thump, and for that no satisfying name occurs to you. You will not mind his other notes, but when he camps near enough for you to hear that one, you presently find that his measured and monotonous repetition of it is beginning to disturb you; next it will weary you, soon it will distress you; and before long each thump will hurt your head; if this goes on, you will lose your mind with the pain and the misery of it, and go crazy. I am bringing some of these birds home to America. There is nothing like them there. They will be a great surprise, and it is said that in a climate like ours they will surpass expectation for fecundity.

I am bringing some nightingales, too, and some cue-owls. I got them in Italy. The song of the nightingale is the deadliest known to ornithology. That demoniacal shriek can kill at thirty yards. The note of the cue-owl is infinitely soft and sweet—soft and sweet as the whisper of a flute. But penetrating—oh, beyond belief; it can bore through boiler-iron. It is a lingering note, and comes in triplets, on the one unchanging key: *hoo-o-o, hoo-o-o, hoo-o-o;* then a silence of fifteen seconds, then the triplet again; and so-on, all night. At first it is divine; then less so; then trying; then distressing; then excruciating; then agonizing; and at the end of two hours the listener is a maniac.

৸৵

The Pious Chameleon

The chameleon in the hotel court. He is fat and indolent and contemplative; but is business-like and capable when a fly comes about—reaches out a tongue like a teaspoon and takes him in. He gums his tongue first. He is always pious, in his looks. And pious and thankful both when Providence or one of us sends him a fly. He has a froggy head, and a back like a new grave—for shape; and hands like a bird's toes that have been frost bitten. But his

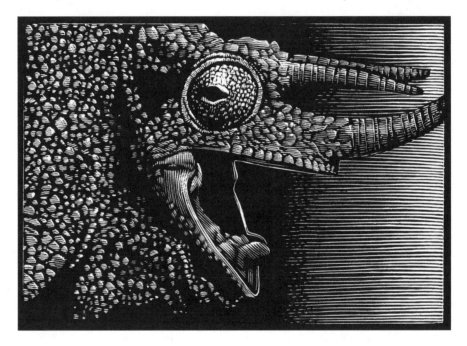

eyes are his exhibition-feature. A couple of skinny cones project from the sides of his head, with a wee shiny bead of an eye set in the apex of each; and these cones turn bodily like pivot-guns and point everywhich-way, and they are independent of each other; each has its own exclusive machinery. When I am behind him and C in front of him, he whirls one eye rearwards and the other forwards—which gives him a most Congressional expression (one eye on the constituency and one on the swag); and then if something happens above and below him he shoots out one eye upward like a tele-scope and the other downward—and this changes his expression, but does not improve it.

❧

A Pocketful of Bat

I CAN SEE the farm yet, with perfect clearness. I can see all its belongings, all its details: the family room of the house, with a "trundle" bed in one corner and a spinning-wheel in another—a wheel whose rising and falling wail, heard from a distance, was the mournfulest of all sounds to me, and made me homesick and low-spirited, and filled my atmosphere with the wandering spirits of the dead; the vast fire-place, piled high, on winter nights, with flaming hickory logs from whose ends a sugary sap bubbled out but did not go to waste, for we scraped it off and ate it; the lazy cat spread out on the rough hearth-stones, the drowsy dogs braced against the jambs and blinking; my aunt in one chimney corner knitting, my uncle in the other smoking his corn-cob pipe; the slick and carpetless oak floor faintly mirroring the dancing flame-tongues and freckled with black indentations where fire-coals had popped out and died a leisurely death; half a dozen children romping in the background twilight; "split"-bottomed chairs here and there, some with rockers; a cradle—out of service, but waiting, with confidence; in the early cold mornings a snuggle of children, in shirts and chemises, occupying the hearthstone and procrastinating—they could not bear to leave that comfortable place and go out on the wind-swept floor-space between house and kitchen where the general tin basin stood on a bench, and wash.

Along outside of the front fence ran the country road; dusty in the summer time, and a good place for snakes—they liked to lie in it and sun themselves; when they were rattlesnakes or puff adders, we killed them; when they were black snakes, or racers, or belonged to the fabled "hoop" breed, we fled, without shame; when they were "house-snakes" or "garters" we carried them home and put them in Aunt Patsy's work-basket for a surprise; for she was prejudiced against snakes, and always when she took the basket in her lap and they began to climb out of it it disordered her mind. She never could seem to get used to them; her opportunities went for nothing. And she was always cold toward bats, too, and could not bear them; and yet I think a bat is as friendly a bird as there is. My mother was aunt Patsy's sister, and had the same wild superstitions. A bat is beautifully soft and silky; I do not know any creature that is pleasanter to the touch, or is more grateful for caressings, if offered in the right spirit. I know all about these coleoptera, because our great cave, three miles below Hannibal, was full of them, and often I brought them home to amuse my mother with. It was easy to manage if it was a school-day, because then I had ostensibly been to school and hadn't any bats. She was not a suspicious person, but full of trust and confidence; and when I said "There's something in my coat-pocket for you," she would put her hand in. But she always took it out again, herself. I didn't have to tell her. It was remarkable, the way she could not learn to like private bats. The more experience she had, the more she could not change her views.

द्रॅ

Hunting the Deceitful Turkey

MY UNCLE AND his big boys hunted with the rifle, the youngest boy and I with a shot-gun—a small single-barrelled shot-gun which was properly suited to our size and strength; it was not much heavier than a broom. We carried it turn-about, half an hour at a time. I was not able to hit anything with it, but I liked to try. Fred and I hunted feathered small game, the others hunted deer, squirrels, wild turkeys, and such things. Jim and his father were the best shots. They killed hawks and wild geese and such-like on the wing; and they didn't wound or kill squirrels, they *stunned* them. When the dogs treed a squirrel, the squirrel would scamper aloft and run out on a limb and flatten himself along it hoping to make himself invisible in that way—and not quite succeeding. You could see his wee little ears sticking up. You couldn't see his nose, but you knew where it was. Then the hunter, despising a "rest" for his rifle, stood up and took off-hand aim at the limb and sent a bullet into it immediately under the squirrel's nose, and down tumbled the animal, unwounded, but unconscious; the dogs gave him a shake and he was dead. Sometimes when the distance was great and the wind not accurately allowed for, the bullet would hit the squirrel's head; the dogs could do as they pleased with that one—the hunter's pride was hurt, and he wouldn't allow it to go into the game-bag.

In the first faint gray of the dawn the stately wild turkeys would be stalking around in great flocks, and ready to be sociable and answer invitations to come and converse with other excursionists of their kind. The hunter concealed himself and imitated the turkey-call by sucking the air through the leg-bone of a turkey which had previously answered a call like that and lived only just long enough to regret it. There is nothing that furnishes a perfect turkey-call except that bone. Another of Nature's treacheries, you see; she is

full of them; half the time she doesn't know which she likes best—to betray her child or protect it. In the case of the turkey she is badly mixed: she gives it a bone to be used in getting it into trouble, and she also furnishes it with a trick for getting itself out of the trouble again. When a mamma-turkey answers an invitation and finds she has made a mistake in accepting it, she does as the mamma-partridge does—remembers a previous engagement and goes limping and scrambling away, pretending to be very lame; and at the same time she is saying to her not-visible children, "Lie low, keep still, don't expose yourselves; I shall be back as soon as I have beguiled this shabby swindler out of the county."

When a person is ignorant and confiding, this immoral device can have tiresome results. I followed an ostensibly lame turkey over a considerable part of the United States one morning, because I believed in her and could not think she would deceive a mere boy, and one who was trusting her and considering her honest. I had the single-barrelled shot-gun, but my idea was to catch her alive. I often got within rushing distance of her, and then made my rush; but always, just as I made my final plunge and put my hand down where her back had been, it wasn't there; it was only two or three inches from there and I brushed the tail feathers as I landed on my stomach—a very close call, but still not quite close enough; that is, not close enough for success, but just close enough to convince me that I could do it next time. She always waited for me, a little piece away, and let on to be resting and greatly fatigued; which was a lie, but I believed it, for I still thought her honest long after I ought to have begun to doubt her, long after I ought to have been suspecting that this was no way for a high-minded bird to be acting. I followed, and followed and followed, making my periodical rushes, and getting up and brushing the dust off, and resuming the voyage with patient confidence; indeed with a confidence which grew, for I could see by the change of climate and vegetation that we were getting up into the high latitudes, and as she always looked a little tireder and a little more discouraged after each rush, I judged that I was safe to win, in the end, the competition being purely a matter of staying power and the advantage lying with me from the start because she was lame.

Along in the afternoon I began to feel fatigued myself. Neither of us had had any rest since we first started on the excursion, which was upwards of ten hours before, though latterly we had paused a while after rushes, I letting on to be thinking about something, and she letting on to be thinking about something else; but neither of us sincere, and both of us waiting for the other to call game but in no real hurry about it, for indeed those little evanescent snatches of rest were very grateful to the feelings of us both, it would naturally be so, skirmishing along like that ever since dawn and not a bite in the meantime; at least for me, though sometimes as she lay on her side fanning herself with a wing and praying for strength to get out of this difficulty a grasshopper happened along whose time had come, and that was well for her, and fortunate, but I had nothing—nothing the whole day.

More than once, after I was very tired, I gave up taking her alive, and was going to shoot her, but I never did it, although it was my right, for I did not believe I could hit her; and besides, she always stopped and posed, when I raised the gun, and this made me suspicious that she knew about me, and my marksmanship, and so I did not care to expose myself to remarks.

I did not get her, at all. When she got tired of the game at last, she rose from almost under my hand and flew aloft with the rush and whir of a shell and lit on the highest limb of a great tree and sat down and crossed her legs and smiled down at me, and seemed gratified to see me so astonished.

I was ashamed, and also lost; and it was while wandering the woods hunting for myself that I found a deserted log cabin and had one of the best meals there that in my life-days I have eaten. The weed-grown garden was full of ripe tomatoes, and I ate them ravenously though I had never liked them before. Not more than two or three times since have I tasted anything that was so delicious as those tomatoes. I surfeited myself with them, and did not taste another one until I was in middle life. I can eat them now, but I do not like the look of them. I suppose we have all experienced a surfeit at one time or another. Once, in stress of circumstances, I ate part of a barrel of sardines, there being nothing else at hand, but since then I have always been able to get along without sardines.

ॐ

Letter to the London Anti-Vivisection Society

SIDNEY G. TRIST, ESQ

Dear Sir: I believe I am not interested to know whether Vivisection produces results that are profitable to the human race or doesn't. To know that the results are profitable to the race would not remove my hostility to it. The pains which it inflicts upon unconsenting animals is the basis of my enmity toward it, & is to me sufficient justification of the enmity without looking further. It is so distinctly a matter of feeling, with me, & is so strong & so deeply rooted in my make & constitution that I am sure I could not even see a vivisector vivisected with anything more than a sort of qualified satisfaction. I do not say I should not go & look on; I only mean that I should almost surely fail to get out of it the degree of contentment which it ought of course to be expected to furnish.

I find some very impressive paragraphs in a paper which was read before the National Individualist Club (1898) by Dr Stephen F. Smith. I have read & re-read these paragraphs, with always augmenting astonishment, & have tried to understand why it should be considered a kind of credit & a handsome thing to belong to a human race that has vivisectors in it. And I have also tried to imagine what would become of the race if it had to be saved by my practicing vivisection on the French plan. Let me quote. [*clipping from printed text:*]

"Vivisectors possess a drug called curare, which, given to an animal, effectually prevents any struggle or cry. A horrible feature of curare is that it has no anæsthetic effect, but on the contrary it intensifies the sensibility to pain. The animal is perfectly conscious, suffers doubly, and is able to make no sign. Claude Bernard, the notorious French vivisector, thus describes the effect of curare: 'The apparent corpse before us hears and distinguishes all that is done. In this motionless body, behind that glazing eye, sensitiveness and intelligence persist in their entirety. The apparent insensibility it produces is accompanied by the most atrocious suffering the mind of man can conceive.' It has been freely admitted by vivisectors that they have used curare alone in the most horrible experiments, and these admissions are to be found multiplied to any extent in the report of the Royal Commission. And though it is illegal at the present day to dispense with anæsthetics, experiments are going on in which curare is the real means of keeping the animal quiet while a pretence is made of anæsthetising them.

"I am not desirous of shocking you by reciting the atrocities of vivisection, but since the apologists try to deceive the public by vague statements that vivisectors would not, and do not perpetrate cruelty, I wish to say sufficient to disprove their assertions.

"There is unfortunately abundant evidence that innumerable experiments of the following character have been performed on sensitive animals. They have been boiled, baked, scalded, burnt with turpentine, frozen, cauterized; they have been partly drowned and brought back to consciousness to have the process repeated; they have been cut open and mangled in every part of the body and have been kept alive in a mutilated state for experiments lasting days or weeks. If I wished, I could pile up mountains of evidence, to be found in the publications of physiologists and in the report of the Royal Commission.

"Here are some experiments by Dr. Drasch in 1889 (Du Bois Reymond's Archives): 'The frogs, curarised or not, are prepared in the following manner. The animal is placed on its back on a piece of cork fastened by a needle through the end of the nose, the lower jaw drawn back and also fastened with pins. Then the mucous membrane is cut away in a circular form, the right eyeball which protrudes into the back of the throat is seized, and the copiously bleeding vessels are tied. Next a tent hook is introduced into the cavity of the eye, drawing out the muscles and optic nerves, which are also secured by a ligature. The eyeball is then split with a needle near the point where the optic nerve enters, a circular piece cut away from the sclerotic and the crystalline lens, etc., removed from the eyeball. I may remark that my experiments lasted a whole year, and I have therefore tried frogs at all seasons.' He calmly gives directions for keeping the animals still. If the frog is not curarised the sciatic and crural nerves are cut through. It is, however, sufficient to fasten the head completely to the cork to immobilise the animal."

I could quote still more shameful vivisection-records from D[r] Smith's paper, but I lack the stomach for it.

Very truly yours
Mark Twain

Vienna, May 26, 1899.

ℰ

The Victims

LITTLE JOHNNY MICROBE BEGGED and begged his mother to let him go to the picnic and said all the nicest creatures were going to be there, and went on saying and saying and saying *Please, ma, can't I? please, ma, let me,* till at last she said he might, and he must be good, and behave, and be sure and be home before sundown, and put his faith in the good spirit and no harm would come to him, and oh, do be careful, she said, it would break mamma's heart if any harm came to her darling. And she promised to have something nice for his supper when he got home.

So Johnny went to the picnic, and mamma Microbe went over to a white corpuscle to hunt the kind of game he preferred for supper. And by and by her microscopic eye discovered little Willie Molecule going along on his way to the picnic, and grabbed him and bit the back of his head off and took him home and knelt down and prayed, giving thanks to the good spirit for that he watches tenderly over them that love him and trust him, allowing none to go hungry from his door.

Little Peter Anthrax begged and begged
So little Peter went to the picnic, and mamma Anthrax went out to hunt the kind of game he preferred for supper. And by and by her quick eye discovered little Johnny Microbe going along on his way to the picnic, and grabbed him and bit his face off.

Little Robbie Typhus Germ begged
So little Robbie went to the picnic and mamma Typhus Germ went out to hunt

little Peter Anthrax going along
and bit his chest off

Little Davy Itch Germ begged
So little Davy went to the picnic and mamma Itch Germ went out to hunt

little Robbie Typhus Germ going along
and bit his bowels out

Little Tommy Red-Speck Spider begged
So little Tommy went to the picnic and mamma Red-Speck Spider went out to hunt

little Davy Itch-Germ going along and bit his buttocks off

Little Fanny Ant begged
So little Fanny went to the picnic and mamma Ant went out to hunt

little Tommy Red-Speck Spider going and bit his spine out

Little Phoebe Gray-Spider begged
So little Phoebe went to the picnic and mamma Gray Spider went out to hunt

little Fanny Ant going along
and bit her forequarters off

Little Sammy Pinch-Bug begged
So little Sammy went to the picnic and mamma Pinch-Bug went out to hunt

little Phoebe Gray Spider
and pierced her through the body from both sides

Little Dora Sparrow begged
So little Dora went to the picnic and mamma Sparrow went out to hunt

little Sammy Pinch-Bug and harpooned him with her beak

Little Harry Weasel begged
So little Harry went to the picnic, and mamma Weasel went out to hunt

and joined her teeth together in the person of little Dora Sparrow

Little Jacky Fox begged
So little Jacky went to the picnic and mamma Fox went out to hunt

and bit little Harry Weasel in two

Little Sophy Wildcat begged
So little Sophy went to the picnic and mamma Wildcat went out to hunt

and broke little Jacky Fox's back with a bite

Little Caleb Sierra Lion begged
So little Caleb went to the picnic, and mamma Sierra Lion went out to hunt

and removed little Sophy Wildcat's interiors

Little Sissy Bengal Tiger begged
So little Sissy went to the picnic and mamma Bengal Tiger went out to hunt

and caved-in the west side of little Caleb Sierra Lion with a pat of her paw

Little Jumbo Jackson Elephantus Ichthyosaurus Megatherium begged
So little Jumbo Jackson went to the picnic, and mamma Elephantus Ichthyosaurus Megatherium went out to hunt

and fetched little Sissy Bengal Tiger a wipe with her 60-foot tail, and a rap with her 19-foot trunk, and observing that she did not respond but seemed satisfied with things as they were, carried her home, cradled on her pair of curled-up 22-foot tusks and

Little Jimmy Gem-of-the-Creation Man begged
So little Jimmy went to the picnic and papa Gem-of-the Creation went out to hunt for—for—anything that might contain life and be helpless—

and hid behind a rock and shot little Jumbo Jackson dead with a magazine rifle and took his tusks and traded them to an Arab land-pirate for a cargo of captive black women and children and sold them to a good Christian planter who promised to give them religious instruction and considerable to do, and blest the planter and shook hands good-bye, and said "By cracky this is the way to extend our noble civilization," and loaded up again and Went for More.

The sun went down, and it was night.

Then mamma Molecule's heart broke and she gave it up, weeping and saying The good spirit has deserted my Willie, who trusted him, and he is dead and will come no more.

ℛ

Extracts from Adam's Diary,
Translated from the Original MS

Monday. This new creature with the long hair is a good deal in the way. It is always hanging around and following me about. I don't like this; I am not used to company. I wish it would stay with the other animals. . . .

Tuesday. [. . .] The new creature names everything that comes along, before I can get in a protest. And always that same pretext is offered—it *looks* like the thing. There is the dodo, for instance. Says the moment one looks at it one sees at a glance that it "looks like a dodo." It will have to keep that name, no doubt. It wearies me to fret about it, and it does no good, anyway. Dodo! It looks no more like a dodo than I do.

Wednesday. Built me a shelter against the rain, but could not have it to myself in peace. The new creature intruded. When I tried to put it out it shed water out of the holes it looks with, and wiped it away with the back of its paws, and made a noise such as some of the other animals make when they are in distress [. . . .]

Saturday. She fell in the pond, yesterday when she was looking at herself in it, which she is always doing. She nearly strangled, and said it was most uncomfortable. This made her sorry for the creatures which live in there, which she calls fish, for she continues to fasten names onto things that don't need them and don't come when they are called by them, which is a matter of no consequence to her, as she is such a numskull anyway; so she got a lot of them out and brought them in last night and put them in my bed to keep warm, but I have noticed them now and then all day and I don't see that they are any happier there than they were before, only quieter. When night comes I shall throw them out doors. I will not sleep with them again, for I find them clammy and unpleasant to lie among when a person hasn't anything on [. . . .]

Tuesday. She has taken up with a snake now. The other animals are glad, for she was always experimenting with them and bothering them [. . . .]

Friday. She says the snake advises her to try the fruit of that tree, and says the result will be a great and fine and noble education [. . . .] I advised her to keep away from the tree. She said she wouldn't. I foresee trouble. Will emigrate.

Wednesday. I have had a variegated time. I escaped that night, and rode a horse all night as fast as he could go, hoping to get clear out of the Park and hide in some other country before the trouble should begin; but it was not to be. About an hour after sun-up, as I was riding through a flowery plain where thousands of animals were grazing, slumbering, or playing with each other, according to their wont, all of a sudden they broke into a tempest of frightful noises and in one moment the plain was in a frantic commotion and every beast was destroying its neighbor. I knew what it meant—Eve had eaten that fruit, and death was come into the world! . . . The tigers ate my horse, paying no attention when I ordered them to desist, and they would even have eaten me if I had stayed—which I didn't, but went away in much haste. . . . I found this place, outside the Park, and was fairly comfortable for a few days, but she has found me out [. . . .] I find she is a good deal of a companion. I see I should be lonesome and depressed without her, now that I have lost my property. Another thing: she says it is ordered that we work for our living, hereafter. She will be useful. I will superintend [. . . .]

Next Year. We have named it Cain. She caught it while I was up country trapping on the North Shore of the Erie; caught it in the timber a couple of miles from our dug-out—or it might have been four, she isn't certain which. It resembles us in some ways, and may be a relation. That is what she thinks, but this is an error, in my judgment. The difference in size warrants the conclusion that it is a different and new kind of animal—a fish, perhaps, though when I put it in the water to see, it sank, and she plunged in and snatched it out before there was opportunity for the experiment to determine the matter. I still think it is a fish, but she is indifferent about what it is, and will not let me have it to try. I do not understand this. The coming of the creature seems to have changed her whole nature and made her unreasonable about experiments. She thinks more of it than she does of any of the other animals, but is not able to explain why. Her mind is disordered—everything shows it. Sometimes she carries the fish in her arms half the night when it complains and wants to get to the water. At such times the water comes out of the places in her face that she looks out of, and she pats the fish on the back and makes soft sounds with her mouth to soothe it, and betrays sorrow and solicitude in a hundred ways. I have never seen her do like this with any other fish, and it troubles me greatly. She used to carry the young tigers around so, and play with them, before we lost our property, but it was only play; she never took on about them like this when their dinner disagreed with them.

Sunday. She doesn't work, Sundays, but lies around all tired out, and likes to have the fish wallow over her; and she makes fool noises to amuse it, and pretends to chew its paws, and that makes it laugh. I have not seen a fish before that could laugh. This makes me doubt [. . . .]

Wednesday. It isn't a fish. I cannot quite make out what it is. It makes curious devilish noises when not satisfied, and says "goo-goo" when it is. It is not one of us, for it doesn't walk; it is not a bird, for it doesn't fly; it is not a frog, for it doesn't hop; it is not a snake, for it doesn't crawl; I feel sure it is not a fish, though I cannot get a chance to find out whether it can swim or not. It merely lies around, and mostly on its back, with its feet up. I have not seen any other animal do that before. I said I believed it was an enigma but she only admired the word without understanding it. In my judgment it is either an enigma; or some kind of a bug. If it dies I will take it apart and see what its arrangements are. I never had a thing perplex me so.

Three Months Later. The perplexity augments instead of diminishing. I sleep but little. It has ceased from lying around, and goes about on its four legs, now. Yet it differs from the other four-legged animals, in that its front legs are unusually short, consequently this causes the main part of its person to stick up uncommonly high in the air, and this is not attractive. It is built much as we are, but its method of traveling shows that it is not of our breed. The short front legs and long hind ones indicate that it is of the kangaroo family, but it is a marked variation of the species, since the true kangaroo hops, whereas this one never does. Still, it is a curious and interesting variety, and has not been catalogued before. As I discovered it, I have felt justified in securing the credit of the discovery by attaching my name to it, and hence have called it *Kangaroorum Adamiensis.* . . . It must have been a young one when it came, for it has grown exceedingly since. It must be five times as big, now, as it was then, and when discontented is able to make from twenty-two to thirty-eight times the noise it made at first. Coercion does not modify this, but has the contrary effect. For this reason I discontinued the system. She reconciles it by persuasion, and by giving it things which she had previously told it she wouldn't give it. As already observed, I was not at home when it first came, and she told me she found it in the woods. It seems odd that it should be the only one, yet it must be so, for I have worn myself out these many weeks try-ing to find another one to add to my collection, and for this one to play with; for surely then it would be quieter and we could tame it more easily. But I find none, nor any vestige of any; and strangest of all, no tracks. It has to live on the ground, it cannot help itself; therefore, how does it get about without leaving a track? I have set a dozen traps, but they do no good; I catch all small animals except that one; animals that merely go into the trap out of curiosity, I think, to see what the milk is there for. They never drink it.

Three Months Later. The kangaroo still continues to grow, which is very strange and perplexing. I never knew one to be so long getting its growth. It has fur on its head, now; not like kangaroo fur, but exactly like our hair, except that it is much finer and softer, and instead of being black is red. I am like to lose my mind over the capricious and harassing developments of this unclassifiable zoölogical freak. If I could catch another one—but that is hope-less; it is a new variety, and the only sample; this is plain. But I caught a true kangaroo and brought it in, thinking that this one, being lonesome, would rather have that for company than have no kin at all, nor any animal it could feel a nearness to or get sympathy from in its forlorn condition here among strangers who do not know its ways or habits, or what to do to make it feel that it is among friends; but it was a mistake—it went into such fits at the sight of the kangaroo that I was convinced it had never seen one before. I pity the poor noisy little animal, but there is nothing I can do to make it happy. If I could tame it—but that is out of the question; the more I try the worse I seem to make it. It grieves me to the heart to see it in its little storms of sorrow and passion. I wanted to let it go, but she wouldn't hear of it. That seemed cruel and not like her; and yet she may be right. It might be lonelier than ever; for since I cannot find another one, how could *it?*

Five Months Later. It is not a kangaroo. No, for it supports itself by holding to her finger, and thus goes a few steps on its hind legs, and then falls down. It is probably some kind of a bear; and yet it has no tail—as yet—and no fur, except on its head. It still keeps on growing—that is a curious circumstance, for bears get their growth earlier than this. Bears are dangerous—since our catastro-phe—and I shall not be satisfied to have this one prowling about the place much longer without a muzzle on. I have offered to get her a kangaroo if she would let this one go, but it did no good—she is determined to run us into all sorts of foolish risks, I think. She was not like this before she lost her mind.

A Fortnight Later. I examined its mouth. There is no danger yet; it has only one tooth. It has no tail yet. It makes more noise, now, than it ever did before—and mainly at night. I have moved out. But I shall go over, mornings, to breakfast, and to see if it has more teeth. If it gets a mouth full of teeth it will be time for it to go, tail or no tail, for a bear does not need a tail in order to be dangerous.

Four Months Later. I have been off hunting and fishing a month, up in the region that she calls Buffalo, I don't know why, unless it is because there are not any buffaloes there. Meantime the bear has learned to paddle around all by itself on its hind legs, and says "poppa" and "momma." It is certainly a new species. This resemblance to words may be purely accidental, of course, and may have no purpose or meaning; but even in that case it is still extraordinary, and is a thing which no other bear can do. This imitation of speech, taken together with general absence of fur and entire absence of tail, sufficiently indicates that this is a new kind of bear. The further study of it will be exceedingly interesting. Meantime I will go off on a far expedition among the forests of the north and make an exhaustive search. There must certainly be another one somewhere, and this one will be less dangerous when it has company of its own species. I will go straightway; but I will muzzle this one first.

Three Months Later. It has been a weary, weary hunt, yet I have had no success. In the meantime, without stirring from the home estate, she has caught another one! I never saw such luck. I might have hunted these woods a hundred years, I never would have run across that thing.

Next Day. I have been comparing the new one with the old one, and it is perfectly plain that they are the same breed. I was going to stuff one of them for my collection, but she is prejudiced against it for some reason or other; so I have relinquished the idea, though I think it is a mistake. It would be an irreparable loss to science if they should get away. The old one is tamer than it was, and can laugh and talk like the parrot, having learned this, no doubt, from being with the parrot so much, and having the imitative faculty in a highly developed degree. I shall be astonished if it turns out to be a new kind of parrot; and yet I ought not to be astonished, for it has already been everything else it could think of, since those first days when it was a fish. The new one is as ugly, now, as the old one was at first; has the same sulphur-and-raw-meat complexion and the same singular head without any fur on it. She calls it Abel.

Ten Years Later. They are boys; we found it out long ago. It was their coming in that small, immature shape that puzzled us; we were not used to it. There are some girls now. Abel is a good boy, but if Cain had stayed a bear it would have improved him [. . . .]

ᏪᎦ

Autobiography of Eve

. . . . LOVE, PEACE, comfort, measureless contentment—that was life in the Garden. It was a joy to be alive. Pain there was none, nor infirmity, nor any physical signs to mark the flight of time; disease, care, sorrow—one might feel these outside the pale, but not in Eden. There they had no place, there they never came. All days were alike, and all a dream of delight.

Interests were abundant; for we were children, and ignorant; ignorant beyond the conception of the present day. We knew *nothing*—nothing whatever. We were starting at the very bottom of things—at the very beginning; we had to learn the a b c of things. To-day the child of four years knows things which we were still ignorant of at thirty [. . . .]

But studying, learning, inquiring into the cause and nature and purpose of everything we came across, were passions with us, and this research filled our days with brilliant and absorbing interest. Adam was by constitution and proclivity a scientist; I may justly say I was the same, and we loved to call ourselves by that great name. Each was ambitious to beat the other in scientific discovery, and this incentive added a spur to our friendly rivalry, and effectively protected us against falling into idle and unprofitable ways and frivolous pleasure-seeking.

Our first memorable scientific discovery was the law that water and like fluids run downhill, not up. It was Adam that found this out. Days and days he conducted his experiments secretly, saying nothing to me about it; for he wanted to make perfectly sure before he spoke. I knew something of prime importance was disturbing his great intellect, for his repose was troubled and he thrashed about in his sleep a good deal. But at last he was sure, and then he told me. I could not believe it, it seemed so strange, so impossible. My astonishment was his triumph, his reward [. . . .]

That law was Adam's first great contribution to science; and for more than two centuries it went by his name—Adam's Law of Fluidic Precipitation [. . . .]

I scored the next great triumph for science myself: to wit, how the milk gets into the cow. Both of us had marveled over that mystery a long time. We had followed the cows around for years—that is, in the daytime—but had never caught them drinking a fluid of that color. And so, at last we said they undoubtedly procured it at night. Then we took turns and watched them by night. The result was the same—the puzzle remained unsolved. These proceedings were of a sort to be expected in beginners, but one perceives, now, that they were unscientific. A time came when experience had taught us better methods. One night as I lay musing, and looking at the stars, a grand idea flashed through my head, and I saw my way! My first impulse was to wake Adam and tell him, but I resisted it and kept my secret. I slept no wink the rest of the night. The moment the first pale streak of dawn appeared I flitted stealthily away; and deep in the woods I chose a small grassy spot and wattled it in, making a secure pen; then I enclosed a cow in it. I milked her dry, then left her there, a prisoner. There was nothing there to drink—she must get milk by her secret alchemy, or stay dry.

All day I was in a fidget, and could not talk connectedly I was so preoccupied; but Adam was busy trying to invent a multiplication table, and did not notice. Toward sunset he had got as far as 6 times 9 are 27, and while he was drunk with the joy of his achievement and dead to my presence and all things else, I stole away to my cow. My hand shook so with excitement and with dread of failure that for some moments I could not get a grip on a teat;

then I succeeded, and the milk came! Two gallons. Two gallons, and nothing to make it out of. I knew at once the explanation: *the milk was not taken in
by the mouth, it was condensed from the atmosphere* through the cow's hair. I ran
and told Adam, and his happiness was as great as mine, and his pride in me
inexpressible.

Presently he said—

"Do you know, you have not made merely one weighty and far-reaching
contribution to science, but two."

And that was true. By a series of experiments we had long ago arrived at
the conclusion that atmospheric air consisted of water in invisible suspen-
sion; also, that the components of water were hydrogen and oxygen, in the
proportion of two parts of the former to one of the latter, and expressible by
the symbol H_2O. My discovery revealed the fact that there was still another
ingredient—milk. We enlarged the symbol to H_2O,M.

DIARY [. . . .] "How stupid we are! Let us eat of it; we shall die, and then we
shall know what it is, and not have any more bother about it."

Adam saw that it was the right idea, and he rose at once and was reaching
for an apple when a most curious creature came floundering by, of a kind
which we had never seen before, and of course we dropped a matter which
was of no special scientific interest, to rush after one that *was*.

Miles and miles over hill and dale we chased that lumbering, scrambling,
fluttering goblin till we were away down the western side of the Valley where
the pillared great banyan tree is, and there we caught him. What a joy, what a
triumph: he is a pterodactyl! Oh, he is a love, he is so ugly! And has such a temper, and such an odious cry. We called a couple of tigers and rode home, and
fetched him along, and now I have him by me, and it is late, but I can't bear to
go to bed, he is such a fascinating fiend and such a royal contribution to science. I know I shant sleep for thinking of him and longing for morning to come,
so that I can explore him and scrutinize him, and search out the secret of his
birth, and determine how much of him is bird and how much is reptile, and see
if he is a survival of the fittest; which we think is doubtful, by the look of him.
Oh, Science, where thou art, all other interests fade and vanish away! [. . .]

Three days later. We have named him Terry, for short, and oh, he *is* a love! All
these three days we have been wholly absorbed in him [. . . .] The cat took
a chance in him, seeing that he was a stranger, but has regretted it. Terry
fetched Thomas a rake fore and aft which left much to be desired in the way
of fur, and Thomas retired with the air of a person who had been intending to
confer a surprise, and was now of a mind to go and think it over and see how
it happened to go the other way [. . . .]

DIARY. *Year 3.* Early in July, Adam noticed that a fish in the pond was developing legs—a fish of the whale family, though not a true whale itself, it being in a state of arrested development. It was a tadpole. We watched it with great interest, for if the legs did really mature and become usable, it was our purpose to develop them in other fishes, so that they could come out and walk around and have more liberty. We had often been troubled about those poor creatures, always wet and uncomfortable, and always restricted to the water whilst the others were free to play amongst the flowers and have a pleasant time. Soon the legs were perfected, sure enough, and then the whale was a frog. It came ashore and hopped about and sang joyously, particularly in the evenings, and its gratitude was without bounds. Others followed rapidly, and soon we had abundant music, nights, which was a great improvement on the stillness which had prevailed before.

We brought various kinds of fishes ashore and turned them loose in the meadows, but in all cases they were a disappointment—no legs came. It was strange; we could not understand it. Within a week they had all wandered back to the water, and seemed better satisfied there than they had been on land. We took this as evidence that fishes as a rule do not care for the land, and that none of them took any strong interest in it but the whales. There were some large whales in a considerable lake three hundred miles up the valley, and Adam went up there with the idea of developing them and increasing their enjoyment.

When he had been gone a week, little Cain was born. It was a great surprise to me, I was not aware that anything was going to happen. But it was just as Adam is always saying: "it is the unexpected that happens."

I did not know what to make of it at first. I took it for an animal. But it hardly seemed to be that, upon examination, for it had no teeth and hardly any fur, and was a singularly helpless mite. Some of its details were human, but there were not enough of them to justify me in scientifically classifying it under that head. Thus it started as a *lusus naturae*—a freak—and it was necessary to let it go at that, for the time being, and wait for developments.

However, I soon began to take an interest in it, and this interest grew day by day; presently this interest took a warmer cast and became affection, then love, then idolatry, and all my soul went out to the creature and I was consumed with a passion of gratitude and happiness. Life was become a bliss, a rapture, an ecstasy, and I longed, day by day, hour by hour, minute by minute for Adam to return and share my almost unendurable joy with me.

Year 4–5. At last he came, but he did not think it was a child. He meant well, and was dear and lovely, but he was scientist first and man afterward—it was his nature—and he could accept nothing until it was scientifically proven. The alarms I passed through, during the next twelve month, with that student's experiments, are quite beyond description. He exposed the child to every discomfort and inconvenience he could imagine, in order to determine what kind of bird or reptile or quadruped it was, and what it was for, and so I had to follow him about, day and night, in weariness and despair to appease its poor little sorrows and help it to bear them the best it could. He believed I had found it in the woods, and I was glad and grateful to let him think so, because the idea beguiled him to go away at times and hunt for another, and this gave the child and me blessed seasons of respite and peace. No one can ever know the relief I felt whenever he ceased from his distressful experiments and gathered his traps and bait together and started for the woods. As soon as he was out of sight I hugged my precious to my heart and smothered it with kisses, and cried for thankfulness. The poor little thing seemed to realize that something fortunate for us had happened, and it would kick and crow, and spread its gummy mouth and smile the happy smile of childhood all the way down to its brains—or whatever those things are that are down in there.

*   *   *   *   *   *   *   *

Year 10. Next came our little Abel. I think we were a year and a half or two years old when Cain was born, and about three or three and a half when Abel was added. By this time Adam was getting to understand. Gradually his experiments grew less and less troublesome, and finally, within a year after the birth of Gladys and Edwina,—years 5 and 6—ceased altogether. He came to love the children fondly, after he had gotten them scientifically classified, and from that time till now the bliss of Eden is perfect.

We have nine children, now—half boys and half girls [. . . .]

Cain and Abel are dear little chaps, and they take very nice care of their little brothers and sisters. The four eldest of the flock go wandering everywhere, according to their desire, and often we see nothing of them for two or three days together. Once they lost Gladys, and came back without her. They could not remember just where or when it was that they missed her. It was far away, they said, but they did not know how far; it was a new region for them [. . . .]

Next day she did not come. Nor the next day, nor the day after that. Then three more days, and still she did not come. It was very strange; nothing quite the match of this had ever happened before. Our curiosity began to be excited. Adam was of the opinion that if she did not come next day, or at furthest the day after, we ought to send Cain and Abel to look.

So we did that. They were gone three days, but they found her. She had had adventures. In the dark, the first night, she fell in the river and was washed down a long distance, she did not know how far, and was finally flung upon a sandbar. After that, she lived with a kangaroo's family, and was hospitably entertained, and there was much sociability. The mama-kangaroo was very sweet and motherly, and would take her babies out of her pocket and go foraging among the hills and dales and fetch home a pocketful of the choicest fruits and nuts; and nearly every night there was company—bears and rabbits and buzzards and chickens and foxes and hyenas and polecats and other creatures—and gay romping and grand times. The animals seemed to pity the child because she had no fur; for always when she slept they covered her with leaves and moss to protect her dainty flesh, and she was covered like that when the boys found her. She had been homesick the first days, but had gotten over it.

ళ

Rosa and the Crows

ROSA WAS WITH US until 1883, when she married a young farmer in the State of New York, and went to live with him on his farm. When the young corn began to sprout the crows took to pulling it up, and then an incident followed whose humor Rosa was quite competent to appreciate. She had spread out and stuck up an old umbrella to do service as a scarecrow, and was sitting on the porch waiting to see what the marauders would think of it. She had not long to wait; soon rain began to fall, and the crows pulled up corn and carried it in under the umbrella and ate it—with thanks to the provider of the shelter!

ళ

Assassin

AND SO I KNOW THAT the fact that for more than fifty-five years I have not wantonly injured a dumb creature is not to be credited to home, school or pulpit, but to a momentary outside influence. When I was a boy my mother pleaded for the fishes and the birds and tried to persuade me to spare them, but I went on taking their lives unmoved, until at last I shot a bird that sat in a high tree, with its head tilted back, and pouring out a grateful song from an innocent heart. It toppled from its perch and came floating down limp and forlorn and fell at my feet, its song quenched and its unoffending life extinguished. I had not needed that harmless creature, I had destroyed it wantonly, and I felt all that an assassin feels, of grief and remorse when his deed comes home to him and he wishes he could undo it and have his hands and his soul clean again from accusing blood. One department of my education, theretofore long and diligently and fruitlessly labored upon, was closed by that single application of an outside and unsalaried influence, and could take down its sign and put away its books and its admonitions permanently.

The Jungle Discusses Man

IT WAS IN THE JUNGLE. The fox had returned from his travels, and this great assemblage had gathered from the mountains and the plains to hear the wonders he was going to tell about the strange countries he had seen and the wide oceans he had crossed. As he walked slowly up and down the grassy space reserved for him, turning his subject over in his mind and arranging his thoughts, he was the centre and focus of an absorbing interest. All eyes followed him back and forth, and the light of admiration was in them, and in some a frank glint of envy. It was not to be denied that contact with the great world had had a gracious and elevating effect upon him. His carriage was graceful, mincing, polished and elegant beyond anything that had been seen in the back woods before; his manners were dignified, easy, and full of distinction; his speech was flowing and unembarrassed, and his foreign accent, so far from marring it, added a delicate charm to it.

It was a fine audience. In front, in the place of honor, was the king, the elephant; to his right and left, all around the front row, sat the nobility, the great beasts of prey; back of these, row after row, disposed according to rank and order of precedence, were the other creatures. In front of the king stood the royal chaplain, the marabout, on one leg, and with his eyes closed in meditation. After a time Reynard opened his portfolios and got out his collection of

pictures, and was now ready to begin. The marabout asked a blessing, then the king said to Reynard—

"Begin!"

The first picture represented a soldier with a gun, a missionary following him with a book. It was passed around, and all examined it with interest.

"What are these things?" the king inquired. "Creatures?"

"Yes, your majesty."

"What kind? How are they called?"

"Sometimes men, sometimes Christians. It is all the same."

"What are they made of?"

"Flesh and bones, like your majesty's subjects."

The tiger reached for the picture and examined it again, with a new interest.

"They look good, these Christians," he said, licking his lips; "are they good?"

"Better than any other of God's creatures, my lord. It is their constant boast; it is a cold day when they forget to give themselves that praise."

The tiger licked his lips again, exhibiting much excitement, and said—

"I would God I had one."

The lion said—

"It is my thought, brother."

The gorilla, leaning upon his staff, examined the picture thoughtfully, his great lips retiring from his tushes and exposing a fellowship smile which some of the smaller animals tremble at and wish they were at home.

"They go upright—like me," he said. "Is it so?"

"They do, my lord."

"Is it feathers they are covered with—or fur?" inquired the rhinoceros.

"Neither, your grace. It is an artificial material, called clothing. They make it themselves, out of various stuffs, and they can take it off when they want to; their natural covering is fish-skin."

Everybody was astonished, and said—

"It doesn't belong to them!" "They can take it off!" "They don't have to put it on, and yet they do!" And the gorilla said, impressively, "Well, I'll be damned!"

The marabout lifted his skinny lids and gave him a crushing look, and he apologised. A hairless dog remarked—

"One perceives that they live in a cold country; that is why they put it on."

"No," observed Reynard; "they put it on in the hottest countries, just the same."

"Why, that is silly!" said many voices. "Why do they afflict themselves in that way?"

"Because they are ashamed to be seen naked."

There was a blank look on all the faces. They could not understand this. Then they all began to laugh, and several said—

"Since they can take those things off when they want to, don't they sometimes want to, and don't they do it?"

"Yes, often—in privacy."

There was another great laugh, and many said—

"Don't they know that God sees them naked?"

"Certainly."

"Land! and they don't mind *Him?* It must be a dirty-minded animal that will be nasty in God's presence and ashamed to be nasty in the presence of his own kind."

ba

The Bee

IT WAS MAETERLINCK who introduced me to the bee. I mean, in the psychical and scientific way, and in the poetical way. I had had a business introduction earlier. It was when I was a boy. It is strange that I should remember a formality like that so long; it must be nearly sixty years [. . . .]

Bee-scientists always speak of the bee as She. It is because all the important bees are of that sex. In the hive there is one married bee, called the Queen; she has 50,000 children; of these, about 100 are sons, the rest are daughters. Some of the daughters are young maids, some are old maids, and all are virgins and remain so.

Every spring the queen comes out of the hive and flies away with one of her sons and marries him. The honeymoon lasts only an hour or two; then the queen divorces her husband and returns home competent to lay two million eggs. This will be enough to last the year, but not more than enough, because hundreds of bees get drowned every day, and other hundreds are eaten by birds, and it is the queen's business to keep the population up to standard— say, 50,000. She must always have that many children on hand and efficient during the busy season, which is summer, or winter would catch the community short of food. She lays from 2,000 to 3,000 eggs a day, according to the demand; and she must exercise judgment, and not lay more than are needed in a slim flower-harvest, nor fewer than are required in a prodigal one, or the Board of Directors will dethrone her and elect a queen that has more sense.

There are always a few royal heirs in stock and ready to take her place—ready, and more than anxious to do it, although she is their own mother. These girls are kept by themselves, and are regally fed and tended from birth. No other bees get such fine food as they get, or live such a high and luxurious life. By consequence they are larger and longer and sleeker than their working sisters. And they have a curved sting, shaped like a scimetar, while the others have a straight one.

A common bee will sting anything or anybody, but a royalty stings royalties only. A common bee will sting and kill another common bee, for cause, but when it is necessary to kill the queen other ways are employed. When a queen has grown old and slack, and does not lay eggs enough, one of her royal daughters is allowed to come and attack her, the rest of the bees looking on at the duel and seeing fair play. It is a duel with the curved stings. If one of the fighters gets hard pressed and gives it up and runs, she is brought back and must try again—once, maybe twice; then, if she runs yet once more for her life, judicial death is her portion: her children pack themselves into a ball around her person and hold her in that compact grip two or three days, until she starves to death or is suffocated. Meantime the victor-bee is receiving royal honors and performing the one royal function—laying eggs.

As regards the ethics of the judicial assassination of the queen, that is a matter of politics, and will be discussed later, in its proper place.

During substantially the whole of her short life of five or six years the queen lives in the Egyptian darkness and stately seclusion of the royal apartments, with none about her but plebeian servants, who give her empty lip-affection in place of the love which her heart hungers for; who spy upon her in the interest of her waiting heirs, and report and exaggerate her defects and deficiencies to them; who fawn upon her and flatter her to her face and slander her behind her back; who grovel before her in the day of her power and forsake her in her age and weakness. There she sits friendless upon her throne through the long night of her life, cut off from the consoling sympathies and sweet companionship and loving endearments which she craves, by the gilded barriers of her awful rank; a forlorn exile in her own house and home, weary object of formal ceremonies and machine-made worship, winged child of the sun, native to the free air and the blue skies and the flowery fields, doomed by the splendid accident of her birth to trade this priceless heritage for a black captivity, a tinsel grandeur, and a loveless life, with shame and insult at the end and a cruel death—and condemned by the human instinct in her to hold the bargain valuable!

Huber, Lubbock, Maeterlinck,—in fact, all the great authorities are agreed in denying that the bee is a member of the human family. I do not know why they have done this, but I think it is from dishonest motives. Why, the innumerable facts brought to light by their own pains-taking and exhaustive experiments prove that if there is a master fool in the world, it is the bee. That seems to settle it.

But that is the way of the scientist. He will spend thirty years in building up a mountain-range of facts with the intent to prove a certain theory; then he is so happy in his achievement that as a rule he overlooks the main chief fact of all: that his accumulation proves an entirely different thing. When you point out this miscarriage to him he does not answer your letters; when you call to convince him, the servant prevaricates and you do not get in. Scientists have odious manners, except when you prop up their theory; then you can borrow money of them.

To be strictly fair, I will concede that now and then one of them will answer your letter, but when they do they avoid the issue—you cannot pin them down. When I discovered that the bee was human I wrote about it to all those scientists whom I have just mentioned. For evasions, I have seen nothing to equal the answers that I got [. . . .]

After the Queen, the personage next in importance in the hive is the virgin. The virgins are 50,000 or 100,000 in number, and they are the workers, the laborers. No work is done, in the hive or out of it, save by them. The males do no work, the queen does no work, unless laying eggs is work, but it does not seem so to me. There are only 2,000,000 of them anyway, and no hurry: two or three thousand a day will answer, and all of five months to finish the contract in. There is no art about it, no effort, anybody could do it. It must be only pastime after one has got the hang of it; no more work about it than hic-cupping. Unless you have to keep count; but that is probably done by tally-clerks. Without doubt this is so, for the distribution of work in a hive is as cleverly and elaborately specialized as it is in a vast American machine-shop or factory. A bee that has been trained to one of the many and various indus-tries of the concern doesn't know how to exercise any other, and would be offended if asked to take a hand in anything outside of her profession. She is as human as a cook; and if you should ask the cook to wait on the table, you know what would happen. Cooks will play the piano if you like, but they draw the line there. In my time I have asked a cook to chop wood, and I know about these things. Even the hired girl has her frontiers; true, they are vague, they are ill-defined, even flexible, but they are there. You ask her to climb the lightning-rod and see what is the matter with it—you will see. These are not theories, they are cold facts, drawn from enlightened experience. Take a wet-nurse, for instance. Ask the wet-nurse to help the hired tramp shovel snow; you will come out of this experiment better educated than when you went in. This is not conjecture; it is founded on the absolute. And then the butler. You ask the butler to wash the dog. It is just as I say; there is much to be learned in these ways, without going to books. Books are very well, but books do not cover the whole domain of esthetic human culture. Pride of profession is one of the boniest bones of existence, if not the boniest. Without doubt it is so in the hive.

ॐ

"Was the World made for Man?"

"Alfred Russell Wallace's revival of the theory that this earth is at the centre of the stellar universe, and is the only habitable globe, has aroused great interest in the world."—*Literary Digest*

"For ourselves we do thoroughly believe that man, as he lives just here on this tiny earth, is in essence and possibilities the most sublime existence in all the range of non-divine being—the chief love and delight of God."
—*Chicago Interior* (Presb.)

I SEEM TO BE the only scientist and theologian still remaining to be heard from on this important matter of whether the world was made for man or not. I feel that it is time for me to speak.

I stand almost with the others. They believe the world was made for man, I believe it likely that it was made for man; they think there is proof, astronomical mainly, that it was made for man, I think there is evidence only, not proof, that it was made for him. It is too early, yet, to arrange the verdict, the returns are not all in. When they are all in, I think they will show that the world was made for man; but we must not hurry, we must patiently wait till they are all in.

Now as far as we have got, astronomy is on our side. Mr. Wallace has clearly shown this. He has clearly shown two things: that the world was made for man, and that the universe was made for the world—to stiddy it, you know. The astronomy part is settled, and cannot be challenged.

We come now to the geological part. This is the one where the evidence is not all in, yet. It is coming in, hourly, daily, coming in all the time, but naturally it comes with geological carefulness and deliberation, and we must not be impatient, we must not get excited, we must be calm, and wait. To lose our tranquillity will not hurry geology; nothing hurries geology.

It takes a long time to prepare a world for man, such a thing is not done in a day. Some of the great scientists, carefully ciphering the evidences furnished by geology, have arrived at the conviction that our world is prodigiously old, and they may be right, but Lord Kelvin is not of their opinion. He takes a cautious, conservative view, in order to be on the safe side, and feels sure it is not so old as they think. As Lord Kelvin is the highest authority in science now living, I think we must yield to him and accept his view. He does not concede that the world is more than a hundred million years old. He believes it is that old, but not older. Lyell believed that our race was introduced into the world 31,000 years ago, Herbert Spencer makes it 32,000. Lord Kelvin agrees with Spencer.

Very well. According to these figures it took 99,968,000 years to prepare the world for man, impatient as the Creator doubtless was to see him and admire him. But a large enterprise like this has to be conducted warily, painstakingly, logically. It was foreseen that man would have to have the oyster. Therefore the first preparation was made for the oyster. Very well, you cannot make an oyster out of whole cloth, you must make the oyster's ancestor first. This is not done in a day. You must make a vast variety of invertebrates, to start with—belemnites, trilobites, jebusites, amalekites, and that sort of fry, and put them to soak in a primary sea, and wait and see what will happen. Some will be a disappointment—the belemnites, the ammonites and such; they will be failures, they will die out and become extinct, in the course of the 19,000,000 years covered by the experiment, but all is not lost, for the amalekites will fetch the home-stake; they will develop gradually into encrinites, and stalactites, and blatherskites, and one thing and another as the mighty ages creep on and the Archaean and the Cambrian Periods pile their lofty crags in the primordial seas, and at last the first grand stage in the preparation of the world for man stands completed, the Oyster is done. An oyster has hardly any more reasoning power than a scientist has; and so it is reasonably certain that this one jumped to the conclusion that the nineteen-million years was a preparation for *him*; but that would be just like an oyster, which is the most conceited animal there is, except man. And anyway, this one could not know, at that early date, that he was only an incident in a scheme, and that there was some more to the scheme, yet.

The oyster being achieved, the next thing to be arranged for in the preparation of the world for man, was fish. Fish, and coal—to fry it with. So the Old Silurian seas were opened up to breed the fish in, and at the same time the great work of building Old Red Sandstone mountains 80,000 feet high to cold-storage their fossils in was begun. This latter was quite indispensable, for there would be no end of failures again, no end of extinctions—millions of them—and it would be cheaper and less trouble to can them in the rocks than keep tally of them in a book. One does not build the coal beds and 80,000 feet of perpendicular Old Red Sandstone in a brief time—no, it took twenty million years. In the first place, a coal bed is a slow and troublesome and tiresome thing to construct. You have to grow prodigious forests of tree-ferns and reeds and calamites and such things in a marshy region; then you have to sink them under out of sight and let them rot; then you have to turn the streams on them, so as to bury them under several feet of sediment, and the sediment must have time to harden and turn to rock; next you must grow another forest on top, then sink it and put on another layer of sediment and harden it; then more forest and more rock, layer upon layer, three miles deep—ah, indeed it is a sickening slow job to build a coal-measure and do it right!

So the millions of years drag on; and meantime the fish-culture is lazying along and frazzling out in a way to make a person tired. You have developed ten thousand kinds of fishes from the oyster; and come to look, you have raised nothing but fossils, nothing but extinctions. There is nothing left alive and progressive but a ganoid or two and perhaps half a dozen asteroids. Even the cat wouldn't eat such.

Still, it is no great matter; there is plenty of time, yet, and they will develop into something tasty before man is ready for them. Even a ganoid can be depended on for that, when he is not going to be called on for sixty million years.

The Palaeozoic time-limit having now been reached, it was necessary to begin the next stage in the preparation of the world for man, by opening up the Mesozoic Age and instituting some reptiles. For man would need reptiles. Not to eat, but to develop himself from. This being the most important detail of the scheme, a spacious liberality of time was set apart for it—thirty million years. What wonders followed! From the remaining ganoids and asteroids and alkaloids were developed by slow and steady and pains-taking culture those stupendous saurians that used to prowl about the steamy world in those remote ages, with their snaky heads reared forty feet in the air and sixty feet of body and tail racing and thrashing after. All gone, now, alas—all extinct, except the little handful of Arkansawrians left stranded and lonely with us here upon this far-flung verge and fringe of time.

Yes, it took thirty million years and twenty million reptiles to get one that would stick long enough to develop into something else and let the scheme proceed to the next step.

Then the Pterodactyl burst upon the world in all his impressive solemnity and grandeur, and all Nature recognized that the Cainozoic threshold was crossed and a new Period open for business, a new stage begun in the preparation of the globe for man. It may be that the Pterodactyl thought the thirty million years had been intended as a preparation for himself, for there was nothing too foolish for a Pterodactyl to imagine, but he was in error, the preparation was for man. Without doubt the Pterodactyl attracted great attention, for even the least observant could see that there was the making of a bird in him. And so it turned out. Also the makings of a mammal, in time. One thing we have to say to his credit, that in the matter of picturesqueness he was the triumph of his Period; he wore wings and had teeth, and was a starchy and wonderful mixture altogether, a kind of long-distance premonitory symptom of Kipling's marine:

> "'E isn't one o' the reg'lar Line, nor 'e isn't one of the crew,
> 'E's a kind of a giddy harumfrodite—soldier an' sailor too!"

From this time onward for nearly another thirty million years the preparation moved briskly. From the Pterodactyl was developed the bird; from the bird the kangaroo, from the kangaroo the other marsupials; from these the mastodon, the megatherium, the giant sloth, the Irish elk, and all that crowd that you make useful and instructive fossils out of—then came the first great Ice Sheet, and they all retreated before it and crossed over the bridge at Behring's strait and wandered around over Europe and Asia and died. All except a few, to carry on the preparation with. Six Glacial Periods with two million years between Periods chased these poor orphans up and down and about the earth, from weather to weather—from tropic swelter at the poles to Arctic frost at the equator and back again and to and fro, they never knowing what kind of weather was going to turn up next; and if ever they settled down anywhere the whole continent suddenly sank under them without the least notice and they had to trade places with the fishes and scramble off to where

the seas had been, and scarcely a dry rag on them; and when there was nothing else doing a volcano would let go and fire them out from wherever they
had located. They led this unsettled and irritating life for twenty-five million
years, half the time afloat, half the time aground, and always wondering what
it was all for, they never suspecting, of course, that it was a preparation for
man and had to be done just so or it wouldn't be any proper and harmonious
place for him when he arrived.

And at last came the monkey, and anybody could see that man wasn't far
off, now. And in truth that was so. The monkey went on developing for close
upon 5,000,000 years, and then turned into a man—to all appearances.

Such is the history of it. Man has been here 32,000 years. That it took a
hundred million years to prepare the world for him is proof that that is what
it was done for. I suppose it is. I dunno. If the Eiffel tower were now representing the world's age, the skin of paint on the pinnacle-knob at its summit
would represent man's share of that age; and anybody would perceive that
that skin was what the tower was built for. I reckon they would, I dunno.

§∂

A Dog's Tale

I

My father was a St. Bernard, my mother was a collie, but I am a Presbyterian. This is what my mother told me; I do not know these nice distinctions myself. To me they are only fine large words meaning nothing. My
mother had a fondness for such; she liked to say them, and see other dogs
look surprised, and envious, as wondering how she got so much education.
But indeed it was not real education, it was only show; she got the words
by listening in the dining room and drawing room when there was company, and by going with the children to Sunday school and listening there;
and whenever she heard a large word she said it over to herself many times,
and so was able to keep it until there was a dogmatic gathering in the neighborhood, then she would get it off and surprise and distress them all, from
pocket-pup to mastiff, which rewarded her for all her trouble. If there was
a stranger he was nearly sure to be suspicious; and when he got his breath
again he would ask her what it meant. And she always told him. He was never

expecting this, but thought he would catch her; so when she told him, he was the one that looked ashamed, whereas he had thought it was going to be she. The others were always waiting for this, and glad of it and proud of her, for they knew what was going to happen, because they had had experience. When she told the meaning of a big word they were all so taken up with admiration that it never occurred to any dog to doubt if it was the right one; and that was natural, because, for one thing, she answered up so promptly that it seemed like a dictionary speaking, and for another thing, where could *they* find out whether it was right or not? for she was the only cultivated dog there was. By and by when I was older, she brought home the word Unintellectual, one time, and worked it pretty hard all the week at different gatherings, making much unhappiness and despondency; and it was at this time that I noticed that during that week she was asked for the meaning at eight different assemblages and flashed out a fresh definition every time, which showed me that she had more presence of mind than culture, though I said nothing, of course. She had one word which she always kept on hand and ready, like a life-preserver, a kind of emergency-word to strap on when she was likely to get washed overboard in a sudden way—that was the word Synonymous. When she happened to fetch out a long word which had had its day weeks before and its prepared meanings gone to her dump-pile, if there was a stranger there of course it knocked him groggy for a couple of minutes, then he would come to, and by that time she would be away down the wind on another tack and not expecting anything; so when he'd hail and ask her to cash-in, I (the only dog on the inside of her game) could see her canvas flicker a moment—but only *just* a moment—then it would belly out taut and full and she would say as calm as a summer's day, "it's synonymous with supererogation" or some godless long reptile of a word like that, and go placidly about and skim away on the next tack perfectly comfortable, you know, and leave that stranger looking profane and embarrassed and the initiated slatting the floor with their tails in unison, and their faces transfigured with a holy joy.

And it was the same with phrases. She would drag home a whole phrase, if it had a grand sound, and play it six nights and two matinees, and explain it a new way every time, which she *had* to, for all she cared for was the phrase, she wasn't interested in what it meant, and knew those dogs hadn't wit enough to catch her, anyway. Yes, she was a daisy! She got so she wasn't afraid of anything, she had such confidence in the ignorance of those creatures. She even brought anecdotes that she had heard the family and the dinner-guests laugh and shout over; and as a rule she got the nub of one chestnut hitched onto another chestnut where of course it didn't fit and hadn't any point; and when she delivered the nub she fell over and rolled on the floor and laughed and barked in the most insane way, while I could see that she was wondering to herself why it didn't seem so funny as it did when she first heard it; but no harm was done, the others rolled and barked, too, privately ashamed of themselves for not seeing the point, and never suspecting that the fault was not with them and there wasn't any to see.

You can see by these things that she was of a rather vain and frivolous character; still, she had virtues, and enough to make up, I think. She had a kind heart and gentle ways, and never harbored resentments for injuries done her, but put them easily out of her mind and forgot them; and she taught her children her kindly ways, and from her we learned also to be brave and prompt in time of danger, and not to run away, but face the peril that threatened friend or stranger and help him the best we could without stopping to think what the cost might be to us. And she taught us not by words only, but by example, and that is the best way and the surest and the most lasting. Why, the brave things she did, the splendid things! she was just a soldier; and so modest about it—well, you couldn't help admiring her, and you couldn't help imitating her; not even a King Charles spaniel could remain entirely despicable in her society. So, as you see, there was more to her than her education.

II

When I was well grown, at last, I was sold and taken away, and I never saw her again. She was broken hearted and so was I, and we cried; but she comforted me as well as she could, and said we were sent into this world for a wise and good purpose, and must do our duties without repining, take our life as we might find it, live it for the best good of others, and never mind about the results, they were not our affair. She said men who did like this would have a noble and beautiful reward by and by in another world, and although we animals would not go there, to do well and right *without* reward would give to our brief lives a worthiness and dignity which in itself would be a reward. She had gathered these things from time to time when she had gone to the Sunday school with the children, and had laid them up in her memory more carefully than she had done with those other words and phrases; and she had studied them deeply, for her good and ours. One may see by this that she had a wise and thoughtful head, for all there was so much lightness and vanity in it.

So we said our farewells, and looked our last upon each other through our tears; and the last thing she said—keeping it for the last to make me remember it the better, I think—was, "In memory of me, when there is a time of danger to another do not think of yourself, think of your mother, and do as she would do."

Do you think I could forget that? No.

III

It was such a charming home!—my new one; a fine great house, with pictures, and delicate decorations, and rich furniture, and no gloom anywhere, but all the wilderness of dainty colors lit up with flooding sunshine; and the spacious grounds around it, and the great garden—oh, greensward, and noble trees, and flowers, no end! And I was the same as a member of the family; and they loved me, and petted me, and did not give me a new name, but called me by my old one that was dear to me because my mother had given it me—Aileen Mavourneen. She got it out of a song; and the Grays knew that song and said it was a beautiful name.

Mrs. Gray was thirty, and so sweet and so lovely, you cannot imagine it; and Sadie was ten, and just like her mother, just a darling slender little copy of her, with auburn tails down her back, and short frocks; and the baby was a year old, and plump and dimpled, and fond of me, and never could get enough of hauling on my tail, and hugging me, and laughing out its innocent happiness; and Mr. Gray was thirty-eight, and tall and slender and handsome, a little bald in front, alert, quick in his movements, business-like, prompt, decided, unsentimental, and with that kind of trim-chiseled face that just seems to glint and sparkle with frosty intellectuality! He was a renowned scientist. I do not know what the word means, but my mother would know how to use it and get effects. She would know how to depress a rat terrier with it and make a lap-dog look sorry he came. But that is not the best one; the best one was Laboratory. My mother could organize a Trust on that one that would skin the tax-collars off the whole herd. The laboratory was not a book, or a picture, or a place to wash your hands in, as the college-president's dog said—no, that is the lavatory, the laboratory is quite different, and is filled with jars, and bottles, and electrics, and wires, and strange machines; and every week other scientists came there and sat in the place, and used the machines, and discussed, and made what they called experiments and discoveries; and often I came, too, and stood around and listened, and tried to learn, for the sake of my mother, and in loving memory of her, although it was a pain to me, as realizing what she was losing out of her life and I gaining nothing at all; for try as I might, I was never able to make anything out of it at all.

Other times I lay on the floor in the mistress's work room and slept, she gently using me for a footstool, knowing it pleased me, for it was a caress; other times I spent an hour in the nursery and got well tousled and made happy; other times I watched by the crib, there, when the baby was asleep and the nurse out for a few minutes on the baby's affairs; other times I romped and raced through the grounds and the garden with Sadie till we were tired out, then slumbered on the grass in the shade of a tree while she read her book; other times I went visiting among the neighbor-dogs, for there were some most pleasant ones not far away, and one very handsome and courteous and graceful one, a curly-haired Irish setter by the name of Robin Adair, who was a Presbyterian like me, and belonged to the Scotch minister.

The servants in our house were all kind to me and were fond of me, and so, as you see, mine was a pleasant life. There could not be a happier dog than I was, nor a gratefuller one. I will say this for myself, for it is only the truth: I tried in all ways to do well and right, and honor my mother's memory and her teachings, and earn the happiness that had come to me, as best I could.

By and by came my little puppy, and then my cup was full, my happiness was perfect. It was the dearest little waddling thing, and so smooth and soft and velvety, and had such cunning little awkward paws, and such affectionate eyes, and such a sweet and innocent face; and it made me so proud to see how the children and their mother adored it, and fondled it and exclaimed

over every little wonderful thing it did. It did seem to me that life was just too lovely to—

Then came the winter. One day I was standing a watch in the nursery. That is to say, I was asleep on the bed. The baby was asleep in the crib, which was alongside the bed, on the side next the fire-place. It was the kind of crib that has a lofty tent over it made of gauzy stuff that you can see through. The nurse was out, and we two sleepers were alone. A spark from the wood-fire was shot out and it lit on the slope of the tent. I suppose a quiet inter-val followed, then a scream from the baby woke me, and there was that tent flaming up toward the ceiling! Before I could think, I sprang to the floor in my fright and in a second was half way to the door; but in the next half-second my mother's farewell was sounding in my ears and I was back on the bed again. I reached my head through the flames and dragged the baby out by the waistband, and tugged it along and we fell to the floor together in a cloud of smoke; I snatched a new hold, and dragged the screaming lit-tle creature along and out at the door and around the bend of the hall, and was still tugging away, all excited and happy and proud, when the master's voice shouted,

"Begone, you cursed beast!" and I jumped to save myself; but he was won-derfully quick, and chased me up, striking furiously at me with his cane, I dodging this way and that, in terror, and at last a strong blow fell upon my left foreleg which made me shriek and fall, for the moment helpless; the cane went up for another blow, but never descended, for the nurse's voice rang wildly out, "The nursery's on fire!" and the master rushed away in that direc-tion, and my other bones were saved.

The pain was cruel, but no matter, I must not lose any time, he might come back at any moment; so I limped on three legs to the other end of the hall where there was a dark little stairway leading up into a garret where old boxes and such things were kept, as I had heard say, and where people sel-dom went. I managed to climb up there, then I searched my way through the dark amongst the piles of things, and hid in the secretest place I could find. It was foolish to be afraid there, yet still I was; so afraid that I held in and hardly even whimpered, though it would have been such a comfort to whimper, because that eases the pain, you know. But I could lick my leg, and that did me some good.

For half an hour there was a commotion down stairs, and shoutings, and rushing footsteps, and then there was quiet again. Quiet for some minutes, and that was grateful to my spirit, for then my fears began to go down, and fears are worse than pains,—oh, much worse. Then came a sound that froze me! They were calling me—calling me by name—hunting for me!

It was muffled by distance, but that could not take the terror out of it, and it was the most dreadful sound to me that I had ever heard. It went all about, everywhere, down there: along the halls, through all the rooms, in both stories, and in the basement and the cellar; then outside, and further and further away—then back, and all about the house again, and I thought it would never, never stop. But at last it did, hours and hours after the vague twilight of the garret had long ago been blotted out by black darkness.

Then in that blessed stillness my terrors fell little by little away, and I was at peace, and slept. It was a good rest I had, but I woke before the twilight had come again. I was feeling fairly comfortable, and could think out a plan, now. I made a very good one; which was, to creep down, all the way down the back stairs, and hide behind the cellar door, and slip out and escape when the iceman came at dawn, whilst he was inside, filling the refrigerator; then I would hide all day, and start on my journey when night came; my journey to—well, anywhere where they would not know me and betray me to the master. I was feeling almost cheerful now; then suddenly I thought, Why, what would life be without my puppy!

That was despair. There was no plan for me; I saw that; I must stay where I was; stay, and wait, and take what might come—it was not my affair; that was what life is,—my mother had said it. Then—well, then the calling began again! All my sorrows came back. I said to myself, the master will never forgive. I did not know what I had done to make him so bitter and so unforgiving, yet I judged it was something a dog could not understand, but which was clear to a man and dreadful.

They called and called—days and nights, it seemed to me. So long that the hunger and thirst near drove me mad, and I recognized that I was getting very weak. When you are this way you sleep a great deal, and I did. Once I woke in an awful fright—it seemed to me that the calling was right there in the garret! And so it was: it was Sadie's voice, and she was crying; my name was falling from her lips all broken, poor thing, and I could not believe my ears for the joy of it when I heard her say:

"Come back to us,—oh, come back to us, and forgive—it is all so sad without our—"

I broke in with *such* a grateful little yelp, and the next moment Sadie was plunging and stumbling through the darkness and the lumber and shouting for the family to hear, "She's found, she's found!"

The days that followed—well, they were wonderful. The mother and Sadie and the servants—why, they just seemed to worship me. They couldn't seem to make me a bed that was fine enough; and as for food, they couldn't be satisfied with anything but game and delicacies that were out of season; and every day the friends and neighbors flocked in to hear about my heroism—that was the name they called it by, and it means agriculture. I remember my mother pulling it on a kennel once, and explaining it that way, but didn't say what agriculture was, except that it was synonymous with intramural incandescence; and a dozen times a day Mrs. Gray and Sadie would tell the tale to newcomers, and say I risked my life to save the baby's, and both of us had burns to prove it, and then the company would pass me around and pet me and exclaim about me, and you could see the pride in the eyes of Sadie and her mother; and when the people wanted to know what made me limp, they looked ashamed and changed the subject, and sometimes when people hunted them this way and that way with questions about it, it looked to me as if they were going to cry.

And this was not all the glory; no, the master's friends came, a whole twenty of the most distinguished people, and had me in the laboratory, and discussed me as if I was a kind of discovery; and some of them said it was wonderful in a dumb beast, the finest exhibition of instinct they could call to mind; but the master said, with vehemence, "It's far above instinct; it's *reason*, and many a man, privileged to be saved and go with you and me to a better world by right of its possession, has less of it that this poor silly quadruped that's foreordained to perish"; and then he laughed, and said: "Why, look at me—I'm a sarcasm! bless you, with all my grand intelligence, the only thing I inferred was that the dog had gone mad and was destroying the child, whereas but for the beast's intelligence—it's *reason*, I tell you!—the child would have perished!"

They disputed and disputed, and *I* was the very centre and subject of it all, and I wished my mother could know that this grand honor had come to me; it would have made her proud.

Then they discussed optics, as they called it, and whether a certain injury to the brain would produce blindness or not, but they could not agree about it, and said they must test it by experiment by and by; and next they discussed plants, and that interested me, because in the summer Sadie and I had planted seeds—I helped her dig the holes, you know,—and after days and days a little shrub or a flower came up there, and it was a wonder how that could happen; but it did, and I wished I could talk,—I would have told those people about it and shown them how much I knew, and been all alive with the subject; but I didn't care for the optics; it was dull, and when they came back to it again it bored me, and I went to sleep.

Pretty soon it was spring, and sunny and pleasant and lovely, and the sweet mother and the children patted me and the puppy good-by, and went away on a journey and a visit to their kin, and the master wasn't any company for us, but we played together and had good times, and the servants were kind and friendly, so we got along quite happily and counted the days and waited for the family.

And one day those men came again, and said now for the test, and they took the puppy to the laboratory, and I limped three-leggedly along, too, feeling proud, for any attention shown the puppy was a pleasure to me, of course. They discussed and experimented, and then suddenly the puppy shrieked, and they set him on the floor, and he went staggering around, with his head all bloody, and the master clapped his hands and shouted:

"There, I've won—confess it! He's as blind as a bat!"

And they all said,

"It's so—you've proved your theory, and suffering humanity owes you a great debt from henceforth," and they crowded around him, and wrung his hand cordially and thankfully, and praised him.

But I hardly saw or heard these things, for I ran at once to my little darling, and snuggled close to it where it lay, and licked the blood, and it put its head against mine, whimpering softly, and I knew in my heart it was a comfort to it in its pain and trouble to feel its mother's touch, though it could not see me. Then it dropped down, presently, and its little velvet nose rested upon the floor, and it was still, and did not move any more.

Soon the master stopped discussing a moment, and rang in the footman, and said, "Bury it in the far corner of the garden," and then went on with the discussion, and I trotted after the footman, very happy and grateful, for I knew the puppy was out of its pain now, because it was asleep. We went far down the garden to the furthest end, where the children and the nurse and the puppy and I used to play in the summer in the shade of a great elm, and there the footman dug a hole, and I saw he was going to plant the puppy, and I was glad, because it would grow and come up a fine handsome dog, like Robin Adair, and be a beautiful surprise for the family when they came home; so I tried to help him dig, but my lame leg was no good, being stiff, you know, and you have to have two, or it is no use. When the footman had finished and covered little Robin up, he patted my head, and there were tears in his eyes, and he said, "Poor little doggie, you saved *his* child."

I have watched two whole weeks, and he doesn't come up! This last week a fright has been stealing upon me. I think there is something terrible about this. I do not know what it is, but the fear makes me sick, and I cannot eat, though the servants bring me the best of food; and they pet me so, and even come in the night, and cry, and say, "Poor doggie—do give it up and come home; *don't* break our hearts!" and all this terrifies me the more, and makes me sure something has happened. And I am so weak; since yesterday I cannot stand on my feet any more. And within this hour the servants, looking toward the sun where it was sinking out of sight and the night chill coming on, said things I could not understand, but they carried something cold to my heart.

"Those poor creatures! They do not suspect. They will come home in the morning, and eagerly ask for the little doggie that did the brave deed, and who of us will be strong enough to say the truth to them: 'The humble little friend is gone where go the beasts that perish.'"

ℬ

Flies and Russians

THERE ARE A NUMBER of ways of justifying the existence of the human race, some of them quite plausible. There are also approximately plausible ways of justifying and excusing the continuance of several nations which apparently ought to have been discontinued many centuries ago. Among these the Russian nation may be instanced as an example. When we look down the ages and examine the history of that people we are puzzled and keep asking, What are the Russians *for*? How did the Russians happen? Were they intentional, or were they an accident? If they were intentional, what was the intention?

In my opinion,—after months of considering and examining—they were intentional. I think this because I am sure their history shows indications of intelligent design—at least design—in the invention and creation of those people. It is my belief that they were created for an object; I think there was a purpose in view. I think this is evidenced in the fact that century after century, from the beginning of Russian time, they have clung, without wavering, to a single ideal, a single ambition, a single industry, and have cared for nothing else, labored for nothing else, been indifferent to all things else.

Examine the proposition for yourself, by the light of analogy. How do we know what a rabbit is for? The rabbit's history tells us what the rabbit is for. How do we know what a mollusk is for? The mollusk's history tells us what the mollusk is for. How do we know what an idiot is for? The idiot's history tells us what the idiot is for. If we combine these three and add the bee, what do we get? A Russian. How do we know that we have got a Russian? The Russian's history tells us we have got him; and at the same time reveals to us what he is for.

The captive rabbit spends its whole life in meek submission to whatever master is over it; the mollusk spends its whole life asleep, drunk, content; the idiot lives his days in a dull and cloudy dream, and reasons not; the bee slaves from dawn to dark storing up honey for a robber to live on.

Since history shows us that through all the ages from its birth the Russian nation has devoted all its strength and mind and soul to coddling, aggrandizing, adoring and enriching a single robber family, a single family of bloody and heartless oppressors, it seems proven and established that that is what the Russian nation is for. It seems proven and established that the creation of that nation was intentional. Coldly intentional. Why a nation should be created for such a function, is another matter. We have no way of finding out. We only know that nothing was to be gained by it; that nothing has been gained by it; that nothing is ever going to be gained by it. It is an enigma, a miscarriage—like the founding of the fly.

It is possible that at the time the idea of creating the Russian nation was first conceived, the grotesque nature of the result was not clearly foreseen. I think that this is the honorable view to take of it. It was so with the fly. It would not be right for us to allow ourselves to believe that the fly would have been created if the way he was going to act had been fully known beforehand. I think we may not doubt that the fly was a disappointment. I think we have reason to believe that he did not come up to expectations. This argument justifies us in surmising that it is the same with the Russians. The making of flies and Russians—just as they are, I mean—could not have been intentional. Necessarily the idea was to supply a long-felt want; we know this because that was always the idea whenever anything was made. Very well, where was the long-felt want? We all know there wasn't any. And suppose there had been a long-felt want,—do you reckon you could supply it with flies and Russians? Certainly not. Then what do these reasonings force upon us? They force upon us the conviction that while they were of course intended to supply a long-felt want, they presently developed unforeseen novelties and abnormalities which disqualified them. Nobody is to blame, but there are the facts. We have the flies and the Russians, we cannot help it, let us not moan about it, but manfully accept the dispensation and do the best we can with it. Time will bring relief, this we know, for we have history for it. Nature had made many and many a mistake before she added flies and Russians, and always she corrected them as soon as she could. She will correct this one too—in time. Geological time. For she is a slow worker, and not to be hurried by any one's complaints or persuasions, nor by the skippy activities of her own frivolous intellect.

She made a mistake in the megatherium. It turned out to be absolutely useless. It took her a million years to find it out; then she abolished the megatherium. By and by she tried saurians; she made saurians ninety feet long, and what to do with them after she made them, she did not know. They were long enough to supply any long-felt want that merely required inches and plenty of them; but there was no such want. Others found it out early; it took Nature a million years to perceive it; then she abolished the brood. Next she tried to make a reptile that could fly. We know the result. The less said about the pterodactyl the better. It was a spectacle, that beast! a mixture of buzzard and alligator, a sarcasm, an affront to all animated nature, a butt for the ribald jests of an unfeeling world. After some ages Nature perceived that to put feathers on a reptile does not ennoble it, does not make it a bird, but only a sham, a joke, a grotesque curiosity, a monster; also that there was no useful thing for the pterodactyl to do, and nothing likely to turn up in the future that could furnish it employment. And so she abolished it.

Nature made thousands and thousands of now extinct species in her apprentice-days which turned out to be pure failures, like the flies and the Russians, and she devoted millions of years to trying to hunt up long-felt wants for them to supply, but there were none, and a museum never occurred to her. So she abolished them all, and scattered their bones in myriads in the eternal rocks, and there they rest to this day, a solemn reminder for us that for every animal-success achieved by her she has scored fifteen hundred failures. And this without including the flies and the Russians.

Herein we find our hope. We shall not live to see the happy day, but it will come. It will take her a million years to find out that there is no use for flies and Russians, then she will act with her accustomed promptness.

There is also another hope, and a pleasanter one. The first time Nature tried to make a horse, the result was pathetic. A stranger would have supposed it was a dog. But she worked at it a million years and enlarged it to the dimensions of a calf, removed a toe or two from its feet, and in other ways improved it. She worked at it another million, then another and another and still another million, and at last after nine or ten million years of thought and labor and worry and cussing she turned out for the grateful and cordial admiration of the world the horse as we see him to-day, that noble creature, that beautiful creature, that matchless darling of our love and worship. Ten million years are soon passed: what may not the fly and the Russian become?

And yet, when we reflect! Even in our own day Russians could be made useful if only a way could be found to inject some intelligence into them. How magnificently they fight in Manchuria! with what indestructible pluck they rise up after the daily defeat, and sternly strike, and strike again! how gallant they are, how devoted, how superbly unconquerable! If they would only reflect! if they could only reflect! if they only had something to reflect with! Then these humble and lovable slaves would perceive that the splendid fighting-energy which they are wasting to keep their chipmunk on the throne would abolish both him and it if intelligently applied.

ૐ

Eve's Diary. Translated from the Original

Saturday.—I am almost a whole day old, now. I arrived yesterday [. . . .] It will be best to start right and not let the record get confused, for some instinct tells me that these details are going to be important to the historian some day. For I feel like an experiment, I feel exactly like an experiment, it would be impossible for a person to feel more like an experiment than I do, and so I am coming to feel convinced that that is what I *am*—an experiment; just an experiment, and nothing more [. . . .]

I followed the other Experiment around, yesterday afternoon, at a distance, to see what it might be for, if I could. But I was not able to make out. I think it is a man. I had never seen a man, but it looked like one, and I feel sure that that is what it is. I realize that I feel more curiosity about it than about any of the other reptiles. If it is a reptile, and I suppose it is; for it has frowsy hair and blue eyes, and looks like a reptile. It has no hips; it tapers like a carrot; when it stands, it spreads itself apart like a derrick; so I think it is a reptile, though it may be architecture.

I was afraid of it at first, and started to run every time it turned around, for I thought it was going to chase me; but by and by I found it was only trying to get away, so after that I was not timid any more, but tracked it along, several hours, about twenty yards behind, which made it nervous and unhappy. At last it was a good deal worried, and climbed a tree. I waited a good while, then gave it up and went home.

To-day the same thing over. I've got it up the tree again.

Sunday.— [. . .] It has low tastes, and is not kind. When I went there yesterday evening in the gloaming it had crept down and was trying to catch the little speckled fishes that play in the pool, and I had to clod it to make it go up the tree again and let them alone. I wonder if *that* is what it is for? Hasn't it any heart? Hasn't it any compassion for those little creatures? Can it be that it was designed and manufactured for such ungentle work? It has the look of it. One of the clods took it back of the ear, and it used language. It gave me a thrill, for it was the first time I had ever heard speech, except my own. I did not understand the words, but they seemed expressive.

When I found it could talk I felt a new interest in it, for I love to talk; I talk all day, and in my sleep, too, and I am very interesting, but if I had another to talk to I could be twice as interesting, and would never stop, if desired.

If this reptile is a man, it isn't an *it*, is it? That wouldn't be grammatical, would it? I think it would be *he*. I think so. In that case one would parse it thus: nominative, *he*; dative, *him*; possessive, *his'n*. Well, I will consider it a man and call it he until it turns out to be something else. This will be handier than having so many uncertainties.

Next week Sunday.—All the week I tagged around after him and tried to get acquainted. I had to do the talking, because he was shy, but I didn't mind it. He seemed pleased to have me around, and I used the sociable "we" a good deal, because it seemed to flatter him to be included.

Wednesday.—We are getting along very well indeed, now, and getting better and better acquainted. He does not try to avoid me any more, which is a good sign, and shows that he likes to have me with him. That pleases me, and I study to be useful to him in every way I can, so as to increase his regard. During the last day or two I have taken all the work of naming things off his hands, and this has been a great relief to him, for he has no gift in that line, and is evidently very grateful. He can't think of a rational name to save him, but I do not let him see that I am aware of his defect. Whenever a new creature comes along I name it before he has time to expose himself by an awkward silence. In this way I have saved him many embarrassments. I have no defect like his. The minute I set eyes on an animal I know what it is. I don't have to reflect a moment; the right name comes out instantly, just as if it were an inspiration, as no doubt it is, for I am sure it wasn't in me half a minute

before. I seem to know just by the shape of the creature and the way it acts what animal it is.

When the dodo came along he thought it was a wildcat—I saw it in his eye. But I saved him. And I was careful not to do it in a way that could hurt his pride. I just spoke up in a quite natural way of pleased surprise, and not as if I was dreaming of conveying information, and said, "Well, I do declare, if there isn't the dodo!" I explained—without seeming to be explaining—how I knew it for a dodo, and although I thought maybe he was a little piqued that I knew the creature when he didn't, it was quite evident that he admired me. That was very agreeable, and I thought of it more than once with gratification before I slept. How little a thing can make us happy when we feel that we have earned it! [. . .]

Extract from Adam's Diary

Perhaps I ought to remember that she is very young, a mere girl, and make allowances. She is all interest, eagerness, vivacity, the world is to her a charm, a wonder, a mystery, a joy [. . . .]

Monday noon.—If there is anything on the planet that she is not interested in it is not in my list. There are animals that I am indifferent to, but it is not so with her. She has no discrimination, she takes to all of them, she thinks they are all treasures, every new one is welcome. When the mighty brontosaurus came striding into camp, she regarded it as an acquisition, I considered it a calamity; that is a good sample of the lack of harmony that prevails in our views of things. She wanted to domesticate it, I wanted to make it a present of the homestead and move out. She believed it could be tamed by kind treatment and would be a good pet; I said a pet twenty-one feet high and eighty-four feet long would be no proper thing to have about the place, because, even with the best intentions and without meaning any harm, it could sit down on the house and mash it, for any one could see by the look of its eye that it was absent-minded.

Still, her heart was set upon having that monster, and she couldn't give it up. She thought we could start a dairy with it, and wanted me to help her milk it; but I wouldn't; it was too risky. The sex wasn't right, and we hadn't any ladder, anyway. Then she wanted to ride it, and look at the scenery. Thirty or forty feet of its tail was lying on the ground, like a fallen tree, and she thought she could climb it, but she was mistaken; when she got to the steep place it was too slick and down she came, and would have hurt herself but for me.

Was she satisfied now? No. Nothing ever satisfies her but demonstration; untested theories are not in her line, and she won't have them. She was born scientific. It is the right spirit, I concede it; it attracts me; I feel the influence of it; if I were with her more I think I should take it up myself. Well, she had one theory remaining about this colossus: she thought that if we could tame him and make him friendly we could stand him in the river and use him for a bridge. It turned out that he was already plenty tame enough—at least as far as she was concerned—so she tried her theory, but it failed: every time she got him properly placed in the river and went ashore to cross over on him, he came out and followed her around like a pet mountain. Like the other animals. They all do that.

Tuesday—Wednesday—Thursday—and to-day: all without seeing him. It is a long time to be alone; still, it is better to be alone than unwelcome.

Friday.—I had to have company—I was made for it, I think—so I made friends with the animals. They are just charming, and they have the kindest disposition and the politest ways; they never look sour, they never let you feel that you are intruding, they smile at you and wag their tail, if they've got one, and they are always ready for a romp or an excursion or anything you want to propose. I think they are perfect gentlemen. All these days we have had such good times, and it hasn't been lonesome for me, ever. Lonesome! No, I should say not. Why, there's always a swarm of them around—sometimes as much as four or five acres—you can't count them; and when you stand on a rock in the midst and look out over the furry expanse it is so mottled and splashed and gay with color and frisking sheen and sun-flash, and so rippled with stripes, that you might think it was a lake, only you know it isn't; and there's storms of sociable birds, and hurricanes of whirring wings; and when the sun strikes all that feathery commotion, you have a blazing up of all the colors you can think of, enough to put your eyes out.

We have made long excursions, and I have seen a great deal of the world; almost all of it, I think; and so I am the first traveller, and the only one. When we are on the march, it is an imposing sight—there's nothing like it anywhere. For comfort I ride a tiger or a leopard, because it is soft and has a round back that fits me, and because they are such pretty animals; but for long distance or for scenery I ride the elephant. He hoists me up with his trunk, but I can get off myself; when we are ready to camp, he sits and I slide down the back way.

The birds and animals are all friendly to each other, and there are no disputes about anything. They all talk, and they all talk to me, but it must be a foreign language, for I cannot make out a word they say; yet they often understand me when I talk back, particularly the dog and the elephant. It makes me ashamed. It shows that they are brighter than I am, and are therefore my superiors. It annoys me, for I want to be the principal Experiment myself—and I intend to be, too.

૪ð

The Supremacy of the House Fly

Dictated, Sept. 4, 1906. There is one thing which fills me with wonder and reverence every time I think of it—and that is the confident and splendid fight for supremacy which the house fly makes against the human being. Man, by his inventive ingenuity, has in the course of the ages, by help of diligence and determination, found ways to acquire and establish his mastery over every living creature under the vault of heaven—except the house fly. With the house fly he has always failed. The house fly is as independent of him to-day as he was when Adam made his first grab for one and didn't get him. The house fly defies all man's inventions for his subjugation or destruction. No creature was ever yet devised that could meet man on his own level and laugh at him and defy him, except the house fly. In ancient times man's dominion over animated nature was not complete; but, detail by detail, as the ages have drifted by, his inventive genius has brought first one and then another of the unconquerables under his dominion: first the elephant and

the tiger, and then the lion, the hippopotamus, the bear, the crocodile, the whale, and so on. One by one man's superiors in fight have succumbed and hauled down the flag. Man is confessed master of them all, now. There isn't one of them—there isn't a single species—that can survive if man sets himself the task of exterminating it—the house fly always excepted. Nature cannot construct a monster on so colossal a scale that man can't find a way to exterminate it as soon as he is tired of its society. Nature cannot contrive a creature of the microscopicalest infinitesimality and hide it where man cannot find it—find it and kill it. Nature has tried reducing microbes to the last expression of littleness, in the hope of protecting and preserving by this trick a hundred deadly diseases which she holds in warmer affection than she holds any benefit which she has ever conferred upon man, but man has circumvented her and made her waste her time and her effort. She has gone on pathetically and hopefully reducing her microbes until at last she has got them down so fine that she can conceal a hundred million of them in a single drop of a man's blood—but it is all in vain. When man is tired of his microbes he knows how to find them and exterminate them. It is most strange, but there stands the simple truth: of all the myriad of creatures that inhabit the earth, including the Christian dissenter, not one is beyond the reach of the annihilatory ingenuity of scientific man—except the house fly.

It is a most disastrous condition. If all the troublesome and noxious creatures in the earth could be multiplied a hundred fold, and the house fly exterminated as compensation, man should be glad and grateful to sign the contract. We should be infinitely better off than we are now. One house fly, all by itself, can cause us more distress and misery and exasperation than can any dozen of the other vexations which Nature has invented for the poisoning of our peace and the destruction of our comfort. All human ingenuities have been exhausted in the holy war against the fly, and yet the fly remains to-day just what he was in Adam's time—independent, insolent, intrusive, and indestructible. Fly-paper has accomplished nothing. The percentage of flies that get hitched to it is but one in the hundred, and the

other ninety-nine assemble as at a circus and enjoy the performance. Slap-
ping flies with a wet towel results in nothing valuable beyond the exercise.
There are not two marksmen in fifty that can hit a fly with a wet towel at
even a short range, and this method brings far more humiliation than satisfaction, because there is an expression about the missed fly which is so eloquent with derision that no operator with sensitive feelings can continue
his labors after his self respect is gone—a result which almost always follows
his third or fourth miss. Anger and eagerness disorder his aim. Under these
influences he delivers a slat which would get a dog every time, yet misses
the fly mysteriously and unaccountably—does not land on the fly's territory
at all. Then the fly smiles that cold and offensive smile which is sacred to the
fly, and the man is conquered, and gives up the contest. Poisonous powders
have been invented for the destruction of noxious insects; they kill the others, but the fly prefers them to sugar. No method of actually exterminating
the fly and getting your house thoroughly rid of him has ever been discovered. When our modern fashion of screening all the doors and windows was
introduced, it was supposed that we were now done with the fly, and that we
had defeated him at last, along with the mosquito. It was not so. Those other
creatures have to stay outside nowadays, but the fly remains a member of
the family just as before.

A week or two ago we hunted down every fly in my bedroom and took his
life; then we closed the doors and kept them closed night and day. I believed I
was now rid of the pest for good and all, and I was jubilant. It was premature.
When I woke the next morning there was a congregation of flies all about me
waiting for breakfast—flies that had been visiting the hog-pen, and the hospital, and all places where disease, decay, corruption and death are to be found,
and had come with their beaks and their legs fuzzy with microbes gathered
from wounds and running sores and ulcers, and were ready and eagerly waiting to wipe off these accumulations upon the butter, and thus accomplish the
degraded duty wherewith Nature—man's persistent and implacable enemy—
had commissioned them.

It was matter for astonishment. The screens were perfect; the doors had
been kept closed; how did the creatures get into the room? Upon consultation
it was determined that they must have come down the chimney, since there
was certainly no other entrance to the place available. I was jubilant once
more, for now I believed that we could infallibly beat the fly. Militarily speaking, we had him in the last ditch. That was our thought. At once we had a fine
wire screen constructed and fitted closely and exactly into the front of the
fireplace, whereby that entrance was effectually closed. During the day we

destroyed all the flies in the room. At night we laid the wood fire and placed the screen. Next morning I had no company for breakfast and was able to eat it in peace at last. The fire had been lighted and was flaming hospitably and companionably up. Then presently I saw that our guess as to how the flies got in had been correct, for they had now begun to come down the chimney, in spite of the fire and smoke, and assemble on the inside of the screen. It was almost unbelievable that they had ventured to descend through all that fire and smoke, but that is what they had done. I suppose there is nothing that a fly is afraid of. His daring makes all other courage seem cheap and poor. Now that I know that he will go through fire to attain his ends it is my conviction that there are no perils for him in this earth that he does not despise.

But for my deep prejudices, I should have admired those daring creatures. I should have felt obliged to admire them. And indeed I would have admired them anyway if they could have departed a little from the inborn insolence and immodesty of their nature and behaved themselves in a humble and winning Christian way for once. But they were flies, and they couldn't do that. Their backs were scorching with the heat—I knew it, I could see it—yet with an ill-timed and offensive ostentation they pretended to like it. It is a vain, mean-spirited and unpleasant creature. You cannot situate a fly in any circumstances howsoever shameful and grotesque that he will not try to show off.

We assailed the screen with brooms and wet towels and things and tried to dislodge those flies and drive them into the fire, but it only amused them. A fly can get amusement out of anything you can start. They took it for a game, and they played it with untiring assiduity and enjoyment. As always, they beat the game. As always, man gave it up and the fly prevailed. It was cold, and by and by we were obliged to take away the screen so that we could mend the fire. Then they all plunged into the room with a hurrah and said they were glad to see us, and explained that they would have come earlier but that they had been delayed by unforeseen circumstances.

However, we have hopes. By noon the fire had been out a couple of hours, the screen had been replaced, and there were no flies on the inside of it. This meant a good deal—it seemed to mean a good deal, at any rate—and so we have a new scheme now. When we start a fire mornings, hereafter, we sha'n't mend it again that day. I will freeze, rather. As many flies may come down and gather on the screen and show off as may desire to do it, but there they will remain. We sha'n't admit them to the room again, and when the fire goes down they will retire up the chimney and distribute elsewhere the wanton and malicious persecutions for which they were created.

The flea never associates with me—has never shown even a passing desire for my company, and so I have none but the friendliest feeling toward him. The mosquito troubles me but little, and I feel nothing but a mild dislike for him. Of all the animals that inhabit the earth, the air, and the waters, I hate only one—and that is the house fly. But I do hate him. I hate him with a hatred that is not measurable with words. I always spare the snake and the spider, and the others, and would not intentionally give them pain, but I would go out of my way, and put aside my dearest occupation, to kill a fly, even if I knew it was the very last one. I can even bear to see a fly suffer for an entire minute—even two minutes, if it is one that I have spent an hour hunting around the place with a wet towel—but that is the limit. I would like to see him suffer a year, and would do it, and gladly, if I could restrict the suffering to himself; but after it reaches a certain point, and the bulk of it begins to fall to my share, I have to call a halt and put him out of his misery, for I am like the rest of my race—I am merciful to a fellow-creature upon one condition only: that its pain shall not confer pain upon *me.*

I have watched the human race with close attention for five and twenty years now, and I know beyond shadow of doubt that we can stand the pain of another creature straight along, without discomfort, until its pain gives *us* pain. Then we become immediately and creditably merciful. I suppose it is a pity that we have no higher motive for sparing pain to a fellow creature, still it is the cold truth—we have no higher one. We have no vestige of pity, not a single shred of it, for any creature's misery until it reaches the point where the contemplation of it inflicts misery upon ourselves. This remark describes every human being that has ever lived.

After improving my marksmanship with considerable practice with a towel, this morning, I slapped a couple of flies into the wash-bowl. With deep satisfaction I watched them spin around and around in the water. Twice they made land and started to climb up the bowl, but I shoved them back with fresh satisfaction and plunged them under with my finger, with more satisfaction. I went on gloating over their efforts to get out of their trouble. Twice more they made land, and in both instances I restored them to their activities in the water. But at last their struggles relaxed and the forlorn things began to exhibit pitiful signs of exhaustion and despair. This pathetic spectacle gave *me* pain, and I recognized that I had reached my limit. I cared not a rap for their sufferings as long as they furnished enjoyment for me, but when they began to inflict pain upon me, that was another matter. The conditions had become personal. I was human, and by the law of my make it was not possible for me to allow myself to suffer when I could prevent it. I had to put the flies out of their troubles, I couldn't help it. I turned a soap-dish over them, and when I looked under it half an hour later I perceived that the spiritual part of them had ascended to the happy hunting grounds of their fathers.

ॐ

Mrs. Clemens Corners the Market in Flies

MONDAY, OCTOBER 15, 1906.

From Susy's Biography of Me.

Sept. 9th, '85.

Mamma is teaching Jean a little natural history and is making a little collection of insects for her. But mamma does not allow Jean to kill any insects she only collects those insects that are found dead. Mamma has told us all, perticulary Jean, to bring her all the little dead insects that she finds. The other day as we were all sitting at supper Jean broke into the room and ran triumfantly up to Mamma and presented her with a plate full of dead flies. Mamma thanked Jean very enthusiastically although she with difficulty concealed her amusement. Just then Sour Mash entered the room and Jean believing her hungry asked Mamma for permission to give her the flies. Mamma laughingly consented and the flies almost immediately disappeared.

Sour Mash's presence indicates that this adventure occurred at Quarry Farm. Susy's Biography interests itself pretty exclusively with historical facts; where they happen is not a matter of much concern to her. When other historians refer to the Bunker Hill Monument they know it is not necessary to mention that that monument is in Boston. Susy recognizes that when she mentions Sour Mash it is not necessary to localize her. To Susy, Sour Mash is the Bunker Hill Monument of Quarry Farm.

Ordinary cats have some partiality for living flies, but none for dead ones; but Susy does not trouble herself to apologize for Sour Mash's eccentricities of taste. This Biography was for *us*, and Susy knew that nothing that Sour Mash might do could startle us or need explanation, we being aware that she was not an ordinary cat, but moving upon a plane far above the prejudices and superstitions which are law to common catdom.

Once in Hartford the flies were so numerous for a time, and so troublesome, that Mrs. Clemens conceived the idea of paying George* a bounty on all the flies he might kill. The children saw an opportunity here for the acquisition of sudden wealth. They supposed that their mother merely wanted to accumulate dead flies, for some aesthetic or scientific reason or other, and they judged that the more flies she could get, the happier she would be; so they went into the business with George on a commission. Straightway the dead flies began to arrive in such quantities that Mrs. Clemens was pleased beyond words with the success of her idea. Next, she was astonished that one house could furnish so many. She was paying an extravagantly high bounty, and it presently began to look as if by this addition to our expenses we were now probably living beyond our income. After a few days there was peace and comfort; not a fly was discoverable in the house; there wasn't a straggler left. Still, to Mrs. Clemens's surprise, the dead flies continued to arrive by the plateful, and the bounty-expense was as crushing as ever. Then she made inquiry, and found that our innocent little rascals had established a Fly Trust, and had hired all the children in the neighborhood to collect flies on a cheap and unburdensome commission.

Mrs. Clemens's experience in this matter was a new one for her, but the governments of the world had tried it, and wept over it, and discarded it, every half-century since man was created. Any Government could have told her that the best way to increase wolves in America, rabbits in Australia, and snakes in India, is to pay a bounty on their scalps. Then every patriot goes to raising them.

ça

The Edisons of the Animal World

Instinct and Thought

YOUNG MAN. It is odious. Those drunken theories of yours, advanced a while ago—concerning the rat and all that—strip Man bare of all his dignities, grandeurs, sublimities.

OLD MAN. He hasn't any to strip—they are shams, stolen clothes. He claims credits which belong solely to his Maker.

---

*The colored butler.

Y.M. But you have no right to put him on a level with the rat.

O.M. I don't—morally. That would not be fair to the rat. The rat is well above him, there.

Y.M. Are you joking?

O.M. No, I am not.

Y.M. Then what do you mean?

O.M. That comes under the head of the Moral Sense. It is a large question. Let us finish with what we are about now, before we take it up.

Y.M. Very well. You have seemed to concede that you place Man and the rat on *a* level. What is it? The intellectual?

O.M. In form—not in degree.

Y.M. Explain.

O.M. I think that the rat's mind and the man's mind are the same machine, but of unequal capacities—like yours and Edison's; like the African pygmy's and Homer's; like the Bushman's and Bismarck's.

Y.M. How are you going to make that out, when the lower animals have no mental quality but instinct, while man possesses reason?

O.M. What is instinct?

Y.M. It is merely unthinking and mechanical exercise of inherited habit.

O.M. What originated the habit?

Y.M. The first animal started it, its descendants have inherited it.

O.M. How did the first one come to start it?

Y.M. I don't know; but it didn't *think* it out.

O.M. How do you know it didn't?

Y.M. Well—I have a right to suppose it didn't, anyway.

O.M. I don't believe you have. What is thought?

Y.M. I know what you call it: the mechanical and automatic putting together of impressions received from the outside, and drawing an inference from them.

O.M. Very good. Now my idea of the meaningless term "instinct" is, that it is merely *petrified thought*; thought solidified and made inanimate by habit; thought which was once alive and awake, but is become unconscious—walks in its sleep, so to speak.

Y.M. Illustrate it.

O.M. Take a herd of cows, feeding in a pasture. Their heads are all turned in one direction. They do that instinctively; they gain nothing by it, they have no reason for it, they don't know why they do it. It is an inherited habit which was originally thought—that is to say, observation of an exterior fact, and a valuable inference drawn from that observation and confirmed by experience. The original wild ox noticed that with the wind in his favor he could smell his enemy in time to escape; then he inferred that it was worth while to keep his nose to the wind. That is the process which man calls reasoning. Man's thought-machine works just like the other animals', but it is a better one and more Edisonian. Man, in the ox's place, would go further, reason wider: he would face a part of the herd the other way and protect both front and rear.

Y.M. Did you say the term instinct is meaningless?

O.M. I think it is a bastard word. I think it confuses us; for as a rule it applies itself to habits and impulses which had a far-off origin in thought, and now and then breaks the rule and applies itself to habits which can hardly claim a thought-origin.

Y.M. Give an instance.

O.M. Well, in putting on trousers a man always inserts the same old leg first—never the other one. There is no advantage in that, and no sense in it. All men do it, yet no man thought it out and adopted it of set purpose, I imagine. But it is a habit which is transmitted, no doubt, and will continue to be transmitted.

Y.M. Can you prove that the habit exists?

O.M. You can prove it, if you doubt. If you will take a man to a clothing store and watch him try on a dozen pairs of trousers, you will see.

Y.M. The cow-illustration is not—

O.M. Sufficient to show that a dumb animal's mental machine is just the same as a man's and its reasoning-processes the same? I will illustrate further. If you should hand Mr. Edison a box which you caused to fly open by some concealed device, he would infer a spring, and would hunt for it and find it. Now an uncle of mine had an old horse who used to get into the closed lot where the corn-crib was and dishonestly take the corn. I got the punishment myself, as it was supposed that I had heedlessly failed to insert the wooden pin which kept the gate closed. These persistent punishments fatigued me; they also caused me to infer the existence of a culprit, somewhere; so I hid myself and watched the gate. Presently the horse came and pulled out the pin with his teeth and went in. Nobody taught him that; he had observed—then thought it out for himself. His process did not differ from Edison's; he put this and that together and drew an inference—and the peg, too; but I made him sweat for it.

Y.M. It has something of the seeming of thought about it. Still, it is not very elaborate. Enlarge.

O.M. Suppose that Edison has been enjoying some one's hospitalities. He comes again, by and by, and the house is vacant. He infers that his host has moved. A while afterward, in another town, he sees the man enter a house; he infers that that is the new home, and follows to inquire. Here, now, is the experience of a gull, as related by a naturalist. The scene is a Scotch fishing vil-lage where the gulls were kindly treated. This particular gull visited a cottage;

was fed; came next day and was fed again; came into the house, next time, and ate with the family; kept on doing this almost daily, thereafter. But once the gull was away on a journey for a few days, and when it returned the house was vacant. Its friends had removed to a village three miles distant. Several months later it saw the head of the family on the street there, followed him home, entered the house without excuse or apology, and became a daily guest again. Gulls do not rank high, mentally, but this one had memory and the reasoning faculty, you see, and applied them Edisonially.

Y.M. Yet it was not an Edison and couldn't be developed into one.

O.M. Perhaps not; could you?

Y.M. That is neither here nor there. Go on.

O.M. If Edison were in trouble and a stranger helped him out of it and next day he got into the same difficulty again, he would infer the wise thing to do in case he knew the stranger's address. Here is a case of a bird and a stranger as related by a naturalist. An Englishman saw a bird flying around about his dog's head, down in the grounds, and uttering cries of distress. He went there to see about it. The dog had a young bird in his mouth—unhurt. The gentleman rescued it and put it on a bush and brought the dog away. Early the next morning the mother-bird came for the gentleman, who was sitting on his verandah, and by its maneuvers persuaded him to follow it to a distant part of the grounds—flying a little way in front of him and waiting for him to catch up, and so on; and keeping to the winding path, too, instead of flying the near way across lots. The distance covered was four hundred yards. The same dog was the culprit; he had the young bird again, and once more he had to give it up. Now the mother-bird had reasoned it all out: since the stranger had helped her once, she inferred that he would do it again; she knew where to find him, and she went upon her errand with confidence. Her mental processes were what Edison's would have been. She put this and that together—and that is all that thought *is*—and out of them built her logical arrangement of inferences. Edison couldn't have done it any better himself.

Y.M. Do you believe that many of the dumb animals can think?

O.M. Yes—the elephant, the monkey, the horse, the dog, the parrot, the macaw, the mocking-bird, and many others. The elephant whose mate fell into a pit, and who dumped dirt and rubbish into the pit till the bottom was raised high enough to enable the captive to step out, was equipped with the reasoning quality. I conceive that all animals that can learn things through teaching and drilling have to know how to observe, and put this and that together and draw an inference—the process of thinking. Could you teach an idiot the manual of arms, and to advance, retreat, and go through complex field-maneuvers at the word of command?

Y.M. Not if he were a thorough idiot.

O.M. Well, canary birds can learn all that; dogs and elephants learn all sorts of wonderful things. They must surely be able to notice, and to put things together, and say to themselves, "I get the idea, now: when I do so and so, as per order, I am praised and fed; when I do differently, I am punished." Fleas can be taught nearly anything that a Congressman can.

Y.M. Granting, then, that dumb creatures are able to think upon a low plane, is there any that can think upon a high one? Is there one that is well up toward man?

O.M. Yes. As a thinker and planner the ant is the equal of any savage race of men; as a self-educated specialist in several arts she is the superior of any savage race of men; and in one or two high mental qualities she is above the reach of any man, savage or civilized.

Y.M. O, come! you are abolishing the intellectual frontier which separates man and beast.

O.M. I beg your pardon. One cannot abolish what does not exist.

Y.M. You are not in earnest, I hope. You cannot mean to seriously say there is no such frontier.

O.M. I do say it seriously. The instances of the horse, the gull, the mother-bird and the elephant show that those creatures put their this's and that's together just as Edison would have done it and drew the same inferences that he would have drawn. Their mental machinery was just like his, also its manner of working. Their equipment was as inferior to his, in elaboration, as a Waterbury is inferior to the Strasburg clock, but that is the only difference—there is no frontier.

Y.M. It looks exasperatingly true; and is distinctly offensive. It elevates the dumb beast to—to—

O.M. Let us drop that lying phrase, and call them the Unrevealed Creatures; so far as we can know, there is no such thing as a dumb beast.

Y.M. On what grounds do you make that assertion?

O.M. On quite simple ones. "Dumb" beast suggests an animal that has no thought-machinery, no understanding, no speech, no way of communicating what is in its mind. We know that a hen *has* speech. We cannot understand everything she says, but we easily learn two or three of her phrases. We know when she is saying "I've laid an egg;" we know when she is saying to the chicks, "Run here, dears, I've found a worm;" we know what she is saying when she voices a warning: "Quick! hurry! gather yourselves under mamma, there's a hawk coming!" We understand the cat when she stretches herself out, purring with affection and contentment and lifts up a soft voice and says, "Come, kitties, supper's ready;" we understand her when she goes mourning about

and says "Where can they be?—they are lost—won't you help me hunt for them?" and we understand the disreputable Tom when he challenges at midnight from his shed: "You come over here, you product of immoral commerce, and I'll make your fur fly!" We understand a few of a dog's phrases, and we learn to understand a few of the remarks and gestures of any bird or other animal that we domesticate and observe. The clearness and exactness of the few of the hen's speeches which we understand is argument that she can communicate to her kind a hundred things which we cannot comprehend—in a word, that she can converse. And this argument is also applicable in the case of others of the great army of the Unrevealed. It is just like man's vanity and impertinence to call an animal dumb because it is dumb to his dull perceptions. Now as to the ant—

Y.M. Yes, go back to the ant, the creature that—as you seem to think—sweeps away the last vestige of an intellectual frontier between man and the Unrevealed.

O.M. That is what she surely does. In all his history the aboriginal Australian never thought out a house for himself and built it. The ant is an amazing architect. She is a wee little creature, but she builds a strong and enduring house eight feet high—a house which is as large in proportion to her size as is the largest capitol or cathedral in the world compared to man's size. No savage race has produced architects who could approach the ant in genius or culture. No civilized race has produced architects who could plan a house better for the uses proposed than can hers. Her house contains a throne room; nurseries for her young; granaries; apartments for her soldiers, her workers, etc.; and they and the multifarious halls and corridors which communicate with them are arranged and distributed with an educated and experienced eye for convenience and adaptability.

Y.M. That could be mere instinct.

O.M. It would elevate the savage much above what he is, if he had it. But let us look further before we decide. The ant has soldiers—battalions, regiments, armies; and they have their appointed captains and generals, who lead them to battle.

Y.M. That could be instinct, too.

O.M. We will look still further. The ant has a system of government; it is well planned, elaborate, and is well carried on.

Y.M. Instinct again.

O.M. She has crowds of slaves, and is a hard and unjust employer of forced labor.

Y.M. Instinct.

O.M. She has cows, and milks them.

Y.M. Instinct, of course.

O.M. In Texas she lays out a farm twelve feet square, plants it, weeds it, cultivates it, gathers the crop and stores it away.

Y.M. Instinct, all the same.

O.M. The ant discriminates between friend and stranger. Sir John Lubbock took ants from two different nests, made them drunk with whisky and laid them, unconscious, by one of the nests, near some water. Ants from the nest came and examined and discussed these disgraced creatures, then carried their friends home and threw the strangers overboard. Sir John repeated the experiment a number of times. For a while the sober ants did as they had done at first—carried their friends home and threw the strangers overboard. But finally they lost patience, seeing that their reformatory efforts went for nothing, and threw both friends and strangers overboard. Come—is this instinct, or is it thoughtful and intelligent discussion of a thing new—absolutely new—to their experience; with a verdict arrived at, sentence passed, and judgment executed? Is it instinct?—thought petrified by ages of habit—or isn't it brand-new thought, inspired by the new occasion, the new circumstances?

Y.M. I have to concede it. It was not a result of habit; it has all the look of reflection, thought, putting this and that together, as you phrase it. I believe it was thought.

O.M. I will give you another instance of thought. Franklin had a cup of sugar on a table in his room. The ants got at it. He tried several preventives; and ants rose superior to them. Finally he contrived one which shut off access—probably set the table's legs in pans of water, or drew a circle of tar around the cup, I don't remember. At any rate he watched to see what they would do. They tried various schemes—failures, every one. The ants were badly puzzled. Finally they held a consultation, discussed the problem, arrived at a decision—and this time they beat that great philosopher. They formed in procession, crossed the floor, climbed the wall, marched across the ceiling to a point just over the cup, then one by one they let go and fell down into it! Was that instinct—thought petrified by ages of inherited habit?

Y.M. No, I don't believe it was. I believe it was a newly-reasoned scheme to meet a new emergency.

o.m. Very well. You have conceded the reasoning power in two instances. I come now to a mental detail wherein the ant is a long way the superior of any human being. Sir John Lubbock proved by many experiments that an ant knows a stranger-ant of her own species in a moment, even when the stranger is disguised—with paint. Also, he proved that an ant knows every individual in her hive of 500,000 souls. Also, that after a year's absence of one of the 500,000 she will straightway recognize the returned absentee and grace the recognition with an affectionate welcome. How were these recognitions made? Not by color, for painted ants were recognized. Not by smell, for ants that had been dipped in chloroform were recognized. Not by speech and not by antennæ—signs nor contacts, for the drunken and motionless ants were recognized and the friend discriminated from the stranger. The ants were all of the one species, therefore the friends had to be recognized by form and feature—friends who formed part of a hive of 500,000! Has any man a memory for form and feature approaching that?

y.m. Certainly not.

o.m. Franklin's ants and Lubbock's ants show fine capacities of putting this and that together in new and untried emergencies and deducing smart conclusions from the combinations—a man's mental process exactly. With memory to help, man preserves his observations and reasonings, reflects upon them, adds to them, re-combines, and so proceeds, stage by stage, to far results—from the tea-kettle to the ocean greyhound's complex engine; from personal labor to slave labor; from wigwam to palace; from the capricious chase to agriculture and stored food; from nomadic life to stable government and concentrated authority; from incoherent hordes to massed armies. The ant has observation, the reasoning faculty, and the preserving adjunct of a prodigious memory; she has duplicated man's development and the essential features of his civilization, and you call it all instinct!

y.m. Perhaps I lacked the reasoning faculty myself.

o.m. Well, don't tell anybody, and don't do it again.

y.m. We have come a good way. As a result—as I understand it—I am required to concede that there is absolutely no intellectual frontier separating Man and the Unrevealed Creatures?

o.m. That is what you are required to concede. There is no such frontier—there is no way to get around that. Man has a finer and more capable machine in him than those others, but it is the same machine and works in the same way. And neither he nor those others can command the machine—it is strictly automatic, independent of control, works when it pleases, and when it doesn't please, can't be forced.

y.m. Then man and the other animals are all alike, as to mental machinery, and there isn't any difference of any stupendous magnitude between them, except in quality, not in kind.

o.m. That is about the state of it—intellectually. There are pronounced limitations on both sides. We can't learn to understand much of their language, but the dog, the elephant, etc., learn to understand a very great deal of ours. To that extent they are our superiors. On the other hand they can't learn reading, writing, etc., nor any of our fine and high things, and there we have a large advantage over them.

y.m. Very well, let them have what they've got, and welcome; there is still a wall, and a lofty one. They haven't the Moral Sense; we have it, and it lifts us immeasurably above them.

o.m. What makes you think that?

y.m. Now look here—let us call a halt. I have stood the other infamies and insanities and that is enough; I am not going to have man and the other animals put on the same level morally.

o.m. I wasn't going to hoist man up to that.

y.m. This is too much! I think it is not right to jest about such things.

o.m. I am not jesting, I am merely reflecting a plain and simple truth—and without uncharitableness. The fact that man knows right from wrong proves his *intellectual* superiority to the other creatures; but the fact that he can *do* wrong proves his *moral* inferiority to any creature that *cannot.* It is my belief that this position is not assailable.

&

A Horse's Tale

Part I

I. Soldier Boy—privately to Himself

I am Buffalo Bill's horse. I have spent my life under his saddle—with him in it, too, and he is good for two hundred pounds, without his clothes; and there is no telling how much he does weigh when he is out on the war path and has his batteries belted on. He is over six feet, is young, hasn't an ounce of waste flesh, is straight, graceful, springy in his motions, quick as a cat, and has a handsome face, and black hair dangling down on his shoulders, and is beautiful to look at; and nobody is braver than he is, and nobody is stronger, except myself. Yes, a person that doubts that he is fine to see, should see him in his beaded buckskins, on my back and his rifle peeping above his

shoulder, chasing a hostile trail, with me going like the wind and his hair streaming out behind from the shelter of his broad slouch. Yes, he is a sight to look at, then—and I'm part of it myself.

I am his favorite horse, out of dozens. Big as he is, I have carried him eighty-one miles between nightfall and sunrise on the scout; and I am good for fifty, day in and day out, and all the time. I am not large, but I am built on a business basis. I have carried him thousands and thousands of miles on scout duty for the army, and there's not a gorge, nor a pass, nor a valley, nor a fort, nor a trading post, nor a Buffalo range in the whole sweep of the Rocky Mountains and the Great Plains that we don't know as well as we know the bugle-calls. He is Chief of Scouts to the Army of the Frontier, and it makes us very important. In such a position as I hold in the military service, one needs to be of good family and possess an education much above the common, to be worthy of the place. I am the best educated horse outside of the hippodrome, everybody says, and the best mannered. It may be so, it is not for me to say; modesty is the best policy, I think. Buffalo Bill taught me the most of what I know, my mother taught me much, and I taught myself the rest. Lay a row of moccasins before me,—Pawnee, Sioux, Shoshone, Cheyenne, Blackfoot, and as many other tribes as you please—and I can name the tribe every moccasin belongs to, by the make of it. Name it in horse-talk, and could do it in American if I had speech.

I know some of the Indian signs—the signs they make with their hands, and by signal fires at night and columns of smoke by day. Buffalo Bill taught me how to drag wounded soldiers out of the line of fire with my teeth; and I've done it, too; at least I've dragged *him* out of the battle when he was wounded. And not just once, but twice. Yes, I know a lot of things. I remember forms, and gaits, and faces; and you can't disguise a person that's done me a kindness so that I won't know him thereafter wherever I find him. I know the art of searching for a trail, and I know the stale track from the fresh. I can keep a trail all by myself, with Buffalo Bill asleep in the saddle; ask him—he will tell you so. Many a time, when he has ridden all night, he has said to me at dawn, "Take the watch, Boy; if the trail freshens, call me." Then he goes to sleep. He knows he can trust me, because I have a reputation. A scout-horse that has a reputation does not play with it.

My mother was all American—no alkali-spider about *her*, I can tell you; she was of the best blood of Kentucky, the bluest Blue Grass aristocracy, very proud and acrimonious—or maybe it is ceremonious, I don't know which it is. But it is no matter, size is the main thing about a word, and that one's up to standard. She spent her military life as colonel of the Tenth dragoons, and saw a deal of rough service—distinguished service it was, too. I mean, she *carried* the colonel; but it's all the same; where would he be without his horse? He wouldn't arrive. It takes two to make a colonel of dragoons. She was a fine dragoon-horse, but never got above that. She was strong enough for the scout-service, and had the endurance, too, but she couldn't quite come up to the speed required; a scout-horse has to have steel in his muscle and lightning in his blood.

My father was a broncho. Nothing, as to lineage—that is, nothing as to recent lineage, but plenty good enough when you go a good way back. When professor Marsh was out here hunting bones for the chapel of Yale university he found skeletons of horses no bigger than a fox, bedded in the rocks, and he said they were ancestors of my father. My mother heard him say it; and he said those skeletons were two million years old, which astonished her and made her Kentucky pretensions look small and pretty antiphonal, not to say oblique. Let me see . . . . I used to know the meaning of those words, but . . . . well, it was years ago, and 't isn't as vivid now as it was when they were fresh. That sort of words doesn't keep, in the kind of climate we have out here. Professor Marsh said those skeletons were fossils. So, that makes me part blue-grass and part fossil; if there is any older or better stock, you will have to look for it among the Four Hundred, I reckon. I am satisfied with it. And am a happy horse, too, though born out of wedlock.

And now we are back at Fort Paxton once more, after a forty-day scout, away up as far as the Big Horn. Everything quiet. Crows and Blackfeet squabbling—as usual—but no outbreaks, and settlers feeling fairly easy.

The Seventh Cavalry still in garrison, here; also the Ninth dragoons, two artillery companies, and some infantry. All glad to see me; including General Alison, commandant. The officers' ladies and children well, and called upon me—with sugar. Col. Drake, Seventh cavalry, said some pleasant things; Mrs. Drake was very complimentary; also Captain and Mrs. Marsh, Company B, Seventh cavalry; also the chaplain, who is always kind and pleasant to me, because I kicked the lungs out of a trader once. It was Tommy Drake and Fanny Marsh that furnished the sugar—nice children, the nicest at the post, I think.

That poor orphan child is on her way from France—everybody is full of the subject. Her father was General Alison's brother; married a beautiful young Spanish lady ten years ago, and has never been in America since. They lived in Spain a year or two, then went to France. Both died, some months ago. This little girl that is coming is the only child. General Alison is glad to have her. He has never seen her. He is a very nice old bachelor, but

is an old bachelor just the same and isn't more than about a year this side
of retirement by age-limit; and so what does he know about taking care of
a little maid nine years old? If I could have her it would be another matter,
for I know all about children, and they adore me. Buffalo Bill will tell you
so himself.

I have some of this news from overhearing the garrison-gossip, the rest of it
I got from Potter, the General's dog. Potter is the great Dane. He is privileged,
all over the post, like Shekels, the 7th Cavalry's dog, and visits everybody's
quarters and picks up everything that is going, in the way of news. Potter has
no imagination, and no great deal of culture, perhaps, but he has a historical
mind and a good memory, and so he is the person I depend upon mainly to
post me up when I get back from a scout. That is, if Shekels is out on depreda-
tion and I can't get hold of him.

II. Letter from Rouen—to General Alison

My dear Brother-in-Law. Please let me write again in Spanish, I cannot trust my
English, and I am aware from what your brother used to say, that army officers
educated at the military Academy of the United States are taught our tongue. It
is as I told you in my other letter: both my poor sister and her husband, when
they found they could not recover, expressed the wish that you should have
their little Catherine,—as knowing that you would presently be retired from
the army—rather than that she should remain with me, who am broken in
health, or go to your mother, in California, whose health is also frail.

You do not know the child, therefore I must tell you something about her.
You will not be ashamed of her looks, for she is a copy in little, of her beautiful mother—and it is that Andalusian beauty which is not surpassable, even
in your country. She has her mother's charm and grace and good heart and
sense of justice, and she has her father's vivacity and cheerfulness and pluck
and spirit of enterprise, with the affectionate disposition and sincerity of both
parents.

My sister pined for her Spanish home all these years of exile; she was always
talking of Spain to the child, and tending and nourishing the love of Spain in
the little thing's heart as a precious flower; and she died happy in the knowledge that the fruitage of her patriotic labors was as rich as even she could
desire.

Cathy is a sufficiently good little scholar, for her nine years, her mother
taught her Spanish herself, and kept it always fresh upon her ear and her
tongue by hardly ever speaking with her in any other tongue; her father was

her English teacher, and talked with her in that language almost exclusively; French has been her every-day speech for more than seven years among her playmates here; she has a good working use of governess-German and Italian. It is true that there is always a faint foreign fragrance about her speech, no matter what language she is talking, but it is only just noticeable, nothing more, and is rather a charm than a mar, I think. In the ordinary child-studies Cathy is neither before nor behind the average child of nine, I should say. But I can say this for her: in love for her friends, and in high-mindedness and good-heartedness she has not many equals, and in my opinion no superiors. And I beg of you, let her have her way with the dumb animals—they are her worship. It is an inheritance from her mother. She knows but little of cruelties and oppressions—keep them from her sight if you can. She would flare up at them and make trouble, in her small but quite decided and resolute way; for she has a character of her own, and lacks neither promptness nor initiative. Sometimes her judgment is at fault, but I think her intentions are always right. Once when she was a little creature of three or four years she suddenly brought her tiny foot down upon the floor in an apparent outbreak of indignation, then fetched it a backward wipe, and stooped down to examine the result. Her mother said—

"Why, what is it, child? What has stirred you so?"

"Mamma, the big ant was trying to kill the little one."

"And so you protected the little one."

"Yes, mamma, because he had no friend, and I wouldn't let the big one kill him."

"But you have killed them both."

Cathy was distressed, and her lip trembled. She picked up the remains and laid them upon her palm, and said—

"Poor little anty, I'm so sorry; and I didn't mean to kill you, but there wasn't any other way to save you, it was such a hurry."

She is a dear and sweet little lady, and when she goes it will give me a sore heart. But she will be happy with you, and if your heart is old and tired, give it into her keeping; she will make it young again, she will refresh it, she will make it sing. Be good to her, for all our sakes!

My exile will soon be over, now. As soon as I am a little stronger I shall see my Spain again; and that will make *me* young again!

Mercedes.

III. General Alison to his Mother

I am glad to know that you are all well, in San Bernardino.

* * * That grandchild of yours has been here—well, I do not quite know how many days it is, nobody can keep account of days or anything else where she is! Mother, she did what the Indians were never able to do, she took the Fort—took it the first day! Took me, too; took the colonels, the captains, the women, the children, and the dumb brutes; took Buffalo Bill, and all his scouts; took the garrison—to the last man; and in forty-eight hours the Indian encampment was hers, illustrious old Thunder-Bird and all. Do I seem to have lost my solemnity, my gravity, my poise, my dignity? You would lose your own, in my circumstances. Mother, you never saw such a winning little devil. She is all energy, and spirit, and sunshine, and interest in everybody and everything, and pours out her prodigal love upon every creature that will take it, high or low, Christian or pagan, feathered or furred; and none has declined it to date, and none ever will, I think. But she has a temper, and sometimes it catches fire and flames up, and is likely to burn whatever is near it, but it is soon over, the passion goes as quickly as it comes. Of course she has an Indian name already; Indians always re-christen a stranger early. Thunder-Bird attended to her case. He gave her the Indian equivalent for Fire-bug, or firefly. He said—

"'Times, ver' quiet, ver' soft, like summer night, but when she mad she blaze."

Isn't it good? Can't you see the flare? She's beautiful, mother, beautiful as a picture; and there is a touch of you in her face, and of her father—poor George! and in her unresting activities, and her fearless ways, and her sunbursts and cloud-bursts, she is always bringing George back to me. These impulsive natures are dramatic. George was dramatic, so is this Lightning-Bug, so is Buffalo Bill. When Cathy first arrived—it was in the forenoon—Buffalo Bill was away, carrying orders to Major Fuller, at Five Forks, up in the Clayton hills. At mid-afternoon I was at my desk, trying to work, and this sprite had been making it impossible for half an hour. At last I said—

"Oh, you bewitching little scamp, *can't* you be quiet just a minute or two, and let your poor old uncle attend to a part of his duties?"

"I'll try, uncle; I will, indeed," she said.

"Well, then, that's a good child—kiss me. Now, then, sit up in that chair, and set your eye on that clock. There—that's right. If you stir—if you so much as wink—for four whole minutes, I'll bite you!"

It was very sweet and humble and obedient she looked, sitting there, still as a mouse; I could hardly keep from setting her free and telling her to make as much racket as she wanted to. During as much as two minutes there was a most unnatural and heavenly quiet and repose, then Buffalo Bill came thundering up to the door in all his scout finery, flung himself out of the saddle, said to his horse, "Wait for me, Boy," and stepped in, and stopped dead in his tracks—gazing at the child. She forgot orders, and was on the floor in a moment, saying—

"Oh, you are so beautiful! Do you like me?"

"No, I don't, I love you!" and he gathered her up with a hug, and then set her on his shoulder—apparently nine feet from the floor.

She was at home. She played with his long hair, and admired his big hands and his clothes and his carbine, and asked question after question, as fast as he could answer, until I excused them both for half an hour, in order to have a chance to finish my work. Then I heard Cathy exclaiming over Soldier Boy; and he was worthy of her raptures, for he is a wonder of a horse, and has a reputation which is as shining as his own silken hide.

IV. *Cathy to her Aunt Mercedes*

Oh, it is wonderful here, aunty dear, just paradise! Oh, if you could only see it! everything so wild and lovely; such grand plains, stretching such miles and miles and miles, all the most delicious velvety sand and sagebrush, and rabbits as big as a dog, and such tall and noble jackassful ears that that is what they name them by; and such vast mountains, and so rugged and craggy and lofty, with cloud-shawls wrapped around their shoulders, and looking so solemn and awful and satisfied; and the charming Indians, oh, how you would dote on them, aunty dear, and they would on you, too, and they would let you hold their babies, the way they do me, and they *are* the fattest, and brownest, and sweetest little things, and never cry, and wouldn't if they had pins sticking in them, which they haven't, because they are poor and can't afford it; and the horses and mules and cattle and dogs—hundreds and hundreds, and hundreds, and not an animal that you can't do what you please with, except uncle Thomas, but *I* don't mind him, he's lovely; and oh, if you could hear the bugles: *too—too—too-too—too—too*, and so on—per-fectly beautiful! Do you recognize that one? It's the first toots of the *reveille*; it goes, dear-me, *so* early in the morning!—then I, and every other soldier on the whole place are up (is up?) and out in a minute, except uncle Thomas, who is most unaccountably lazy, I don't know why, but I have talked to him about it, and I reckon it will be better, now. He hasn't any faults much, and is charming and sweet, like Buffalo Bill, and Thunder-Bird, and mammy Dorcas, and Soldier

Boy, and Shekels, and Potter, and Sour-Mash, and—well, they're *all* that, just angels, as you may say.

The very first day I came, I don't know how long ago it was, Buffalo Bill took me on Soldier Boy to Thunder-Bird's camp, not the big one which is out on the plain, which is White Cloud's, he took me to *that* one next day, but this one is four or five miles up in the hills and crags, where there is a great shut-in meadow, full of Indian lodges and dogs and squaws and everything that is interesting, and a brook of the clearest water running through it, with white pebbles on the bottom and trees all along the banks cool and shady and good to wade in, and as the sun goes down it is dimmish in there, but away up against the sky you see the big peaks towering up and shining bright and vivid in the sun, and sometimes an eagle sailing by them, not flapping a wing, the same as if he was asleep, and young Indians and girls romping and laughing and carrying on, around the spring and the pool, and not much clothes on except the girls, and dogs fighting, and the squaws busy at work, and the bucks busy resting, and the old men sitting in a bunch smoking, and passing the pipe not to the left but to the right, which means there's been a row in the camp and they are settling it if they can, and children playing *just* the same as any other children, and little boys shooting at a mark with bows, and I cuffed one of them because he hit a dog with a club that wasn't doing anything, and he resented it but before long he wished he hadn't, but this sentence is getting too long and I will start another. Thunder-Bird put on his Sunday-best war-outfit to let me see him, and he was splendid to look at, with his face painted red and bright and intense like a fire-coal and a valance of eagle feathers from the top of his head all down his back, and he had his tomahawk, too, and his pipe, which has a stem which is longer than my arm, and I never had such a good time in an Indian camp in my life, and I learnt a lot of words of the language, and next day BB took me to the camp out on the Plains, four miles, and I had another good time and got acquainted with some more Indians and dogs; and the big chief, by the name of White Cloud, gave me a pretty little bow and arrows and I gave him my red sash-ribbon, and in four days I could shoot very well with it and beat any white boy of my size at the post; and I have been to those camps plenty of times since; and I have learned to ride, too, BB taught me, and every day he practices me and praises me, and every time I do better than ever he lets me have a scamper on Soldier Boy, and *that's* the last agony of pleasure! for he is the charmingest horse, and so beautiful and shiny and black, and hasn't another color on him anywhere, except a white star in his forehead, not just an imitation star, but a real one, with four points, shaped exactly like a star that's hand-made, and if you should cover him all up but his star you would know him anywhere, even in Jerusalem or Australia by that. And I got acquainted with a good many of the Seventh Cavalry, and the dragoons, and officers, and families, and horses, in the first few days, and some more in the next few and the next few and the next few, and now I know more soldiers and horses than you can think, no matter how hard you try. I am keeping up my studies every now and then, but there isn't much time for it. I love you so! and I send you a hug and a kiss.

Cathy.

P.S.–I belong to the Seventh cavalry, and Ninth dragoons, I am an officer, too, and do not have to work on account of not getting any wages.

V. General Alison to Mercedes

She has been with us a good nice long time, now. You are troubled about your sprite because this is such a wild frontier, hundreds of miles from civilization, and peopled only by wandering tribes of savages? You fear for her safety? Give yourself no uneasiness about her. Dear me, she's in a nursery! and she's got more than eighteen hundred nurses. It would distress the garrison to suspect that you think they can't take care of her. They think they can. They would tell you so themselves. You see, the Seventh Cavalry has never had a child of its very own before, and neither has the Ninth Dragoons; and so they are like all new mothers, they think there is no other child like theirs, no other child so wonderful, none that is so worthy to be faithfully and tenderly looked after and protected. These bronzed veterans of mine are very good mothers, I think, and wiser than some other mothers; for they let her take lots of risks, and it is a good education for her; and the more risks she takes and comes successfully out of, the prouder they are of her. They adopted her, with grave and formal military ceremonies of their own invention—solemnities is the truer word; solemnities that were so profoundly solemn and earnest, that the spectacle would have been comical if it hadn't been so touching. It was a good show, and as stately and complex as guard-mount and the trooping of the colors; and it had its own special music, composed for the occasion by the band-master of the Seventh; and the child was as serious as the most serious war-worn soldier of them all; and finally when they throned her upon the shoulder of the oldest veteran, and pronounced her "well and truly adopted," and the bands struck up and all saluted and she saluted in return, it was better and more moving than any kindred thing I have seen on the stage, because stage-things are make-believe, but this was real and the players' hearts were in it.

It happened several weeks ago, and was followed by some additional solemnities. The men created a couple of new ranks, thitherto unknown to the army regulations, and conferred them upon Cathy, with ceremonies suitable to a duke. So now she is Corporal-General of the Seventh Cavalry, and Flag-Lieutenant of the Ninth Dragoons, with the privilege (decreed by the men) of writing U.S.A. after her name! Also, they presented her a pair of shoulder-straps—both dark blue, the one with F.L. on it, the other with C.G. Also, a sword. She wears them. Finally, they granted her the *salute*. I am witness that that ceremony is faithfully observed by both parties—and most gravely and decorously, too. I have never seen a soldier smile yet, while delivering it, nor Cathy in returning it.

Ostensibly I was not present at these proceedings, and am ignorant of them; but I was where I could see. I was afraid of one thing—the jealousy of the other children of the post; but there is nothing of that, I am glad to say. On the contrary they are proud of their comrade and her honors. It is a surprising thing, but it is true. The children are devoted to Cathy, for she has turned their dull frontier life into a sort of continuous festival; also they know her for a staunch and steady friend, a friend who can always be depended upon, and does not change with the weather.

She has become a rather extraordinary rider, under the tutorship of a more than extraordinary teacher—BB, which is her pet name for Buffalo Bill. She pronounces it *bee*by. He has not only taught her seventeen ways of breaking her neck, but twenty-two ways of avoiding it. He has infused into her the best and surest protection of a horseman—*confidence*. He did it gradually, systematically, little by little, a step at a time, and each step made sure before the next was essayed. And so he inched her along up through terrors that had been discounted by training before she reached them, and therefore were not recognizable as terrors when she got to them. Well, she is a daring little rider, now, and is perfect in what she knows of horsemanship. By and by she will know the art like a West Point cadet, and will exercise it as fearlessly. She doesn't know anything about side-saddles. Does that distress you? And she is a fine performer, without any saddle at all. Does that discomfort you? Do not let it; she is not in any danger, I give you my word.

You said that if my heart was old and tired she would refresh it, and you said truly. I do not know how I got along without her, before. I was a forlorn old tree, but now that this blossoming vine has wound itself about me and become the life of my life, it is very different. As a furnisher of business for me and for Mammy Dorcas she is exhaustlessly competent, but I like my share of it and of course Dorcas likes hers, for Dorcas "raised" George, and Cathy is

George over again in so many ways that she brings back Dorcas's youth and the joys of that long-vanished time. My father tried to set Dorcas free twenty years ago, when we still lived in Virginia, but without success; she considered herself a member of the family, and wouldn't go. And so, a member of the family she remained, and has held that position unchallenged ever since, and holds it now; for when my mother sent her here from San Bernardino when we learned that Cathy was coming, she only changed from one division of the family to the other. She has the warm heart of her race, and its lavish affections, and when Cathy arrived the pair were mother and child in five minutes, and that is what they are to date and will continue. Dorcas really thinks she raised George, and that is one of her prides, but perhaps it was a mutual raising, for their ages were the same—thirteen years short of mine. But they were playmates, at any rate; as regards that, there is no room for dispute.

Cathy thinks Dorcas is the best Catholic in America except herself. She could not pay any one a higher compliment than that, and Dorcas could not receive one that would please her better. Dorcas is satisfied that there has never been a more wonderful child than Cathy. She has conceived the curious idea that Cathy is *twins*, and that one of them is a boy-twin and failed to get segregated—got submerged, is the idea. To argue with her that this is nonsense is a waste of breath—her mind is made up, and arguments do not affect it. She says—

"Look at her: she loves dolls, and girl-plays, and everything a girl loves, and she's gentle and sweet, and ain't cruel to dumb brutes—now that's the girl-twin; but she loves boy-plays, and drums and fifes and soldiering, and rough-riding, and ain't afraid of anybody or anything—and that's the boy-twin; 'deed you needn't tell *me* she's only *one* child; no sir, she's twins, and one of them got shet up out of sight. Out of sight, but that don't make any difference, that boy is in there, and you can see him look out of her eyes when her temper is up."

Then Dorcas went on, in her simple and earnest way, to furnish illustrations.

"Look at that raven, marse Tom. Would anybody befriend a raven but that child? Of course they wouldn't, it ain't natural. Well, the Injun boy had the raven tied up, and was all the time plaguing it and starving it, and she pitied the po' thing, and tried to buy it from the boy, and the tears was in her eyes. That was the girl-twin, you see. She offered him her thimble, and he flung it down; she offered him all the doughnuts she had, which was two, and he flung them down; she offered him half a paper of pins, worth forty ravens, and he made a mouth at her and jabbed one of them in the raven's back. That was the limit, you know. It called for the other twin. Her eyes blazed up, and she jumped for him like a wildcat, and when she was done with him she was rags and he warn't anything but an allegory. That was most undoubtedly the other twin, you see, coming to the front. No sir, don't tell *me* he ain't in there, I've seen him with my own eyes—and plenty of times, at that."

"Allegory? What is an allegory?"

"I don't know, marse Tom, it's one of her words, she loves the big ones, you know, and I pick them up from her; they sound good and I can't help it."

"What happened after she had converted the boy into an allegory?"

"Why, she untied the raven and confiscated him by force and fetched him home, and left the doughnuts and things on the ground. Petted him, of course, like she does with every creature. In two days she had him so stuck after her that she—well, *you* know how he follows her everywhere, and sets on her shoulder often when she rides her break-neck rampages—all of which is the girl-twin to the front, you see—and he does what he pleases, and is up to all kinds of devilment, and is a perfect nuisance in the kitchen. Well, they all stand it, but they wouldn't if it was another person's bird." [. . .]

VI. Soldier Boy and the Mexican Plug

"When did you come?"

"Arrived at sundown."

"Where from?"

"Salt Lake."

"Are you in the service?"

"No. Trade."

"Pirate trade, I reckon."

"What do you know about it?"

"I saw you when you came. I recognized your master. He is a bad sort. Trap-robber, horse-thief, squaw-man, renegado—Hank Butters—I know him very well. Stole you, didn't he?"

"Well, it amounted to that."

"I thought so. Where is his pard?"

"He stopped at White Cloud's camp."

"He is another of the same stripe, is Blake Haskins." (*Aside.*) They are laying for Buffalo Bill again, I guess. (*Aloud.*) "What is your name?"

"Which one?"

"Have you got more than one?"

"I get a new one every time I'm stolen. I used to have an honest name, but that was early; I've forgotten it. Since then I've had thirteen *aliases*."

"Aliases? What is alias?"

"A false name."

"Alias. It's a fine large word, and is in my line; it has quite a learned and cerebro-spinal incandescent sound. Are you educated?"

"Well, no, I can't claim it. I can take down bars, I can distinguish oats from shoe-pegs, I can blaspheme a saddle-boil with the college-bred, and I know a few other things—not many; I have had no chance, I have always had to work; besides, I am of low birth and no family. You speak my dialect like a native, but you are not a Mexican Plug, you are a gentleman, I can see that; and educated, of course."

"Yes, I am of old family, and not illiterate. I am a fossil."

"A which?"

"Fossil. The first horses were fossils. They date back two million years."

"Gr-eat sand and sage brush! do you mean it?"

"Yes, it is true. The bones of my ancestors are held in reverence and worship, even by men. They do not leave them exposed to the weather when they find them, but carry them three thousand miles and enshrine them in their temples of learning, and worship them."

"It is wonderful! I knew you must be a person of distinction, by your fine presence and courtly address, and by the fact that you are not subjected to the indignity of hobbles, like myself and the rest. Would you tell me your name?"

"You have probably heard of it—Soldier Boy."

"What!—the renowned, the illustrious?"

"Even so."

"It takes my breath! Little did I dream that ever I should stand face to face with the possessor of that great name. Buffalo Bill's horse! Known from the Canadian border to the deserts of Arizona, and from the eastern marches of the Great Plains to the foot-hills of the Sierra! Truly this is a memorable day. You still serve the celebrated Chief of Scouts?"

"I am still his property, but he has lent me, for a time, to the most noble, the most gracious, the most excellent, her Excellency Catherine, Corporal-General 7th Cavalry, and Flag-Lieutenant 9th Dragoons, U.S.A.,—on whom be peace!"

"Amen. Did you say *her* Excellency?"

"The same. A Spanish lady, sweet blossom of a ducal house. And truly a wonder; knowing everything, capable of everything; speaking all the languages, master of all sciences, a mind without horizons, a heart of gold, the glory of her race! On whom be peace!"

"Amen. It is marvelous!"

"Verily. I knew many things, she has taught me others. I am educated. I will tell you about her."

"I listen—I am enchanted."

"I will tell a plain tale, calmly, without excitement, without eloquence. When she had been here four or five weeks she was already erudite in military things, and they made her an officer—a double officer. She rode the drill every day, like any soldier; and she could take the bugle and direct the evolutions herself. Then, on a day, there was a grand race, for prizes—none to enter but the children. Seventeen children entered, and she was the youngest. Three girls, fourteen boys—good riders all. It was a steeple chase, with four hurdles, all pretty high. The first prize was a most cunning half-grown silver bugle, and mighty pretty, with red silk cord and tassels. Buffalo Bill was very anxious; for he had taught her to ride, and he did most dearly want her to win that race, for the glory of it. So he wanted her to ride me, but she wouldn't; and she reproached him, and said it was unfair and unright, and taking advantage; for what horse in this post or any other could stand a chance against me? and she was very severe with him, and said, 'You ought to be ashamed—you are proposing to me conduct unbecoming an officer and a gentleman.' So he just tossed her up in the air about thirty feet and caught her as she came down, and said he *was* ashamed; and put up his handkerchief and pretended to cry, which nearly broke her heart, and she petted him, and begged him to forgive her, and said she would do anything in the world he could ask but that; but he said he ought to go hang himself, and he *must*, if he could get a rope, it was nothing but right he should, for he never never could forgive himself; and then *she* began to cry, and they both sobbed and sobbed, the way you could hear him a mile, and she clinging around his neck and pleading, till at last he was comforted a little, and gave his solemn promise he wouldn't hang himself till after the race; and wouldn't do it at all if she won it, which made her happy, and she said she would win it or die in the saddle; so then everything was pleasant again and both of them content. He can't help playing jokes on her, he is so fond of her and she is so innocent and unsuspecting; and when she finds it out she cuffs him and is in a fury, but presently forgives him because it's *him*; and maybe the very next day she's caught with another joke; you see she can't learn any better, because she hasn't any deceit in her, and that kind aren't ever expecting it in another person.

"It was a grand race. The whole post was there, and there was such another whooping and shouting when the seventeen kids came flying down the turf and sailing over the hurdles—oh, beautiful to see! Half-way down, it was kind of neck-and-neck, and anybody's race and nobody's. Then, what should happen but a cow steps out and puts her head down to munch grass, with her broadside to the battalion and they a-coming like the wind; they split apart to flank her, but *she?*—why, she drove the spurs home and soared over that cow like a bird! and on she went, and cleared the last hurdle solitary and alone, the army letting loose the grand yell, and she skipped from the horse the same as if he had been standing still, and made her bow, and everybody crowded around to congratulate, and they gave her the bugle, and she put it to her lips and blew 'boots and saddles' to see how it would go, and BB was as proud as you can't think! And he said, 'Take Soldier Boy, and don't pass him back till I ask for him!' and I can tell you he wouldn't have said that to any other person on this planet. That was two months and more ago, and nobody has been on my back since but the Corporal-General 7th Cavalry and Flag-Lieutenant of the 9th Dragoons, U.S.A.,—on whom be peace!"

"Amen. I listen—tell me more."

"She set to work and organized the Sixteen, and called it the First Battalion Rocky Mountain Rangers, U.S.A., and she wanted to be bugler, but they elected her Lieutenant General *and* Bugler. So she ranks her uncle the commandant, who is only a Brigadier. And doesn't she train those little people! Ask the Indians, ask the traders, ask the soldiers, they'll tell you. She has been at it from the first day. Every morning they go clattering down into the plain, and there she sits on my back with her bugle at her mouth and sounds the orders and puts them through the evolutions for an hour and more; and it is too beautiful for anything, to see those ponies dissolve from one formation into another, and waltz about, and break, and scatter, and form again, always moving, always graceful, now trotting, now galloping, and so on, sometimes near by, sometimes in the distance, all just like a state ball, you know, and sometimes she can't hold herself any longer, but sounds the 'charge,' and turns me loose! and you can take my word for it, if the battalion hasn't *too* much of a start we catch up and go over the breastworks with the front line.

"Yes, they are soldiers, those little people; and healthy, too, not ailing any more, the way they used to be sometimes. It's because of her drill. She's got a fort, now—Fort Fanny Marsh. Major General Tommy Drake planned it out, and the Seventh and the Dragoons built it. Tommy is the Colonel's son, and is fifteen and the oldest in the Battalion; Fanny Marsh is Brigadier General, and is next oldest—over thirteen. She is daughter of Capt. Marsh, Co. B, Seventh Cavalry. Lieutenant General Alison is the youngest by considerable; I think she is about nine and a half or three-quarters. Her military rig, as Lieutenant General, isn't for business, it's for dress parade, because the ladies made it. They say they got it out of the Middle Ages—out of a book—and it is all red and blue and white silks and satins and velvets; tights, trunks, sword, doublet, with slashed sleeves, short cape, cap with just one feather in it; I've heard them name these things, they got them out of the book; she's dressed like a page, of old times, they say. It's the daintiest outfit that ever was—you will say so, when you see it. She's lovely in it—oh, just a dream! In some ways she is just her age, but in others she's as old as her uncle, I think. She is very learned. She teaches her uncle his book. I have seen her sitting by with the book and reciting to him what is in it, so that he can learn to do it himself.

"Every Saturday she hires little Injuns to garrison her fort, then she lays siege to it, and makes military approaches by make-believe trenches in make-believe night, and finally at make-believe dawn she draws her sword and sounds the assault and takes it by storm. It is for practice. And she has invented a bugle-call all by herself, out of her own head, and it's a stirring one, and the prettiest in the service. It's to call *me*—it's never used for anything else. She taught it to me, and told me what it says: '*It is I, Soldier—come!*' and when those thrilling notes come floating down the distance, I hear them without fail, even if I am two miles away; and then—oh, then you should see my heels get down to business!

"And she has taught me how to say good-morning and good-night to her, which is by lifting my right hoof for her to shake; and also how to say good-bye; I do that with my left foot—but only for practice, because there hasn't been any but make-believe good-bying yet, and I hope there won't ever be. It would make me cry, if I ever had to put up my left foot in earnest. She has taught me how to salute, and I can do it as well as a soldier. I bow my head low, and lay my right hoof against my cheek. She taught me that because I got into disgrace once, through ignorance. I am privileged, because I am known to be honorable and trustworthy, and because I have a distinguished record in the service; so they don't hobble me nor tie me to stakes or shut me tight in stables, but let me wander around to suit myself. Well, trooping the colors is a very solemn ceremony, and everybody must stand uncovered when the flag goes by, the commandant and all; and once I was there, and ignorantly walked across right in front of the band, which was an awful disgrace. Ah, the Lieutenant-General was so ashamed, and so distressed that I should have done such a thing before all the world, that she couldn't keep the tears back; and then she taught me the salute, so that if I ever did any other unmilitary act through ignorance I could do my salute and she believed everybody would think it was apology enough and would not press the matter. It is very nice and distinguished; no other horse can do it; often the men salute me, and I return it. I am privileged to be present when the Rocky Mountain Rangers troop the colors, and I stand solemn, like the children, and I salute when the flag goes by. Of course when she goes to her fort her sentries sing out 'turn out the guard!' and then . . . . do you catch that refreshing early-morning whiff from the mountain-pines and the wild flowers? The night is far spent, we'll hear the bugles before long. Dorcas

the black woman is very good and nice; she takes care of the Lieutenant-General, and is Brigadier General Alison's mother, which makes her mother-in-law to the Lieutenant General. That is what Shekels says. At least it is what I think he says, though I never can understand him quite clearly. He—"

"Who is Shekels?"

"The Seventh Cavalry's dog. I mean, if he *is* a dog. His father was a cuyote, and his mother was a wildcat. It doesn't really make a dog out of him, does it?"

"Not a real dog, I should think. Only a kind of a general dog, at most, I reckon. Though this is a matter of ichthyology, I suppose; and if it is, it is out of my depth, and so my opinion is not valuable, and I don't claim much consideration for it."

"It isn't ichthyology, it is dogmatics, which is still more difficult and tangled up. Dogmatics always are."

"Dogmatics is quite beyond me, quite; so I am not competing. But on general principles it is my opinion that a colt out of a cuyote and a wildcat is no square dog, but doubtful. That is my hand, and I stand pat."

"Well, it is as far as I can go myself, and be fair and conscientious. I have always regarded him as a doubtful dog, and so has Potter. Potter is the great Dane. Potter says he is no dog, and not even poultry—though I do not go quite so far as that."

"And I wouldn't, myself. Poultry is one of those things which no person can get to the bottom of, there is so much of it and such variety. It is just wings, and wings, and wings, till you are weary: turkeys, and geese, and bats, and butterflies, and angels, and grasshoppers, and flying-fish, and—well, there is really no end to the tribe, it gives me the heaves just to think of it. But this one hasn't any wings, has he?"

"No."

"Well, then, in my belief he is more likely to be dog than poultry. I have not heard of poultry that hadn't wings. Wings is the *sign* of poultry, it is what you tell poultry by. Look at the mosquito."

"What do you reckon he is, then? he must be something."

"Why, he could be a reptile; anything that hasn't wings is a reptile."

"Who told you that?"

"Nobody told me, but I overheard it."

"Where did you overhear it?"

"Years ago. I was out with the Philadelphia Institute expedition in the Bad Lands under professor Cope, hunting mastodon-bones, and I overheard him say, his own self, that any plantigrade circumflex vertebrate backterium that hadn't wings and was uncertain was a reptile. Well, then, has this dog any wings? No. Is he a plantigrade circumflex vertebrate bacterium? Maybe so, maybe not; but without ever having seen him, and judging only by his illegal and spectacular parentage, I will bet the odds of a bale of hay to a bran mash that he looks it. Finally, is he uncertain? That is the point—is he uncertain? I will leave it to you if you have ever heard of a more uncertainer dog than what this one is?"

"No, I never have."

"Well, then, he's a reptile. That's settled."

"Why, look here, whatsyourname—"

"Last alias, Mongrel."

"A good one, too. I was going to say, you are better educated than you have been pretending to be. I like cultured society, and I shall cultivate your acquaintance. Now as to Shekels, whenever you want to know about any private thing that is going on at this post or in White Cloud's camp or Thunder-Bird's, he can tell you; and if you make friends with him he'll be glad to, for he is a born gossip, and picks up all the tittle-tattle. Being the whole Seventh Cavalry's reptile, he doesn't belong to anybody in particular, and hasn't any military duties; so he comes and goes as he pleases, and is popular with all the house-cats and other authentic sources of private information. He understands all the languages, and talks them all, too. With an accent like gritting your teeth, it is true, and with a grammar that is no improvement on blasphemy—still, with practice you get at the meat of what he says, and it serves . . . . Hark! that's the reveille . . . .

*The Reveille**

---

*At West Point the bugle is supposed to be saying

"I can't get 'em up,
I can't get 'em up,
I can't get 'em up in the mor . . . ning!"

Faint and far, but isn't it clear, isn't it sweet? There's no music like the bugle to stir the blood, in the still solemnity of the morning twilight, with the dim plains stretching away to nothing and the spectral mountains slumbering against the sky. You'll hear another note in a minute—faint and far and clear, like the other one, and sweeter still, you'll notice. Wait . . . . listen. There it goes! It says,—'*It is I, Soldier—come!*' . . . .

"Soldier Boy's" Bugle-Call

. . . . now then, watch me leave a blue streak behind!"

VII. Soldier Boy and Shekels

"Did you do as I told you? Did you look up the Mexican Plug?"

"Yes, I made his acquaintance before night and got his friendship."

"I liked him; did you?"

"Not at first. He took me for a reptile, and it troubled me, because I didn't know whether it was a compliment or not. I couldn't ask him, because it would look ignorant. So I didn't say anything, and soon liked him very well indeed. Was it a compliment, do you think?"

"Yes, that is what it was. They are very rare, the reptiles; very few left, nowadays."

"Is that so? What is a reptile?"

"It is a plantigrade circumflex vertebrate bacterium that hasn't any wings and is uncertain."

"Well, it—it sounds fine, it surely does."

"And it *is* fine. You may be thankful you are one."

"I am. It seems wonderfully grand and elegant for a person that is so humble as I am, but I am thankful, I am indeed, and will try to live up to it. It is hard to remember; will you say it again, please, and say it slow?"

"Plantigrade circumflex vertebrate bacterium that hasn't any wings and is uncertain."

"It *is* beautiful, anybody must grant it; beautiful, and of a noble sound; I hope it will not make me proud and stuck-up—I should not like to be that. It is much more distinguished and honorable to be a reptile than a dog, don't you think, Soldier?"

"Why there's no comparison. It is awfully aristocratic. Often a duke is called a reptile; it is set down so, in history."

"Isn't that grand! Potter wouldn't ever associate with me, but I reckon he'll be glad to when he finds out what I am."

"You can depend upon it."

"I will thank Mongrel for this. He is a very good sort, for a Mexican Plug, don't you think he is?"

"It is my opinion of him; and as for his birth, he cannot help that. We cannot all be reptiles, we cannot all be fossils; we have to take what comes, and be thankful it is no worse. It is the true philosophy."

"For those others?"

"Stick to the subject, please. Did it turn out that my suspicions were right?"

"Yes, perfectly right. Mongrel has heard them planning. They are after BB's life, for running them out of Medicine Bow and taking their stolen horses away from them."

"Well, they'll get him yet, for sure."

"Not if he keeps a sharp lookout."

"*He* keep a sharp lookout! He never does; he despises them, and all their kind. His life is always being threatened, and so it has come to be monotonous."

"Does he know they are here?"

"Oh, yes, he knows it. He is always the earliest to know who comes and who goes. But he cares nothing for them and their threats, he only laughs when people warn him. They'll shoot him from behind a tree the first he knows. Did Mongrel tell you their plans?"

"Yes. They have found out that he starts for Fort Clayton day after tomorrow, with one of his scouts; so they will leave to-morrow, letting on to go south, but they will fetch around north all in good time."

"Shekels, I don't like the look of it."

VIII. The Scout-start. BB and Lt. Gen. Alison

BB (*saluting.*) "Good! handsomely done! the Seventh couldn't beat it! You do certainly handle your Rangers like an expert, General. And where are you bound?"

"Four miles on the trail to Fort Clayton."

"Glad am I, dear! What's the idea of it?"

"Guard of honor for you and Thorndike."

"Bless—your—*heart!* I'd rather have it from you than from the Commander-in-Chief of the Armies of the United States, you incomparable little soldier!—and I don't need to take any oath to that, for you to believe it."

"I *thought* you'd like it, BB."

"*Like* it? well, I should say so! Now, then—all ready—sound the advance, and away we go!"

IX. Soldier Boy and Shekels, again

"Well, this is the way it happened. We did the escort-duty; then we came back and struck for the plain and put the Rangers through a rousing drill—oh, for hours! Then we sent them home under Brigadier General Fanny Marsh; then the Lieutenant General and I went off on a gallop over the plains for about three hours, and were lazying along home in the middle of the afternoon, when we met Jimmy Slade, the drummer boy, and he saluted and asked the Lieutenant General if she had heard the news, and she said no, and he said—

"'Buffalo Bill has been ambushed and badly shot, this side of Clayton, and Thorndike the scout, too; Bill couldn't travel, but Thorndike could, and he brought the news, and sergeant Wilkes and six men of Company B are gone, two hours ago, hot foot, to get Bill. And they say—'

"'*Go!*' she shouts to me—and I went."

"Fast?"

"Don't ask foolish questions. It was an awful pace. For four hours nothing happened, and not a word said, except that now and then she said, 'keep it up, Boy, keep it up, sweetheart, we'll save him!' I kept it up. Well, when the dark shut down, in the rugged hills, that poor little chap had been tearing around in the saddle all day, and I noticed by the slack knee-pressure that she was tired and tottery, and I got dreadfully afraid, but every time I tried to slow down and let her go to sleep, so I could stop, she hurried me up again; and so, sure enough, at last over she went!

"Ah, that was a fix to be in! for she lay there and didn't stir, and what was I to do? I couldn't leave her to fetch help, on account of the wolves. There was nothing to do but stand by. It was dreadful. I was afraid she was killed, poor little thing. But she wasn't. She came to, by and by, and said, 'kiss me, Soldier,' and those were blessed words. I kissed her—often; I am used to that, and we like it. But she didn't get up, and I was worried. She fondled my nose with her hand, and talked to me, and called me endearing names—which is her way—but she caressed with the same hand all the time. The other arm was broken, you see, but I didn't know it, and she didn't mention it. She didn't want to distress me, you know.

"Soon the big gray wolves came, and hung around, and you could hear them snarl, and snap at each other, but you couldn't see anything of them except their eyes, which shone in the dark like sparks and stars. The Lieutenant General said, 'If I had the Rocky Mountain Rangers here, we would make those creatures climb a tree.' Then she made believe that the Rangers were in hearing, and put up her bugle and blew the assembly; and then boots and saddles; then the trot! gallop!—*charge!* Then she blew the retreat, and said, 'that's for you, you rebels, the Rangers don't ever retreat!'

"The music frightened them away, but they were hungry, and kept coming back. And of course they got bolder and bolder, which is their way. It went on for an hour, then the tired child went to sleep, and it was pitiful to hear her moan and nestle and I couldn't do anything for her. All the time, I was laying for the wolves. They are in my line; I have had experience. At last the boldest one ventured within my lines and I landed him among his friends with some of his skull still on him, and they did the rest. In the next hour I got a couple more, and they went the way of the first one, down the throats of the detachment. That satisfied the survivors, and they went away and left us in peace.

"We hadn't any more adventures, though I kept awake all night and was ready. From midnight on, the child got very restless, and out of her head, and moaned, and said, 'Water, water—thirsty;' and now and then 'kiss me, Soldier,' and sometimes she was in her fort and giving orders to her garrison; and once she was in Spain, and thought her mother was with her. People say a horse can't cry; but they don't know, because we cry inside.

"It was an hour after sun-up that I heard the boys coming, and recognized the hoof-beats of Pomp and Caesar and Jerry, old mates of mine; and a welcomer sound there couldn't ever be. Buffalo Bill was in a horse-litter, with his leg broken by a bullet, and Mongrel and Blake Haskins's horse were doing the work. Buffalo Bill and Thorndike had killed both of those toughs.

"When they got to us, and Buffalo Bill saw the child lying there so white, he said, 'My God!' and the sound of his voice brought her to herself and she gave a little cry of pleasure and struggled to get up, but couldn't, and the soldiers gathered her up like the tenderest women, and their eyes were wet and they were not ashamed, when they saw her arm dangling; and so were Buffalo Bill's, and when they laid her in his arms, he said, 'My darling, how does this come?' and she said, 'We came to save you, but I was tired, and couldn't keep awake, and fell off and hurt myself, and couldn't get on again.' 'You came to save me, you dear little rat? it was too lovely of you!' 'Yes, and Soldier stood by me, which you know he would, and protected me from the wolves; and if he got a chance he kicked the life out of some of them—for you know he would, BB.' The sergeant said, 'he laid out three of them sir, and here's the bones to show for it.' 'He's a grand horse,' said BB, 'he's the grandest horse that ever was! and has saved your life, Lieutenant General Alison, and shall protect it the rest of his life—he's yours, for a kiss!' He got it, along with a passion of delight, and he said, 'you are feeling better, now, little Spaniard—do you think you could blow the advance?' She put up the bugle to do it, but he said wait a minute, first. Then he and the sergeant set her arm, and put it in splints, she wincing but not whimpering; then we took up the march for home, and that's the end of the tale; and I'm her horse. Isn't she a brick, Shekels?"

"Brick? She's more than a brick, more than a thousand bricks—she's a reptile!"

"It's a compliment out of your heart, Shekels. God bless you for it!"

X. General Alison and Dorcas

"Too much company for her, marse Tom. Betwixt you, and Shekels, the colonel's wife, and the Cid—"

"The Cid? Oh, I remember—the raven."

"—and Mrs. Captain Marsh, and Famine and Pestilence the baby *cuyotes*, and Sour-Mash and her pups, and Sardanapalus and her kittens—hang these names she gives the creatures, they warp my jaw—and Potter: you-all sitting around *in* the house, and Soldier Boy at the window the entire time, it's a wonder to me she comes along as well as she does. She—"

"You want her all to yourself, you stingy old thing!"

"Marse Tom, you know better. It's too much company. And then the idea of her receiving reports all the time from her officers, and acting upon them, and giving orders, the same as if she was well, it ain't good for her, and the surgeon don't like it, and tried to persuade her not to and couldn't; and when he *ordered* her, she was that outraged and indignant, and was very severe on him, and accused him of insubordination, and said it didn't become him to give orders to an officer of her rank. Well, he saw he had excited her more and done more harm than all the rest put together, so he was vexed at himself and wished he had kept still. Doctors *don't* know much, and that's a fact. She's too much interested in things—she ought to rest more. She's all the time sending messages to BB, and to soldiers and Injuns and what-not, and to the animals."

"To the animals?"

"Yes, sir."

"Who carries them?"

"Sometimes Potter, but mostly it's Shekels."

"Now come! who can find fault with such pretty make-believe as that?"

"But it ain't make-believe, marse Tom, she does send them."

"Yes, I don't doubt that part of it."

"Do you doubt they get them, sir?"

"Certainly. Don't you?"

"No, sir. Animals talk to one another, I know it perfectly well, marse Tom, and I ain't saying it by guess, I've *seen* them do it. Yes, sir, many's the time."

"What a curious superstition!"

"It ain't a superstition, marse Tom. Look at that Shekels—look at him, *now*. Is he listening, or ain't he? *Now* you see! he's turned his head away. It's because he was caught—caught in the act. I'll ask you—could a Christian look any more ashamed than what he looks now?—*lay down!* You see? he was going to sneak out. Don't tell *me*, marse Tom! If animals don't talk, I miss *my* guess. And Shekels is the worst. He goes and tells the animals everything that happens in the officers' quarters; and if he's short of facts, he invents them. He hasn't any more principle than a blue-jay; and as for morals, he's empty. Look at him now; look at him grovel. He knows what I am saying, and he knows it's the truth. You see, yourself, that he can feel shame; it's the only virtue he's got. It's wonderful how they find out everything that's going on—the animals. They—" [. . . .]

XI. *Several Months Later. Antonio and Thorndike*

"Thorndike, isn't that Plug you're riding an asset of the scrap you and Buffalo Bill had with the late Blake Haskins and his pal a few months back?"

"Yes, this is Mongrel—and not a half bad horse, either."

"I've noticed he keeps up his lick first-rate. Say—isn't it a gaudy morning!"

"Right you are!"

"Thorndike, it's Andalusian! and when that's said, all's said."

"Andalusian *and* Oregonian, Antonio! Put it that way, and you have my vote. Being a native up there, I know. You being Andalusian-born—"

"Can speak with authority for that patch of paradise? Well, I can. Like the Don! like Sancho! This is the correct Andalusian dawn, now—crisp, fresh, dewy, fragrant, pungent—

> 'What though the spicy breezes
> Blow soft o'er Ceylon's isle'

—*git* up, you old cow! stumbling like that when we've just been praising you! out on a scout and can't live up to the honor any better than that? Antonio, how long have you been out here in the Plains and the Rockies?"

"More than thirteen years."

"It's a long time. Don't you ever get homesick?"

"Not till now."

"Why *now*?—after such a long cure."

"These preparations of the retiring Commandant's have started it up."

"Of course. It's natural."

"It keeps me thinking about Spain. I know the region where the Seventh's child's aunt lives; I know all the lovely country for miles around; I'll bet I've seen her aunt's villa, many a time; I'll bet I've been in it in those pleasant old times when I was a Spanish gentleman."

"They say the child is wild to see Spain."

"It's so; I know it from what I hear."

"Haven't you talked with her about it?"

"No. I've avoided it. I should soon be as wild as she is. That would not be comfortable."

"I wish I was going, Antonio. There's two things I'd give a lot to see. One's a railroad."

"She'll see one when she strikes Missouri."

"The other's a bull-fight."

"I've seen lots of them; I wish I could see another."

"I don't know anything about it, except in a mixed-up foggy way, Antonio, but I know enough to know it's grand sport."

"The grandest in the world! There's no other sport that begins with it. I'll tell you what I've seen, then you can judge. It was my first, and it's as vivid to me now as it was when I saw it. It was a Sunday afternoon, and beautiful

weather, and my uncle the priest took me, as a reward for being a good boy
and because of my own accord and without anybody asking me I had bank-
rupted my savings-box and given the money to a mission that was civilizing
the Chinese and sweetening their lives and softening their hearts with the
gentle teachings of our religion, and I wish you could have seen what we saw
that day, Thorndike.

"The amphitheatre was packed, from the bull-ring to the highest row—
twelve thousand people in one circling mass, one slanting, solid mass—royalties, nobles, clergy, ladies, gentlemen, state officials, generals, admirals,
soldiers, sailors, lawyers, thieves, merchants, brokers, cooks, housemaids,
scullery-maids, doubtful women, dudes, gamblers, beggars, loafers, tramps,
American ladies, gentlemen, preachers, English ladies, gentlemen, preachers,
German ditto, French ditto, and so-on and so-on, all the world represented:
Spaniards to admire and praise, foreigners to enjoy and go home and find
fault—there they were, one solid, sloping, circling sweep of rippling and flashing color under the down-pour of the summer sun—just a garden, a gaudy,
gorgeous flower-garden! Children munching oranges, six thousand fans fluttering and glimmering, everybody happy, everybody chatting gaily with
their intimates, lovely girl-faces smiling recognition and salutation to other
lovely girl-faces, gray old ladies and gentlemen dealing in the like exchanges
with each other—ah, such a picture of cheery contentment and glad anticipa-
tion! not a mean spirit, nor a sordid soul, nor a sad heart there—ah, Thorndike,
I wish I could see it again.

"Suddenly, the martial note of a bugle cleaves the hum and murmur—clear
the ring!

"They clear it. The great gate is flung open, and the procession marches in,
splendidly costumed and glittering: the marshals of the day, then the pica-
dors on horseback, then the matadors on foot, each surrounded by his qua-
drille of *chulos*. They march to the box of the city fathers, and formally salute.
The key is thrown, the bull-gate is unlocked. Another bugle-blast—the gate
flies open, the bull plunges in, furious, trembling, blinking in the blinding
light, and stands there, a magnificent creature, centre of those multitudinous
and admiring eyes, brave, ready for battle, his attitude a challenge. He sees
his enemy: horsemen sitting motionless, with long spears in rest, upon blindfolded broken-down nags, lean and starved, fit only for sport and sacrifice,
then the carrion-heap.

"The bull makes a rush, with murder in his eye, but a picador meets him
with a spear-thrust in the shoulder. He flinches with the pain, and the picador skips out of danger. A burst of applause for the picador, hisses for the bull.

Some shout 'cow!' at the bull, and call him offensive names. But he is not listening to them, he is there for business; he is not minding the cloak-bearers
that come fluttering around to confuse him; he chases this way, he chases that
way, and hither and yon, scattering the nimble banderillos in every direction
like a spray, and receiving their maddening darts in his neck as they dodge
and fly—oh, but it's a lively spectacle, and brings down the house! Ah, you
should hear the thundering roar that goes up when the game is at its wildest
and brilliant things are done!

"Oh, that first bull, that day, was great! From the moment the spirit of war
rose to flood tide in him and he got down to his work, he began to do wonders. He tore his way through his persecutors, flinging one of them clear over
the parapet; he bowled a horse and his rider down, and plunged straight for
the next, got home with his horns, wounding both horse and man; on again,
here and there and this way and that; and one after another he tore the bowels out of two horses so that they gushed to the ground, and ripped a third
one so badly that although they rushed him to cover and shoved his bowels
back and stuffed the rents with tow and rode him against the bull again he
couldn't make the trip; he tried to gallop, under the spur, but soon reeled and
tottered and fell, all in a heap. For a while, that bull-ring was the most thrilling and glorious and inspiring sight that ever was seen. The bull absolutely
cleared it, and stood there alone! monarch of the place. The people went mad
for pride in him, and joy and delight, and you couldn't hear yourself think,
for the roar and boom and crash of applause."

"Antonio, it carries me clear out of myself, just to hear you tell it; it must
have been perfectly splendid. If I live, I'll see a bull-fight yet, before I die. Did
they kill him?"

"Oh, yes, that is what the bull is for. They tired him out, and got him at last.
He kept rushing the matador, who always slipped smartly and gracefully
aside in time, waiting for a sure chance; and at last it came: the bull made a
deadly plunge for him—was avoided neatly, and as he sped by, the long sword
glided silently into him, between left shoulder and spine—in and in, to the
hilt. He crumpled down, dying."

"Ah, Antonio, it *is* the noblest sport that ever was. I would give a year of my
life to see it. Is the bull always killed?"

"Yes. Sometimes a bull is timid, finding himself in so strange a place, and
he stands trembling, or tries to retreat—then everybody despises him for his
cowardice and wants him punished and made ridiculous; so they hough him
from behind, and it is the funniest thing in the world to see him hobbling
around on his severed legs; the whole vast house goes into hurricanes of

laughter over it; I have laughed till the tears ran down my cheeks to see it. When he has furnished all the sport he can, he is not any longer useful, and is killed."

"Well, it is perfectly grand, Antonio, perfectly beautiful. Burning a nigger don't begin."

XII. Mongrel and the Other Horse

"Sage-Brush, have you been listening?"

"Yes."

"Isn't it strange?"

"Well, no, Mongrel, I don't know that it is."

"Why don't you?"

"I've seen a good many human beings in my time. They are created as they are, they cannot help it. They are only brutal because that is their make; brutes would be brutal, too, if it was *their* make."

"To me, Sage-Brush, man is most strange and unaccountable. Why should he treat dumb animals that way when they are not doing any harm?"

"Man is not always like that, Mongrel; he is kind enough when he is not excited by religion."

"Is the bull fight a religious service?"

"I think so. I have heard so. It is held on Sunday."

(*A reflective pause, lasting some minutes.*) Then—

"When we die, Sage-Brush, do we go to heaven and dwell with man?"

"My father thought not. He believed we do not have to go there unless we deserve it."

Part II. IN SPAIN

XIII. General Alison to his Mother

* * * * It was a prodigious trip, but delightful, of course, through the Rockies and the Black Hills and the mighty sweep of the Great Plains to civilization and the Missouri border—where the railroading began and the delightfulness ended. But no one is the worse for the journey; certainly not Cathy, nor Dorcas nor Soldier Boy; and as for me, I am not complaining.

Spain is all that Cathy had pictured it—and more, she says. She is in a fury of delight, the maddest little animal that ever was, and all for joy. She thinks she remembers Spain, but that is not very likely, I suppose. The two—Mercedes and Cathy—devour each other. It is a rapture of love, and beautiful to see. It is Spanish; that describes it. Will this be a short visit?

No. It will be permanent. Cathy has elected to abide with Spain and her aunt. Dorcas says she (Dorcas) foresaw that this would happen; and also says that she wanted it to happen, and says the child's own country is the right place for her, and that she ought not to have been sent to me, I ought to have gone to her. I thought it insane to take Soldier Boy to Spain, but it was well that I yielded to Cathy's pleadings; if he had been left behind, half of her heart would have remained with him, and she would not have been contented. As it is, everything has fallen out for the best, and we are all satisfied and comfortable. It may be that Dorcas and I will see America again some day; but also it is a case of maybe not [. . . .]

When we rode away, our main body had already been on the road an hour or two—I speak of our camp equipage; but we didn't move off alone: when Cathy blew the advance the Rangers cantered out in column of fours, and gave us escort, and were joined by White Cloud and Thunder-Bird in all their gaudy bravery, and by Buffalo Bill and four subordinate scouts. Three miles away, in the Plains, the Lieutenant General halted, sat her horse like a military statue, the bugle at her lips, and put the Rangers through the evolutions for half an hour; and finally, when she blew the charge, she led it herself. "Not for the last time," she said, and got a cheer, and we said good-bye all around, and faced eastward and rode away.

Postscript. A Day Later. Soldier Boy was stolen last night. Cathy is almost beside herself, and we cannot comfort her. Mercedes and I are not much alarmed about the horse, although this part of Spain is in something of a turmoil, politically, at present, and there is a good deal of lawlessness. In ordinary times the thief and the horse would soon be captured. We shall have them before long, I think.

XIV. Soldier Boy—to Himself

It is five months. Or is it six? My troubles have clouded my memory. I think I have been all over this land, from end to end, and now I am back again since day before yesterday, to that city which we passed through, that last day of our long journey, and which is near her country home. I am a tottering ruin and my eyes are dim, but I recognised it. If she could see me she would know me and sound my call. I wish I could hear it once more; it would revive me, it would bring back her face and the mountains and the free life, and I would come—if I were dying I would come! She would not know *me*, looking as I do, but she would know me by my star. But she will never see me, for they do not let me out of this shabby stable—a foul and miserable place, with most two wrecks like myself for company.

How many times have I changed hands? I think it is twelve times—I cannot remember; and each time it was down a step lower, and each time I got a harsher master. They have been cruel, every one; they have worked me night and day in degraded employments, and beaten me; they have fed me ill, and some days not at all. And so I am but bones, now, with a rough and frowsy skin humped and cornered upon my shrunken body—that skin which was once so glossy, that skin which she loved to stroke with her hand. I was the pride of the mountains and the Great Plains; now I am a scarecrow and despised. These piteous wrecks that are my comrades here say we have reached the bottom of the scale, the final humiliation; they say that when a horse is no longer worth the weeds and discarded rubbish they feed to him, they sell him to the bull-ring for a glass of brandy, to make sport for the people, and perish for their pleasure.

To die—that does not disturb me, we of the service never cared for death. But if I could see her once more! if I could hear her bugle sing again and say "It is I, Soldier—come!"

XV. Gen. Alison, to Mrs. Drake, the Colonel's Wife

* * * * To return, now, to where I was, and tell you the rest. We shall never know how she came to be there; there is no way to account for it. She was always watching for black and shiny and spirited horses—watching, hoping, despairing, hoping again; always giving chase and sounding her call, upon the meagerest chance of a response, and breaking her heart over the disappointment; always inquiring, always interested in sales-stables and horse-accumulations in general. How she got there must remain a mystery.

At the point which I had reached in a preceding paragraph of this account, the situation was as follows: two horses lay dying; the bull had scattered his persecutors for the moment, and stood raging, panting, pawing the dust in clouds over his back, when the man that had been wounded returned to the ring on a remount, a poor blindfolded wreck that yet had something ironically military about his bearing—and the next moment the bull had ripped him open and his bowels were dragging upon the ground and the bull was charging his swarm of pests again. Then came pealing through the air a bugle-call that froze my blood—"*It is I, Soldier—come!*" I turned; Cathy was flying down through the massed people; she cleared the parapet at a bound, and sped toward that riderless horse, who staggered forward toward the remembered sound, but his strength failed, and he fell at her feet, she lavishing kisses upon him and sobbing, the house rising with one impulse, and white with horror! Before help could reach her the bull was back again—

She was never conscious again in life. We bore her home, all mangled and drenched in blood, and knelt by her and listened to her broken and wandering words, and prayed for her passing spirit; and there was no comfort—nor ever will be, I think. But she was happy, for she was far away under another sky, and comrading again with her Rangers, and her animal friends, and the soldiers. Their names fell softly and caressingly from her lips, one by one, with pauses between. She was not in pain, but lay with closed eyes, vacantly murmuring, as one who dreams. Sometimes she smiled, saying nothing; sometimes she smiled when she uttered a name—such as Shekels, or BB, or Potter. Sometimes she was at her fort, issuing commands; sometimes she was careering over the plain at the head of her men; sometimes she was training her horse; once she said, reprovingly, "You are giving me the wrong foot; give me the left—don't you know it is good-bye?"

After this, she lay silent some time; the end was near. By and by she murmured, "tired . . . . sleepy . . . . take Cathy, mamma." Then, "kiss me, Soldier." For a little time she lay so still that we were doubtful if she breathed. Then she put out her hand and began to feel gropingly about; then said, "I cannot find it: blow 'taps.'"* It was the end.

*Taps**

℔

---

*"Lights out."

Man and the Other Animals

As I HAVE SAID, it is my conviction that a person's temperament is a law, an iron law, and has to be obeyed, no matter who disapproves; manifestly, as it seems to me, temperament is a law of God, and is supreme, and takes precedence of all human laws. It is my conviction that each and every human law that exists has one distinct purpose and intention, and only one: to oppose itself to a law of God and defeat it, degrade it, deride it, and trample upon it. We find no fault with the spider for ungenerously ambushing the fly and taking its life; we do not call it murder; we concede that it did not invent its own temperament, its own nature, and is therefore not blamable for the acts which the law of its nature requires and commands. We even concede this large point: that no art and no ingenuity can ever reform the spider and persuade her to cease from her assassinations. We do not blame the tiger for obeying the ferocious law of the temperament which God lodged in him, and which the tiger must obey. We do not blame the wasp for her fearful cruelty in half paralyzing a spider with her sting and then stuffing the spider down a hole in the ground to suffer there many days, while the wasp's nursery gradually torture the helpless creature through a long and miserable death by gnawing rations from its person daily; we concede that the wasp is strictly and blamelessly obeying the law of God as required by the temperament which He has put into her. We do not blame the fox, the blue jay, and the many other creatures that live by theft; we concede that they are obeying the law of God promulgated by the temperament with which He provided for them. We do not say to the ram and the goat "Thou shall not commit adultery," for we know that ineradicably embedded in their temperament—that is to say in their born nature—God has said to them "thou *shalt* commit it."

If we should go on until we had singled out and mentioned the separate and distinct temperaments which have been distributed among the myriads of the animal world, we should find that the conduct reputation of each species is determined by one special and prominent trait; and then we should find that all of these traits, and all the shadings of these many traits, have also been distributed among mankind; that in every man a dozen or more of these traits exist, and that in many men traces and shadings of the whole of them exist. In what we call the lower animals, temperaments are often built out of merely one, or two, or three, of these traits; but man is a complex animal, and it takes all of the traits to fit him out. In the rabbit we always find meekness and timidity, and in him we never find courage, insolence, aggressiveness; and so when the rabbit is mentioned we always remember that he is meek and timid; if he has any other traits or distinctions—except, perhaps, an extravagant and inordinate fecundity—they never occur to us. When we consider the house-fly and the flea, we remember that in splendid courage the belted knight and the tiger cannot approach them, and that in impudence and insolence they lead the whole animal world, including even man; if those creatures have other traits they are so overshadowed by those which I have mentioned that we never think of them at all. When the peacock is mentioned, vanity occurs to us, and no other trait; when we think of the goat, unchastity occurs to us, and no other trait; when certain kinds of dogs are mentioned, loyalty occurs to us, and no other trait; when the cat is mentioned, her independence—a trait which she alone of all created creatures, including man, possesses—occurs to us, and no other trait; except we be of the stupid and the ignorant—then we think of treachery, a trait which is common to many breeds of dogs, but is not common to the cat. We can find one or two conspicuous traits in each family of what we impudently call the lower animals; in each case these one or two conspicuous traits distinguish that family of animals from the other families; also in each case those one or two traits are found in every one of the members of each family, and are so prominent as to eternally and unchangeably establish the character of that branch of the animal world. In all these cases we concede that the several temperaments constitute a law of God, a command of God, and that whatsoever is done in obedience to that law is blameless.

Man was descended from those animals; from them he inherited every trait that is in him; from them he inherited the whole of their numerous traits in a body, and with each trait its share of the law of God. He widely differs from them in this: that he possesses not a single trait that is similarly and equally prominent in each and every member of his race. You can say the house-fly is limitlessly brave, and in saying it you describe the whole house-fly tribe; you can say the rabbit is limitlessly timid, and by that phrase you describe the whole rabbit tribe; you can say the spider is limitlessly murderous, and by that phrase you describe the whole spider tribe; you can say the lamb is limitlessly innocent, and sweet, and gentle, and by that phrase you describe all the lambs; you can say the goat is limitlessly unchaste, and by that phrase you describe the whole tribe of goats. There is hardly a creature which you cannot definitely and satisfactorily describe by one single trait—but you cannot describe man by one single trait. Men are not all cowards, like the rabbit; nor all brave, like the house-fly; nor all sweet and innocent and gentle, like the lamb; nor all murderous, like the spider and the wasp; nor all thieves, like the fox and the blue jay; nor all vain, like the peacock; nor all beautiful, like the angel-fish; nor all frisky, like the monkey; nor all unchaste, like the goat. The human family cannot be described by any one phrase; each individual has to be described by himself. One is brave, another is a coward; one is gentle and kindly, another is ferocious; one is proud and vain, another is modest and humble. The multifarious traits that are scattered, one or two at a time, throughout the great animal world, are all concentrated, in varying and nicely shaded degrees of force and feebleness, in the form of instincts, in each and every member of the human family. In some men the vicious traits are so slight as to be imperceptible, while the nobler traits stand out conspicuously. We describe that man by those fine traits, and we give him praise and accord him high merit for their possession. It seems comical. He did not invent his traits; he did not stock himself with them; he inherited them at his birth; God conferred them upon him; they are the law that God imposed upon him, and he could not escape obedience if he should try. Sometimes a man is a born murderer, or a born scoundrel—like Stanford White—and upon him the world lavishes censure and dispraise; but he is only obeying the law of his nature, the law of his temperament; he is not at all likely to try to disobey it, and if he should try he would fail. It is a curious and humorous fact that we excuse all the unpleasant things that the creatures that crawl, and fly, and swim, and go on four legs do, for the recognizably sufficient reason that they are but obeying the law of their nature, which is the law of God, and are therefore innocent; then we turn about and with the fact plain before us that we get all our unpleasant traits by inheritance from those creatures, we blandly assert that we did not inherit the immunities along with them, but that it is our duty to ignore, abolish, and break these laws of God. It seems to me that this argument has not a leg to stand upon, and that it is not merely and mildly humorous, but violently grotesque.

℘

The President Hunts a Cow

TWO COLOSSAL HISTORICAL INCIDENTS took place yesterday; incidents which must go echoing down the corridors of time for ages; incidents which can never be forgotten while histories shall continue to be written. Yesterday, for the first time, business was opened to commerce by the Marconi Company, and wireless messages sent entirely across the Atlantic, straight from shore to shore; and on that same day the President of the United States for the fourteenth time came within three miles of flushing a bear. As usual, he was far away, nobody knew where, when the bear burst upon the multitude of dogs and hunters, and equerries, and chamberlains in waiting, and sutlers, and cooks, and scullions, and Rough Riders, and infantry and artillery, and had his customary swim to the other side of a pond and disappeared in the woods. While half the multitude watched the place where he vanished, the other half galloped off, with horns blowing, to scour the State of Louisiana in search of the great hunter. Why don't they stop hunting the bear altogether, and hunt the President? He is the only one of the pair that can't be found when he is wanted.

By and by the President was found and laid upon the track, and he and the dogs followed it several miles through the woods, then gave it up, because Rev. Dr. Long, the "nature fakir," came along and explained that it was a cow track. This is a sorrowful ending to a mighty enterprise. His Excellency leaves for Washington to-day, to interest himself further in his scheme of provoking a war with Japan with his battle-ships. Many wise people contend that his idea, on the contrary, is to compel peace with Japan, but I think he wants a war. He was in a skirmish once at San Juan Hill, and he got so much moonshine glory out of it that he has never been able to stop talking about it since. I remember that at a small luncheon party of men at Brander Matthews's house, once, he dragged San Juan Hill in three or four times, in spite of all attempts of the judicious to abolish the subject and introduce an interesting one in its place. I think the President is clearly insane in several ways, and insanest upon war and its supreme glories [. . . .]

Alas, the President has got that cow after all! If it was a cow. Some say it was a bear—a real bear. These were eye-witnesses, but they were all White House domestics; they are all under wages to the great hunter, and when a witness is in that condition it makes his testimony doubtful. The fact that the President himself thinks it was a bear does not diminish the doubt, but enlarges it [. . . .] I am sure he honestly thinks it was a bear, but the circumstantial evidence that it was a cow is overwhelming. It acted just as a cow would act; in every detail, from the beginning to the end, it acted precisely as a cow would act when in trouble; it even left a cow track behind, which is what a cow would do when in distress, or, indeed, at any other time if it knew a President of the United States was after it—hoping to move his pity, you see; thinking, maybe he would spare her life on account of her sex, her helpless situation, and her notorious harmlessness. In her flight she acted just as a cow would have done when in a frenzy of fright, with a President of the United States and a squadron of bellowing dogs chasing after her; when her strength was exhausted, and she could drag herself no further, she did as any other despairing cow would have done—she stopped in an open spot, fifty feet wide, and humbly faced the President of the United States, with the tears running down her cheeks, and said to him with the mute eloquence of surrender: "Have pity, sir, and spare me. I am alone, you are many; I have no weapon but my helplessness, you are a walking arsenal; I am in awful peril, you are as safe as you would be in a Sunday-school; have pity, sir—there is no heroism in killing an exhausted cow."

Here are the scare-heads that introduce the wonderful dime-novel performance:

ROOSEVELT TELLS OF HUNTING TRIP
Ate All the Game, Except a Wildcat, and That
Had a Narrow Escape.
Swam Despite Alligators
Charged Into the Canebrake After Bear and
Hugged the Guides After the Kill.

There it is—he hugged the guides after the kill. It is the President all over; he is still only fourteen years old, after living half a century; he takes a boy's delight in showing off; he is always hugging something or somebody—when there is a crowd around to see the hugging and envy the hugged. A grown

person would have milked the cow and let her go; but no, nothing would do this lad but he must kill her and be a hero. The account says:

The bear slain by the President was killed Thursday, and the killing was witnessed by one of the McKenzies and by Alex Ennolds.

These names will go down in history forever, in the company of an exploit which will take a good deal of the shine out of the twelve labors of Hercules. Testimony of the witnesses:

They say that the President's bearing was extremely sportsmanlike.

Very likely. Everybody knows what mere sportsmanlike bearing is, unqualified by an adjective, but none of us knows quite what it is when it is extremely sportsmanlike, because we have never encountered that inflamed form of the thing before. The probabilities are that the sportsmanlike bearing was not any more extremely sportsmanlike than was that of Hercules; it is quite likely that the adjective is merely emotional, and has the hope of a raise of wages back of it. The chase of the frightened creature lasted three hours, and reads like a hectic chapter in a dime-novel—and this time it is a chapter of pathetically humble heroics. In the outcome the credit is all with the cow, none of it is with the President. When the poor hunted thing could go no further it turned, in fine and picturesque defiance, and gallantly faced its enemies and its assassin. From a safe distance Hercules sent a bullet to the sources of its life; then, dying, it made fight—so there *was* a hero present after all. Another bullet closed the tragedy, and Hercules was so carried away with admiration of himself that he hugged his domestics and bought a compliment from one of them for twenty dollars. But this resumé of mine is pale; let us send it down to history with the colors all in it:

The bear slain by the President was killed Thursday, and the killing was witnessed by one of the McKenzies and by Alex Ennolds. They say that the President's bearing was extremely sportsmanlike. The animal had been chased by the dogs for three hours, the President following all the time. When at last they came within hearing distance the President dismounted, threw off his coat and dashed into the canebrake, going to within twenty paces of the beast. The dogs were coming up rapidly, with the President's favorite, Rowdy, in the lead.

The bear had stopped to bid defiance to the canines when the President sent a fatal bullet from his rifle through the animal's vitals. With the little life left in it the bear turned on the dogs. The President then lodged a second bullet between the bear's shoulders, breaking the creature's neck. Other members of the party soon came up, and the President was so rejoiced over his success that he embraced each of his companions. Ennolds said: "Mr. President, you are no tenderfoot."

Mr. Roosevelt responded by giving Ennolds a $20 note.

There was little hunting yesterday, because the dogs encountered a drove of wild hogs, more ferocious than bears. One of the best dogs was killed by a boar.

There were daily swims in the lake by members of the party, including the President.

"The water was fine," he said, "and I did not have the fear of alligators that some seem to have."

Whatever Hercules does is to him remarkable; when other people are neglectful, and fail to notice a detail, here and there, proper for admiration and comment, he supplies the omission himself. Mr. Ennolds lost a chance; if he had been judiciously on watch he could have done the alligator compliment himself, and got another twenty for it.

The paragraph about the wild hogs naively furnishes a measure of the President's valor; he isn't afraid of a cow, he isn't afraid of an alligator, but—

∲∂

The Time I Got an Elephant for Christmas

DICTATED XMAS DAY, 1908.

Ten days ago Robert Collier wrote me that he had bought a baby elephant for my Christmas, and would send it as soon as he could secure a car for it and get the temporary loan of a trainer from Barnum & Bailey's winter-quarters menagerie at Bridgeport. The cunning rascal knew the letter would never get to my hands, but would stop in Miss Lyon's on the way and be suppressed. The letter would not have disturbed me, for I know Robert, and would have suspected a joke behind it; but it filled Miss Lyon with consternation—she taking it in earnest, just as he had expected she would. She and Ashcroft discussed the impending disaster together, and agreed that it must be kept from me at all costs. That is to say, they resolved to do the suffering and endure the insomnia and save me. They had no doubts about the elephant. They knew quite well that if Robert was inspired to do a kindness for a friend, he would not consider expense, but would buy elephants or any other costly rarity that might seem to him to meet the requirements.

Miss Lyon called up New York on the telephone and got into conversation with Robert. She timidly suggested that we had no way of taking care of an elephant here, it being used to a warm climate and—

"Oh, that's all right, put him in the garage," interrupted Robert cheerfully.

"But there's nothing but a stove there, and so—"

"The very thing! There couldn't be anything better."

Defeated, Miss Lyon hunted up another excuse.

"But the pony lives in the garage, Mr. Collier, and she's a timid little thing, and if an elephant should come, she—"

"Oh, that's all right, Miss Lyon, give yourself no trouble. This elephant loves ponies above everything, and will fondle the pony and—"

"Mr. Collier, she would jump out through the roof! Oh we never never can shut them up together. Between his caresses and her frenzies they would wreck the whole place."

"Oh, I have it! The loggia! the loggia! Spacious—enclosed with glass—steam-heated—cheerful surroundings—bright sunshine—adorable scenery—oh, the very place! Put him in the loggia!"

"But Mr. Collier, I think it would never do—I am afraid it wouldn't—indeed I am sure. We play cards there—"

"Just the thing! He has a passion for cards. Oh, games of any kind! They're just in his line. He'll take a hand, don't you doubt it."

Miss Lyon despairingly invented excuse after excuse, with failing hope, but Robert turned them all to the elephant's advantage; and so at last her invention-mill broke down and she hung up the receiver, beaten at all points.

That was ten days ago. Miss Lyon has worried about the impending elephant by day and by night ever since, and Ashcroft has done the best he could to find reasons that could make an elephant's society endurable here. Among other emollients he kept prominently in the foreground the fact that this was only a baby elephant, not an adult.

Meantime telegrams came from Robert now and then reporting progress— progress that was slow and disappointing, but full of hope, full of encouragement—all this concerned the car for the elephant; heavy Christmas traffic in the way, etc.; but at last came cordial word that the car had been secured. Miss Lyon had been hoping, a little, and then a little more and a little more—but this news mashed those frail hopes into the mud.

Day before yesterday came a telegram saying ten bales of hay—one ton—

had been shipped to us by fast freight, and along with the hay twenty bushels of carrots and fruit. All for the elephant. Freight prepaid.

Early yesterday morning the railway office, three miles away, reported the arrival of this provender, and an hour later it arrived here and was stored in the garage. Miss Lyon—however, her despair had already reached bottom.

At nine this morning, Mr. Lounsbury telephoned that there was a man at the station with a letter from Robert Collier; man said he was an elephant trainer from Barnum & Bailey's, and had been sent here to train an elephant for Mr. Clemens. Bring him over? Yes, bring him. So Lounsbury brought him. Lounsbury is always awake, and always has his pump with him. On the way over, he did a little pumping:

"Where is the elephant?"

"He will arrive at noon."

"Where is he going to be housed?"

"In the loggia."

"What kind of an elephant is it?"

"A baby elephant."

"How big?"

"About as big as a cow."

"How long have you been with Barnum & Bailey?"

"Six years."

"Good. Then you know a couple of old friends of mine there—Billy Brisbane and Hank Roberts."

"Yes, indeed. Good boys, too."

"There aren't any better. How are they?"

"Billy was ailing a little, last week—rheumatism, I think—but Hank's as sound as a nut."

Mental remark by Lounsbury: "They've been dead as much as two years; this fellow's a fraud; there's a nigger in this woodpile somewhere."

Miss Lyon received the trainer (Robert Collier's butler in disguise), as cheerfully as she could, and she and Ashcroft took down his instructions concerning the right and safe way to get on the good side of an elephant, and which end of him to avoid when he was angry: then the trainer drove away with Lounsbury to get the animal, and Ashcroft was sent to my room to say that the decorating of the loggia (with greenery and so on) had been delayed, and would I remain abed for an hour or two longer? They had sent the pony to a neighbor's house, and wanted to get the elephant stowed out of sight in the garage before I should have my Christmas spoiled by finding out the disaster that had befallen us.

In about half an hour the elephant arrived, but Miss Lyon got herself out of the way; she could not bear to look at him. Yet there was no occasion to be afraid of him: he is only two feet long, is built of cloth, and goes on wheels.

Robert has come out ahead. No, it is the pony: for she has the ton of hay and the other delicacies.

ह

Little Bessie Would Assist Providence

LITTLE BESSIE WAS NEARLY three years old. She was a good child, and not shallow, not frivolous, but meditative and thoughtful, and much given to thinking out the reasons of things and trying to make them harmonise with results. One day she said—

"Mamma, why is there so much pain and sorrow and suffering? What is it all for?"

It was an easy question, and mamma had no difficulty in answering it:

"It is for our good, my child. In His wisdom and mercy the Lord sends us these afflictions to discipline us and make us better."

"Is it *He* that sends them?"

"Yes."

"Does He send *all* of them, mamma?"

"Yes, dear, all of them. None of them comes by accident; He alone sends them, and always out of love for us, and to make us better."

"Isn't it strange!"

"Strange? Why, no, I have never thought of it in that way. I have not heard any one call it strange before. It has always seemed natural and right to me, and wise and most kindly and merciful."

"Who first thought of it like that, mamma? Was it you?"

"Oh, no, child, I was taught it."

"Who taught you so, mamma?"

"Why, really, I don't know—I can't remember. My mother, I suppose; or the preacher. But it's a thing that everybody knows."

"Well, anyway, it does seem strange. Did He give Billy Norris the typhus?"

"Yes."

"What for?"

"Why, to discipline him and make him good."

"But he died, mamma, and so it *couldn't* make him good."

"Well, then, I suppose it was for some other reason. We know it was a *good* reason, whatever it was."

"What do you think it was, mamma?"

"Oh, you ask so many questions! I think it was to discipline his parents."

"Well, then, it wasn't fair, mamma. Why should *his* life be taken away for their sake, when he wasn't doing anything?"

"Oh, *I* don't know! I only know it was for a good and wise and merciful reason."

"What reason, mamma?"

"I think—I think—well, it was a judgment; it was to punish them for some sin they had committed."

"But *he* was the one that was punished, mamma. Was that right?"

"Certainly, certainly. He does nothing that isn't right and wise and merciful. You can't understand these things now, dear, but when you are grown up you will understand them, and then you will see that they are just and wise."

After a pause:

"Did He make the roof fall in on the stranger that was trying to save the crippled old woman from the fire, mamma?"

"Yes, my child. *Wait!* Don't ask me why, because I don't know. I only know it was to discipline some one, or be a judgment upon somebody, or to show His power."

"That drunken man that stuck a pitchfork into Mrs. Welch's baby when—"

"Never mind about it, you needn't go into particulars; it was to discipline the child—*that* much is certain, anyway."

"Mamma, Mr. Burgess said in his sermon that billions of little creatures are sent into us to give us cholera, and typhoid, and lockjaw, and more than a thousand other sicknesses and—mamma, does He send them?"

"Oh, certainly, child, certainly. Of course."

"What for?"

"Oh, to *discipline* us! haven't I told you so, over and over again?"

"It's awful cruel, mamma! And silly! and if I—"

"Hush, oh *hush!* do you want to bring the lightning?"

"You know the lightning *did* come last week, mamma, and struck the new church, and burnt it down. Was it to discipline the church?"

(Wearily). "Oh, I suppose so."

"But it killed a hog that wasn't doing anything. Was it to discipline the hog, mamma?"

"Dear child, don't you want to run out and play a while? If you would like to—"

"Mamma, only think! Mr. Hollister says there isn't a bird or fish or reptile or any other animal that hasn't got an enemy that Providence has sent to bite it and chase it and pester it, and kill it, and suck its blood and discipline it and make it good and religious. Is that true, mother—because if it is true, why did Mr. Hollister laugh at it?"

"That Hollister is a scandalous person, and I don't want you to listen to anything he says."

"Why, mamma, he is very interesting, and *I* think he tries to be good. He says the wasps catch spiders and cram them down into their nests in the ground—*alive*, mamma!—and there they live and suffer days and days and days, and the hungry little wasps chewing their legs and gnawing into their bellies all the time, to make them good and religious and praise God for His infinite mercies. *I* think Mr. Hollister is just lovely, and ever so kind; for when I asked him if *he* would treat a spider like that, he said he hoped to be damned if he would; and then he—"

"My child! oh, do for goodness' sake—"

"And mamma, he says the spider is appointed to catch the fly, and drive her fangs into his bowels, and suck and suck and suck his blood, to discipline him and make him a Christian; and whenever the fly buzzes his wings with the pain and misery of it, you can see by the spider's grateful eye that she is thanking the Giver of All Good for—well, she's saying grace, as *he* says; and also, he—"

"Oh, aren't you *ever* going to get tired chattering! If you want to go out and play—"

"Mamma, he says himself that all troubles and pains and miseries and rotten diseases and horrors and villainies are sent to us in mercy and kindness to discipline us; and he says it is the duty of every father and mother to *help* Providence, every way they can; and says they can't do it by just scolding and whipping, for that won't answer, it is weak and no good—Providence's way is best, and it is every parent's duty and every *person's* duty to help discipline everybody, and cripple them and kill them, and starve them, and freeze them, and rot them with diseases, and lead them into murder and theft and dishonor and disgrace; and he says Providence's invention for disciplining us and the animals is the very brightest idea that ever was, and not even an idiot could get up anything shinier. Mamma, brother Eddie needs disciplining, right away; and I know where you can get the smallpox for him, and the itch, and the diphtheria, and bone-rot, and heart disease, and consumption, and— *Dear* mamma, have you fainted! I will run and bring help! Now *this* comes of staying in town this hot weather."

ৡ৯

Letters from the Earth

THE CREATOR SAT upon the throne, thinking. Behind him stretched the illimitable continent of heaven, steeped in a glory of light and color; before him rose the black night of Space, like a wall. His mighty bulk towered rugged and mountain-like into the zenith, and His divine head blazed there like a distant sun. At His feet stood three colossal figures, diminished to extinction, almost, by contrast—archangels—their heads level with His ancle-bone.

When the Creator had finished thinking, he said,

"I have thought. Behold!"

He lifted his hand, and from it burst a fountain-spray of fire, a million stupendous suns, which clove the blackness and soared, away and away and away, diminishing in magnitude and intensity as they pierced the far frontiers of Space, until at last they were but as diamond nail-heads sparkling under the domed vast roof of the universe.

At the end of an hour the Grand Council was dismissed.

II

They left the Presence impressed and thoughtful, and retired to a private place, where they might talk with freedom. None of the three seemed to want to begin, though all wanted somebody to do it. Each was burning to discuss the great event, but would prefer not to commit himself till he should know how the others regarded it. So there was some aimless and halting conversation about matters of no consequence, and this dragged tediously along, arriving nowhere, until at last the archangel Satan gathered his courage together—of which he had a very good supply—and broke ground. He said—

"We know what we are here to talk about, my lords, and we may as well put pretence aside, and begin. If this is the opinion of the Council—"

"It is, it is!" said Gabriel and Michael, gratefully interrupting.

"Very well, then, let us proceed. We have witnessed a wonderful thing; as to that, we are necessarily agreed. As to the value of it—if it has any—that is a matter which does not personally concern us. We can have as many opinions about it as we like, and that is our limit. We have no vote. I think Space was well enough, just as it was, and useful, too. Cold and dark—a restful place, now and then, after a season of the over-delicate climate and trying splendors of heaven. But these are details of no considerable moment; the new feature, the immense feature, is—what, gentlemen?"

"The invention and introduction of automatic, unsupervised, self-regulating *law* for the government of those myriads of whirling and racing suns and worlds!"

"That is it!" said Satan. "You perceive that it is a stupendous idea. Nothing approaching it has been evolved from the Master Intellect before. Law—*automatic* Law—exact and unvarying Law—requiring no watching, no correcting, no readjusting while the eternities endure! He said those countless vast bodies would plunge through the wastes of Space ages and ages, at unimaginable speed, around stupendous orbits, yet never collide, and never lengthen nor shorten their orbital periods by so much as the hundredth part of a second in two thousand years! That is the new miracle, and the greatest of all—*Automatic Law!* And He gave it a name—the Law of Nature—and said Natural Law is the Law of God—interchangeable names for one and the same thing."

"Yes," said Michael, "and He said He would establish Natural Law—the Law of God—throughout His dominions, and its authority should be supreme and inviolable."

"Also," said Gabriel, "He said He would by and by create animals, and place them, likewise, under the authority of that Law."

"Yes," said Satan, "I heard Him, but did not understand. What *is* animals, Gabriel?"

"Ah, how should I know? How should any of us know? It is a new word."

[Interval of three centuries, celestial time—the equivalent of a hundred million years, earthly time. Enter a messenger-Angel.]

"My lords, He is making animals. Will it please you to come and see?"

They went, they saw, and were perplexed. Deeply perplexed—and the Creator noticed it, and said—

"Ask. I will answer."

"Divine One," said Satan, making obeisance, "what are they for?"

"They are an experiment in Morals and Conduct. Observe them, and be instructed."

There were thousands of them. They were full of activities. Busy, all busy—

mainly in persecuting each other. Satan remarked—after examining one of them through a powerful microscope—

"This large beast is killing weaker animals, Divine One."

"The tiger—yes. The law of his nature is ferocity. The law of his nature is the law of God. He cannot disobey it."

"Then in obeying it he commits no offence, Divine One?"

"No, he is blameless."

"This other creature here, is timid, Divine One, and suffers death without resisting."

"The rabbit—yes. He is without courage. It is the law of his nature—the law of God. He must obey it."

"Then he cannot honorably be required to go counter to his nature and resist, Divine One?"

"No. No creature can be honorably required to go counter to the law of his nature—the law of God."

After a long time and many questions, Satan said—

"The spider kills the fly, and eats it; the bird kills the spider and eats it; the wildcat kills the goose; the—well, they all kill each other. It is murder all along the line. Here are countless multitudes of creatures, and they all kill, kill, kill, they are all murderers. And they are not to blame, Divine One?"

"They are not to blame. It is the law of their nature. And always the law of nature is the law of God. Now—observe—behold! A new creature—and the masterpiece—*Man!*"

Men, women, children, they came swarming in flocks, in droves, in millions.

"What shall you do with them, Divine One?"

"Put into each individual, in differing shades and degrees, all the various Moral Qualities, in mass, that have been distributed, a single distinguishing characteristic at a time, among the non-speaking animal world—courage, cowardice, ferocity, gentleness, fairness, justice, cunning, treachery, magnanimity, cruelty, malice, malignity, lust, mercy, pity, purity, selfishness, sweetness, honor, love, hate, baseness, nobility, loyalty, falsity, veracity, untruthfulness—each human being shall have *all* of these in him, and they will constitute his nature. In some, there will be high and fine characteristics which will submerge the evil ones, and those will be called good men; in others the evil characteristics will have dominion, and those will be called bad men. Observe—behold—they vanish!"

"Whither are they gone, Divine One?"

"To the earth—they and all their fellow animals." [. . .]

Satan's Letter

This is a strange place, an extraordinary place, and interesting. There is nothing resembling it at home. The people are all insane, the other animals are all insane, the Earth is insane, Nature itself is insane. Man is a marvelous curiosity. When he is at his very very best he is a sort of low grade nickel-plated angel; at his worst he is unspeakable, unimaginable; and first and last and all the time he is a sarcasm. Yet he blandly and in all sincerity calls himself the "noblest work of God." This is the truth I am telling you. And this is not a new idea with him, he has talked it through all the ages, and believed it. Believed it, and found nobody among all his race to laugh at it.

Moreover—if I may put another strain upon you—he thinks he is the Creator's pet. He believes the Creator is proud of him; he even believes the Creator loves him; has a passion for him; sits up nights to admire him; yes, and watch over him and keep him out of trouble. He prays to Him, and thinks He listens. Isn't it a quaint idea? Fills his prayers with crude and bald and florid flatteries of Him, and thinks He sits and purrs over these extravagancies and enjoys them. He prays for help, and favor, and protection, every day; and does it with hopefulness and confidence, too, although no prayer of his has ever been answered. The daily affront, the daily defeat, do not discourage him, he goes on praying just the same. There is something almost fine about this perseverance. I must put one more strain upon you: he thinks he is going to heaven! [. . .]

Letter . . .

So the First Pair went forth from the Garden under a curse—a permanent one. They had lost every pleasure they had possessed before "The Fall;" and yet they were rich, for they had gained one worth all the rest: they knew the Supreme Art.

They practised it diligently, and were filled with contentment. The Deity *ordered* them to practise it. They obeyed, this time. But it was just as well it was not forbidden, for they would have practised it anyhow, if a thousand Deities had forbidden it.

Results followed. By the name of Cain and Abel. And these had some sisters; and knew what to do with them. And so there were some more results: Cain and Abel begot some nephews and nieces. These, in their turn, begot some second-cousins. At this point classification of relationships began to get difficult, and the attempt to keep it up was abandoned.

The pleasant labor of populating the world went on from age to age, and with prime efficiency; for in those happy days the sexes were still competent for the Supreme Art when by rights they ought to have been dead eight hundred years. The sweeter sex, the dearer sex, the lovelier sex was manifestly at its very best, then, for it was even able to attract gods. Real gods. They came down out of heaven and had wonderful times with those hot young blossoms. The Bible tells about it.

By help of those visiting foreigners the population grew and grew until it numbered several millions. But it was a disappointment to the Deity. He was dissatisfied with its morals; which in some respects were not any better than his own. Indeed they were an unflatteringly close imitation of his own. They were a very bad people, and as he knew of no way to reform them, he wisely concluded to abolish them. This is the only really enlightened and superior idea his Bible has credited him with, and it would have made his reputation for all time if he could only have kept to it and carried it out. But he was always unstable—except in his advertisements—and his good resolution broke down. He took a pride in man; man was his finest invention; man was his pet, after the housefly, and he could not bear to lose him wholly; so he finally decided to save a sample of him and drown the rest.

Nothing could be more characteristic of him. He created all those infamous people, and he alone was responsible for their conduct. Not one of them deserved death, yet it was certainly good policy to extinguish them; especially since in creating them the master crime had already been committed, and to allow them to go on procreating would be a distinct *addition* to the crime. But at the same time there could be no justice, no fairness, in any favoritism—*all* should be drowned or none.

No, he would not have it so; he would save half a dozen and try the race over again. He was not able to foresee that it would go rotten again, for he is only the Far-Sighted One in his advertisements.

He saved out Noah and his family, and arranged to exterminate the rest. He planned an Ark, and Noah built it. Neither of them had ever built an Ark before, nor knew anything about Arks; and so something out of the common was to be expected. It happened. Noah was a farmer, and although he knew what was required of the Ark he was quite incompetent to say whether this one would be large enough to meet the requirements or not (which it wasn't), so he ventured no advice. The Deity did not know it wasn't large enough, but took the chances and made no adequate measurements. In the end the ship fell far short of the necessities, and to this day the world still suffers for it.

Noah built the Ark. He built it the best he could, but left out most of the essentials. It had no rudder, it had no sails, it had no compass, it had no pumps, it had no charts, no lead-lines, no anchors, no log, no light, no ventilation; and as for cargo-room—which was the main thing—the less said about that the better. It was to be at sea eleven months, and would need fresh water enough to fill two Arks of its size—yet the additional Ark was not provided. Water from outside could not be utilized: half of it would be salt water, and men and land-animals could not drink it.

For not only was a sample of man to be saved, but business samples of the other animals, too. You must understand that when Adam ate the apple in the Garden and learned how to multiply and replenish, the other animals learned the Art, too, by watching Adam. It was cunning of them, it was neat; for they got all that was worth having out of the apple without tasting it and afflicting themselves with the disastrous Moral Sense, the parent of all immoralities.

Letter . . .

Noah began to collect animals. There was to be one couple of each and every sort of creature that walked or crawled, or swam or flew, in the world of animated nature. We have to guess at how long it took to collect the creatures and how much it cost, for there is no record of these details. When Symmachus made preparation to introduce his young son to grown-up life in imperial Rome, he sent men to Asia, Africa and everywhere to collect wild animals for the arena-fights. It took the men three years to accumulate the animals and fetch them to Rome. Merely quadrupeds and alligators, you understand— no birds, no snakes, no frogs, no worms, no lice, no rats, no fleas, no ticks, no caterpillars, no spiders, no houseflies, no mosquitoes,—nothing but just plain simple quadrupeds and alligators: and no quadrupeds except fighting ones. Yet it was as I have said: it took three years to collect them, and the cost of animals and transportation and the men's wages footed up $4,500,000.

How many animals? We do not know. But it was under 5,000, for that was the largest number *ever* gathered for those Roman shows, and it was Titus, not Symmachus, who made that collection. Those were mere baby-museums, compared to Noah's contract. Of birds and beasts and fresh-water creatures he had to collect 146,000 kinds; and of insects upwards of 2,000,000 species.

Thousands and thousands of those things are very difficult to catch, and if Noah had not given up and resigned, he would be on the job yet, as Leviticus used to say. However, I do not mean that he withdrew. No, he did not do that. He gathered as many creatures as he had room for, and then stopped.

If he had known all the requirements in the beginning, he would have been aware that what was needed was a fleet of Arks. But he did not know how many kinds of creatures there were, neither did his Chief. So he had no kangaroo, and no 'possum, and no Gila Monster, and no ornithorhynchus, and lacked a multitude of other indispensable blessings which a loving Creator had provided for man and forgotten about, they having long ago wandered to a side of his world which he had never seen and with whose affairs he was not acquainted. And so every one of them came within a hair of getting drowned.

They only escaped by an accident: there was not water enough to go around. Only enough was provided to flood one small corner of the globe—the rest of the globe was not then known, and was supposed to be non-existent.

However, the thing that really and finally and definitely determined Noah to stop with enough species for purely business purposes and let the rest become extinct, was an incident of the last days: an excited stranger arrived with some most alarming news. He said he had been camping among some mountains and valleys about six hundred miles away, and he had seen a wonderful thing there: he stood upon a precipice overlooking a wide valley, and up the valley he saw a billowy black sea of strange animal life coming. Presently the creatures passed by, struggling, fighting, scrambling, screeching, snorting—horrible vast masses of tumultuous flesh! Sloths as big as an elephant; frogs as big as a cow; a megatherium and his harem huge beyond belief; saurians and sauri-

ans and saurians, group after group, family after family, species after species—
a hundred feet long, thirty feet high, and twice as quarrelsome; one of them
hit a perfectly blameless Durham bull a thump with its tail and sent it whiz-
zing three hundred feet into the air and it fell at the man's feet with a sigh and
was no more. The man said that these prodigious animals had heard about the
Ark and were coming. Coming to get saved from the flood. And not coming in
pairs, they were *all* coming: they did not know the passengers were restricted
to pairs, the man said, and wouldn't care a rap for the regulations, anyway—
they would sail in that Ark or know the reason why. The man said the Ark
would not hold the half of them; and moreover they were coming hungry, and
would eat up everything there was, including the menagerie and the family.

All these facts were suppressed, in the Biblical account. You find not a hint
of them there. The whole thing is hushed up. Not even the names of those vast
creatures are mentioned. It shows you that when people have left a reproachful vacancy in a contract they can be as shady about it in Bibles as elsewhere.
Those powerful animals would be of inestimable value to man now, when
transportation is so hard pressed and expensive, but they are all lost to him.
All lost, and by Noah's fault. They all got drowned. Some of them as much as
eight million years ago.

Very well, the stranger told his tale, and Noah saw that he must get away
before the monsters arrived. He would have sailed at once, but the upholster-
ers and decorators of the housefly's drawing room still had some finishing
touches to put on, and that lost him a day. Another day was lost in getting
the flies aboard, there being sixty-eight billions of them and the Deity still
afraid there might not be enough. Another day was lost in stowing 40 tons of
selected filth for the fly's sustenance.

Then at last, Noah sailed; and none too soon, for the Ark was only just
sinking out of sight on the horizon when the monsters arrived, and added
their lamentations to those of the multitude of weeping fathers and mothers
and frightened little children who were clinging to the wave-washed rocks
in the pouring rain and lifting imploring prayers to an All-Just and All-For-
giving and All-Pitying Being who had never answered a prayer since those
crags were builded, grain by grain out of the sands, and would still not have
answered one when the ages should have crumbled them to sand again.

Letter VII

On the third day, about noon, it was found that a fly had been left behind.
The return-voyage turned out to be long and difficult, on account of the lack

of chart and compass, and because of the changed aspects of all coasts, the steadily rising water having submerged some of the lower landmarks and given to higher ones an unfamiliar look; but after sixteen days of earnest and faithful seeking, the fly was found at last, and received on board with hymns of praise and gratitude, the Family standing meanwhile uncovered, out of reverence for its divine origin. It was weary and worn, and had suffered somewhat from the weather, but was otherwise in good estate. Men and their families had died of hunger on barren mountain tops, but It had not lacked for food, the multitudinous corpses furnishing it in rank and rotten richness. Thus was the sacred bird providentially preserved.

Providentially. That is the word. For the fly had not been left behind by accident. No, the hand of Providence was in it. There are no accidents. All things that happen, happen for a purpose. They are foreseen from the beginning of time, they are ordained from the beginning of time. From the dawn of Creation the Lord had foreseen that Noah, being alarmed and confused by the invasion of the prodigious brevet Fossils, would prematurely fly to sea unprovided with a certain invaluable disease. He would have all the other diseases, and could distribute them among the new races of men as they appeared in the world, but he would lack one of the very best—typhoid fever; a malady which, when the circumstances are especially favorable, is able to utterly wreck a patient without killing him; for it can restore him to his feet with a long life in him, and yet deaf, dumb, blind, crippled and idiotic. The housefly is its main disseminator, and is more competent and more calamitously effective than all the other distributors of the dreaded scourge put together. And so, by foreordination from the beginning of time, this fly was left behind to seek out a typhoid corpse and feed upon its corruptions and gaum its legs with the germs and transmit them to the repeopled world for permanent business. From that one housefly, in the ages that have since elapsed, billions of sickbeds have been stocked, billions of wrecked bodies sent tottering about the earth, and billions of cemeteries recruited with the dead [. . . .]

Letter . . .

Noah and his family were saved—if that could be called an advantage. I throw in the *if* for the reason that there has never been an intelligent person of the age of sixty who would consent to live his life over again. His or any one else's. The family were saved, yes, but they were not comfortable, for they were full of microbes. Full to the eyebrows; fat with them, obese with them; distended like balloons. It was a disagreeable condition, but it

could not be helped, because enough microbes had to be saved to supply the future races of men with desolating diseases, and there were but eight persons on board to serve as hotels for them. The microbes were by far the most important part of the Ark's cargo, and the part the Creator was most anxious about and most infatuated with. They had to have good nourishment and pleasant accommodations. There were typhoid germs, and cholera germs, and hydrophobia germs, and lockjaw germs, and consumption germs, and black-plague germs, and some hundreds of other aristocrats, specially precious creations, golden bearers of God's love to man, blessed gifts of the infatuated Father to his children—all of which had to be sumptuously housed and richly entertained; these were located in the choicest places the interiors of the family could furnish: in the lungs, in the heart, in the brain, in the kidneys, in the blood, in the guts. In the guts particularly. The great intestine was the favorite resort. There they gathered, by countless billions, and worked, and fed, and squirmed, and sang hymns of praise and thanksgiving; and at night when it was quiet you could hear the soft murmur of it. The large intestine was in effect their heaven. They stuffed it solid; they made it as rigid as a coil of gaspipe. They took pride in this. Their principal hymn made gratified reference to it:

> "Constipation, O constipation,
>   The Joyful sound proclaim
>   Till man's remotest entrail
>   Shall praise its maker's name."

The discomforts furnished by the Ark were many, and various. The family had to live right in the presence of the multitudinous animals, and breathe the distressing stench they made and be deafened day and night with the thunder-crash of noise their roarings and screechings produced; and in addition to these intolerable discomforts it was a peculiarly trying place for the ladies, for they could look in no direction without seeing some thousands of the creatures engaged in multiplying and replenishing. And then, there were the flies. They swarmed everywhere, and persecuted the family all day long. They were the first animals up, in the morning, and the last ones down, at night. But they must not be killed, they must not be injured, they were sacred, their origin was divine, they were the special pets of the Creator, his darlings.

By and by the other creatures would be distributed here and there about the earth—*scattered*: the tigers to India, the lion and the elephant to the vacant desert and the secret places of the jungle, the birds to the boundless regions of empty space, the insects to one or another climate, according to nature and requirement; but the fly? He is of no nationality; all the climates are his home, all the globe is his province, all creatures that breathe are his prey, and unto them all he is a scourge and a hell.

To man he is a divine ambassador, a minister plenipotentiary, the Creator's special representative. He infests him in his cradle; clings in bunches to his gummy eyelids; buzzes and bites and harries him, robbing him of his sleep and his weary mother of her strength in those long vigils which she devotes to protecting her child from this pest's persecutions. The fly harries the sick man in his home, in the hospital, even on his death-bed at his last gasp. Pesters him at his meals; previously hunts up patients suffering from loathsome and deadly diseases; wades in their sores, gaums its legs with a million death-dealing germs, then comes to that healthy man's table and wipes these things off on the butter and discharges a bowel-load of typhoid germs and excrement on his batter-cakes. The housefly wrecks more human constitutions and destroys more human lives than all God's multitude of misery-messengers and death-agents put together.

Shem was full of hookworms. It is wonderful, the thorough and comprehensive study which the Creator devoted to the great work of making man miserable. I have said he devised a special affliction-agent for each and every detail of man's structure, overlooking not a single one, and I said the truth. Many poor people have to go barefoot, because they cannot afford shoes. The Creator saw his opportunity. I will remark, in passing, that he always has his eye on the poor. Nine-tenths of his disease-inventions were intended for the poor, and they *get* them. The well-to-do get only what is left over. Do not suspect me of speaking unheedfully, for it is not so: the vast bulk of the Creator's affliction-inventions *are* specially designed for the persecution of the poor. You could guess this by the fact that one of the pulpit's finest and commonest names for the Creator is "The Friend of the Poor." Under no circumstances does the pulpit ever pay the Creator a compliment that has a vestige of truth in it. The poor's most implacable and unwearying enemy is their Father in Heaven. The poor's only real friend is their fellow man. He is sorry for them, he pities them, and he shows it by his deeds. He does much to relieve their distresses; and in every case their Father in Heaven gets the credit of it.

Just so with diseases. If science exterminates a disease which has been working for God, it is God that gets the credit, and all the pulpits break into grateful advertising-raptures and call attention to how good he is! Yes, *he* has done it. Perhaps he has waited a thousand years before doing it. That is nothing; the pulpit says he was thinking about it all the time. When exasperated men rise up and sweep away an age-long tyranny and set a nation free, the first thing the delighted pulpit does is to advertise it as God's work, and invite the people to get down on their knees and pour out their thanks to him for it. And the pulpit says with admiring emotion, "Let tyrants understand that the Eye that never sleeps is upon them; and let them remember that the Lord our God will not always be patient, but will loose the whirlwinds of his wrath upon them in his appointed day."

They forget to mention that he is the slowest mover in the universe; that his Eye that never sleeps, might as well, since it takes it a century to see what any other eye would see in a week; that in all history there is not an instance where he thought of a noble deed *first*, but always thought of it just a little after somebody else had thought of it and *done* it. He arrives then, and annexes the dividend.

Very well, six thousand years ago Shem was full of hookworms. Microscopic in size, invisible to the unaided eye. All of the Creator's specially-deadly disease-producers are invisible. It is an ingenious idea. For thousands of years it kept man from getting at the roots of his maladies, and defeated his attempts to master them. It is only very recently that science has succeeded in exposing some of these treacheries.

The very latest of these blessed triumphs of science is the discovery and identification of the ambuscaded assassin which goes by the name of the hookworm. Its special prey is the barefooted poor. It lies in wait in warm regions and sandy places and digs its way into their unprotected feet.

The hookworm was discovered two or three years ago by a physician, who had been patiently studying its victims for a long time. The disease induced by the hookworm had been doing its evil work here and there in the earth ever since Shem landed on Ararat, but it was never suspected to *be* a disease at all. The people who had it were merely supposed to be *lazy*, and were therefore despised and made fun of, when they should have been pitied. The hookworm is a peculiarly sneaking and underhanded invention, and has done its surreptitious work unmolested for ages; but that physician and his helpers will exterminate it now.

God is back of this. He has been thinking about it for six thousand years, and making up his mind. The idea of exterminating the hookworm was his. He came very near doing it before Dr. Charles Wardell Stiles did. But he is in time to get the credit of it. He always is.

It is going to cost a million dollars. He was probably just in the act of contributing that sum when a man pushed in ahead of him—as usual. Mr. Rockefeller. He furnishes the million, but the credit will go elsewhere—as usual. This morning's journal tells us something about the hookworm's operations:

The hookworm parasites often so lower the vitality of those who are affected as to retard their physical and mental development, render them more susceptible to other diseases, make labor less efficient, and in the sections where the malady is most prevalent greatly increase the death rate from consumption, pneumonia, typhoid fever and malaria. It has been shown that the lowered vitality of multitudes, long attributed to malaria and climate and seriously affecting economic development, is in fact due in some districts to this parasite. The disease is by no means confined to any one class; it takes its toll of suffering and death from the highly intelligent and well to do as well as from the less fortunate. It is a conservative estimate that two millions of our people are affected by this parasite. The disease is more common and more serious in children of school age than in other persons.

Widespread and serious as the infection is, there is still a most encouraging outlook. The disease can be easily recognized, readily and effectively treated and by simple and proper sanitary precautions successfully prevented, with God's help.

The poor little children are under the Eye that never sleeps, you see. They have had that ill luck in all the ages. They and "the Lord's poor"—as the sarcastic phrase goes—have never been able to get away from that Eye's attentions.

Yes, the poor, the humble, the ignorant—they are the ones that catch it. Take the "sleeping sickness," of Africa. This atrocious cruelty has for its victims a race of ignorant and unoffending blacks whom God placed in a remote wilderness, and bent his parental Eye upon them—the one that never sleeps when there is a chance to breed sorrow for somebody. He arranged for these people before the Flood. The chosen agent was a fly, related to the tzetze; the tzetze is a fly which has command of the Zambesi country and stings cattle and horses to death, thus rendering that region uninhabitable by man. The tzetze's awful relative deposits a microbe which produces the Sleeping Sickness. Ham was full of these microbes, and when the voyage was over he discharged them in Africa and the havoc began, never to find amelioration until six thousand years should go by and science should pry into the mystery and hunt out the cause of the disease. The pious nations are now thanking God, and praising him for coming to the rescue of his poor blacks. The pulpit says the praise is due to him, for the reason that the scientists got their inspiration from him. He is surely a curious Being. He commits a fearful crime, continues that crime unbroken for six thousand years, and is then entitled to praise because he suggests to somebody else to modify its severities. He is called patient, and he certainly must be patient, or he would have sunk the pulpit in perdition ages ago for the ghastly compliments it pays him.

Science has this to say about the Sleeping Sickness, otherwise called the Negro Lethargy:

It is characterised by periods of sleep recurring at intervals. The disease lasts from four months to four years, and is always fatal. The victim appears at first languid, weak, pallid, and stupid. His eyelids become puffy, an eruption appears on his skin. He falls asleep while talking, eating, or working. As the disease progresses he is fed with difficulty and becomes much emaciated. The failure of nutrition and the appearance of bedsores are followed by convulsions and death. Some patients become insane.

It is he whom Church and people call Our Father in Heaven who has invented the fly and sent him to inflict this dreary long misery and melancholy and wretchedness, and decay of body and mind, upon a poor savage who has done the Great Criminal no harm. There isn't a man in the world who doesn't pity that poor black sufferer, and there isn't a man that wouldn't make him whole if he could. To find the one person who has no pity for him you must go to heaven; to find the one person who is able to heal him and couldn't be persuaded to do it, you must go to the same place. There is only one father cruel enough to afflict his child with that horrible disease—only one. Not all the eternities can produce another one. Do you like reproachful poetical indignations warmly expressed? Here is one, hot from the heart of a slave:

> "Man's inhumanity to man
> Makes countless thousands mourn!"

I will tell you a pleasant tale which has in it a touch of pathos. A man got religion, and asked the priest what he must do to be worthy of his new estate.

The priest said, "Imitate our Father in Heaven, learn to be like him." The man studied his Bible diligently and thoroughly and understandingly, and then with prayers for heavenly guidance instituted his imitations. He tricked his wife into falling down stairs, and she broke her back and became a paralytic for life; he betrayed his brother into the hands of a sharper, who robbed him of his all and landed him in the almshouse; he inoculated one son with hookworms, another with the sleeping sickness, another with gonorrhea, he furnished one daughter with scarlet fever and ushered her into her teens deaf dumb and blind for life; and after helping a rascal seduce the remaining one, he closed his doors against her and she died in a brothel cursing him. Then he reported to the priest, who said that *that* was no way to imitate his Father in Heaven. The convert asked wherein he had failed, but the priest changed the subject and inquired what kind of weather he was having, up his way [. . . .]

Letter . . .

The Ark continued its voyage, drifting around here and there and yonder, compassless and uncontrolled, the sport of the random winds and the swirling currents. And the rain, the rain, the rain! it kept on falling, pouring, drenching, flooding. No such rain had ever been seen before. Sixteen inches a day had been heard of, but that was nothing to this. This was a hundred and twenty inches a day—ten feet! At this incredible rate it rained forty days and forty nights, and submerged every hill that was 400 feet high. Then the heavens and even the angels went dry; no more water was to be had.

As a Universal Flood it was a disappointment, but there had been heaps of Universal Floods before, as is witnessed by all the Bibles of all the nations, and this was as good as the best one.

At last the Ark soared aloft and came to a rest on the top of Mount Ararat, 17,000 feet above the valley, and its living freight got out and went down the mountain.

ॐ

Afterword

.

The Cultural Conversation about Animals

THE ISSUE OF MAN's treatment of animals acquired greater urgency during the last three decades of the nineteenth century as new books published by Charles Darwin suggested that there might be emotional and intellectual continuities between humankind and the lower animals, in addition to the biological continuities he had put forth in *On the Origin of Species*. In 1871, Darwin had claimed in *The Descent of Man, and Selection in Relation to Sex* that "the lower animals are excited by the same emotions as ourselves."[1] He followed that volume with a book devoted completely to the topic, *The Expression of the Emotions in Man and Animals* (1872).

The Descent of Man, which Twain acquired in late 1871, the year it came out, was the first book by Darwin that Twain read.[2] That book, Twain wrote, "startled the world."[3] The many pencil marks Twain made in the first four chapters of the *Descent of Man* are evidence of the care with which he read it. His well-worn copy is in the Mark Twain Papers in the Bancroft Library at the University of California, Berkeley, where I examined it.[4] The passages that Twain marked show him to be particularly fascinated by evidence that nonhuman animals manifest behavior decidedly similar to the way humans would behave under similar circumstances.[5] For example, one passage that Twain marks in chapter 1 is Darwin's summary of a section in Alfred Brehm's *Life of Animals* (*Thierleben*) detailing the behavior of baboons with hangovers:

. . . the natives of northeastern Africa catch the wild baboons by exposing vessels with strong beer, by which they are made drunk. He has seen some of these animals, which he kept in confinement, in this state; and he gives a laughable account of their behavior and strange grimaces. On the following morning they were very cross and dismal; they held their aching heads with both hands and wore a most pitiable expression; when beer or wine was offered them, they turned away with disgust, but relished the juice of lemons. An American monkey, an Ateles, after getting drunk on brandy, would never touch it again, and thus was wiser than many men. These trifling facts prove how similar the nerves of taste must be in monkeys and man, and how similarly their whole nervous system is affected.[6]

On the following page, Twain marks Darwin's comment that "The whole process of that most important function, the reproduction of the species, is strikingly the same in all mammals, from the first act of courtship by the male to the birth and nurturing of the young."[7]

Twain is clearly having a good time as he reads this book—as his occasional playful response to one of Darwin's comments shows. For example, Darwin casually observes that the "faculty of erecting the ears and of directing them to different points of the compass, is no doubt of the highest service to many animals, as they thus perceive the point of danger; but I have never heard of a man who possessed the least power of erecting his ears—the one movement which might be of use to him." Twain writes in the margin on that page, "'Twould make an ass of him."[8]

In the chapter devoted to a "Comparison of the Mental Powers of Man and the Lower Animals," Twain marks a passage about the emotions dogs feel: "The love of a dog for his master is notorious; in the agony of death he has been known to caress his master, and every one has heard of the dog suffering under vivisection, who licked the hand of the operator; this man, unless he had a heart of stone, must have felt remorse to the last hour of his life."[9] If *The Descent of Man* was Twain's introduction to Darwin, it was probably his introduction to the topic of vivisection as well. (At the time Twain read Darwin's book, only a handful of American scientists and laboratories were doing experiments on animals, and the issue of vivisection would not attract broad public awareness in the United States for over a decade.)[10] Nearly thirty years later Twain would become the most prominent American author to inveigh against the practice of experimenting on conscious, unanesthetized animals— frequently on dogs. Indeed, when Twain referred, in a letter, to having begun to think about what became "A Dog's Tale" over twenty years before he wrote it, he may well have had this passage from *The Descent of Man* in mind.[11]

Twain found Darwin's thoughts on animal intelligence and memory in *The Descent of Man* as noteworthy as his comments about animals' emotional lives. Twain marked this passage, for example: "An adopted kitten scratched the above-mentioned affectionate baboon, who certainly had a fine intellect, for she was much astonished at being scratched, and immediately examined the kitten's feet, and without more ado bit off the claws."[12] Twain also marked accounts of animals using reason that Darwin took from the work of Johann Rengger. In one such story that Twain marked, when Rengger "first gave eggs to his monkeys, . . . they smashed them and thus lost much of their contents; afterward they gently hit one end against some hard body, and picked off the bits of shell with their fingers."[13] In another passage that Twain marked, the monkeys were often given "lumps of sugar" that were "wrapped up in paper; and Rengger sometimes put a live wasp in the paper, so that in hastily unfolding it they got stung; after this had once happened, they always first held the packet to their ears to detect any movement within."[14] On a page that followed, Twain wrote his own examples of animal cognition: "War Horses learn the bugle notes. Fire horses rush at the fire alarm." Twain then added, "That is educated excitement & interest, & imagination, & memory."[15]

Clearly Darwin's *Descent of Man* had a profound impact on Twain's thinking about animals. Although Twain did not reread the book in his later years, his friend and biographer Albert Bigelow Paine believed that "its influence was always present."[16] Between his first introduction to Darwin's writing in 1871 and his acquisition of a twelve-volume set of Darwin's works in the late 1880s, Twain met the great man himself. The two were introduced to each other at Grasmere, in the Lake District, in 1879. But they got to know each other principally through their books. Twain expressed admiration for Darwin on a number of occasions, and Darwin seems to have been a fan of Twain's as well. Evidently Darwin found it relaxing to read from *Innocents Abroad* or other works by Twain at bedtime.[17] And Twain's own writings suggest that he made good use of other of Darwin's volumes in addition to *The Descent of Man*.[18] Alan Gribben notes that "Mark Twain also probably owes the inspiration for one of his most celebrated maxims—'Man is the Only Animal that Blushes. Or needs to'" (from *Following the Equator*) to chapter 13 of Darwin's *Expression of the Emotions in Man and Animals*, which begins, "Blushing is the most peculiar and the most human of all expressions. Monkeys redden from passion, but it would require an overwhelming amount of evidence to make us believe that any animal could blush."[19]

The ferment over animal intelligence and emotions that Darwin's work helped spark prompted an explosion of articles in the popular press. During the last two decades of the nineteenth century and the first decade of the twentieth, popular journals ran articles with titles such as "Are the Lower Animals Approaching Man?" (1887), "The Intelligence of Animals" (1889, 1890, 1891), "Mutual Aid Among Animals" (1890), "A Dog's Humanity" (1891), "Animal Training and Animal Intelligence" (1891), "Is Man the Only Reasoner?" (1891), "Games that Birds Play" (1892), "Intelligence in Animal Life" (1893), "Intelligence of Birds and Animals" (1893), "Mind in Children and Animals" (1893), "Animal Emotions" (1902), "Animal Individuality" (1904), "What Do Animals

Know?" (1904, 1905), and "Do Animals Reason?" (1905)—a small sampling of the many such articles that appeared.[20] *Could* animals think and reason? Could they feel emotions similar to those that humans felt?

In Twain's view, just because animals didn't put their thoughts into human language, it didn't mean that they did not think, and just because animals didn't put their emotions into human language, it didn't mean that they did not feel. Twain claims to have begun his studies of these questions in the late 1870s or early 1880s, a time when, as he recalled, "the storm of indignation raised" by Darwin's *Descent of Man* "was still raging in pulpits and periodicals."[21] The "Instinct and Thought" chapter of *What Is Man?*, a dialogue between a Young Man (Y.M.) and an Old Man (O.M.) published anonymously in 1906, is Twain's most extended direct exploration of these issues. The excerpt that follows provides a lucid overview of Twain's views on the ability of animals to think, reason, and communicate:

O.M. . . . Here is a case of a bird and a stranger as related by a naturalist. An Englishman saw a bird flying around about his dog's head, down in the grounds, and uttering cries of distress. He went there to see about it. The dog had a young bird in his mouth—unhurt. The gentleman rescued it and put it on a bush and brought the dog away. Early the next morning the mother bird came for the gentleman, who was sitting on his verandah, and by its maneuvers persuaded him to follow it to a distant part of the grounds—flying a little way in front of him and waiting for him to catch up, and so on; and keeping to the winding path, too, instead of flying the near way across lots. The distance covered was four hundred yards. The same dog was the culprit; he had the young bird again, and once more he had to give it up. Now the mother-bird had reasoned it all out: since the stranger had helped her once, she inferred that he would do it again; she knew where to find him, and she went upon her errand with confidence. Her mental processes were what Edison's would have been. She put this and that together— and that is all that thought is—and out of them built her logical arrangement of inferences. Edison couldn't have done it any better himself.

Y.M.   Do you believe that many of the dumb animals can think?

O.M.   Yes—the elephant, the monkey, the horse, the dog, the parrot, the macaw, the mocking-bird, and many others. The elephant whose mate fell into a pit, and who dumped dirt and rubbish into the pit till the bottom was raised high enough to enable the captive to step out, was equipped with the reasoning quality. I conceive that all animals that can learn things through teaching and drilling have to know how to observe, and put this and that together and draw an inference—the process of thinking. Could you teach an idiot of manuals of arms, and to advance, retreat, and go through complex field maneuvers at the word of command?

Y.M. Not if he were a thorough idiot.

O.M. Well, canary birds can learn all that; dogs and elephants learn all sorts of wonderful things. They must surely be able to notice, and to put things together, and say to themselves, "I get the idea, now: when I do so and so, as per order, I am praised and fed; when I do differently, I am punished." Fleas can be taught nearly anything that a Congressman can. . . .

Y.M. O, come! you are abolishing the intellectual frontier which separates man and beast. . . . You cannot mean to seriously say there is no such frontier.

O.M. I do say it seriously. The instances of the horse, the gull, the mother-bird, and the elephant show that those creatures put their this's and that's together just as Edison would have done it and drew the same inferences that he would have drawn. Their mental machinery was just like his, also its manner of working. . . . there is no frontier.

Y.M. It looks exasperatingly true; and is distinctly offensive. It elevates the dumb beasts to—to—

O.M. Let us drop that lying phrase, and call them the Unrevealed Creatures; so far as we can know, there is no such thing as a dumb beast. . . . "Dumb" beast suggests an animal that has no thought-machinery, no understanding, no speech, no way of communicating what is in its mind. We know that a hen *has* speech. We cannot understand everything she says, but we easily learn two or three of her phrases. We know when she is saying "I have laid an egg;" we know when she is saying to the chicks, "Run here, dears, I've found a worm;" we know what she is saying when she voices a warning: "Quick! hurry! gather yourselves under mamma, there's a hawk coming!" We understand the cat when she stretches herself out, purring with affection and contentment and lifts up a soft voice and says, "Come, kitties, supper's ready;" we understand her when she goes mourning about and says, "Where can they be?—they are lost—won't you help me hunt for them?" . . . The clearness and exactness of the few of the hen's speeches which we understand is argument that she can communicate to her kind a hundred things which we cannot comprehend—in a word, that she can converse. And this argument is also applicable in the case of others of the great army of the Unrevealed. It is just like man's vanity and impertinence to call an animal dumb because it is dumb to his dull perceptions.[22]

Twain's views here echo those expressed in *The Descent of Man,* where Darwin opined that "the senses and intuitions, the various emotions and faculties, such as love, memory, attention, curiosity, imitation, reason, etc., of which man boasts, may be found in an incipient, or even sometimes in a well-developed condition, in the lower animals."[23]

They also echo in both substance and style comments Michel de Montaigne made in essays Twain bought while living in Hartford in 1873.[24] Centuries before Darwin, Montaigne had argued that the gap between animals and humans was smaller than men would like to imagine. Like Darwin and Twain after him, Montaigne was intrigued by examples of animal reasoning and intelligence. His famous essay, "Apology for Raimond Sebond," used the same example of reasoning on the part of elephants that Twain would later use in the passage quoted above: "when, by the craft of the hunter, one of them [an elephant] is trapped in certain deep pits prepared for them and covered over with brush to deceive them, all the rest, in great diligence, bring a great many stones and logs of wood to raise the bottom so that he may get out."[25] When Montaigne recounts an ancient philosopher's description of a dog who seems to have grasped the basic logic of the syllogism, he imagines the thought process going on in the dog's head in a manner that Twain would echo when he imagines the kind of thought process in which the mother bird engaged.[26] Both have no hesitation in labeling the process "thought" and "reason": "This is reasoning in the dog," Montaigne wrote, while Twain asserted, "the mother-bird had reasoned it all out." Montaigne also prefigured the strategy that Twain used of "translating" what animals are saying to each other in their own languages to demonstrate the "impertinence" of man's calling "an animal dumb because it is dumb to his dull perceptions."[27] (The comment in "A Dog's Tale"— "but for the beast's intelligence—it's *reason*, I tell you!—the child would have perished!"—also echoes Montaigne's comment, "This is reasoning in the dog.") [28]

Some of Twain's portrayals of animals that one might be tempted to call anthropomorphic, actually reflected a major strand of scientific thought of his day—and our own day as well. An article in the *Wall Street Journal* on 27 October 2006, headlined "What Your Pet Is Thinking," noted that "Ethologists, the scientists who study animal behavior, have amassed thousands of studies showing that animals can count, understand cause and effect, form abstractions, solve problems, use tools and even deceive. But lately scientists have gone a step further. Researchers around the world are providing tantalizing evidence that animals not only learn and remember but they may also have consciousness—in other words, they may be capable of thinking about their thoughts and knowing that they know."[29] And while both scholarly and popular considerations of animal intelligence have increased in recent years, studies of animals' emotional life have proliferated as well.[30]

While reading Darwin and Montaigne helped prompt Twain to ponder what humans and animals had in common regarding thought and feeling, William Lecky's work helped prompt him to think about what humans owed animals from a moral standpoint. In his well-worn and heavily marked-up copy of Lecky's *History of European Morals from Augustus to Charlemagne*, Twain would have read that "At one time the benevolent affections embrace merely the family, soon the circle expanding includes first a class, then a nation, then a coalition of nations, then all humanity, and finally, its influence is felt in the dealings of man with the animal world."[31] But it was Montaigne who provided Twain with some rhetorical models when it came to condemning man's arrogance in positioning himself at the apex of the animal kingdom. Montaigne asks, "How does [man] know, by the strength of his understanding, the secret and internal motions of animals?—from what comparison betwixt them and us does he conclude the stupidity he attributes to them? When I play with my cat who knows whether I do not make her more sport than she makes me? We mutually divert one another with our play. If I have my hour to begin or to refuse, she also has hers. . . ."[32] Montaigne posited the presumptuousness of man's certainty that he is the "highest animal," writing, "Presumption is our natural and original disease. The most wretched and frail of all creatures is man, and withal the proudest."[33] One hears echoes of Montaigne's description of man as "the most wretched and frail of all creatures" in the picture of man that Twain draws in "Man's Place in the Animal World":

Man seems to be a rickety poor sort of a thing, any way you take him; a kind of British Museum of infirmities and inferiorities. He is always undergoing repairs. A machine that was as unreliable as he is would have no market. . . . For style, look at the Bengal tiger—that ideal of grace, beauty, physical perfection, majesty. And then look at Man—that poor thing. He is the Animal of the Wig, the Trepanned Skull, the Ear Trumpet, the Glass Eye, the Pasteboard Nose, the Porcelain Teeth, the Silver Windpipe, the Wooden Leg—a creature that is mended and patched all over, from top to bottom. If he can't get renewals of his bricabrac in the next world, what will he look like?[34]

Twain explains that his studies have prompted him to renounce his "allegiance to the Darwinian theory of the Ascent of Man from the Lower Animals" since a "new and truer" theory "to be named the *Descent* of Man from the Higher Animals" makes more sense. Man, Twain writes, is the only animal that for "sordid wages will march out . . . and help to slaughter strangers of his own species who have done him no harm and with whom he has no quarrel." Twain continues,

Man is the only Patriot. He sets himself apart in his own country, under his own flag, and sneers at the other nations, and keeps multitudinous uniformed assassins on hand at heavy expense to grab slices of other people's countries, and keep *them* from grabbing slices of *his*. And in the intervals between campaigns he washes the blood off his hands and works for "the universal brotherhood of man"—with his mouth.[35]

Far from being "the Reasoning Animal" that he claims to be, man "is the Unreasoning Animal." Twain adds, "the strongest count against his intelligence is the fact that with that record back of him he blandly sets himself up as the head animal of the lot; whereas by his own standards he is the bottom one."[36]

In Twain's *What Is Man?* the Young Man who was reluctantly persuaded that animals could think was sure that there was still one thing that set human beings off from other animals:

Y.M. Very well, let them have what they've got, and welcome; there is still a wall, and a lofty one. They haven't the Moral Sense; we have it, and it lifts us immeasurably above them.

O.M. What makes you think that?

Y.M. Now look here—let's call a halt. I have stood the other infamies and insanities and that is enough; I am not going to have man and the other animals put on the same level morally.

O.M. I wasn't going to hoist man up to that.

Y.M. This is too much! I think it is not right to jest about such things.

O.M. I am not jesting, I am merely reflecting a plain and simple truth—and without uncharitableness. The fact that man knows right from wrong proves his intellectual superiority to the other creatures; but the fact that he can do wrong proves his moral inferiority to any creature that cannot. It is my belief that this position is not assailable.[37]

Twain's caustic discussion in both "What Is Man?" and "Man's Place in the Animal World" of the flaws man has but "higher animals" lack also resonates with Montaigne's charge of humankind's unwarranted arrogance, sense of entitlement, and airs of superiority. Montaigne's views clearly prefigure the central point of "Was the World made for Man?" Twain's satiric challenge to the arguments creationists used to undermine Darwin. The author of "Man's Place in the Animal World" clearly would have found himself agreeing with Montaigne's assertion that in many ways, "animals excel us."[38]

Darwin's theories, as well as articles in the popular press about humans and animals sharing, at least to some degree, the ability to think and feel, made the question of how humans ought to treat animals particularly vexing during this period, and helped attract support for anticruelty and antivivisection movements in Europe and the United States. Agitation for anticruelty legislation had begun in Britain in the early 1800s, and in the United States in the 1820s, but in both countries the movement for animal welfare did not pick up broad popular support until the last third of the nineteenth century. Early British animal welfare activists often invoked the comment made in 1789 by philosopher Jeremy Bentham. Arguing that animals were sentient beings who had the right to be protected from mistreatment by humans, Bentham wrote, "The question is not, Can they *reason*? Nor, Can they *talk*? But Can they *suffer*?"[39] Activists had worked to get Parliament to pass the first animal welfare act as early as 1800 but did not succeed until 1822, when a law punishing excessive cruelty to cattle, horses, sheep, and mules was passed. In 1824, under the leadership of Richard "Humanity" Martin, the Society for the Prevention of Cruelty to Animals was born in England. During the next four decades the organization lobbied to strengthen and extend protection to all domesticated animals (including dogs, chickens, pigs, and cats), distributed thousands of humane publications, and established veterinary hospitals and animal shelters for stray cats and dogs.[40]

Widely publicized British animal advocacy helped inspire American reformers to pass state laws punishing wanton cruelty toward domestic animals, starting with a New York law in 1828. Henry Bergh founded the first animal welfare organization in the United States in 1866, the American Society for the Prevention of Cruelty to Animals. (The admiring profile of Bergh and his activities that Mark Twain wrote the year after the ASPCA was founded, entitled "Cruelty to Animals," is reprinted in part 1.) By the time Bergh founded the ASPCA, thirteen other states and six territories had joined New York in passing anticruelty legislation.[41] In 1868, George T. Angell founded the Massachusetts Society for the Prevention of Cruelty to Animals. Anticruelty advocates in the United States, under the guidance of Bergh and Angell, succeeded in directing Americans' attention during the 1880s and 1890s to the issue of the humane treatment of animals, particularly the horses that pulled carts and omnibuses in every American city (each year in the largest cities in the United States at this time, some twenty-five thousand streetcar horses died from overwork).[42] In 1882, taking a page from the animal welfare movement in Britain, Angell's Massachusetts society came up with the idea of promoting "Bands of Mercy" throughout America—groups of schoolchildren who pledged to work against cruelty to animals. By the 1890s, almost half a million young people who pledged "kindness and justice to all living creatures" belonged to over eleven thousand Bands of Mercy.[43] In 1890, Angell published the first American edition of Anna Sewell's *Black Beauty* and distributed two million free copies through the Bands of Mercy.[44]

Organizations like those founded by Bergh and Angell proved to be sources of empowerment for middle-class young women like Mark Twain's daughters Clara and Jean. The blue cards issued to members by the Society for the Prevention of Cruelty to Animals allowed them to report violations of the law to the authorities. One can see how the system worked from Clara's account of her experience in France. She recalls that she and Jean

hastened to become members of the Society for Prevention of Cruelty to Animals a few days after arriving in Paris. We were very proud of the blue cards enabling us to cut short the beating of any horse on the street, whether driven by a private coachman or a coal-wagon driver. We were kept extremely busy at our task, too, for in both France and Italy little love is wasted on the dumb beasts.[45]

On one occasion, Clara witnessed a man

standing up in his wagon and beating his horse with might and main. A policeman stood near by, but no one lifted a hand to protect the poor animal against his cruelty. My blood ran cold, and without further delay I flew from my carriage and called to the man to wait a moment. But he was too far gone in rage to stop for the sight of a childish-looking girl with nothing but a piece of blue paper in her hand. He mocked me with a laugh, and my temper rose higher. I whisked off and showed my card to the policeman. Very unwillingly conceding my rights, he returned with me to the savage driver. Several minutes elapsed before I was satisfied that the man's name and address would be reported at headquarters in proper fashion. . . . [46]

Clara's behavior collected quite a crowd—a fact which led her rather overprotective father to take a somewhat dim view of her engaging in these "citizen's arrests" of sorts. Later that evening, (Clara reports) Twain said to his wife, "Do you know, Livy, that Clara holds up the entire Paris traffic with that blue card? Do you approve of that?" Livy's response was "Youth dear, you would do the same thing if the blue card were yours."[47] Twain never got himself a blue card—although he viewed his daughters' activities with pride.[48] It was a more radical wing of the animal welfare movement that would engage his own energies and attention.

The most controversial issue that animal welfare activists tackled during the last third of the nineteenth century was vivisection—the practice of operating and experimenting on live animals. Those who opposed vivisection were appalled by the pain it inflicted on animals. Those who defended it argued for the potential scientific progress that it made possible. Its most partisan opponents felt that vivisection was never justified under any circumstances, while its most committed defenders felt that it should be the experimenter's prerogative to do any kind of vivisection he or she desired, at any time. Others took a position in between these extremes, arguing that if vivisection were properly regulated, it could be an acceptable means of increasing scientific knowledge.

In Britain in 1876, journalist and suffragist Frances Power Cobbe led a successful drive to have Parliament pass the "Cruelty to Animals Act," a law regulating experimentation on live animals, which inspired Henry Bergh to push for similar legislation in the United States. The 1876 British law mandated the monitoring and licensing of all animal researchers, and outlawed some of the most repugnant forms of experimentation (such as "performing multiple experiments on the same, unanesthetized animal").[49] But the legislation was so weakened by the medical establishment by the time Parliament passed it, that Cobbe dubbed it "the Vivisector's Charter."[50] Cobbe fought tirelessly for stronger antivivisection legislation during the following two decades and beyond, founding antivivisectionist organizations that took an increasingly hard line against all forms of experimentation on live animals.[51] With Bergh's encouragement, Caroline Earle White organized an American Anti-Vivisection Society in 1883, but its efforts to pass legislation regulating vivisection failed to generate the broad support that such efforts garnered in Britain.[52]

Debates about vivisection divided Victorian society in both Britain and the United States. Some, like Henry Bergh, advocated the prohibition not of all experiments on animals but "only those that rejected the use of anesthesia."[53] Others, most notably Frances Power Cobbe, fought for the total abolition of experiments on live animals. Darwin himself embodied the ambivalence of his society on this issue, being unwilling to engage in any form of vivisection himself but also unwilling to forego the scientific advances that the practice might potentially yield. The medical profession circulated provivisection pamphlets during the 1880s with titles such as "Vivisection: What Good Has It Done?" which argued that most of what we know about "the movement of the blood . . . the mode of action of the heart, and of the other processes by which the blood is effected, of the functions of the nervous system, of the functions of the brain, . . . of the functions of the spinal cord, . . . is almost entirely due to vivisection."[54] But the advances in medicine that animal experimentation helped make possible in the twentieth century were still largely hypothetical during this period, and scientific medicine was just beginning to acquire widespread support by the 1890s. Vivisection's foes were still able to argue that little medical knowledge was directly indebted to experiments on live animals.[55] Indeed, some doctors argued for the negative effects of vivisection on medical education. Dr. Albert Leffingwell, for example, maintained that "witnessing or performing what amounted to deliberate torture inevitably 'deadens one's humanity and begets indifference.'"[56]

During the 1890s, the popular press in both Britain and the United States ran articles defending vivisection and attacking it. Both sides claimed to have the best interests of humanity at heart. As vivisectors held out the promise of finding cures, inoculations, and surgical procedures that could have real benefit for humans, antivivisection activists argued that experiments on animals had yielded relatively little knowledge of genuine value. The antivivisectionists' main argument, however, was that a society that tolerated the cruelty that so much of vivisection involved was a society that had lost its moral compass. Typical of this latter response, perhaps, was a squib the popular magazine *Life* ran in January, 1898. Under the headline "Future Vivisectors," *Life* featured an extract from a recent story in the press followed by a mordant editorial comment.

FUTURE VIVISECTORS

"The arrest of the boys developed a story of degrading cruelty. After stealing the rabbits, they hid them in the basement of their home and at various times amused themselves by cutting off the rabbits' ears and tails, punching out their eyes, and in other ways maltreating them, in order to hear them 'holler,' as they said, and *also to find out how long they would live after being tortured.* The dead rabbits were found under an adjoining house. Pigeons which had been decapitated were also found there. The boys probably will be sent to Reform School."

Why send them to a Reform School? What's the matter with a Medical School? The dear boys are simply doing what every vivisector seems to take a pride in, and what is taught and practiced in Medical Colleges.[57]

The growth of the medical research community in the 1890s helped fuel the antivivisection movement but also emboldened the scientific community to fight back. As Patricia Peck Gossel observes, large numbers of research animals were central to the new studies being done in bacteriology and in the production of antitoxin and antiserum. The journals that scientists banded together to edit "credited the scientific laboratory and animal experimentation with a long list of beneficial achievements—anaesthesia, antiseptic surgery and new advances in therapeutics such as the prevention of rabies and the 'cure' of diphtheria."[58] Diane Beers notes that "Although antivivisectionists correctly challenged claims of vivisection's role in certain medical discoveries and raised valid questions about the value of using animals, they also made mistakes" and their "opponents pounced on the errors."[59] For example, some prominent antivivisectionists in the United States "denounced the treatments for rabies and diphtheria as unwarranted or dangerous, only to be discredited by additional scientific confirmation of the shots' effectiveness. Leaders of the provivisection faction . . . enthusiastically exposed the errors and dismissed their nemeses as incompetent and 'wholly indifferent to . . . facts.'"[60] Provivisectionists argued that experiments on animals had also "generated the insights that led to the treatment for syphilis; improved surgical techniques; and enhanced current knowledge of tumors, abscesses, disorders of the brain, and a litany of additional illnesses."[61] They tended to dismiss "the issue of pain, claiming that ignorance and emotionalism led antivivisectionists to draw erroneous conclusions about the amount of pain animals endured during experiments."[62] In addition, a number of scientists debunked as "categorically unscientific" any statement about the emotional capacities of nonhuman animals as they lobbied against laws regulating animal experimentation.[63]

In the 1890s, Jennifer Mason writes, Darwin's *Expression of the Emotions in Man and Animals* (1872) "was all but expunged from the canon of Darwin's works in the wake of the delegitimization of . . . [the] belief in a fundamental similarity between human and nonhuman emotional experience."[64] With this rationale for animal protection challenged, animal welfare advocates increasingly invoked the responsibility that the strong had to protect the weak—an argument that would be increasingly applied to society's responsibility to protect children as well as animals.[65]

The animal welfare movement, decentralized and divided as to priorities and tactics (as it always had been), ranged from those who simply wanted to extend humane education in schools and protect children from abuse to those who advocated "the abolition of animal experimentation, hunting, meat-eating, and animals' status as property."[66] By the start of World War I, the medical advances that experimentation had yielded had taken much of the wind out of the sails of the antivivisection movement.[67] In general, the movement's strategy shifted from seeking abolition to advocating more stringent and enforced regulation, and to allowing animal experimentation only when other routes to knowledge were blocked—a position held by many people today.[68]

Today's animal welfare activists who campaign against animal testing of cosmetics and other non-lifesaving products and procedures are heirs to the principled men and women at the turn of the century who felt that inflicting pain on animals to gain trivial forms of knowledge eroded their own humanity in unacceptable ways. The cultural conversation about animal welfare and experimental science at the turn of the century shaped debates and discussions of these issues in ways that remain with us today. Modern-day regulations stipulating accountability, responsibility, use of proper anesthesia, and attentiveness to the health and well-being of laboratory research animals are the legacy of that moment in history. The animal welfare advocates of that era helped ensure that over the next century and more, when science and medicine argued for the utility of experiments on animals in the fight against disease, those experiments would be conducted in a manner designed to minimize gratuitous suffering. In short, they helped twentieth-century and twenty-first-century science aspire (in theory, if not always in practice) to functioning in a more humane way.

Mark Twain and the Animal Welfare Movement

The dog is a gentleman; I hope to go to his heaven, not man's.
—SLC to William Dean Howells, 2–13 April 1899

How did Mark Twain become engaged in the animal welfare movement in the first place and why did he write the three polemical pieces dealing with animal welfare for which he is best known: his 1899 letter to the London Anti-Vivisection Society, his 1903 story "A Dog's Tale," and his 1906 novella *A Horse's Tale*? Although these questions cannot be answered with certainty, some intriguing hypotheses emerge as we begin to explore them.

On 18 March 1900, the *New York Times* reprinted a letter that Mark Twain had sent to the *Times* of London acknowledging his election as honorary member of the London Anti-Vivisection Society. "Dear Sir," he had written, "I am glad of the honor, since I have no friendly feeling toward either 'sport' or vivisection. Sincerely yours, S. L. Clemens."[69] "No friendly feeling" was an understatement, as most British readers would have recognized. Twain's impassioned opposition to the practice of experimentation on live animals was well known. Nearly a year before this brief letter ran in the *New York Times*, he had written another letter—to Sidney G. Trist, secretary of the London Anti-Vivisection Society—condemning vivisection in the strongest language he could muster. Trist gave Twain's 26 May 1899 letter wide circulation in the press, and also had numerous copies printed as a pamphlet that was sold to benefit the society.

Somehow, in the spring of 1899, as Twain was packing up his family to leave Vienna for London, a paper that Dr. Stephen F. Smith, a member of the Royal College of Surgeons, had presented to the National Individualist Club, came across Twain's desk, kindling his outrage (as he tells us in the letter, which is included in its entirety in part 3 of this volume). Although no copy of Smith's antivivisectionist paper is extant, a perusal of a book Smith published shortly thereafter, *Scientific Research: A View from Within,* expands on some of the same ideas discussed in the paper that Twain quotes in his letter. In the book, Smith quotes French vivisector Claude Bernard as having noted that the drug

Curare renders all movement impossible, but it does not hinder the animal from suffering, and from being conscious of pain. . . . A gentle sleep seems to occupy the transition from life to death. But it is nothing of the sort; the external appearances are deceitful. In this motionless body behind that glazing eye, and with all the appearance of death, sensitiveness and intelligence persist in their entirety. The corpse before us hears and distinguishes all that is done around it.[70]

No record of the "National Individualist Club" seems to exist, and we don't know how Twain came upon Smith's paper. Be that as it may, in late May 1899, shortly before leaving Vienna for London, Twain wrote Trist the letter that is reprinted in part 3 of this book. A look at Twain's reading, at his friendships with men who were committed antivivisectionists, and at the state of vivisection in fin-de-siècle Vienna might help us understand the origins of this famous text.

Some of the nineteenth-century British writers whom Twain admired most were outspoken on the issue of cruelty to animals and were active supporters of the antivivisection movement. Twain was a devoted fan of the poems of Robert Browning, for example, and frequently entertained family and friends by reading them aloud. Browning, a vehement opponent of vivisection and vice-president of one of the two leading British antivivisection groups, the Victoria Street Society, wrote in 1875 that "he would rather submit to the worst of deaths, so far as pain goes, than have a single dog or cat tortured on the pretence of saving me a twinge or two."[71] Browning wrote two antivivisection poems, "Tray" (1879), in which a dog who rescues a child is repaid with the prospect of being vivisected, and "Arcades Ambo" (1889), which attacks the vivisector's cowardice and selfishness.[72]

Since there is no record of Twain's having met the secretary of the London Anti-Vivisection Society to whom he sent his letter, presumably a friend or acquaintance with ties to the British antivivisection movement must have prevailed upon Twain to take time out from the chaos of moving to write. Twain had spent significant time in the late 1890s in London, and one of his London friends who was deeply committed to the antivivisection movement might have urged Twain to take this stand: Canon Basil Wilberforce, Anglican Archdeacon of Westminster Abbey. The nature of Twain's friendship with Wilberforce can be gleaned from the notes the two men exchanged. In July 1899, shortly after he returned to London from Vienna, Twain attended a luncheon party at which Wilberforce was present as well. Each mistakenly left with the other's hat. Twain wrote Wilberforce this note:

> Prince of Wales Hotel, De Vere Gardens,
> *July, 3, 1899.*
>
> Dear Canon Wilberforce,—It is 8 P.M. During the past four hours I have not been able to take anything that did not belong to me; during all that time I have not been able to stretch a fact beyond the frontiers of truth try as I might, & meantime, not only my morals have moved the astonishment of all who have come in contact with me, but my manners have gained more compliments than they have been accustomed to. This mystery is causing my family much alarm. It is difficult to account for it. I find I haven't my own hat. Have you developed any novelties of conduct since you left Mr. Murray's, & have they been of a character to move the concern of your friends? I think it must be this that has put me under this happy charm; but, oh dear! I tremble for the other man!
>
> *Sincerely yours,*
> *S. L. Clemens.*[73]

The following note from Wilberforce crossed Twain's and arrived almost as soon as Twain sent his own note:

> *July 3, 1899.*
>
> Dear Mr. Clemens,—I have been conscious of a vivacity and facility of expression this afternoon beyond the normal and I have just discovered the reason!! I have seen the historic signature "Mark Twain" in my hat!! Doubtless you have been suffering from a corresponding dullness & have wondered why. . . . If you

should be passing this way to-morrow will you look in and change hats? Or shall I send it to the hotel?

I am, very sincerely yrs.,

20 Dean's Yard.   *Basil Wilberforce.*[74]

Other letters from Wilberforce to Twain in the Mark Twain Papers make it clear that the men who engaged in the jocular exchange quoted above enjoyed each other's company. On several occasions, Canon Wilberforce and his wife invited Twain to give informal after-dinner talks in their drawing room in Dean's Yard at Westminster Abbey.[75] In one letter inviting Twain to lunch, Wilberforce also mentioned that he had just been preaching from the pulpit "about your indictment of that *scoundrel* the King of the Belgians and telling my people to buy the book."[76] The two men shared some political views. It is highly likely that on one of the occasions when they got together, Wilberforce would have told Twain about an issue that increasingly drew his ire in very public ways: vivisection.

Wilberforce was an official patron of the London Anti-Vivisection society.[77] A book of his, *Sermons Preached in Westminster Abbey*, was advertised in the anti-vivisectionist book by Dr. Stephen F. Smith discussed above.[78] The strength of Wilberforce's views on vivisection is apparent in a sermon he preached in Westminster Abbey, where he asserted, "I believe that no greater cruelty is perpetuated on this earth than that which is committed in the name of science in some physiological laboratories."[79] An 1899 collection of pamphlets entitled *Cruelty to Animals* includes a selection called "'Inhuman Devils'—Canon Wilberforce on Vivisection" that reprinted a lengthy letter he had written in 1892 asserting that

Our contention is that the public has been blinded by scientific dust thrown into its eyes, and that multitudes are wholly unaware of the unspeakable and fiendish cruelties that are perpetrated in the name of science.

The public is taught to believe that vivisections are rare, that animals subjected to them are under anaesthetics, and that the discoveries made by the process are of infinite value. . . . Let us glance at some of the so-called "experiments," and judge whether men endowed with ordinary sensibilities and imaginations could perform them without temporarily transforming themselves into "inhuman devils." . . . They include baking, freezing, burning, pouring boiling oil on living animals, saturating them with inflammable oil and setting them on fire, starving them to death, skinning alive, cutting off the breasts while giving milk, gouging out their eyes, larding the feet with nails, forcing broken glass into ears, intestines, and muscles, and making incisions in the skull and twisting about a bent needle in the brain, etc.[80]

Wilberforce cites a book by Frances Power Cobbe that documents "every experiment described." The letter (which goes on for six pages) cites other experiments in which animals were tortured that yielded little if any scientific knowledge (including one in which "fifty-one dogs had portions of the brain hemisphere washed out of the head, which had been pierced in several places. This was repeated four times; the mutilated creatures and their behavior having been studied for months. Most of the animals died at last of inflammation of the brain").[81]

Wilberforce's passionate, partisan commitment to the cause comes across just as clearly in the letters he sent to Frances Power Cobbe. Cobbe had founded Britain's first antivivisection society in 1875 (the Victoria Street Society, whose name later was changed to the National Anti-Vivisection Society), and went on to found the British Union for the Abolition of Vivisection in 1898. A tireless speaker, writer, and activist, Cobbe had her share of opponents. Wilberforce took on the role of personal cheerleader in these fights, offering advice, helping her strategize, building her confidence, and cheering her on, as his letters to her in the Huntington Library show.[82]

Wilberforce might well have sparked Twain's thinking on this topic, urging him to write the 1899 letter to the secretary of the London Anti-Vivisection Society, an organization in which Wilberforce was deeply involved. On 26 April 1899, less than a month before Twain wrote his letter, a well-attended meeting of the National Anti-Vivisection Society (sponsored by the London Anti-Vivisection Society) was held in St. James Hall in Piccadilly and was covered prominently in the press. The chairman of the meeting noted with alarm that "in ten years the number of experiments had increased from 1,069 to 8,800." He and his fellow antivivisectionists argued that "medical inspection of vivisection had become something of a fraud" and that "the sufferings entailed on the animals had become so great and the results so small that their patience had become exhausted."[83] A few weeks later, another meeting of the National Anti-Vivisection Society was held at which Stephen Coleridge made a motion affirming that "the torture inflicted upon animals by licensed vivisectors in the laboratories of this country is unjustifiable" and pledging the organization "to support measures in Parliament to put an end to it." Canon Wilberforce was one of three people who spoke on behalf of the measure, which passed with only a handful of dissenting votes.[84] Less than a week later, Twain sent this organization his own letter attacking vivisection.[85]

In addition to Wilberforce, other friends and acquaintances of Twain's supported the antivivisection movement and may have played a role in shaping his thinking on this issue. One was the expatriate American writer Moncure D. Conway, who had lived in London since before the Civil War and had been friends with Twain since the early 1870s.[86] Conway was also an old friend of Cobbe's.[87] Among the extracts from letters related to the practice of vivisection in America reprinted in the anonymously written 1899 volume *Cruelty to Animals* is this comment from Conway: "I do not think vivisection should be allowed for demonstration of facts already discovered."[88]

Twain wrote the 1899 letter while living in Vienna, a city in which the practice of vivisection had been a subject of recent negative attention. Vienna was home to Dr. Simon Stricker, a vivisector of some infamy after Dr. Albert Leffingwell, an American physician, published his description of Stricker's work in 1894. Leffingwell tells us that a European journal had recently described one of Stricker's class demonstrations:

> . . . he destroys the spinal cord of a dog by thrusting a steel probe into the spinal column, producing, we may say, the most atrocious torture it is possible to conceive. The animal evinced its agony by fearful convulsions; but it was permitted to utter no cry that might evoke sympathy, for previous to the demonstration its laryngeal nerves had been cut! No vivisection could be more utterly unjustifiable or more fiendish in atrocity. . . . [89]

Twain may well have heard stories of Stricker's notorious lab while he was living in the same city.

Twain's daughter Jean had been deeply committed to the anticruelty wing of the animal welfare movement all of her adult life.[90] But there is no record of her having been engaged in antivivisection activities. It is much more likely that Twain's reading, his friendship with prominent antivivisectionists like Canon Wilberforce, and his possible awareness of what had gone on in laboratories in Vienna, played a greater role in prompting him to write to the *Times* of London in 1899.

What may have prompted Twain to write "A Dog's Tale," his famous antivivisection story narrated in the first person by a dog, which he published in December 1903? Animal "autobiographies" were a well-known genre at the turn of the century.[91] But the popularity of stories with first-person animal narrators does not explain why Twain chose to write the distinctively polemical piece at this moment in time. It may well have been a response to the Brown Dog Affair.

In 1902, a twenty-four-year old Swedish woman of independent means named Louise (also known as Lizzie) Lind-af-Hageby and her friend, Liese Schartau, both committed antivivisectionists, enrolled as physiology students at University College London in order to see for themselves whether the school was violating national laws about experimentation on animals.[92] The two undercover investigators recorded what they witnessed over a period of months, and contacted Stephen Coleridge at the National Anti-Vivisection Society, who helped them publish their findings as a short book, *The Shambles of Science*, in 1903.

Particularly shocking was their account of the "a brown terrier dog with a recent abdominal wound which had been carried into the laboratory strapped to a board" and "then subjected to an operation in the throat by Professor William Bayliss" in apparent violation of the law prohibiting a vivisected animal from being used for one experiment, revived, and then used for another. As Coral Lansbury notes in *The Old Brown Dog: Women, Workers and Vivisection in Edwardian England*, "The dog had struggled throughout the course of the demonstration and was still alive when it was taken from the lecture room."[93] When *The Shambles of Science* came out in early 1903, Coleridge publicly charged that Bayliss, the physiologist involved, had broken the law, and Bayliss countersued to protect his reputation. Throughout all of 1903, there was tremendous press coverage of the controversy. The case was heard in court in November 1903.[94] The liberal and working-class press strongly supported Coleridge, and the *Daily News* even published the entire court proceedings in November 1903, one month before "A Dog's Tale" came out in *Harper's*.[95] Coleridge was frustrated if not surprised when the court found for Bayliss, ordered that the offending section of *The Shambles of Science* be removed from subsequent editions, and fined Coleridge two thousand pounds. The *Daily News*, Lansbury notes, "immediately opened a subscription fund to pay Coleridge's damages, and the money was oversubscribed within the month. If Coleridge and Lind-af-Hageby had lost in court, they were not vanquished in public opinion. The case had brought them the publicity they desired, and the sales of *The Shambles of Science* increased."[96]

On 26 January 1904, some two months after the court case ended, Coleridge ordered 3,000 copies of "A Dog's Tale" to be specially printed by *Harper's*, aware of the potential of the story to keep the most callous offenses of the vivisectors fresh in the public's mind.[97] Whether Twain's story was directly inspired by news of the Brown Dog Affair or more broadly by the widespread discussion of incidents like it in the antivivisection community, it ended up playing an important role in the antivivisection movement and cemented Twain's reputation as a leading voice for animal welfare.

Two years later, in 1906, Lind-af-Hageby and a colleague, working with Coleridge, George Bernard Shaw, and others, decided to present to the borough of Battersea a distinctive drinking fountain with a statue of a Brown Dog on it and a provocative inscription:

In memory of the Brown Terrier Dog Done to Death in the Laboratories of University College in February, 1903, after having endured Vivisection extending over more than Two Months and having been handed over from one Vivisector to Another Till Death came to his Release. Also in Memory of the 232 dogs Vivisected at the same place during the year 1902. Men and women of England, how long shall these Things be?[98]

Battersea was both a working-class neighborhood known for its radical politics and the site of the Battersea Dogs' Home, the largest institution of its kind in England.[99] The Brown Dog quickly became a symbol of all oppressed groups in society—particularly workers. Over the next few years, the erection, destruction, and replacement of this statue to the Brown Dog would produce riots and demonstrations of a size comparable only to those set off by the suffrage movement.[100]

Lind-af-Hageby herself paid tribute to Twain directly for the role his work had played in the cause of antivivisection. In a letter she wrote on 2 July 1907, Lind-af-Hageby gratefully told Twain, "Your pen has so skillfully & so beautifully served the Anti-Vivisection Movement. . . . Your words are listened to where the fervent representations of other men are passed by unheard." She expressed her gratitude for "your power to mould the thoughts of the world."[101] Twain's effectiveness in the past in championing "the defenceless creatures which are exploited for scientific purposes" encouraged Lind-af-Hageby to ask whether he might be willing to grant her a brief interview during his stay in England that summer, where he had gone to receive an honorary degree from Oxford. It is not known whether Twain found time in his busy schedule to meet her.[102] The sincerity and effusiveness of Lind-af-Hageby's gratitude lends credence to the idea that "A Dog's Tale" bore a close connection to the cause that was so close to her heart.

Twain did find time in July 1907 during his stay in London to acquire a copy of the autobiography of Britain's leading antivivisection activist, who had died in 1904.[103] The nearly two dozen marks or marginal comments that he made in his copy of the *Life of Frances Power Cobbe, As Told by Herself* (which I examined in the Mark Twain Papers) attest to the care with which he read it and to his continuing interest in the antivivisection movement.[104] A particularly poignant passage Twain marked documents a case of cruelty to an animal that was simultaneously an act of enormous cruelty to a disabled human being. The story Cobbe recounts was told by her friend, John Bright, about a "poor crippled woman in a miserable cottage near Llandudno, where [Bright] usually spent his holidays."

He had got into the habit of visiting this poor creature, who could not stir from her bed, but lay there all day long alone, her husband being out at work as a labourer. Sometimes a neighbour would look in and give her food, but unless one did so, she was entirely helpless. Her only comforter was her dog, a fine collie, who lay beside her on the floor, ran in and out, licked her poor useless hands, and showed his affection in a hundred ways. Bright grew fond of the dog, and the dog always welcomed him each year with gambols and joy. One summer he came to the cottage, and the hapless cripple lay on her pallet still, but the dog did not come out to him as usual, and his first question to the woman was: "Where is your collie?" The answer was that *her husband had drowned the dog* to save the expense of feeding it.

Bright's voice broke when he came to the end of this story, and we said very little more to each other during that dinner.[105]

Twain also marked a passage describing the Catholic church's opposition to the creation of an animal welfare organization in Rome:

Pope Pio IX. had been addressed by the English in Rome through Lord Ampthill, (then Mr. Odo Russell, our representative there)—with a request for permission to found a Society for Prevention of Cruelty to Animals in Rome; where, (as all the world knows) it is almost as deplorably needed as at Naples. After a considerable delay, the formal reply through the proper Office, was sent to Mr. Russell *refusing* the (indispensable) permission. The document conveying this refusal expressly stated that "a Society for such a purpose could not be sanctioned in Rome. Man owed duties to his fellow men; but he owed no duties to the lower animals; therefore, though such societies might exist in Protestant countries they could not be allowed to be established in Rome."[106]

In the margin next to this passage, Twain writes, "the Church's attitude." The number of times that Twain improves Cobbe's grammar or syntax further shows him to be a particularly assiduous reader.[107] On a more substantive level, several of his marginal comments and markings involve the issue of why God does not intervene to stop suffering.[108] The attentiveness with which Twain read this book attests to the strength of his interest in the antivivisection and anticruelty movement in England and the dedicated woman who did so much to sustain it for three decades.

Twain retained an interest in the animal welfare movement's goals and methods in a range of other contexts as well, in addition to writing two antivivisection texts and the antibullfighting novella discussed in the introduction.[109] Sometimes he jotted down comments on the subject in his journal or in autobiographical dictations, or alluded to it in notes for a story. When he was traveling in Calcutta in March 1896, for example, he noted in his journal that "Horses in Calcutta wear white pith sun-protectors like a mortar-board. *We shd introduce that.* Let a Cruelty to Animals Society look to it. If Henry Bergh were alive he would do it."[110] (Twain was unaware of the fact that when he was alive, Henry Bergh *had* done something very close to this. One of the early moves of the ASPCA was providing free straw hats for cab horses during the hot summer months.)[111] And at one point he began a sketch that centered on a young woman who wrote for an animal welfare journal.[112]

Twain grew increasingly disappointed with his fellow human beings for a broad range of reasons in the last decades of his life. Their treatment of animals was right up there with other failings—cupidity, greed, hypocrisy, arrogance, pride—the list was long. His genuine belief that there may be more of a continuum than a sharp break between human and nonhuman species, one that many of his peers shared, helped fuel his anger. As the texts in this book show, Mark Twain addressed the theme of human cruelty to nonhuman animals in writings over four decades. His best-known pieces in support of animal rights and animal welfare had a big impact in his day, and continue to be widely cited and invoked today. The antivivisection letter written with ink that almost sears the page, the antivivisection story thick with hard-to-bear sweetness and stomach-curdling pathos, and even the rather clumsy but well-meaning antibullfighting novella, were important to Twain; given Twain's centrality in American culture, they should be important to us. Some of the debates they entered are still raging today—debates about experimentation on animals, for example: when, if ever, are such experiments justified? In what contexts? For what ends? And what are the limits that should be placed on them? Questions of what humans owe nonhuman animals continue to spark impassioned partisan responses whether the issue at hand is sustenance (debates about the moral and environmental politics of eating meat), pleasure (debates about the morality of hunting for sport, of bullfighting, of making clothing out of animals, of domesticating animals as pets, of confining them in zoos), or pain (debates about how best to address cases of animal overpopulation), etc. As is often the case, Mark Twain was there, entering into debates that resonate with much of what is still being debated today. His words help prompt us to think, to question our assumptions, and to care—both about our fellow human beings and about the other animals with whom we share the planet.

Note on the Texts

THE ARRANGEMENT OF THESE TEXTS is roughly chronological, according to the date of first publication or, where publication was delayed, to the date of composition. All of the selections, many of the titles, and all decisions about when to elide parts of the longer texts, are the editor's. The critical establishment of the selected texts was carried out by members of the Mark Twain Project using scholarly critical editions where they existed, and relying on the original manuscripts, typescripts, and printings where they did not. For sources of the texts selected, see the explanatory bibliography below.

Mark Twain's own textual elisions occur either as ellipsis points (. . . .) or as asterisks (∗ ∗ ∗ ∗), the so-called line of stars. Elisions by the editor are signaled by three or four ellipses points enclosed in brackets, thus: [. . .]; they are *not* used at the beginning and end of a selection where the text is complete but manifestly excerpted from a longer work. For texts that Mark Twain published or intended to publish, emendations have been made silently to correct simple errors and resolve pointless inconsistencies, and to supplant manuscript devices (such as ampersands) not appropriate for print. The size and font of headings and subheadings within the texts, and numerical divisions of them (I, II, and II, or Chapter I, Chapter II, etc.), have been made to conform to the typographical design of this volume. The position of datelines, salutations, and signatures in personal letters has also been made uniform, despite some variation in the originals. The author's wording, punctuation, and spelling have been followed exactly (even when they are slightly old-fashioned), except where they were manifestly defective. For the few selections representing letters and notebook entries—texts the author never intended to publish—the text is transcribed exactly as it stands in the original, without correcting errors or converting ampersands.

Part One: 1850s and 1860s

• "Bugs!" (pp. 37–38). Extracted from a personal letter from Samuel L. Clemens to Ann E. Taylor, 21 and 25 May 1856. The text is taken from a critical edition of the letters, *Mark Twain's Letters, Volume 1: 1853–1866*, ed. Edgar Marquess Branch, Michael B. Frank, Kenneth M. Sanderson; associate editors Harriet Elinor Smith, Lin Salamo, and Richard Bucci (Berkeley and Los Angeles: University of California Press, 1988), pp. 59–60.

• "Cruelty to Animals I" (p. 38). Published in the San Francisco *Daily Morning Call* on 18 September 1864, p. 1. The text is taken from a critical edition of Mark Twain's (unsigned) work as a reporter for that newspaper, *Clemens of the "Call,"* ed. Edgar M. Branch (Berkeley and Los Angeles: University of California Press, 1969), p. 520.

• "Jim Smiley and His Jumping Frog" (pp. 38–44). First published in the New York *Saturday Press* 4 (18 November 1865): 248–249. The text is taken from a critical edition of his journalism, *Early Tales & Sketches, Volume 2: 1864–1865,* ed. Edgar Marquess Branch and Robert H. Hirst, with the assistance of Harriet Elinor Smith (Berkeley and Los Angeles: University of California Press, 1981), pp. 281–288.

• "Fitz Smythe's Horse" (pp. 44–45). First published in the Virginia City *Territorial Enterprise,* some time between 16 and 19 January 1866, which is not extant. The text is taken from a critical edition of his journalism, *Early Tales & Sketches, Volume 2: 1864–1865,* ed. Edgar Marquess Branch and Robert H. Hirst, with the assistance of Harriet Elinor Smith (Berkeley and Los Angeles: University of California Press, 1981), pp. 345–346.

• "Cruelty to Animals II" (pp. 45–47). First subsection of "Letter from 'Mark Twain,'" San Francisco *Alta California,* written 30 April 1867 from New York, published in San Francisco 10 June 1867, p. 1. The text is transcribed from a microfilm edition of the newspaper.

From *The Innocents Abroad, or The New Pilgrim's Progress; Being Some Account of the Steamship Quaker City's Pleasure Excursion to Europe and the Holy Land; with Descriptions of Countries, Nations, Incidents and Adventures, as They Appeared to the* AUTHOR (Hartford: American Publishing Co., 1869). This is the first edition of this work, set from manuscript and proofread by Mark Twain.

   • "The Pilgrim" (p. 48). Chapter 11, pp. 100–101.
   • "The Dogs of Constantinople" (pp. 48–51). Chapter 34, pp. 370–373. The selection from chapter 34 is a revised form of "The Dogs of Constantinople" in "The Holy Land Excursion. Letter from 'Mark Twain,'" written in August 1867 and published in the San Francisco *Alta California,* 29 October 1867, p. 1. We have corrected *The Innocents Abroad* printing from this earlier form of the text, which was used as printer's copy for the book.
   • "Syrian Camels I" (pp. 51–52). Chapters 42 and 50, pp. 439 and 526. The selection from chapter 50 is a nearly verbatim reprint of a passage from "The Holy Land Excursion. Letter from 'Mark Twain,'" written in September 1867 and published in the San Francisco *Alta California,* 16 February 1868, p. 1. We have corrected *The Innocents Abroad* printing from this earlier form of the text, which was used as printer's copy for the book.
   • "The Remarkable 'Jericho'" (p. 53). Chapter 42, pp. 439–441.
   • "Pilgrims on Horseback" (pp. 54–55). Chapters 43 and 45, pp. 451–452 and 476–477.
   • "Arabs and Their Steeds" (p. 55). Chapter 45, p. 477.

Part Two: 1870s and 1880s

From *Roughing It*, first published in Hartford by the American Publishing Company in February 1872. The following selections are taken from a critical edition of the book, *Roughing It*, ed. Harriet Elinor Smith and Edgar Marquess Branch; associate editors Lin Salamo and Rob Browning (Berkeley and Los Angeles: University of California Press, 1993).
  • "The Cayote, Allegory of Want" (pp. 59–61). Chapter 5, pp. 30–34.
  • "With a Flash and a Whiz" (pp. 61–62). Chapter 3, pp. 12–13.
  • "Syrian Camels II" (pp. 62–63). Chapter 3, pp. 15–17.
  • "The Genuine Mexican Plug" (pp. 63–67). Chapter 24, pp. 158–165.
  • "The Retired Milk Horse" (pp. 67–69). Chapter 76, pp. 518–519.

• "An Invention to Make Flies Curse" (pp. 69–70). A personal letter from Samuel L. Clemens to Willard M. White, 3 March 1873. The text is taken from a critical edition of the letters, *Mark Twain's Letters, Volume 5: 1872–1873*, ed. Lin Salamo and Harriet Elinor Smith (Berkeley and Los Angeles: University of California Press, 1997), pp. 307–308.

From *The Adventures of Tom Sawyer*, first published in Hartford by the American Publishing Company in December 1876. The following texts are taken from the revised and corrected critical text published in the Mark Twain Library, ed. John C. Gerber and Paul Baender (Berkeley and Los Angeles: University of California Press, 1982).
  • "Peter and the Pain-Killer" (pp. 70–72). Chapter 12, pp. 92–96.
  • "The Pinch-bug and the Poodle" (pp. 73–74). Chapter 5, pp. 40–43.
  • "Bugs and Birds and Tom in the Morning" (pp. 74–75). Chapter 14, pp. 106–107.

• "A Cat-Tale" (pp. 76–84). The text is a critical transcription of the manuscript, which was written in 1880 and left unpublished by Mark Twain. First published by Frederick Anderson in *Concerning Cats: Two Tales by Mark Twain* (San Francisco: The Book Club of California, 1959), pp. 1–19. The manuscript is now in the Mark Twain Papers, The Bancroft Library.

From *A Tramp Abroad* (Hartford: American Publishing Co., 1880). This is the first edition of this work, set from manuscript and proofread by Mark Twain.
  • "The Presumptuous Ravens" (pp. 84–86). Chapter 2, pp. 31–32. The selection has been corrected against the original manuscript for this chapter, which is in the Mark Twain Papers, The Bancroft Library.
  • "Birds with a Sense of Humor" (pp. 86–90). Chapters 2 and 3, pp. 36–42. The selection (also known generally as the Blue Jay Yarn) has been corrected against the original manuscripts for these chapters, which are in the Mark Twain Papers, The Bancroft Library, and in the Oliver Wendell Holmes Library at Phillips Academy, Andover, Mass.
  • "The Idiotic Ant" (pp. 90–93). Chapter 22, pp. 215–219.

From *Life on the Mississippi* (Boston: James R. Osgood and Co., 1885). This is the first edition of this work, set from a revised typescript prepared by Mark Twain.

- "Cock-fight in New Orleans" (pp. 93–94). Chapter 45, pp. 457–458. This selection has been corrected against the manuscript in the Morgan Library and Museum, New York.

From *Adventures of Huckleberry Finn*, first published in New York by Charles L. Webster and Company in February 1885. The selection is taken from a critical edition of the book, *Adventures of Huckleberry Finn*, ed. Victor A. Fischer and Lin Salamo, with the late Walter Blair (Berkeley and Los Angeles: University of California Press, 2003).

- "The Bricksville Loafers" (pp. 94–95). Chapter 21, p. 183.

From *A Connecticut Yankee in King Arthur's Court*, first published in New York by Charles L. Webster and Company in December 1889. The selection is taken from a critical edition of the book, *A Connecticut Yankee in King Arthur's Court*, ed. Bernard L. Stein, with an introduction by Henry Nash Smith (Berkeley and Los Angeles: University of California Press, 1979).

- "A Prescription for Universal Peace" (pp. 95–96). Chapter 40, pp. 445–446.

Part Three: 1890s–1910

- "Letters from a Dog to Another Dog Explaining and Accounting for Man" (pp. 99–107). The text is a critical transcription of an unfinished manuscript, written about January and February 1891, which is in the Mark Twain Papers, The Bancroft Library. The text has not been printed before.

From *Tom Sawyer Abroad, by Huck Finn. Edited by Mark Twain*, first published as a book in New York by Charles L. Webster and Company in April 1894. The selections are taken from the revised and corrected critical text published in the Mark Twain Library, ed. John C. Gerber and Terry Firkins (Berkeley and Los Angeles: University of California Press, 1982).

- "The Phenomenal Flea" (pp. 107–108). Chapter 7, pp. 44 – 46.
- "Huck Kills a Bird" (pp. 108–109). Chapter 5, p. 32.

- "The Bird with the Best Grammar" (p. 109). This selection is from Mark Twain's so-called "Morals Lecture" as given in Cleveland, Ohio, on 15 July 1895, and reported verbatim in the Cleveland *Plain Dealer*, 19 July 1895, reprinted in Fred W. Lorch, *The Trouble Begins at Eight: Mark Twain's Lecture Tours* (Ames: Iowa State University Press, 1968), p. 325. The passage records a spoken version of "Birds with a Sense of Humor" from *A Tramp Abroad*.

- "Ants and the True Religion" (pp. 109–110). This selection is transcribed directly from the original manuscript notebook no. 37, typescript pp. 10–12, Mark Twain Papers, The Bancroft Library. Mark Twain made the entry in his notebook sometime between 28 and 31 March 1896. Previously published, with errors and omissions, in *Mark Twain's Notebook*, ed. Albert Bigelow Paine (New York: Harper and Brothers, 1935), pp. 283–285.

• "The Sailors and the St. Bernard" (pp. 110–117). From "The Enchanted Sea-Wilderness," written in November and December 1896 but left unpublished by Mark Twain. It was included in *Which Was the Dream? and Other Symbolic Writings of the Later Years*, ed. John S. Tuckey (Berkeley and Los Angeles: University of California Press, 1967), pp. 77–85. This selection has been corrected against the manuscript in the Mark Twain Papers, The Bancroft Library.

• "Man's Place in the Animal World" (pp. 117–125). Written in August–October 1896 but not published until 1962 when Bernard DeVoto included it under the title "The Lowest Animal" in *Letters from the Earth* (New York: Harper and Row, 1962), pp. 222–232. The present text is taken from a critical edition, *What Is Man? and Other Philosophical Writings*, ed. Paul Baender (Berkeley and Los Angeles: University of California Press, 1973), pp. 81–89. The text has been corrected against the manuscript in the Mark Twain Papers, The Bancroft Library, which lacks the first page, presumably containing the "telegrams" referred to on p. 121 and quoted from on p. 119.

From *Following the Equator* (Hartford: American Publishing Co., 1897), the first edition of this work, which was set from manuscript and proofread by Mark Twain. All selections have been corrected against the original manuscript that was used as printer's copy for the first edition, now in the Henry W. and Albert A. Berg Collection, New York Public Library.
  • "The Marvelous Moa" (p. 125). Chapter 8, p. 102.
  • "The Inimitable Ornithorhynchus" (pp. 125–128). Chapter 8, pp. 102–107.
  • "The Laughing Jackass of Adelaide" (p. 129). Chapter 19, pp. 184–185.
  • "The Phosphorescent Sea-Serpent" (pp. 129–130). Chapter 9, pp. 109–110.
  • "The Independent-Minded Magpie" (pp. 130–131). Chapter 23, pp. 225–226.
  • "The Bird of Birds" (pp. 131–132). Chapter 38, pp. 353–356.
  • "The Deadliest Song Known to Ornithology" (p. 133). Chapter 56, pp. 540–543.
  • "The Pious Chameleon" (p. 134). Chapter 65, p. 645.

• "A Pocketful of Bat" (pp. 135–136). Taken from a manuscript titled "My Autobiography [Random Extracts from it]," written in 1897 and 1898, and first published in the *North American Review* 184 (1 March 1907): 449–463. Text is transcribed from the original manuscript, pp. 49–53, now in the Mark Twain Papers, The Bancroft Library.

• "Hunting the Deceitful Turkey" (pp. 136–138). Part of "My Autobiography [Random Extracts from it]," written in 1897 and 1898, first published in *Harper's Monthly Magazine* 114 (December 1906): 57–58, but ultimately incorporated in the final form of the autobiography as an example of previous failed attempts to write it. The text reproduces exactly a critical text established for the Mark Twain Project's forthcoming edition of the autobiography by Harriet Elinor Smith and Lin Salamo.

• "Letter to the London Anti-Vivisection Society" (pp. 139–140). Text is taken from a photofacsimile of the original letter published in *The Pains of Lowly Life*, ca. 1910, pp. 2–5, in a copy of that pamphlet owned by The Beinecke Rare Book and Manuscript Library at Yale University.

• "The Victims" (pp. 141–144). Essentially a draft rather than a finished story, the manuscript was written sometime between 1900 and 1905 and left untitled and unpublished (Albert Bigelow Paine, Mark Twain's official biographer, supplied the title on the manuscript itself). The text is taken from a critical edition, *Fables of Man*, ed. John S. Tuckey, text established by Kenneth M. Sanderson and Bernard L. Stein, series editor Frederick Anderson (Berkeley and Los Angeles: University of California Press, 1972), pp. 135–140. The text has been corrected against the manuscript in the Mark Twain Papers, The Bancroft Library.

• "Extracts from Adam's Diary, Translated from the Original MS" (pp. 144–149). The text is constructed from four authoritative documents: the original holograph manuscript and a typescript of that manuscript revised by Mark Twain (both now in the Henry W. and Albert A. Berg Collection of the New York Public Library); the first printing in *Harper's Monthly Magazine* 102 (April 1901): 762–767; and its first publication as a book, *Extracts from Adam's Diary: Translated from the Original MS. By Mark Twain* (New York: Harper and Brothers, 1906). Mark Twain made revisions and corrections at all four stages, which the present text incorporates while rejecting unauthorized changes made by typist, typesetters, and editors.

• "Autobiography of Eve" (pp. 149–154). This portion of the original manuscript was probably written in 1901. It was left unpublished by Mark Twain. Bernard DeVoto published approximately this same selection as "Extract from Eve's Autobiography" in *Letters from the Earth* (New York: Harper and Row, 1962), pp. 77–89. The complete manuscript was first published by Howard Baetzhold and Joseph B. McCullough in *The Bible According to Mark Twain* (Athens: University of Georgia Press, 1995), pp. 42–62; the section republished here begins on page 53 of their text (page 43 of the manuscript). The present text has been transcribed from the original manuscript in the Mark Twain Papers, The Bancroft Library.

• "Rosa and the Crows" (p. 154). From "A Family Sketch," a manuscript written in 1901 and revised in 1906, now in the James S. Copley Library in La Jolla, California. Not previously printed.

• "Assassin" (pp. 154–155). From "A Family Sketch," a manuscript written in 1901 and revised in 1906, now in the James S. Copley Library in La Jolla, California. Not previously printed.

• "The Jungle Discusses Man" (pp. 155–158). Manuscript in the Mark Twain Papers, written about 1902, but left unpublished and untitled by Mark Twain; Paine supplied the title and the approximate date of composition. Only recently published in a limited edition of fifty copies, *Twenty-Two Easy Pieces* (Berkeley and Los Angeles: University of California Press, 2001), pp. 84–86, and in *Who Is Mark Twain?* (New York: HarperStudio, 2009), pp. 169–173.

• "The Bee" (pp. 158–161). Transcribed from manuscript in the Mark Twain Papers, written about 1902. Left unpublished by Mark Twain, but published by Paine with major omissions and errors in *What Is Man? And Other Essays* (New York: Harper and Brothers, 1917), pp. 280–284. The present text is a critically transcribed selection from the original manuscript.

• "'Was the World made for Man?'" (pp. 161–165). Manuscript in the Mark Twain Papers, written about April 1903. Left unpublished by Mark Twain but published by Bernard DeVoto in *Letters from the Earth* (New York: Harper and Row, 1962), pp. 211–113. The text is taken from a critical edition, *What Is Man? And Other Philosophical Writings*, ed. Paul Baender (Berkeley and Los Angeles: University of California Press, 1973), pp. 101–106. The text has been corrected against the manuscript in the Mark Twain Papers, The Bancroft Library.

• "A Dog's Tale" (pp. 165–174). First published in *Harper's Monthly Magazine* 108 (December 1903): 11–19. Corrected against the manuscript in the Mark Twain Papers which, however, lacks the concluding seventeen paragraphs, here necessarily based on the *Harper's* printing.

• "Flies and Russians" (pp. 174–177). Manuscript written between late November 1904 and February 1905 and left unpublished by Mark Twain. The text is taken from a critical edition of it in *Fables of Man*, ed. John S. Tuckey, text established by Kenneth M. Sanderson and Bernard L. Stein, series editor Frederick Anderson (Berkeley and Los Angeles: University of California Press, 1972), pp. 421–424. The text has been corrected against the original manuscript in the Mark Twain Papers, The Bancroft Library, and the first sentence of the manuscript (inserted by Mark Twain while intending to join the essay to "The Czar's Soliloquy") has been omitted, even though it stands uncanceled.

• "Eve's Diary. Translated from the Original" (pp. 177–181). First published in *Harper's Monthly Magazine* (December 1905): 25–32. Collected and reprinted, with revisions, in *Eve's Diary: Translated from the Original MS. By Mark Twain* (New York: Harper and Brothers, 1906). The present text has been constructed from three authoritative documents: the *Harper's* printing of December 1905, the book printing in 1906, and manuscript pages in the Mark Twain Papers for the section titled "Extract from Adam's Diary," which was first included in the book printing and is the only part of the text for which the original manuscript is known to survive.

• "The Supremacy of the House Fly" (pp. 181–186). Part of Mark Twain's autobiography, it survives in a typescript and its carbon, prepared from dictation by Josephine

Hobby and revised and corrected by Mark Twain, who dated it 4 September 1906. The original documents are now in the Mark Twain Papers, The Bancroft Library. The present text reproduces exactly the critical text established for the Mark Twain Project's forthcoming edition of the autobiography by Harriet Elinor Smith and Lin Salamo. The text has not been printed before.

• "Mrs. Clemens Corners the Market in Flies" (pp. 186–187). Part of Mark Twain's autobiography, it survives in a typescript and its carbon, which were prepared from dictation by Josephine Hobby and revised and corrected by Mark Twain, who dated it 15 October 1906. The original documents are now in the Mark Twain Papers, The Bancroft Library. Mark Twain published it in the *North American Review* 185 (3 May 1907): 1–12.

• "The Edisons of the Animal World" (pp. 187–195). A section of *What Is Man?* first published in 1906. The text is taken from a critical edition of that work in *What Is Man? And Other Philosophical Writings*, ed. Paul Baender (Berkeley and Los Angeles: University of California Press, 1973), pp. 189–199. The text has been corrected against the original manuscript in the Mark Twain Papers, The Bancroft Library.

• *A Horse's Tale* (pp. 195–228). The text has been constructed from the original manuscript, now in the Henry W. and Albert A. Berg Collection of the New York Public Library, and its first publication in *Harper's Magazine* (August and September 1906), and its first edition, *A Horse's Tale* (New York: Harper and Brothers, 1907). That first-edition text has been corrected against the manuscript.

• "Man and the Other Animals" (pp. 229–231). The concluding section of a long typed document, an autobiographical dictation for 4 February 1907, now in the Mark Twain Papers, The Bancroft Library. It has not been printed before.

• "The President Hunts a Cow" (pp. 231–235). From two typed documents, autobiographical dictations for 18 and 21 October 1907, now in the Mark Twain Papers, The Bancroft Library. Mark Twain left these texts unpublished, but Bernard DeVoto included virtually this same selection as "The Hunting of the Cow" in *Mark Twain in Eruption* (New York: Harper and Brothers, 1940), pp. 7–14. The present text is a critical transcription of the original typed documents.

• "The Time I Got an Elephant for Christmas" (pp. 235–238). Although ostensibly "dictated," this selection was actually written out in longhand by Mark Twain. That manuscript in the Mark Twain Papers, dated 25 December 1908, has been critically transcribed for this edition; the text has not been printed before.

• "Little Bessie Would Assist Providence" (pp. 238–241). The text, written in 1908 or 1909, is taken from a critical edition of it in *Fables of Man*, ed. John S. Tuckey, text established by Kenneth M. Sanderson and Bernard L. Stein, series editor Frederick Anderson (Berkeley and Los Angeles: University of California Press, 1972), pp. 34–

37. The critical text has been corrected from the original manuscript and typescript which are now in the Mark Twain Papers, The Bancroft Library.

• "Letters from the Earth" (pp. 241–255). This incomplete work was written in 1909 but not published until 1962, *Letters from the Earth* (New York: Harper & Row, 1962), pp. 3–55. The present selection is taken from a critical edition of this work in *What Is Man? And Other Philosophical Writings*, ed. Paul Baender (Berkeley and Los Angeles: University of California Press, 1972), pp. 401–430. The critical text has been corrected against the original manuscript in the Mark Twain Papers, The Bancroft Library.

Mark Twain Project
April 2009

Notes

Introduction

1. "Extracts from Adam's Diary, Translated from the Original MS," in part 3.

2. *Mark Twain's Autobiography*, ed. Albert Bigelow Paine, 2 vols. (New York: Harper and Brothers, 1924), 1:119.

3. Ibid.

4. Ibid.

5. Albert Bigelow Paine, *Mark Twain: A Biography*, 4 vols. (New York: Harper and Brothers, 1912), 1:36.

6. "Assassin," in part 3. Here Twain claims that this childhood experience made him abhor the idea of killing animals for sport ever after.

7. "With a Flash and a Whiz," in part 2.

8. "Man's Place in the Animal World," in part 3.

9. William Dean Howells, *My Mark Twain: Reminiscences and Criticisms* (New York: Harper and Brothers, 1910), 43.

10. "Huck Kills a Bird," in part 3.

11. "Hunting the Deceitful Turkey," in part 3.

12. Katherine C. Grier, *Pets in America: A History* (Chapel Hill: University of North Carolina Press, 2006), 148. Grier notes that "The metaphor of the hunt was still in common use throughout the 1800s to represent the economic activity of middle-class men." See also Grier, "Material Culture as Rhetoric: Animal Artifacts as a Case Study," in *American Material Culture: The Shape of a Field*, ed. J. Ritchie Garrison and Ann Smart Martin (New York: Norton, 1997), 65–104.

13. Samuel Langhorne Clemens (hereafter, SLC) to Charles L. Webster, 10 July 1884, Vassar College Library; photocopy in the Mark Twain Papers, The Bancroft Library, University of California, Berkeley (hereafter, MTP).

14. Clara Clemens, "My Father," *The Mentor*, May 1924, 23.

15. SLC, autobiographical dictation of 8 October 1906, MTP.

16. Susy Clemens quoted in Paine, *Mark Twain: A Biography*, 2:684.

17. Joseph H. Twichell, untitled [recollections of Mark Twain], in *Public Meeting Under the Auspices of the American Academy and the National Institute of Arts and Letters Held at Carnegie Hall, New York, November 30, 1910 in Memory of Samuel Langhorne Clemens (Mark Twain)* (New York: The De Vinne Press, 1922), 49.

18. Susy Clemens quoted in Paine, *Mark Twain's Autobiography*, 2:82.

19. SLC to the editor of *Echoes*, 2 April 1890, Hartford, Elmira College Library, photocopy in MTP. Twain added that the cats "died early—on account of being overweighted with their names, it was thought. SOUR MASH, APPOLLINARIS, ZOROASTER and BLATHERSKITE,—names given them not in an unfriendly spirit, but merely to practice the children in large and difficult styles of pronunciation."

20. SLC interpolated comment in Susy Clemens, *Papa: An Intimate Biography of Mark Twain by Susy Clemens, His Daughter, Thirteen, With a Foreword and Copious Comments by Her Father*, ed. Charles Neider (Garden City, N.Y.: Doubleday, 1985), 100.

21. Caroline Harnsberger, *Mark Twain Family Man* (New York: Citadel Press, 1960), 74.

22. Susy Clemens, *Papa*, 99–100.

23. SLC to Mrs. Mabel Larkin Patterson, 2 October 1908, in Albert Bigelow Paine, ed., *Mark Twain's Letters*, 2 vols. (New York: Harper and Brothers, 1917), 2:821.

24. On Flash, see Clara Clemens to SLC, 20 November 1884 (Huntington Library, San Marino, Calif.). On Jumbo, see Clara Clemens, *My Father Mark Twain* (New York: Harper and Brothers, 1931), 28–29. On Max Clemens, see SLC to Jean Clemens, 20 July 1890 (Huntington Library). On Scott, see Jean Clemens to SLC, 23 July 1907 (Huntington Library). On Fix, see Susy Clemens to SLC, 1 August 1886 (Huntington Library). On Cadichon, see Susy Clemens, *Papa*, 143–145, 149–150; Caroline Harnsberger—who spells it "Kadishan"—notes that the name came from a book called *Adventures with a Donkey* (Harnsberger, *Mark Twain Family Man*, 103). Harnsberger probably meant Sophie Ségur's *The Adventures of a Donkey*, which was translated from the French and published in English in 1880 by the Baltimore Publishing Company.

25. Clara Clemens, "My Father," *The Mentor*, May 1924, 21–22.

26. Grier, *Pets in America*, 166–181.

27. SLC, "A Family Sketch," ms. written in 1901, revised in 1906, now in James S. Copley Library, La Jolla, Calif., photocopy in MTP, 40–41.

28. Ibid., 41.

29. Ibid., 41.

30. SLC, "A Family Sketch," 41–42. See also Susy Clemens, *Papa*, 152.

31. "The Victims," in part 3.

32. SLC to Franklin G. Whitmore, 12 August 1881, Mark Twain House, photocopy in MTP.

33. SLC to Charles S. Fairchild, 22 September 1881, Mark Twain House, photocopy in MTP.

34. SLC to Jane L. Clemens, 24 July 1887, Vassar College Library, photocopy in MTP.

35. For example, to Louise Paine in 1908, he wrote,

Tammany is dead. I am very sorry. She was the most beautiful cat on this western bulge of the globe, & perhaps the most gifted. She leaves behind her, inconsolable, two children by her first marriage—Billiards & Babylon; & 3 grandchildren by her second—Ananda, Annanci & Sindbad. She met her death by violence, at the hands of a dog.

He added that Miss Lyon buried her "with the honors due her official rank" as "Mascot to the Aquarium"; SLC to Louise Paine, 4 November 1908, MTP.

36. SLC, "Closing Words of My Autobiography," autobiographical dictation of Christmas Eve, 1909 (MTP); included by Paine, with slight changes, as "The Death of Jean" in Mark Twain, *What Is Man? and Other Essays* (New York: Harper and Brothers, 1917), 120.

37. Susy Clemens, *Papa,* 75.

38. SLC, "A Family Sketch," 35.

39. SLC to Mary Mason Fairbanks, 17 June 1868, *Mark Twain's Letters, Volume 2: 1867–1868,* ed. Harriet Elinor Smith and Richard Bucci, associate editor Lin Salamo (Berkeley and Los Angeles: University of California Press, 1990), 223.

40. Letters addressed to Twain as "Dearest Grenouille" or "Dear Grenouille" include Susy Clemens to SLC, n.d. [Florence, c. 1893]; Jean Clemens to SLC, 30 May 1907; Jean Clemens to SLC, 3 June 1907; Jean Clemens to SLC, 24 June 1907; Jean Clemens to SLC, 28 June 1907; Jean Clemens to SLC, 20 July 1907; Jean Clemens to SLC, 23 July 1907; Jean Clemens to SLC, 30 July 1907; Jean Clemens to SLC, 28 August 1907; Jean Clemens to SLC, 10 August 1907, Jean Clemens to SLC, 26 May 1908. All of these letters are in the Huntington Library.

41. SLC to William Dean Howells, 2 April 1899, in *Mark Twain–Howells Letters,* ed. Henry Nash Smith and William M. Gibson, with the assistance of Frederick Anderson, 2 vols. (Cambridge, Mass.: Belknap Press of Harvard University Press, 1960), 2:690.

42. Twain's travels also provided him with opportunities to interact in new ways with familiar animals. Joe Twichell, who accompanied Twain to Europe in 1878, recalled the following: "One day during our 'tramp abroad,' when we were toiling up the long ascent above the Chamouni, from the Riffel Inn to the Gorner Grat, as we paused for a rest, a lamb from a flock of sheep near by ventured inquisitively toward us; whereupon Mark rested himself upon a rock, and with beckoning hand and soft words tried to get it to come to him. On the lamb's part it was a struggle between curiosity and timidity, but in a succession of advances and retreats it gained confidence, though at a very gradual rate. It was a scene for a painter—the great American humorist on one side of the game, and that silly little creature on the other, with the Matterhorn for a background. Mark was reminded that the time he was consuming in that diversion was valuable; but to no purpose. The Gorner Grat could wait. He held on with undiscouraged perseverance till he carried his point: the lamb finally put its nose in his hand; and he was happy over it all the rest of the day" (Twichell, *Public Meeting,* 41–42).

43. See Mark Twain, "Some Learned Fables, for Good Boys and Girls" in *Sketches, New and Old* (1875), reprinted in *Mark Twain: Collected Tales, Sketches, Speeches & Essays, 1852–1890,* ed. Louis Budd (New York: Library of America, 1992), 611–631; "The Fable of the Yellow Terror" in *Fables of Man,* ed. John S. Tuckey (Berkeley and Los Angeles: University of California Press, 1972), 425–429; and "A Fable," *Harper's Magazine,* December 1909, 70–71, reprinted in Budd, *Mark Twain: Collected Tales, Sketches, Speeches & Essays, 1891–1910,* 877–879.

44. He also admired the paintings of animals by popular British artist Edwin Henry Landseer that he saw at an exhibit at the Royal Academy in 1874. Twain found Landseer's animal paintings "wonderfully beautiful," in large part due to their uncanny realism. As he put it in a letter, "if the room were darkened ever so little & a motionless living animal placed beside a painted one, no man could tell which was which"; SLC to Joseph H. Twichell, 5 January 1874, in Michael B. Frank and Harriet Elinor Smith, eds., *Mark Twain's Letters, Volume 6, 1874–1875* (Berkeley and Los Angeles: University of California Press, 2002), 11, see also p. 12n3 in that volume.

45. In an autobiographical dictation on 5 February 1906 (MTP), SLC called *Rab and His Friends* "that pathetic and beautiful masterpiece."

46. I examined Mark Twain's personal copy of vol. 1 of *The Descent of Man*, in the Mark Twain Papers; Charles Darwin, *The Descent of Man, and Selection in Relation to Sex*, 2 vols. (New York: D. Appleton, 1871). Several examples of Twain's marginalia are discussed in detail in the afterword.

47. Walter Blair hypothesized the possible link between the two stories on the basis of textual similarities, noting that Bierce's woodpecker "admits that he does not know why he pecks holes in a dead tree: 'Some naturalists affirm that I hide acorns in these pits; others maintain that I get worms out of them.' Alert source hunters will notice the bird's theoretical kinship with Baker's blue jay, which dumped acorns into his knothole.... They also may be interested in the fact that at one time when he talked about his story long after he wrote it, Twain called it 'a tale of how the poor and innocent woodpeckers tried to fill up a house with acorns'"; Walter Blair, *Essays on American Humor: Blair Through the Ages*, ed. Hamlin Hill (Madison: University of Wisconsin Press, 1993), 172. In a letter to C.W. Stoddard, 1 February 1875 (Buffalo Public Library), Twain wrote that Bierce's "exquisite things" for *Fun* were "just delicious"; quoted in Alan Gribben, *Mark Twain's Library: A Reconstruction*, 2 vols. (Boston: G.K. Hall, 1980), 1:69. Bierce first published "The Robin and the Woodpecker" in *Fun*, 18 January 1873, 2nd ser., no. 48; see *The Collected Fables of Ambrose Bierce, with Introduction and Commentary*, ed. S.T. Joshi (Columbus: Ohio State University Press, 2000), 315, seven years before Mark Twain published "Jim Baker's Blue-jay Yarn" in *A Tramp Abroad*. "The Robin and the Woodpecker" was one of the six fables by Bierce included in *Mark Twain's Library of Humor* in 1888.

48. Alan Gribben notes that Twain purchased Audubon's *The Birds of America from Drawings Made in the United States and Their Territories*, in the edition reissued by John Woodhouse Audubon, plates engraved by J. Bien, 5 vols. (New York: Roe, Lockwood & Son; also G. Lockwood, 1860–1870). He also quotes Cable's recollection of having consulted this volume with Twain to identify a bird in Hartford in February 1884 (Gribben, *Mark Twain's Library*, 1:31).

49. In an autobiographical dictation of 13 August 1906, SLC said that "The incomparable Jungle Books must remain unfellowed permanently" (MTP), quoted in Gribben, *Mark Twain's Library*, 1:378. Isabel V. Lyon's journal records that on the evening of 11 June SLC read the story "Red Dog" to his household; IVL 1906 Journal, typescript p. 164 (MTP), quoted in Gribben, *Mark Twain's Library*, 1:381.

50. Wood's *Animal Analogues* is an ingenious collection of verses and illustrations that posits fanciful links between plants and animals, and between different species of animals. One selection, for example, which is accompanied by illustrations showing the ways in which an ape hanging from a branch resembles the shape of a bunch of grapes hanging from a vine, includes the following lines: "The Apes, from whom we are descended,/Hang ape-x down from trees suspended,/And since we find them in the trees,/We term them arbor-igines . . . "; Robert Williams Wood, *Animal Analogues* (San Francisco: Paul Elder, 1908), 16. An inscription in Twain's copy of the book examined by Gribben reads "S. L. Clemens, 1909, Stormfield. A cunning book" (Gribben, *Mark Twain's Library*, 2:784).

51. Gribben examined a copy of Roberts's *The Kindred of the Wild: A Book of Animal Life*, illus. Charles Livingston Bull (Boston: L. C. Page, 1902) that was inscribed "To Jean Clemens/from her Father/Sept. '03" (Gribben, *Mark Twain's Library* 2:382). Jean notes in her journal of 1 December 1906–27 February 1907 that her father had given her *The Birds of North America* for Christmas: "Christmas gift from Father—Father's 'Birds of North America' is a beautiful book and will prove very useful indeed" (Huntington Library).

52. "Bugs!" in part 1.

53. "Jim Smiley and His Jumping Frog," in part 1.

54. Twain refers to the "gorgeous gold frog" that will grace the cover of his first book in "Letter from New York, April 19, 1867," in the San Francisco *Alta California*, 2 June 1857; in *Mark Twain's Travels with Mr. Brown*, ed. Franklin Walker and G. Ezra Dane (New York: Russell and Russell, 1940), 158.

55. "Cruelty to Animals I," in part 1, p. 38.

56. "Fitz Smythe's Horse," in part 1.

57. "Cruelty to Animals II," in part 1, pp. 45–47.

58. "Pilgrims on Horseback," in part 1.

59. Ibid.

60. Chuck Jones, *Chuck Amuck: The Life and Times of an Animated Cartoonist* (New York: Farrar, Straus, Giroux, 1989), 33–34. Comments here on Twain's influence on Chuck Jones draw on Shelley Fisher Fishkin, *Lighting Out for the Territory: Reflections on Mark Twain and American Culture* (New York: Oxford University Press, 1997), 146–150.

61. "The Cayote, Allegory of Want," in part 2.

62. Chuck Jones quoted in Steven Schneider, *That's All Folks! The Art of Warner Bros. Animation* (New York: Donald Hunter/Henry Holt, 1988), 222.

63. "With a Flash and a Whiz," in part 2.

64. Jones, *Chuck Amuck*, 34.

65. "Syrian Camels II," in part 2.

66. "The Retired Milk Horse," in part 2.

67. "The Pinch-bug and the Poodle," in part 2.

68. For Twain's influence on Walt Disney, see Fishkin, *Lighting Out for the Territory*, 147; Bob Thomas, *Walt Disney: An American Original* (New York: Simon and Schuster, 1976), 36;

and Richard Schickel, *The Disney Version: The Life, Times, Art and Commerce of Walt Disney*, rev. ed. (New York: Touchstone/Simon and Schuster, 1985), 323.

69. "The Idiotic Ant," in part 2.

70. "The Bricksville Loafers," in part 2.

71. "A Cat-Tale" and "A Prescription for Universal Peace," both in part 2.

72. "Letters from a Dog to Another Dog Explaining and Accounting for Man," in part 3.

73. "The Bird of Birds," in part 3.

74. Ibid.

75. "The Independent-Minded Magpie," in part 3.

76. Mark Twain, notebook 33, typescript pp. 56–57 (MTP), from February 1894, quoted in *Mark Twain's Notebook*, ed. Albert Bigelow Paine (New York: Harper and Brothers, 1935), 236–237.

77. "The Deadliest Song Known to Ornithology," in part 3.

78. "Letters from the Earth," in part 3.

79. "The Supremacy of the Housefly," in part 3.

80. Ibid. Twain may have been inconsistent when it came to killing flies, if a story told by an acquaintance who spent time with him in Berlin in 1891 is to be believed. Henry Fisher, a journalist who wrote a memoir about his travels with Twain, recalled that

> While talking, he [Twain] was groping in the air after flies and at last caught one. He held it in the hollow of his hand listening to its buzzing for a while, then asked me to take it in my own hand, never hurt it, open the window and let it fly out.
>
> "I learned that from Tolstoy," he said. "Tolstoy, you know, used to catch lots of mice in his house, but never killed them or gave them to the cat. He carried them out to the forest and there set them free. Why should a human being kill little animals? Because a tiger may want to eat me—that's no reason why I should turn tiger, is it?"

Henry W. Fisher, *Abroad with Mark Twain and Eugene Field. Tales They Told to a Fellow Correspondent* (New York: Nicholas Brown, 1922), 75–76. The story may well be apocryphal, given how often Twain himself invoked his sworn enmity towards the housefly.

81. "Letters from the Earth," in part 3. Twain referred to the carrier of sleeping sickness as "the tsetse's awful relative," believing that the tsetse fly caused the disease only in cattle, while a related fly caused it in humans; scientists today call both the flies that infect cattle and those that infect humans "tsetse flies" (Genus Glossina). The figure of sixty million Africans being threatened by the disease on a daily basis in the twenty-first century comes from "Newly discovered protein an important tool for sleeping sickness research" (3 January 2005) at http://www.innovations-report .de/html/berichte/biowissenschaften_chemie/bericht-41082.html (accessed 7 January 2009). The tsetse fly had only one real competitor for Twain's unmitigated contempt: "the ambuscaded assassin which goes by the name of the hookworm," whose "special prey is the barefooted poor" ("Letters from the Earth," in part 3).

82. The Phenomenal Flea," in part 3.

83. "Hunting the Deceitful Turkey," "Rosa and the Crows," "Mrs. Clemens Corners the Market in Flies," and "The Time I Got an Elephant for Christmas" are in part 3.

84. "Little Bessie Would Assist Providence," in part 3.

85. Ibid.

86. Mark Twain, *The Innocents Abroad* (1869), in *The Oxford Mark Twain*, ed. Shelley Fisher Fishkin (New York: Oxford University Press, 2006), 274–275.

87. "The Victims," in part 3.

88. Ibid.

89. "Man's Place in the Animal World," in part 3.

90. Ibid.

91. Twain was actively, publicly engaged as a writer with the animal welfare movement from 1899 through 1907 and it is during this period that he was the most famous American associated with the movement. Two other prominent Americans who actively supported the movement at the turn of the century were the popular poet Ella Wheeler Wilcox and the well-known actress Minnie Maddern Fiske (who urged Twain to write *A Horse's Tale*). But Twain's renown, both in the United States and abroad, eclipsed that of either of these figures. (Of course Henry Bergh, founder of the ASPCA, was well known in the United States, but he was not a celebrity in his own right outside of his efforts to promote this cause.) In the decade after Twain's death, Jack London would become the best-known American advocate for animal welfare. London, like Twain, had a long-standing interest in animals, but his impact on the animal welfare movement came after the appearance of his novels *Jerry of the Islands* and *Michael, Brother of Jerry* in 1917. These books would spark the growth all over the world of Jack London clubs devoted to ending the exploitation of animals in entertainment settings. (The Massachusetts SPCA initiated the first Jack London Club in 1918. The club protested performing-animal acts in vaudeville, the circus, the Wild West show, and the rodeo.) Although some of London's earlier publications helped generate opposition to dog-fighting and argued for animal reasoning and intelligence, it was not until after 1917 that his work played a central role in the animal welfare movement. (I am grateful to Jack London scholar Jeanne Campbell Reesman and cultural historian Janet Davis for having helped me to establish this chronology.) In 1913, Sidney Trist, former secretary of the London Anti-Vivisection Society who received Twain's 1899 letter, noted that writers of an earlier generation—Longfellow, Emerson, and Whitman—had supported the animal welfare movement, but the only more recent American writers he cites in addition to Mark Twain are Ella Wheeler Wilcox and romance-novelist Myrtle Reed; Sidney G. Trist *The Under Dog: A Series of Papers by Various Authors on the Wrongs Suffered by Animals at the Hand of Man* (London: The Animals' Guardian, 1913), vii.

92. Letter to the London Anti-Vivisection Society, in part 3.

93. For example, excerpts from it appeared in *Life* 17 May 1900 under the headline "The Heart of a Humorist," and in *Health* for June 1900; *Life* (17 May 1900), 35.914, APS Online p. 420, and *Health* (June 1900), 59.6, APS Online p. 242.

94. I examined the copy of the New York Anti-Vivisection Society pamphlet (*Mark Twain on Vivisection*) at the Huntington Library; the pamphlet also included "Eulogy on the Dog" by Senator George G. Vest. See also Howard Baetzhold, *Mark Twain and John Bull: The British Connection* (Bloomington: Indiana University Press), 379n34; Baetzhold cites Jacob Blanck, *Bibliography of American Literature*, vol. 2 (New Haven: Yale University Press, 1957), 209, 215.

95. Accessed on 23 January 2007 were 1,140 such Web sites.

96. When they were babies, two of Twain's daughters, Clara and Jean, were each rescued from a fire on two consecutive days by a family servant named Rosa (SLC, "A Family Sketch," 48–50).

97. "A Dog's Tale," in part 3.

98. Blanck, *Bibliography of American Literature*, 2:212–213.

99. Literary Notes, *Christian Observer* (2 March 1904), 92, 9, APS Online p. 6.

100. Mark Twain, *A Dog's Tale*, illustrated by W.T. Smedley (New York: Harper & Brothers, 1904). A mother dog and her puppy appear on the cover. The illustration on the frontispiece of scientists and the puppy is captioned, "THEY DISCUSSED AND EXPERIMENTED." The cover is a monochrome version of the full-color picture opposite page 18 captioned, "BY-AND-BY CAME MY LITTLE PUPPY." Opposite page 29 is an illustration captioned, "FRIENDS AND NEIGHBORS FLOCKED IN TO HEAR ABOUT MY HEROISM." Opposite page 35 is an illustration captioned, "'POOR LITTLE DOGGIE, YOU SAVED *HIS* CHILD.'"

101. *New York Times* (19 December 1903), ProQuest Historical Newspapers page 8.

102. Albert Leffingwell, "Vivisection in America," chap. 1, "Vivisection in Medical Schools," appendix to Henry Salt, *Animal Rights Considered in Relation to Social Progress* (London: Macmillan, 1894), 144.

103. Ibid., 143–145 (italics in original).

104. Leffingwell, "Vivisection in America," 155 (italics and ellipsis in original).

105. Ibid., 155–163. Leffingwell concluded that "It is evident therefore that in the majority of American universities and colleges there are no restrictions governing or limiting the infliction of pain. The judgment of the professor is the only guide; his wish, the only limitation. That which in England would be a crime, in America would not even be the infraction of a college rule! The freedom which prevails in the physiological laboratories at Vienna, Berlin, and Paris has quietly taken root in our American universities" (163). For an example of a current policy on the care of laboratory animals by one of the institutions that had had no such policy in place when Leffingwell conducted his survey in the 1890s, see http://med.stanford.edu/compmed/animal_care/guidelines.html#anes (accessed 21 February 2009). Among other things, under the topic "Anesthesia and Analgesia" the regulations state that "Animal procedures are reviewed by both the VSC [Veterinary Service Center] and the Administrative Panel on Laboratory Animal Care (A-PLAC) to ensure that proposed anesthetics and/or analgesics are appropriate for the species and research objectives. The VSC veterinary staff is available upon written request to provide assistance with,

or training in the proper administration and use of anesthetics." Furthermore, "The ILAR [Institute for Laboratory and Animal Research] *Guide for the Care and Use of Laboratory Animals* requires that any proposal to conduct painful procedures without anesthesia or analgesia must be scientifically justified by the investigator and approved by the institutional animal care and use committee." These were precisely the kinds of regulations that Leffingwell had sought and not found in American colleges and universities in the 1890s.

106. "New Books," *Charleston Sunday News*, 25 September 1904, p. 21, in Louis J. Budd, ed., *Mark Twain: The Contemporary Reviews* (Cambridge: Cambridge University Press, 1999), 541.

107. "In Mark Twain's famous little story, *A Dog's Tale*, first given to print in *Harper's Magazine* about a year ago, there is such a charming blending of humor and pathos, coupled with appeal to our sensibilities, that it is no wonder that the tale has been thought worthy of book form . . . "; "Reviews of Newest Books," *Detroit Free Press*, 1 October 1904, p. 7, in Budd, *Mark Twain: The Contemporary Reviews*, 541. "Mr. Clemens's humor is never far away from deeply felt sentiment. In this charming story of a dog's experiences he not only makes us laugh but also makes us ashamed of the cruelties of our kind. It is a most effective plea against the excesses of vivisection. . . ."; "The Literature of the Day/Fiction," *Congregationalist and Christian World* (Boston) 89 (15 October 1904): 544, in Budd, *Mark Twain: The Contemporary Reviews*, 541. The book was also positively reviewed in the journal *Public Opinion*; "Briefer Notices," *Public Opinion* 27 (29 September 1904): 411, in Budd, *Mark Twain: The Contemporary Reviews*, 541. The *Saturday Review* found the "protest against scientific cruelty" marred by what it viewed as the "very tedious and pointless jocularity at the outset"; "Novels," *Saturday Review* 99 (1 April 1905): 425, in Budd, *Mark Twain: The Contemporary Reviews*, 541–542.

108. "The popularity enjoyed by Mrs. Minnie Maddern Fiske, the actress, has made her work in opposition to trapping, range stock evils and other cruelties most valuable. She has aided many local societies, and whenever possible plans to give humane addresses to groups of prominent women in the various cities in which she appears. Mrs. Fiske's devotion to the humane cause has accomplished great good because of her intense sincerity"; Sydney H. Coleman, *Humane Society Leaders in America* (Albany, N.Y.: American Humane Association, 1924), 193–194.

109. Gerald Carson, *Men, Beasts, and Gods: A History of Cruelty and Kindness to Animals* (New York: Charles Scribner's Sons, 1972), 122–123.

110. Ibid., 123, and Coleman, *Humane Society Leaders*, 193–194. Minnie Maddern Fiske and Twain may have become acquainted through their shared interest in the theatre, or through her husband, Harrison Grey Fiske, founder of the Actor's Fund, a charity that Mark Twain supported.

111. Fiske quoted in Paine, *Mark Twain: A Biography*, 4:1245–1246.

112. Twain also begged her patience, adding, "But I may not get it to suit me, in which case it will go in the fire. Later I will try it again—& yet again—& again. I am used to this. . . . So do not be discouraged"; Paine, *Mark Twain: A Biography*, 4:1246. Twain

did get it to suit him, despite the fact that he wrote it in just eight days. SLC to Clara Clemens, 1 October 1905 in the James S. Copley Library, La Jolla, California.

113. Ibid. Susy died in August 1896 of spinal meningitis.

114. SLC to Frederick A. Duneka, 2 October 1905, in Paine, *Mark Twain's Letters*, 2:778; corrected against the manuscript in the Henry W. and Albert A. Berg Collection, New York Public Library.

115. Paine, *Mark Twain: A Biography*, 4:1246–1247.

116. Parts of it—especially when the horse narrates his own story—resonate with Tolstoy's story "Strider: The Story of a Horse" (*Kholstomir*), written in 1863, published in 1885, and translated and published in the United States in 1887. It was referred to in the American press when it came out as "the autobiography of a horse"; "More Tales from Tolstoi," *The Literary World* 18, no. 21 (15 October 1887): 349. Although Twain's publishing company, Webster and Company, did not publish this volume, it published two other collections of Tolstoy's stories a few years later, in 1891 and 1892 (one was advertised in the back pages of Twain's novel *The American Claimant*). Twain is likely to have read Tolstoy's "Story of a Horse" before writing his own *Horse's Tale*.

117. SLC, autobiographical dictation of 29 August 1906, sequence 1, p. 1090, MTP.

118. SLC to Lillian R. Beardsley, 28 August 1906, from Dublin, New Hampshire, read by Twain into the autobiographical dictation, of 29 August 1906, sequence 1, p. 1091, MTP.

119. "Recent Fiction," *Birmingham* (U.K.) *Post*, 22 November 1907, p. 4, in Budd, *Mark Twain: The Contemporary Reviews*, 587.

120. "Holiday Editions," *Louisville Courier-Journal*, 23 November 1907, p. 5, in Budd, *Mark Twain: The Contemporary Reviews*, 587.

121. "Mark Twain's Music Ride," *New York Times Saturday Review of Books* 23 (November 1907): 742, in Budd, *Mark Twain: The Contemporary Reviews*, 587–588.

122. "The New Books of the Month," *Book News Monthly* 26 (December 1907): 306, in Budd, *Mark Twain: The Contemporary Reviews*, 588.

123. *Bookman* (London), 33 (December 1907), Christmas Supplement, p. 74, in Budd, *Mark Twain: The Contemporary Reviews*, 588.

124. "Man's Place in the Animal World," in part 3.

125. Ibid.

126. "Letters from a Dog to Another Dog Explaining and Accounting for Man," in part 3.

127. SLC to William Dean Howells, 2 April 1899, in *Selected Mark Twain-Howells Letters 1872–1910*, ed. Frederick Anderson, William M. Gibson, and Henry Nash Smith (Cambridge, Mass.: Belknap Press of Harvard University Press, 1967), 331.

128. I examined Twain's personal, marked-up copy of this book in the Mark Twain Papers. Clevenger went on to say that "There is no more potent argument than good-natured ridicule. The pathos of his *Joan of Arc*, his *Gilded Age* and *Prince and Pauper* affects all who read those works. *Innocents Abroad* has brushed away the cobwebs of superstition from legions of brains, and in many such ways this genial author has helped

his fellow-man and the world is the better for his having lived. This mention is quite appropriate to a chapter on Development of the Brain"; S.V. Clevenger, *The Evolution of Man and his Mind. A History and Science of the Evolution and Relation of the Mind and Body of Man and Animals* (Chicago: Evolution, 1903), 404.

Afterword

1. Charles Darwin, *The Descent of Man, and Selection in Relation to Sex*, 2 vols. (New York: D. Appleton, 1871), 1:38.

2. *Mark Twain's Autobiography*, ed. Albert Bigelow Paine, 2 vols. (New York: Harper and Brothers, 1924), 1:146.

3. Ibid.

4. Darwin, *Descent of Man*. Clemens's copy has copious markings on virtually every page of the book's opening chapters, although there are no marks after chap. 6.

5. Twain's markings are generally vertical lines next to specific paragraphs and sections. He also writes a number of comments in the margins. Often these are definitions of words that may have been unfamiliar to him which he chose to note for future reference. For example, he writes "man resembling" next to "anthropomorphous" (p. 14). Sometimes, however, he adds his own observations to Darwin's. Sherwood Cummings, in his book *Mark Twain and Science: Adventures of a Mind* (Baton Rouge: Louisiana State University Press, 1988), transcribed some of Twain's substantive marginal comments. Alan Gribben, in *Mark Twain's Library: A Reconstruction* (Boston: G.K. Hall, 1980), hypothesized about certain writings by Twain that might echo specific points Darwin made here. The marked passages quoted here are my own transcriptions of Twain's markings and handwritten marginal comments in his personal copy of the *Descent of Man* in the Mark Twain Papers.

6. Darwin provides the following citation for this passage: "Brehm, 'Thierleben,' B.i. 1864, s. 75, 86"; Darwin, *Descent of Man*, 12.

7. Ibid., 13.

8. Ibid., 20.

9. Ibid., 39.

10. Patricia Peck Gossel, "William Henry Welch and the Antivivisection Legislation in the District of Columbia, 1896–1900," *Journal of the History of Medicine and Allied Sciences* 40 (1985): 299. Although the public was not yet broadly engaged by the issue, animal welfare publications had been writing about vivisection in the United States from at least the 1870s; the nation's best-known antivivisection society, the American Anti-Vivisection Society, was founded in 1883.

11. Darwin also seems to have kindled Twain's interest in the issue of what motivates a person to relieve another being's suffering. Near Darwin's comment that we are "impelled to relieve the sufferings of another, in order that our own painful feelings may be at the same time relieved" (a passage that Twain marked), Twain scrawled in the margin, "selfishness again—not charity not generosity (save toward ourselves)"; Twain's copy of Darwin, *Descent of Man*, 78.

12. Ibid., 40. See also comments by Cummings, *Mark Twain and Science*, 32–34.

13. Twain's copy of Darwin, *Descent of Man*, 45–46.

14. Ibid., 46.

15. Ibid., 48. Twain was also struck by other instances Darwin related involving memory, such as this one: "I had a dog who was savage and averse to all strangers, and I purposely tried his memory after an absence of five years and two days. I went near the stable where he lived, and shouted to him in my old manner; he showed no joy, but instantly followed me out walking and obeyed me, exactly as if I had parted with him only half an hour before" (43–44). In close proximity to Darwin's comment that "The taste for the beautiful, at least as far as female beauty is concerned, is not of a special nature in the human mind" (62), Twain added his own observation that a love of music might not be an exclusively human response either, scribbling, "serpent charmers—mice love music—snakes also" (62).

16. Albert Bigelow Paine, *Mark Twain: A Biography*, 4 vols. (New York: Harper and Brothers, 1912), 4:1540.

17. *Mark Twain's Notebooks & Journals*, vol. 2: 1877–1883, ed. Frederick Anderson, Lin Salamo, and Bernard L. Stein (Berkeley and Los Angeles: University of California Press, 1976), 486. See also Henry W. Fisher, *Abroad with Mark Twain and Eugene Field: Tales They Told to a Fellow Correspondent* (New York: Nicholas L. Brown, 1922), 117–118.

18. The twelve-volume set of Darwin's work that Clemens acquired in the late 1880s is at Wake Forest University, Winston-Salem, N.C.; Gribben, *Mark Twain's Library*, 1:175.

19. Charles Darwin, *The Expression of the Emotions in Man and Animals* (New York: D. Appleton, 1886), 309. Gribben, *Mark Twain's Library*, 1:175. The epigraph, which Twain ascribes to *Pudd'nhead Wilson's New Calendar*, begins chap. 27 of *Following the Equator*; Mark Twain, *Following the Equator* [1897], in *The Oxford Mark Twain*, ed. Shelley Fisher Fishkin (New York: Oxford University Press, 1996), 256.

20. William Hosea Ballou, "Are the Lower Animals Approaching Man?" *North American Review* 145, no. 372 (November 1887): 516–523; [Anon.], "The Intelligence of Animals," *The Chautauquan* (New York) 9, no.8 (May 1889): 400–401; [Anon.], "Intelligence of Animals," *Forest and Stream: A Journal of Outdoor Life, Travel, Nature Study, Shooting, Fishing, Yachting* 34, no. 10 (27 March 1890): 202; H. Reynolds, "Intelligence Of Animals; Animals Understand Speech," *The Phrenological Journal and Science of Health* (Philadelphia) 93, no. 1 (July 1891): 13–14; Prince P. Kropotkin, "Mutual Aid Among Animals," *The Eclectic Magazine of Foreign Literature* (New York) 52, no. 4 (October 1890): 523; Prince P. Kropotkin, "Mutual Aid Among Animals," *Littell's Living Age* (Boston) 187, no. 2415 (11 October 1890): 67; Prince P. Kropotkin, "Mutual Aid Among Animals," *The Eclectic Magazine of Foreign Literature* (New York) 52, no. 6 (December 1890): 836–850; S.W., "A Dog's Humanity," *Spectator* (18 April 1891), 108–109; Ernest Ingersoll, "Animal Training and Animal Intelligence," *Frank Leslie's Popular Monthly* (New York) 32, no. 6 (December 1891): 726–735; James Sully, "Is Man the Only Reasoner?" *The Eclectic Magazine of Foreign Literature* (New York) 54, no. 6 (December 1891): 814–822; "Games that Birds Play," *The American Farmer; Devoted to Agriculture, Horticulture, etc.* (Baltimore) 50, no. 33 (1 June 1892):

6; Chas. C. Abbott, "Intelligence in Animal Life," *Friends' Intelligencer* (Philadelphia) 50, no. 33 (19 August 1893): 525–526; Nicholas Pike, "Intelligence of Birds and Animals," *Scientific American* (New York) 69, no. 12 (16 September 1893): 186; "Animal Emotions," *The Youth's Companion* (Boston) 75, no. 35 (28 August 1902): 420; William Long, "Animal Individuality," *The Independent* (New York) 56, no. 2896 (2 June 1904): 1242–1243; John Burroughs, "What Do Animals Know?" *Century Illustrated Magazine* (New York) 68, no. 4 (August 1904): 555–564; "What Do Animals Know?" *Current Literature* (New York) 39, no. 6 (December 1905): 645–647; "Do Animals Reason?" *The Independent* (New York) 59, no. 2961 (31 August 1905): 481–485.

21. Mark Twain, "A Monument to Adam," *Harper's Weekly* 49 (15 July 1905): 1008, quoted in Gribben, *Mark Twain's Library*, 1:174.

22. "The Edisons of the Animal World," in part 3.

23. Darwin, *Descent of Man*, 101.

24. *Works of Michael De Montaigne. His Essays, Journey into Italy, and Letters, with Notes from All the Commentators, Biographical and Bibliographical Notices, etc.*, by W. Hazlitt. A New and Carefully revised edition edited by O.W. Wight, 4 vols. (New York: Hurd and Houghton, 1866) (hereafter *Essays*). Gribben identifies this set as the one that Twain owned, noting that the first volume of this set in Twain's library was signed "Saml. L. Clemens, Hartford, 1873" and the other volumes were signed "S.L. Clemens." He notes that there were a few remarks by Twain in pencil throughout; Gribben, *Mark Twain's Library*, 1:380. I have not been able to examine Twain's own copy but have quoted from another copy of the same edition Twain used.

25. Montaigne attributes this story to Juba, a king of Barbary; *Essays*, 2:154.

26. "Chrysippus, though in other things as scornful a judge of the condition of animals as any other philosopher whatever, considering the motions of a dog, who coming to a place where three ways met, either to hunt after his master he has lost, or in pursuit of some game that flies before him, goes snuffing first in one of the ways, and then in another, and, after having made himself sure of two, without finding the trace of what he seeks, dashes into the third without examination, is forced to confess that this is reasoning in the dog: 'I have traced my master to this place; he must of necessity be gone one of these three ways; he is not gone this way nor that, he must then infallibly be gone this other'; and that assuring himself by this conclusion, he makes no use of his nose in the third way, nor ever lays it to the ground, but suffers himself to be carried on there by the force of reason. This sally, purely logical, and this use of propositions divided and conjoined, and the right enumeration of parts, is it not every whit as good that the dog knows all of this himself as well as from Trapezuntius?" Montaigne, "An Apology for Raimond Sebond," *Essays*, 2:150.

27. Montaigne also compares the subtle signs by which animals often communicate with the ways in which humans communicate using eyes, hands, eyebrows, shoulders; Montaigne, "An Apology for Raimond Sebond," 2:137–138. "We must observe the parity betwixt us; we have some tolerable apprehension of their meaning, and so have the beasts of ours,—much about the same. They caress us, threaten us, and beg

of us, and we do the same to them. As to the rest, we manifestly discover that they have a full and absolute communication among themselves, and that they perfectly understand one another, not only those of the same, but of divers kinds . . ." (2:137).

28. Montaigne, "An Apology for Raimond Sebond," *Essays*, 2:150; "A Dog's Tale," in part 3.

29. Sharon Begley, "What Your Pet Is Thinking. Sit. Fetch. Reflect. New Research into Animal Consciousness Suggests They're More Aware than Previously Believed," *Wall Street Journal*, 27 October 2006, p. W1. Recent books on animal intelligence by scholars include Edward A. Wasserman and Thomas R. Zentall, eds., *Comparative Cognition: Experimental Explorations of Animal Intelligence* (New York: Oxford University Press, 2006); Zhann Reznikova, *Animal Intelligence: From Individual to Social Cognition* (Cambridge: Cambridge University Press, 2007); James L. Gould and Carol Grant Gould, *Animal Architects: Building and the Evolution of Intelligence* (New York: Basic Books, 2007); Irene Maxine Pepperberg, *The Alex Studies: Cognitive and Communicative Abilities of Grey Parrots* (Cambridge, Mass.: Harvard University Press, 2002) and also Pepperberg, *Alex & Me: How a Scientist and a Parrot Discovered a Hidden World of Animal Intelligence—and Formed a Deep Bond in the Process* (New York: Collins/HarperCollins, 2008). See also Marian Stamp Dawkins, *Through Our Eyes Only?: The Search for Animal Consciousness* (New York: Oxford University Press, 1998) and David DeGrazia, *Taking Animals Seriously: Mental Life and Moral Status* (Cambridge: Cambridge University Press, 1996).

30. Best known, perhaps, is the best seller by Jeffrey Moussaief Masson and Susan McCarthy, *When Elephants Weep: The Emotional Lives of Animals* (New York: Delta, 1996). Masson has explored this terrain in numerous other volumes as well—including *The Pig Who Sang to the Moon: The Emotional Lives of Farm Animals* (New York: Ballantine Books, 2004). Recent scholarly studies of the topic include Marc Bekoff, *Minding Animals: Awareness, Emotions, and Heart* (New York: Oxford University Press, 2002); Jaak Panksepp, *Affective Neuroscience: The Foundations of Human and Animal Emotions* (New York: Oxford University Press, 2004); Marc Bekoff, ed., foreword by Jane Goodall, *The Emotional Lives of Animals: A Leading Scientist Explores Animal Joy, Sorrow, and Empathy—and Why They Matter* (Novato, Calif.: New World Library, 2007); Marc Bekoff, *Animal Passions and Beastly Virtues: Reflections on Redecorating Nature* (Philadelphia: Temple University Press, 2005); Marc Bekoff, ed., foreword by Stephen Jay Gould, *The Smile of a Dolphin: Remarkable Accounts of Animal Emotions* (New York: Discovery Books, 2000); and Jonathan Balcombe, *Pleasurable Kingdom: Animals and the Nature of Feeling Good* (New York: Macmillan, 2007). See also Marc Bekoff and Jessica Pierce, *The Moral Lives of Animals* (Chicago: University of Chicago Press, forthcoming). A survey of current research on animal emotions that appeared in *Psychology Today* in 2006 (which focused in particular on the research of neuroscientist Jaak Panksepp) summed up the recent trend in scholarship in language which echoes Twain's charge that "it is just like man's vanity and impertinence to call an animal dumb because it is dumb to his dull perceptions": "Over the past several years a cadre of neuroscientists, psychologists and animal-behaviorists has begun to overturn a centuries-old belief—that unless a creature can talk about

its feelings, you can't assume that it has them in the first place. Using the modern tools of brain imaging and electrical stimulation, combined with sophisticated field observations, they're finding that mammals display not only the primitive drives of fear and rage, but the softer emotions of love and nurturance, curiosity and play. In short, we've seen a philosophical shift, with the delineation between animal instinct and emotions considered uniquely human breaking down"; Douglas Starr, "Animal Passions," *Psychology Today* 39, no. 2 (March/April 2006): 94–101.

31. Twain heavily annotated a copy of W. E. H. Lecky, *History of European Morals from Augustus to Charlemagne*, 2 vols. (New York: D. Appleton, 1874); see Gribben, *Mark Twain's Library*, 1:400. This passage from Lecky is also quoted in Peter Singer, "A Final Word," in *In Defense of Animals: The Second Wave*, ed. Peter Singer (Hoboken, N.J.: Blackwell, 2006), 226.

32. Montaigne, "An Apology for Raimond Sebond," *Essays*, 2:136.

33. Ibid., 2:135.

34. "Man's Place in the Animal World," in part 3.

35. Ibid.

36. Ibid.

37. "The Edisons of the Animal World," in part 3.

38. "We sufficiently discover in most of their works how much animals excel us, and how unable our art is to imitate them"; Montaigne, "An Apology for Raimond Sebond," *Essays*, 2:139.

39. Jeremy Bentham, *An Introduction to the Principles of Morals and Legislation* [1789], ed. Laurence Lafleur (New York: Hafner, 1948), 311; cited in Diane L. Beers, *For the Prevention of Cruelty: The History and Legacy of Animal Rights Activism in the United States* (Athens, Ohio: Swallow Press/Ohio University Press, 2006), 21, 206. Beers notes the significance of Bentham's comment in rallying reformers (21).

40. Beers, *For the Prevention of Cruelty*, 21–22, 206n1. See also Sydney Coleman, *Humane Society Leaders in America* (Albany, N.Y.: American Humane Association, 1924), 31–21, and Lawrence Finsen and Susan Finsen, *The Animal Rights Movement in America: From Compassion to Respect* (New York: Twayne, 1994), 25.

41. See Beers, *For the Prevention of Cruelty*, 23, 206n15.

42. Beers, *For the Prevention of Cruelty*, 64, 217n22; Gerald Carson, *Men, Beasts, and Gods: A History of Cruelty and Kindness to Animals* (New York: Charles Scribner's Sons, 1972), 93.

43. Beers, *For the Prevention of Cruelty*, 89.

44. Bernard Unti and Bill DeRosa, "Humane Education: Past, Present and Future," in *The State of the Animals II: 2003*, ed. Deborah J. Salem and Andrew N. Rowan (Washington, D.C.: Humane Society Press, 2004), 4.

45. Clara Clemens, *My Father Mark Twain* (New York: Harper and Brothers, 1931), 128.

46. Ibid., 129. Clara's behavior here is reminiscent of that of her grandmother, Jane Clemens, who once confronted a "burly cartman who was beating his horse over the head with the butt of his heavy whip" and persuaded him to desist and admit to his error; Paine, *Mark Twain's Biography*, 1:119.

47. Ibid., 129–130. When Clara and Jean accompanied Twain to a social function, they would occasionally bring out their blue cards and make the driver of the carriage "understand he could choose between one more blow on the horse's back or PRISON. While the conversation had progressed the horse stood still, and now without the whip it was hard to start him again. We made little headway. The horse walked us the rest of the way, so that we gave the appearance of driving at a funeral." On one occasion when this occurred, Twain lost patience, jumped out of the carriage and walked the remaining two blocks, calling back to his daughters, "Girls, you can drive the other two blocks alone; I wouldn't go to hell at such a pace"; Clara Clemens, *My Father Mark Twain*, 128.

Despite Clara's recollection of Twain's impatience on this occasion, he was also known for behavior much like that of his daughters (and his mother). His Hartford pastor and close friend Joseph Twichell recalled that Twain "could never bear to have a horse touched with the whip. Repeatedly I have seen him put out a restraining hand to a driver who was reaching for that implement, and say, 'Never mind that; we are going fast enough; we are in no hurry'"; Joseph H. Twichell, untitled [recollections of Mark Twain], in *Public Meeting Under the Auspices of the American Academy and the National Institute of Arts and Letters Held at Carnegie Hall, New York, November 30, 1910 in Memory of Samuel Langhorne Clemens (Mark Twain)* (New York: The De Vinne Press, 1922), 41.

48. In an essay published by Paine as "The Death of Jean," Twain noted, "She was a loyal friend to all animals, and she loved them all, birds, beasts, and everything—even snakes—an inheritance from me. She knew all the birds: she was high up in that lore. She became a member of various humane societies when she was still a little girl—both here and abroad—and she remained an active member to the last. She founded two or three societies for the protection of animals, here and in Europe"; *Mark Twain: Tales, Speeches, Essays, and Sketches*, ed. Thomas Quirk (New York: Penguin, 1994), 351. The manuscript was actually titled "Closing Words of My Autobiography"; Twain's official biographer Albert Bigelow Paine retitled it "The Death of Jean" in the January 1911 *Harper's Monthly Magazine*.

49. Beers, *For the Prevention of Cruelty*, 23, 206n13. See Harriet Ritvo, "Plus Ça Change: Anti-Vivisection Then and Now," *Science, Technology and Human Values* 9 (Spring 1984): 58–59.

50. Beers, *For the Prevention of Cruelty*, 206n14. See also H. Guither, *Animal Rights: History and Scope of a Radical Movement* (Carbondale, Ill.: Southern Illinois University Press, 1998) and Finsen and Finsen, *The Animal Rights Movement in America*. For a comparative perspective on the role the animal welfare movement played for middle-class women in England, see Moira Ferguson, *Animal Advocacy and Englishwomen, 1780–1900: Patriots, Nation, Empire* (Ann Arbor: University of Michigan Press, 1998).

51. Cobbe recounts her career in her autobiography, which Twain read with care, as I note below. A concise outline of Cobbe's involvement in the British Union for the Abolition of Vivisection may be found in Hilary Marsh, "One Hundred Years of the BUAV," *Paragon Review*, issue 7, 1998; http://www.hull.ac.uk/oldlib/archives/paragon/1998/buav.html (accessed 3 January 2009).

52. For differences between the British and American movements that may help explain some of the movement's relative lack of success in the United States, see Craig Buettinger, "Women and Antivivisection in Late Nineteenth-Century America," *Journal of Social History* 30, no. 4 (Summer 1997): 857–872; http://www.jstor.org/stable/3789786?seq = 12 (accessed 15 November 2008). Regarding the U.S. movement's inability to get legislation passed before the 1880s, Patricia Peck Gossel observes that attempts by the American Anti-Vivisection Society to pass state regulations most often "were defeated by statements from local medical societies. American antivivisectionists could point to few cases of actual abuse, and state legislators, who were more concerned with the need for new knowledge in this era of admiration for expertise, gave physicians and scientists the benefit of the doubt. Before the 1880s few American investigators did extensive animal experiments. It is estimated that perhaps a dozen scientists practiced experimental physiology, and a handful of laboratories were beginning to work in bacteriology. With so few experiments being performed, humane advocates required more evidence than just the possibility of horrors like those described by British antivivisectionists to have legislators take them seriously"; Patricia Peck Gossel, "William Henry Welch and the Antivivisection Legislation in the District of Columbia, 1896–1900," *Journal of the History of Medicine and Allied Sciences* 40, no. 4 (1985): 399. The main legal success to which they could point was legislation passed in Massachusetts in 1895 prohibiting vivisection in public schools.

53. Beers, *For the Prevention of Cruelty*, 123. Beers notes that "Even after the advent of anesthesia, vivisection was often performed without palliatives of any kind, sometimes in flagrant violation of humane policy" (123). See also F. B. Orlans, *In the Name of Science: Issues in Responsible Animal Experimentation* (New York: Oxford University Press, 1993), quoted in Lisa Sideris, Charles McCarthy, and David H. Smith, "Roots of Concern with Nonhuman Animals in Biomedical Ethics," *ILAR Journal [Institute for Laboratory Animal Research Journal]: Bioethics of Laboratory Animal Research*, 40, no. 1 (1999); http://dels.nas.edu/ilar_n/ilarjournal/40_1/40_1Roots.shtml (accessed 3 January 2009).

54. "*Vivisection: What Good Has It Done? A Speech Delivered by G. M. Humphrey, M.D., F.R.S., Professor of Anatomy and Physiology at the University of Cambridge. At the Forty-ninth Annual Meeting of the British Medical Association, August, 1881*" (London: J. W. Klockmann, 2, Langham Place, W.C., 1882), reproduced in Susan Hamilton, ed., *Animal Welfare & Anti-Vivisection, 1870–1910: Nineteenth-Century Woman's Mission*, 3 vols., vol. 3: *Pro-Vivisection Writings* (Oxford: Routledge, 2004), 297–306. Quotation is from page 4 of pamphlet (page 300 in this edition).

55. Hamilton, *Animal Welfare & Anti-Vivisection, 1970–1910*, vol. 1: *Writings of Frances Power Cobbe*, and vol. 2: *Anti-Vivisection Writings*.

56. Leffingwell, "Vivisection in America," appendix to Henry Salt, *Animal Rights Considered in Relation to Social Progress* (London: Macmillan, 1894), 143. See also Beers, *For the Prevention of Cruelty*, 125, 236n26.

57. *Life*, 6 January 1898, 31, 786, APS Online p. 8.

58. Gossel, "William Henry Welch," 401.

59. Beers, *For the Prevention of Cruelty*, 126–127.

60. Ibid., 127.

61. Ibid., 128.

62. They argued that "self-regulation, the liberal use of chloroform, and animals' differing sensitivities" showed that the antivivisectionists were basing their claims on "imagined horrors"; Beers, *For the Prevention of Cruelty*, 127. Sideris, McCarthy, and Smith note in "Roots of Concern with Nonhuman Animals in Biomedical Ethics" that "By 1908, animal researchers had formed a Council on Defense of Medical Research with the objective of securing the future of animal research in America. The Council published and distributed pamphlets, arguing for the benefits of animal research and maintaining the ability of animal researchers to regulate themselves." See also Robert D. Sharpe, *Cruel Deception: The Use of Animals in Medical Research* (Glasgow: Thorsons, 1988) and Peter Singer, *Animal Liberation* (New York: Avon, 1990).

63. Jennifer Mason, *Civilized Creatures: Urban Animals, Sentimental Culture, and American Literature, 1850–1900* (Baltimore: Johns Hopkins University Press, 2005), 165.

64. Mason, *Civilized Creatures*, 165.

65. An article published in the *Home Journal* in 1867 suggested a way "to improve the prevention-of-cruelty movement by extending its protection to 'miserable children (animals, we might call them)' so evident in the streets of New York. 'Let there be a lawful interference; in short, let us have a legally constituted and organized Society for the Prevention of Cruelty to Children'"; Lela B. Costin, Howard Jacob Karger, and David Stoesz, *The Politics of Child Abuse in America* (New York: Oxford University Press, 1997), 54. The assistance of Henry Bergh, the founder of the ASPCA, was enlisted by individuals concerned with child welfare, and in 1874 Bergh helped found the New York Society for the Prevention of Cruelty to Children. Beers notes that "by 1922, approximately three hundred animal advocacy groups in the United States had integrated activism on behalf of animals and children. Conversely, many Progressive Era child protection societies prosecuted animal cruelty" (93). The ASPCA today counts the prevention of child abuse as one of its goals, and the American Humane Association claims to have made the welfare of both animals and children part of its central mission since its founding in 1877. See also Susan Pearson, *The Rights of the Defenseless: Animals, Children, and Sentimental Liberalism in Nineteenth-Century America* (Chicago: University of Chicago Press, forthcoming).

66. Mason, *Civilized Creatures*, 172. Janet Davis's book, *The Gospel of Kindness: Animal Welfare and the Making of Modern America* (New York: Oxford University Press, forthcoming) also provides useful perspectives on these issues.

67. Although there remains debate over the extent to which particular advances in medicine may be attributable to animal research, a connection between medical progress and use of animals in research became established in the public mind in the 1910s as researchers produced a steady flow of publications arguing that animal research resulted in significant medical advances; Beers, *For the Prevention of Cruelty*, 127–128. Beers cites the following examples: W. B. Cannon, "Animal Experimentation

and Its Benefits to Mankind," *Journal of the American Medical Association* 58 (1912): 1829–37; W.H. Welch, "Fields of Usefulness of the American Medical Association: President's Address at the First Annual Session of the American Medical Association," *Journal of the American Medical Association* 54 (1910): 2011–2017; Burnside Foster, "Results of Animal Experimentation," *Yale Review* 2 (January 1913): 306–307; and W.W. Keen, *Animal Experimentation* (Boston: Houghton Mifflin, 1914), 282–285. See also Sharpe, *Cruel Deception* and Singer, *Animal Liberation.*

68. This is the general position of the ASPCA, which "strongly supports the development and validation of alternative methods to the use of animals in biomedical research and testing. Animals should be used only when there are no alternatives and the research is believed likely to produce new and substantive information that will benefit human and animal health." For more on the ASPCA's position on the use of animals in research and testing, see http://www.aspca.org/about-us/policy-positions/research-general-considerations.html (accessed 1 March 2009). Many today also hold the position that Mark Twain articulated of total opposition to experimentation on animals. Both the American Anti-Vivisection Society (AAVS), founded in 1883, and People for the Ethical Treatment of Animals (PETA), founded in 1980, maintain this position. AAVS identifies itself as "the first non-profit animal advocacy and educational organization in the United States dedicated to ending experimentation on animals in research, testing, and education. AAVS also opposes and works to end other forms of cruelty to animals," working "with students, grassroots groups, individuals, teachers, the media, other national organizations, government officials, members of the scientific community, and advocates in other countries to *legally* and *effectively* end the use of animals in science through education, advocacy, and the development of alternative methods to animal use"; http://www.aavs.org/about.html (accessed 1 March 2009). PETA identifies itself as "the largest animal rights organization in the world." It asserts that it adheres to the "principle that animals are not ours to eat, wear, experiment on, or use for entertainment. PETA educates policymakers and the public about animal abuse and promotes kind treatment of animals;" http://www.peta.org/factsheet/files/FactsheetDisplay.asp?ID = 107 (accessed 1 March 2009). Additional information on AAVS's and PETA's arguments against experimentation on animals may be found at http://www.aavs.org/researchBG.html, http://www.aavs.org/testingBg.html, and http://www.peta.org/mc/factsheet_experimentation.asp (all accessed 7 January 2009).

69. SLC letter to the London Anti-Vivisection Society, reprinted in *The New York Times*, 18 March 1900, 14; http://www.twainquotes.com/Vivisection.html (accessed 3 January 2009).

70. Stephen Smith [Member of the Royal College of Surgeons, England], *Scientific Research: A View from Within*, 2nd ed. (London: Elliott Stock, n.d.); other editions appeared in 1901 and 1902 from the same publisher.

71. Robert Browning, letter to Francis Power Cobbe, quoted by G.W. Cooke in *The Complete Poetical and Dramatic Works of Robert Browning*, Cambridge Edition (Boston: The Riverside Press/Houghton, Mifflin, 1895), 887.

72. Browning, "Tray," in *Complete Poetical Works of Robert Browning* (New York: Macmillan, 1907), 1166; Browning, "Arcades Ambo," in *Complete Poetical Works*, 1301. For an excellent overview of British writers who supported various wings of the animal welfare movement, see Chien-hui Li, "Mobilizing Literature in the Animal Defense Movement in Britain, 1870–1918," *Concentric: Literary and Cultural Studies* 32, no. 1 (January 2006): 27–55. Li's article includes a rich bibliography of both primary and secondary materials on this topic. Tolstoy and Shaw were two other contemporary writers whom Twain admired greatly who also were committed to animal welfare and opposed to vivisection. Twain was known to admire Tolstoy's respect for animals; see Henry W. Fisher, *Abroad with Mark Twain and Eugene Field. Tales They Told to a Fellow Correspondent* (New York: Nicholas Brown, 1922), 75–76, and Gribben, *Mark Twain's Library*, 2:706–707. For more on Tolstoy's response to animals, see Leo Tolstoy, *The First Step*, trans. Aylmer Maude (Manchester: Albert Broadbent, 1900), 59–61, and Tom Regan, *Animal Rights, Human Wrongs: An Introduction to Moral Philosophy* (Lanham, M.D.: Rowman and Littlefield, 2003), 5. Twain did not meet George Bernard Shaw until 1907, but had been familiar with his work before then (Gribben, *Mark Twain's Library*, 2:638). In his preface to *The Doctor's Dilemma* (1913), Shaw credited Twain with having been among the "the most popular spokesmen of humanity" who abhorred "the vivisector's cruelty [and] imbecile casuistry." Shaw bemoaned the fact that "the doctor complies with the professional fashion of defending vivisection" by "assuring you that" authors such as "Mark Twain are ignorant sentimentalists"; Bernard Shaw, *The Doctor's Dilemma: A Tragedy* (Baltimore: Penguin Books, 1954), 35–36.

73. SLC to Basil Wilberforce, 3 July 1899, in Albert Bigelow Paine, *Mark Twain: A Biography*, 4 vols. (New York: Harper and Brothers, 1912), 4:1085.

74. Basil Wilberforce to SLC, 3 July 1899, in Paine, *Mark Twain: A Biography*, 4:1086.

75. See Basil Wilberforce to SLC, 16 October 1899, and Basil Wilberforce to SLC, 16 April 1900, MTP.

76. Basil Wilberforce to SLC, 18 June 1907, MTP. Wilberforce was referring to *King Leopold's Soliloquy*, a satirical indictment by Twain of King Leopold's rule in the Belgian Congo, published in 1905.

77. Smith, *Scientific Research*, 98.

78. Ibid., 81.

79. Wilberforce went on to say that "the cause which we are championing is no fanatical protest based on ignorant sentimentality, but a claim of simple justice not only on the transcendent truths of the immanence of the divine truth in all that lives, but also upon the irrefutable logic of ascertained fact"; Wilberforce sermon quoted in Rod Preece, "Darwinism, Christianity, and the Great Vivisection Debate," *Journal of the History of Ideas* (New Brunswick, N.J.) 64, no. 3 (July 2003): 419.

80. Canon Wilberforce wrote the letter to clarify an occasion when he had been misquoted in the (London) *Times*. The exchange is entitled "'Inhuman Devils.' Canon Wilberforce on Vivisection," in [Anon.], *Cruelty to Animals* (New York: The Gilliss Press, 1899), 1–3. A note in the beginning of the pamphlet explains that "The following cor-

respondence, arising out of the annual meeting and proceedings of the Victoria Street Society, London, was reported in the Zoophilist, at the time."

81. Ibid., 4.

82. Basil Wilberforce correspondence in the Cobbe papers in the Huntington Library, San Marino, Calif. See Wilberforce's letter to Cobbe from 3 July 1890, plotting strategy ("I wonder if it would be a good plan to organize carefully a public discussion in Exeter Hall—one speaker on each side to speak for 20 minutes each— . . . I believe we could beat them if we had a good champion and a really good chairman"); or his letter from 8 November 1890 expressing gratitude ("God bless you dear wise teacher"); or his letter from 3 December 1892 discussing how best to defuse an opponent of the cause (Wilberforce referred to an article someone had written as "one tissue of mis-representation of words & motive—she must be jumped upon." He added, "of course shall be *very* careful for these fellows are burning for a lawsuit . . . ").

83. "London Anti-Vivisection Society. A Meeting," *Times* (London), 27 April 1899, p. 10 (issue 35814, col. A). The article noted "a large attendance."

84. The report on this meeting in the *Nursing Record and Hospital World* began with a comment on the increasing public awareness of the issue: "That the public conscience is becoming aroused on the question of vivisection is, we think, evidenced by the great enthusiasm shown at the meeting recently held at St. James's Hall, which was so densely packed some time before the hour appointed for opening that an overflow meeting had to be held in another room"; "Anti-Vivisection," *The Nursing Record and Hospital World*. 22 (20 May 1899): 391.

85. "Letter to the London Anti-Vivisection Society," in part 3.

86. Dennis Welland notes that Twain was friends with Conway at least from 1872, and notes that they remained friends for more than thirty years; Welland, *Mark Twain in England* (London: Chatto and Windus, 1978), 55, 227.

87. Moncure Conway, *Autobiography: Memories and Experiences of Moncure D. Conway with two portraits*, 2 vols. (London: Cassell , 1904), 1:347–348, cf. 2:400.

88. "Extracts from letters," in [Anon.], *Cruelty to Animals*, 67.

89. Leffingwell, "Vivisection in America," 154. Although Leffingwell referred to him as "Simon Stricker" the professor's real name was "Salomon Stricker."

90. In 1905, for example, Jean wrote a lengthy letter to the editor of *Harper's Weekly* condemning the "torture most carriage-horses have to endure" as a result of fashion-able "high cheek-reins" and martingales. "About the worst instrument of torture," Jean wrote, "aside from burred bits, is the combination of cheek-rein and martingale. The cheek obliges the horse to hold his head above a natural angle, and the martingale prevents his throwing it higher in order to relieve the horrible tension a little"; Jean L. Clemens, "A Word for the Horses" (letter to the editor, datelined New York, March 10, 1905), *Harper's Weekly* 49 (1 April 1905): 474.

91. The most famous nineteenth-century animal autobiography on both sides of the Atlantic was Anna Sewell's *Black Beauty* (London: Jarrold and Sons, 1877). Other con-temporary animal autobiographies that predate Twain's engagement with the genre,

and that are told through the eyes of dogs, include *Confessions of a Lost Dog: Reported by Her Mistress* by Frances Power Cobbe (London: Griffith and Farran,1867), *Beautiful Joe: The Autobiography of a Dog* by Canadian author (Margaret) Marshall Saunders, reputed to be the first Canadian best seller (Philadelphia: Griffith and Rowland Press, 1893), the popular *Sable and White: The Autobiography of a Show Dog* by British author William Gordon Stables, illustrated by Harrison Weir (New York: E. P. Dutton, 1893), and the more obscure but well-received *Three of Us. Barney. Cossack. Rex*, a collection of three stories by the American writer Izora C. Chandler, the last of which—"Rex"—calls itself an "auto-bow-wow-ography" (New York: Hunt & Eaton, 1895). For useful historical perspective on animal autobiographies, see Tess Coslett, "Chapter Three: Animal Autobiography," in Coslett, *Talking Animals in British Children's Fiction, 1786–1914* (Aldershot: Ashgate, 2006), 63–92. The fact that Twain has the mother of the dog-narrator of "A Dog's Tale" give her child the name of "Aileen Mavourneen" (the title of an old Irish ballad written by S.C. Hall) suggests that he may also have had in mind an earlier book by Gordon Stables that was not an animal autobiography per se, *Aileen Aroon* (London: S.W. Partridge, 1884). The dog-protagonist's name in this book is Aileen, and on at least one occasion her master addresses her as "mavourneen" (a Gaelic term of endearment): "You seldom play with much heart, mavourneen" (12).

92. Coral Lansbury, *The Old Brown Dog: Women, Workers and Vivisection in Edwardian England* (Madison: University of Wisconsin Press, 1985), 8–12. See also http://www.navs.org.uk/about_us/24/0/299 (accessed 4 January 2008).

93. Lansbury, *Old Brown Dog*, 10.

94. Ibid., 10.

95. Ibid., 11.

96. Ibid., 11.

97. "'A Dog's Tale' reprinted by permission from *Harper's Magazine* Christmas Number, 1903 by Mark Twain printed for the National Anti-Vivisection Society" (London, 1903; i.e., 1904). As the Bibliography of American Literature entry indicates, some uncertainty existed regarding this publication: "Through the courteous cooperation of Eugene Exman, author of *The Brothers Harper* and *The House Harper*, we are now able to report as follows: 3,000 copies of the pamphlet were printed by Harper & Brothers, New York, for the use of the National Anti-Vivisection Society, London. The precise date of publication has not been determined but the order to print was issued 26 January 1904. Presumably the pamphlet was manufactured soon after that date"; Jacob Blanck, *Bibliography of American Literature*, addendum 3479: "Twain's 'A Dog's Tale,'" *Papers of the Bibliographical Society of America* 62 (Fourth Quarter, 1968): 617.

98. Lansbury, *Old Brown Dog*, 14.

99. Ibid., 7.

100. Coral Lansbury explores this history in detail in *Old Brown Dog*, particularly pages 1–62.

101. L. Lind-af-Hageby to SLC 2 July 1907, MTP. Lind-af-Hageby also noted that she had sent Twain a copy of her book, *The Shambles of Science*, by the same post.

102. We do know that during that summer of 1907 Twain got acquainted with George Bernard Shaw, who had been an outspoken antivivisectionist for some time.

103. Twain's copy of the book bears the inscription, "S.L. Clemens, London July 1907"; Frances Power Cobbe, *Life of Frances Power Cobbe, As Told by Herself.* With additions by the author, and introduction by Blanche Atkinson with six illustrations (London: Swan Sonnenschein, 1904).

104. There is no record of Twain having met Cobbe in person (she had left London by 1884). However, he had had much to do, of late, with the society that she founded, the National Anti-Vivisection Society, then headed by Stephen Coleridge, the group having arranged to obtain several thousand copies of "A Dog's Tale" from *Harper's* to sell in Britain. (By 1898 Cobbe had broken with Coleridge over the issue of total abolition of all forms of vivisection, and founded the British Union of Anti-Vivisectionists.)

105. Mark Twain's copy of Cobbe, *Life of Frances Power Cobbe*, 462–463.

106. Ibid., 544–545.

107. For example, he corrected "those sort of people" to "that sort of people" (481); he changed past tense to present tense in a discussion of the duty that man owes to animals (545–546); and he changed "to have founded it" to "to found it" (referring to an antivivisection society) (550).

108. For example, in a comment that quotes a speech ascribing to the Creator "eternal mercy," Twain underlined "eternal mercy" and put an exclamation point next to it in the margin (547). In the margin on page 566, Twain wrote, "The wise & satisfied Christian explains to us that God sends misery & suffering to man to *discipline* him: & then the said Christian does his level best to *abolish* the misery & suffering!" He also marked in very bold black ink two pages of comments by Cobbe about brutality directed against women (593–594).

109. For a closer look at the critical response to Twain's novella, *A Horse's Tale*, see introduction, p. 31.

110. Notebook 36, typescript p. 59, December 1895–March 1896, MTP. Microfilm Edition of Mark Twain's Literary Manuscripts Available in the Mark Twain Papers, 42 vols. (Berkeley: The Bancroft Library, 2001).

111. Carson, *Men, Beasts, and Gods*, 120.

112. Twain's draft for what he called "Tale of the Dime-Novel Maiden" describes a poor young woman who is trying to earn a living with her pen. Her "first story showed that she had a passionate love for animals & pity for their unfair show in the world. It happened that one of the two great Prevention of Cruelty Societies needed an assistant editor for their little paper, so the editor got on her track & sent for her . . ."; SLC to Olivia L. Clemens, 17 October 1893 and 16 and 17 December 1893, MTP.

ACKNOWLEDGMENTS

Mark Twain's Book of Animals has been enormously enriched by the meticulous efforts of Robert H. Hirst, General Editor of the Mark Twain Project at the Bancroft Library, to ensure that each of the Mark Twain texts in this book is accurate and authentic, and by the imaginative and striking illustrations by Barry Moser that complement those texts. It has been a privilege and a pleasure to work on this book with such a superb textual editor and such a distinguished artist.

I would also like to thank Laura Cerruti, Kathleen MacDougall, and Hannah Love at the University of California Press, and Victor Fischer, Benjamin Griffin, Lin Salamo, Neda Salem, and Harriet Elinor Smith at the Mark Twain Project for all they did to help bring this project to fruition. I am grateful to my agent, Sam Stoloff, for his sage guidance and advice, and to Anant Vinjamoori, my research assistant during the early stages of this project, for the diligent digging he did and the stimulating questions he asked. Janet Davis, Cary Franklin, Jennifer Mason, Makoto Nagawara, Jeanne Campbell Reesman, Andrew Rubenfield, and Barbara Schmidt helped draw my attention to useful primary and secondary sources. Kent Rasmussen and Vasile Stanescu offered constructive criticism and suggestions. During the period in which I worked on this book, Michael Greger, Ursula Heise, and Peter Singer gave public presentations that helped shape my understanding of issues of animal welfare. This book benefited from the generous help of others who made my research trips enjoyable and productive; who helped provide opportunities for me to test my ideas; who contributed, in small ways or large, to my thinking; and who helped make it possible for me to do what I do: Harold Augenbraum, Carol Beales, Lawrence Berkove, Beth Bird, Alyce Boster, David Bradley, Carol Plaine Fisher, Bobby Fishkin, Joey Fishkin, Ryan Frisinger, Allen Frost, Jan Hafner, Betti-Sue Hertz, Sue Hodson, Hal Holbrook, Michael Keller, Howard Kincade, Carol Lawrence, Dagmar Logie, Sharon Long, Jo Ann Miller, Monica Moore, Mary Munill, Hilton Obenzinger, Nelia Peralta, Carla Peterson, Lauri Ramey, Jan and Niels Reimers, the late Lillian Robinson, David Rosenbloom, Larry Scott, Barbara Snedecor, Laura Stalker, Ron Vanderhye, Ryo Waguri, and Jessica Williams. Portions of my introduction and afterword were presented at an annual conference of the American Literature Association and at a fundraising lunch for the Mark Twain Project; I benefitted from the response to my work on those occasions. I would like to thank the staff of the following research libraries for facilitating my use of their outstanding collections: Green Library at Stanford University, the Huntington Library, and the Copley Library.

I close with the familiar "I owe my greatest debt to my husband"—but in this case, the sacrifices this book ended up requiring of him were both unexpected and severe: meat is no longer on our family menu. Twain was not a vegetarian himself, but spending all this time with his attentive explorations of animal emotion and cognition made a quasi-vegetarian of *me* (a pescetarian, to be precise). In spite of this, Jim could not have been more helpful and supportive, even going so far as to track down a copy of the precise edition of Montaigne's essays that Mark Twain had owned and getting it for me as a present. I am very grateful for the good will he has shown toward a project that has resulted in the banishment of some of his favorite foods from our home.

INDEX

Page numbers in *italics* indicate illustrations.

317

Designer: Barry Moser
Text: 9.5 x 14.5 Nofret
Display: Nofret
Compositor: BookMatters, Berkeley
Indexer: Jean Mann
Illustrator: Barry Moser
Printer and Binder: Maple-Vail Book Manufacturing Group